Stage 2

Operational Cost Accounting

Examination Text

British Library Cataloguing-in-Publication Data

A catalogue record for this book is available from the British Library.

Published by AT Foulks Lynch Ltd
Number 4
The Griffin Centre
Staines Road
Feltham
Middlesex
TW14 OHS

ISBN 0 7483 3405 X

© AT Foulks Lynch Ltd, 1996

Acknowledgements

We are grateful to the Chartered Institute of Management Accountants, the Chartered Association of Certified Accountants and the Institute of Chartered Accountants in England and Wales for permission to reproduce past examination questions. The answers have been prepared by AT Foulks Lynch Ltd.

CONTENTS

PREFACE

The 1996 edition of this textbook has been specifically written for paper 6, Operational Cost Accounting for the CIMA examinations.

CIMA base the examinations set in November 1996 and May 1997 on legislation at 1 June 1996, and this Textbook has been fully updated where necessary for such legislation.

We have also analysed the syllabus guidance notes and the various clarifications issued by CIMA to ensure that all the appropriate items contained therein have been incorporated into the text. CIMA have also kindly provided us with an advance copy of the new syllabus guidance notes to be published in August 1996 and the syllabus changes to be effective from May 1997, and we have incorporated these notes into the text where appropriate.

The text has been written to cover the syllabus in great detail giving appropriate weighting to the various topics. Our texts are, however, very different from a reference book or a more traditional style text book. The texts are focused very closely on the examinations and are written in a way that will help you assimilate the information easily and give you plenty of practice at the various techniques involved.

Particular attention has been paid to producing an interactive text that will maintain your interest with a series of carefully designed features.

- **Activities**. The text involves you in the learning process with a series of activities designed to arrest your attention and make you concentrate and respond.

- **Definitions**. The text clearly defines key words or concepts and where relevant we do of course use CIMA's official terminology. The purpose of including these definitions is **not** that you should learn them - rote learning is not required and is positively harmful. The definitions are included to focus your attention on the point being covered.

- **Conclusions**. Where helpful, the text includes conclusions that summarise important points as you read through the chapter rather than leaving the conclusion to the chapter end. The purpose of this is to summarise concisely the key material that has just been covered so that you can constantly monitor your understanding of the material as you read it.

- **Self test questions**. At the end of each chapter there is a series of self test questions. The purpose of these is to help you revise some of the key elements of the chapter. The answer to each is a paragraph reference, encouraging you to go back and re-read and revise that point.

- **End of chapter questions**. At the end of each chapter we include examination style questions. These will give you a very good idea of the sort of thing the examiner will ask and will test your understanding of what has been covered.

All in all a textbook which will teach you, involve you, interest you and help you revise and, most importantly of all, a textbook that is focused on the examinations.

THE SYLLABUS

ABILITIES REQUIRED IN THE EXAMINATION

Each examination paper contains a number of topics. Each topic has been given a number to indicate the level of ability required of the candidate.

The numbers range from 1 to 4 and represent the following ability levels:

Ability level

Appreciation

To understand a knowledge area at an early stage of learning, or outside the core of management accounting, at a level which enables the accountant to communicate and work with other members of the management team.

1

Knowledge

To have detailed knowledge of such matters as laws, standards, facts and techniques so as to advise at a level appropriate to a management accounting specialist.

2

Skill

To apply theoretical knowledge, concepts and techniques to the solution of problems where it is clear what technique has to be used and the information needed is clearly indicated.

3

Application

To apply knowledge and skills where candidates have to determine from a number of techniques which is the most appropriate and select the information required from a fairly wide range of data, some of which might not be relevant; to exercise professional judgement and to communicate and work with members of the management team and other recipients of financial reports.

4

EXAMINATION PROCEDURE

The examination will be set in accordance with the provisions of relevant UK legislation passed and case law established *up to and including 1 June* preceding the examination. This is especially relevant to the following five papers:

- Business Environment and Information Technology (Stage 1)
- Financial Accounting & Business and Company Law (Stage 2)
- Financial Reporting & Business Taxation (Stage 3)

This means that the Business Taxation paper will be set in accordance with the Finance Act 1996 for both the November 1996 and May 1997 examinations and with the Finance Act 1997 for the November 1997 examination.

The examination will also be set in accordance with relevant Statements of Standard Accounting Practice and Financial Reporting Standards issued up to and including 1 June preceding the examination. These are especially relevant to the following papers:

- Financial Accounting
- Financial Reporting

This criterion also applies to material contained in Exposure Drafts which are especially relevant to the Financial Reporting paper.

Where examinations are not based on UK legislation and practice, overseas candidates may take appropriate opportunities to cite examples of local practice in their answers. Such examples should be supported with references which will validate the answers.

Stage 2, Paper 6: OPERATIONAL COST ACCOUNTING

Syllabus overview

This syllabus covers the underpinning knowledge necessary for a student to apply a range of cost accounting techniques within the context of organisation-wide databases and information systems.

Students should seek the opportunity to learn cost accounting techniques in a computer environment.

Aim

To test the candidate's ability to:

- apply cost accounting principles and techniques to all kinds of organisations

- analyse and critically evaluate information for cost ascertainment, planning, control and decision making

- interpret cost accounting statements.

Content	*Ability required*	*Chapter where covered in this text*
6a COST ACCOUNTING (study weighting 35%)		
Use of relevant, opportunity and notional costs; classification and coding of costs; cost behaviour	3	1, 5, 6, 13
Cost accounting appropriate to service and production-based organisations; design of computerised systems	3	2, 3, 4, 5, 7
Integrated and non-integrated systems, including their reconciliation	3	12
Job, batch, contract and service costing, including work in progress	3	8, 9
Process costing: the principle of equivalent units; treatment of normal and abnormal losses and gains; joint products and by-products; problems of common costs	3	10, 11
6b INFORMATION FOR DECISIONS (study weighting 25%)		
Marginal costing compared with absorption costing	3	6
The concept of contribution; relevant costs	3	14
Product sales pricing and mix	2	15
Break-even analysis, break-even and profit/volume graphs	3	14
Limiting factors, including problems requiring graphical linear programming solutions	2	15, 16
Decisions about alternatives, such as make or buy	3	15, 16

SYLLABUS GUIDANCE NOTES

Stage 2

Paper 6

Operational Cost Accounting (OCA)

Introduction

Chartered management accountants are part of the management team of an organisation, whose role includes the preparation of management accounting information. The information which may be produced depends on the existence of a reliable cost accounting system which is suitable for the organisation concerned.

This paper is intended to build upon the knowledge gained from the study of cost accounting as part of the CQM paper at Stage 1.

The examination paper

The syllabus is divided into sections which represent the cost accounting functions of cost recording, providing information for management decision making, and control of revenues and expenditures. While it is easy to set a question which can be clearly identified within only one of these sections, it should not be assumed that this will always be done. Candidates will be expected to have a thorough understanding of the entire syllabus and to be able to relate the items within each part of the syllabus into a coherent whole.

Wherever possible, cost accounting systems should be considered in the context of a computerised environment, and questions may be set which require candidates to explain how a computer may be used to perform a particular cost accounting function.

The examination paper will be divided into three sections.

Section A will contain one compulsory question composed of ten multiple-choice sub-questions.

Section B will contain compulsory questions.

Section C will offer candidates a choice of questions.

Questions in Section B and Section C may be in either a numerical or essay format or in a combination of these styles.

Content

6 (a) Cost accounting (study weighting 35%)

This section deals with the routine collection and classification of costs and their recording by a cost accounting system appropriate to the organisation concerned, which may be manufacturing, commercial or service-based.

In the examination, candidates may be required to:

- apply the knowledge of basic cost collection and classification from their Stage 1 studies to more complex situations involving detailed preparation and interpretation of cost accounting statements

- demonstrate a knowledge of modern approaches to absorption costing, as well as more traditional methods.

6 (b) Information for decisions (study weighting 25%)

This section of the syllabus builds upon the candidate's understanding from Stage 1 studies of cost behaviour, and the methods used to identify fixed and variable costs. This syllabus tests ability to apply this knowledge in decision making situations.

For the purposes of calculations in providing information for decisions it should be assumed that the organisation's objective is cost minimisation and profit maximisation, unless information is provided to the contrary.

In the examination, candidates may be required to:

- make calculations and form a conclusion based upon the results of those calculations

- make decisions, or recommendations, as to the action to be taken in particular circumstances

- make comments concerning the non-quantitative (ie qualitative) aspects of the decision being made

- demonstrate an appreciation of the effects of pricing policies on decision making, applying basic economic knowledge to discursive elements of a question.

The following items are **not** examinable:

- the use of data to determine optimum selling prices

- linear programming.

6 (c) Budgets and budgetary control (study weighting 20%)

This section builds upon the knowledge gained at Stage 1 and requires candidates to demonstrate a thorough understanding of the budgeting process. Many of the topics are also examinable in the CQM paper at Stage 1, and candidates should not be surprised to learn that questions set at Stage 2 will be more complex and may emphasise the interpretative aspects of budget preparation.

In the examination, candidates may be required to:

- demonstrate an understanding of the role of forecasting, particularly in the determination of the principal budget factor.

The following items are **not** examinable:

- calculations using quantitative forecasting techniques

- the behavioural aspects of budgeting.

6 (d) Standard costing (study weighting 20%)

All of the topics within this section have an ability level of 3. Candidates will be expected to have understood the basic principles of standard costing from their earlier studies, and to be able to apply this knowledge to more complex and varied situations. The entire range of operating variances is within the syllabus at this level (except the fixed overhead volume sub-variances).

In the examination, candidates may be required to:

- prepare profit reconciliation statements using either standard marginal costing or standard absorption costing principles

- prepare ledger accounts for a standard cost book-keeping system which uses either the integrated or interlocking method. In some questions the use of journal entries may be preferred to ledger accounts.

The following items are **not** examinable:

- the materials mix and yield variances

- the distinction between planning and operating variances.

HOTLINE TO THE EXAMINER

AT Foulks Lynch, in common with other training organisations, maintains regular contact with the CIMA examiners to seek clarification of the syllabus. CIMA publishes all such questions and the examiners' answers, and we are grateful to CIMA for permission to reproduce the key questions and answers below.

1   **Will candidates be required to perform detailed ABC calculations (6b)?**

Knowledge of 'modern approaches' to absorption costing is expected at Stage 2. Activity-based costing is therefore included but detailed numeric questions will not be set.

2   **Please confirm whether the algebraic method of cost reapportionment is examinable (6a).**

The Examiner does not envisage setting a question which would require specifically the use of the algebraic method of cost reapportionment. However, service department reapportionment is examinable, and he would consider the algebraic method to be the most efficient use of examination time.

3   **Will candidates be expected to produce multi product P/V (profit/volume) charts?**

These would not be expected.

4   **Will standard process costing questions be set?**

Questions on standard process costing will not be set in OCA; this topic enters CIMA's syllabus at Stage 3.

5   **Please clarify the scope of the following topics in the syllabus:**
   (i)   **cost accounting appropriate to service and production-based organisation (6a);**
   (ii)   **design of computerised systems (6a);**
   (iii)   **product sales pricing (6b).**

(i)   Candidates are expected to have full knowledge of the Stage 1 Cost Accounting syllabus and to be able to apply this knowledge to specific costing methods within the Stage 2 syllabus. Knowledge of job, batch, contract, output and process, and service costing methods is essential.

(ii)   Candidates are expected to be computer-aware and aware of the role of cost accounting in the provision of management information, and the place of accounting systems within information systems. Detailed knowledge of spreadsheets is expected (particularly in the context of budget preparation, standard costs and variance analysis).

(iii) Candidates should be able to answer decision-making problems involving opportunity costs and spare capacity/short term minimum pricing situation. For longer term pricing decisions, candidates will be expected to have an understanding of basic pricing theory from their study of economics, but will not be required to calculate optimum prices using calculus.

6   **Please give some guidance as to the depth to which process costing will be examined.**

Total knowledge of process costing using actual values (ie, not standard process costing), including opening/closing work-in-progress, losses having either no value, a scrap value or a disposal cost, joint products, by products and the sell or process further decision. Losses may be fully or partially complete and questions may be set requiring candidates to deal with any or all of these issues in a single question

7   **Will multi-product breakeven problems be examinable, and if so, to what level?**

Multi-product breakeven charts are not examinable, but calculations involving multiple products with different contribution/sales ratios may be set in the context of budgeting and decision making.

MAY 1997 EXAMINATIONS - SYLLABUS CHANGES

CIMA have announced some minor alterations to certain syllabuses to take effect from May 1997 onwards.

The changes which affect this paper are reproduced below in the form given by CIMA. You should refer to the syllabus on page (v) to appreciate to what these changes refer.

Syllabus
reference

6a: the second item is to become
(3)   Cost accounting appropriate to service and production-based organisations; specification, design and operation of databases for the collection of and storage of cost accounting data; use of relevant applications software to extract data and prepare management information.

6b: the fifth item is to become
(2)   Limiting factors, single scarce resource problems including situations with demand constraints.

6c: the fourth item 'Problems and techniques of forecasting' is to be deleted.

IMPACT ON THE TEXTBOOK

As you read the text these syllabus changes are clearly highlighted.

		To be studied for Nov '96	To be studied for May '97
Pages 118 & 126	Specification, design and operation of databases	Yes	Yes
Page 286	Limiting factors	Yes	Yes
Page 311	Linear programming	Yes	No
Pages 332 & 357	Problems and techniques of forecasting	Yes	No

---

1 INTRODUCTION TO COST ACCOUNTING

INTRODUCTION & LEARNING OBJECTIVES

Syllabus area 6a. Classification and coding of costs. (Ability required 3).

This chapter is concerned with explaining the need for cost accounting and its relationships with other forms of accounting.

When you have studied this chapter you should be able to do the following:

- Explain the importance of cost accounting as part of the management information system.

- Understand the differences between cost units and cost centres and explain these differences using examples.

- Explain the need to use coding systems to facilitate accurate cost collection.

---

1 ACCOUNTING

1.1 Financial, cost and management accounting

The financial accounts record transactions between the business and its customers, suppliers, employees and owners eg, shareholders. The managers of the business must account for the way in which funds entrusted to them have been used and, therefore, records of assets and liabilities are required, as well as a statement of any increase in the total wealth of the business. This is done by presenting a balance sheet, profit and loss account, and cash flow statement at least once every year. The law requires that accounts of certain businesses shall be presented in a specific way and particular details of transactions may be required by the Inspector of Taxes.

However, in performing their job, managers will need to know a great deal about the detailed working of the business. This knowledge must embrace production methods and the cost of processes, products etc. It is not the function of financial accounting to provide such detail and therefore the managers require additional accounting information geared to their own needs.

Cost accounting involves the application of a comprehensive set of principles, methods and techniques to the determination and appropriate analysis of costs to suit the various parts of the organisation structure within a business.

Management accounting is a wider concept involving professional knowledge and skill in the preparation and particularly the presentation of information to all levels of management in the organisation structure. The source of such information is the financial and cost accounts. The information is intended to assist management in its policy and decision-making, planning and control activities.

The particular concern of this text is with the cost accounting branch of management accounting.

1.2   Management accounting

Definition | An integral part of management concerned with identifying, presenting and interpreting information used for:

- formulation of strategy;
- planning and controlling the activities;
- decision taking;
- optimising the use of resources;
- disclosure to shareholders and others external to the entity;
- disclosure to employees;
- safeguarding assets.

The above involves participation in management to ensure that there is effective:

- formulation of plans to meet objectives (strategic planning);

- formulation of short term operations plans (budgeting/profit planning);

- acquisition and use of finance (financial management) and recording of actual transactions (financial accounting and cost accounting);

- communication of financial and operating information;

- corrective action to bring plans and results into line (financial control);

- reviewing and reporting on systems and operations (internal audit, management audit).

1.3   Cost accounting

Definition | The establishment of budgets, standard costs and actual costs of operations, processes, activities or products and the analysis of variances, profitability or social use of funds. The use of the term costing is not recommended except with a qualifying adjective eg, standard costing.

1.4   Profit statements

It may be helpful at this stage to examine a simple trading and profit and loss to consider the work of the cost accountant:

XYZ Company
Trading and profit and loss account for the year ended . . .

		£	£
Sales			200,000
Cost of sales:	Materials consumed	80,000	
	Wages	40,000	
	Production expenses	15,000	135,000
Gross profit			65,000
Marketing expenses		15,000	
General administrative expenses		10,000	
Financing costs		4,000	
			29,000
Net profit before tax			36,000

The above statement may be adequate to provide outsiders with a superficial picture of the trading results of the business, but managers would need much more detail to answer questions such as:

(a)   What are our major products and which ones are most profitable?
(b)   How much has our stock of raw materials increased?
(c)   How does our labour cost per unit compare with last period?
(d)   Are our personnel department expenses more than we expected?

The cost accountant will aim to maintain a system which will provide the answers to those (and many other) questions on a regular and **ad-hoc** basis. In addition, the cost accounts will contain detailed information concerning stocks of raw materials, work-in-progress and finished goods as a basis for the valuation necessary to prepare final accounts.

1.5   Activity

(a)   Distinguish between financial accounting, cost accounting and management accounting.
(b)   What is the work of the cost accountant likely to include in a typical manufacturing situation?

1.6   Activity solution

(a)   In modern business, the three functions of financial, cost and management accounting merge together in many ways. It will be very difficult clearly to define the three terms. However, a generalised definition could be:

(i)   **Financial accounting**

The recording of the financial transactions of a firm and their summary in periodic financial statements for the use of persons outside the organisation who wish to analyse and interpret the firm's financial position.

(ii) **Cost accounting**

Involves a careful evaluation of the resources used within the business. The techniques employed are designed to provide monetary information about the performance of a business and possibly the direction which future operations should take.

(iii) **Management accounting**

(1) has accounting as its essential foundation;

(2) is essentially concerned with offering advice to management based upon information collected;

(3) may include involvement in:

- decision-making;
- planning (budgetary);
- controlling the business.

(b) The cost accountant's work may include the following:

(i) The application of accounting principles and costing principles, methods and techniques in the ascertainment of costs.

(ii) The analysis of savings and excesses as compared with previous experience or with standards.

(iii) Operating costing systems to provide the following information:

(1) Details of product profitability.
(2) Stock valuation records (raw materials, work-in-progress, finished goods).
(3) Labour cost records.
(4) Overhead control records.
(5) Bases for evaluation of selling prices.

1.7 Cost units

The physical measure of product or service for which costs can be determined is called a **cost unit**. In a printing firm, the cost unit would be the specific customer order. For a paint manufacturer, the unit would be a litre (or a thousand litres) of paint.

The ascertainment of the cost per cost unit is important for a variety of reasons:

(a) making decisions about pricing, acceptance of orders, and so on
(b) measuring changes in costs and relative levels of efficiency
(c) inventory valuation for financial reporting
(d) planning future costs (budgeting and standard costs).

1.8 Cost units

Definition A unit of product or service in relation to which costs are ascertained.

1.9   Examples of cost units

The following table provides examples of cost units:

Business	*Cost unit*
Brewing	Barrel/hectolitre
Coal mining	Ton/tonne
Electricity	KWH
Engineering	Contract, job
Gas	Therm
Paper	Ream
Sand & Gravel	Cubic yard/metre
Steel	Tonne/ton/sheet
Airline	Available tonne km
Hotel and catering	Room/cover
Professional service (accountants, architects)	Chargeable hour
Education	(a) Enrolled student (b) Successful student
Healthcare (hospitals)	Bed occupied

1.10   Classification of costs

Costs may be classified using a number of different criteria. Classification is the logical grouping of similar items and the purpose of classifying costs is so that meaningful cost accounting reports may be prepared based upon such costs.

The classification criterion chosen will depend on both the purpose of the classification and the type of organisation.   Some classifications (eg, by element) greatly assist the collection of costs. Different classifications are dealt with below:

(a)   **Elements of cost**

The initial classification of costs is according to the **elements** upon which expenditure is incurred:

- Materials;
- Labour;
- Expenses.

Within the cost elements, costs can be further classified according to the **nature** of expenditure. This is the usual analysis in a financial accounting system eg, raw materials, consumable stores, wages, salaries, rent, rates, depreciation.

(b)   **Direct and indirect costs**

> *Definition*   **Direct costs** are costs which are incurred for, and can be conveniently identified with, a particular cost unit. The aggregate of direct materials, direct wages and direct expenses is known as **prime cost**.

> *Definition*   **Indirect costs** are costs which cannot be associated with a particular unit of output. The total of indirect materials, indirect wages and indirect expenses represents **overheads**.

To ascertain the total cost of a cost unit, indirect costs are allotted to cost centres and cost centre costs are shared over (absorbed by) cost units. The subject of allotment and absorption of overhead costs is explained later.

Direct materials
Direct labour } Prime cost
Direct expenses } Total cost

Indirect materials
Indirect labour } Overhead
Indirect expenses

(c)   **Functional analysis of cost**

(i)   **Overhead classification**

Overheads are usually categorised into the principal activity groups:

- manufacturing;
- administration;
- selling;
- distribution; and
- research.

(ii)   **Prime cost classification**

Prime costs are usually regarded as being solely related to manufacturing, and so are not classified.

(d)   **Normal and abnormal**

An important feature of management reporting is that it should emphasise the areas of the business which require management attention and possible action.

Normal costs are those which are expected; abnormal costs are those which are unusual, either by nature or size and are those to which management's attention should be drawn.

(e)   **Controllable and non-controllable**

A cost is deemed controllable by a manager if they are responsible for it being incurred ie, they authorised the expenditure. Clearly, all costs are controllable at some management level.

When preparing performance reports for appraisal of managers it is vital that costs are classified as controllable or non-controllable. Managers will become disillusioned with cost control if their performance is evaluated on items outside their control.

(f)   **Relevant and irrelevant**

Management needs information to assist them in making the correct choice between alternatives. For these purposes and to ensure that valuable management time is not wasted only those costs affected by the management's decision are important. These are classified as relevant costs.

(g)   **Notional costs and real costs**

A notional cost is a cost which will not result in an outflow of cash either now or in the future. This compares to other 'real' costs which will cause cash outflows. Notional costs are sometimes used when comparing performances of two or more operating units.

The above classifications may be used independently or they may be combined. For example, a material which is used by a production department and which is readily identifiable with the product to which it relates may be classified as

- material;
- production; and
- direct.

Since all direct costs must by definition be production costs, the material described above would usually be classified as **direct materials**.

1.11   Activity

Classify the following cost:

Wages of an employee who supervises the machine operators within a production process which makes engines.

1.12   Activity solution

Production overhead (indirect wages).

1.13   Manufacturing and service industries

Whereas manufacturing industries are concerned with converting raw materials into a product which they sell, service industries do not have a manufactured output. Instead, their output consists of services to a customer. Nevertheless, in the process of providing such services, they may use considerable quantities of consumable materials.

Since there is no manufacturing element, service industries cannot have factory, prime or manufacturing overhead costs.

1.14   Manufacturing cost centres

A **cost centre** is a small part of a business in respect of which costs may be determined and then related to cost units. Terminology varies from organisation to organisation, but the small part of a business could be a whole department or merely a sub-division of a department. A number of departments together would comprise a function. Thus a cost centre could be a location, function or item of equipment or a group or combination of any of these.

It is important to recognise that the ascertainment of cost centre costs, apart from the aspect of calculating unit costs, is necessary for control purposes.

The terms **direct** and **indirect** may be used in relation to a cost centre. For example, a supervisor's salary would be a direct charge to the cost centre in which he is employed, whereas rent would need to be shared between a number of cost centres. Both of these items are, of course, indirect as regards specific cost units.

(Definition)   A cost centre is a production or service, location, function, activity or item of equipment where costs may be attributed to cost units.

1.15   Cost codes

(Definition)   A system of symbols designed to be applied to a classified set of items, to give a brief accurate reference, facilitating entry, collation and analysis.

For example, travelling expenses incurred by a salesman in the Eastern Sales Division may be coded:

TESE

Where TE represents travel (natural classification)
S   represents selling expenses (functional)
E   represents Eastern Division (cost centre)

or

13422

Where 13 represents travel
4   represents selling expenses
22   represents Eastern Division

The main purpose of cost codes are to:

(a)   Assist precise information; incurred costs can be associated with pre-established codes, so reducing variations in classification.

(b)   Reduce clerical work. In the above example the code 13422 will replace the title selling expense - Eastern Division travel, thus simplifying communication and improving accuracy.

(c)   Facilitate electronic data processing. Computer analysis, summarisation and presentation of data can be performed more easily through the medium of codes.

(d)   Facilitate a logical and systematic arrangement of costing records ie, accounts can be arranged in blocks of codes permitting additional codes to be inserted in logical order.

(e)   Simplify comparison of totals of similar expenses rather than all the individual items. This facilitates control.

(f)   Incorporate check codes within the main code to check the accuracy of posting.

1.16   Benefits of cost accounting

The overriding benefit is the provision of information which can be used specifically to:

(a)   disclose profitable and unprofitable activities;
(b)   identify waste and inefficiency;
(c)   analyse movements in profit;
(d)   estimate and fix selling prices;
(e)   value stocks;
(f)   develop budgets and standards to assist planning and control;
(g)   evaluate the cost effects of policy decisions.

Thus, by a **detailed analysis** of expenditure (the terms would include the apportionment of cost, analysis between fixed and variable costs and the association of expenditure with a particular management function) costing becomes an important element of **managerial planning and control**.

2   CHAPTER SUMMARY

This chapter has introduced the reasons for and principles of identifying costs within an organisation.

Cost units and cost centres have been defined, and the need for coding systems explained.

3   SELF TEST QUESTIONS

3.1   What is management accounting? (1.2)

3.2   What is cost accounting? (1.3)

3.3   Describe the inadequacies of trading and profit and loss accounts as a source of management information. (1.4)

3.4   What is a cost unit? (1.8)

3.5   List the possible classifications of total cost. (1.10)

3.6   What is a cost centre? (1.14)

3.7   Explain the purpose of cost codes. (1.15)

4   EXAMINATION TYPE QUESTION

4.1   Definitions

(a)   Define the terms 'cost centre' and 'cost unit'.

(4 marks)

(b)   Distinguish between direct and indirect costs and discuss the factors which should influence whether a particular cost is treated as direct or indirect in relation to a cost unit.

(7 marks)

(Total: 11 marks)

5   ANSWER TO EXAMINATION TYPE QUESTION

5.1   Definitions

(a)   A cost centre is a production or service location, function, activity or item of equipment whose costs may be attributed to cost units. (CIMA terminology).

A cost unit is a unit of product or service in relation to which costs are ascertained. (CIMA terminology).

(b)   Direct costs are all costs which are physically traceable to the finished good in an economically feasible manner. (CT Horngren). All other costs are indirect.

There are several factors which will affect whether a cost is direct or whether it is treated as being indirect. For example, as the definition suggests, certain costs may be traceable to finished goods but it may not be economically worthwhile to do so.

If the cost unit is very large eg, contract costing, then the majority of costs, including depreciation of plant and machinery and foreman's salary will be direct costs for a particular contract. For 'small' cost units where for example, cost units are processed on a machine, the depreciation of the machine is not traceable to individual cost units. If would, therefore, be treated as production overhead and included in unit cost via the overhead absorption rate.

Another cost which may be direct or indirect is overtime premium. It may be possible to, for example, trace which jobs are carried out during overtime hours, and charge the premium to those jobs. However, if overtime is worked to increase the overall volume of production it would not be equitable to charge the premium to certain units. The premium would therefore be treated as a production overhead unless the overtime is worked at the specific request of a customer in which case it would be treated as direct.

Hence, whether costs are direct or indirect depends on the individual circumstances.

2 ACCOUNTING FOR MATERIALS (1)

INTRODUCTION & LEARNING OBJECTIVES

Syllabus area 6a. Cost accounting appropriate to service and production based organisations. (Ability required 3).

This chapter is concerned with the purchasing, storage and usage of materials and the methods used to record these activities.

In this context, the documentation used, and costs associated with these activities will be considered, and related to the objectives of cost accounting described earlier.

When you have studied this chapter you should be able to do the following:

- Define different types of material.

- Explain, using example documentation, the procedures for purchasing materials.

- Explain storekeeping procedures.

- Explain how records of stock movements are kept.

- Value materials issued from stores.

- Explain and quantify the effect on stock valuation and profit of using different methods to value materials issued.

---

1 MATERIALS

In a manufacturing business, materials purchased fall into three main categories:

(a) raw materials from which the product is made eg, sheet steel from which car body sections are made;

(b) consumable stores used in production; eg, grease, nuts, screws;

(c) materials used in operating the business as opposed to making the product eg, machine parts and fuel for power generation.

Categories (b) and (c) are generally treated as indirect materials which form part of overhead costs, so the remainder of this chapter will concentrate on the costing and control procedures relating to direct materials.

2 PURCHASING MATERIALS

2.1 Introduction

Materials can form the largest single item of cost and it is essential that the material purchased is the most suitable for the intended purpose from the aspects of utility and cost. Purchasing a great variety of materials is expensive and ideally the business should seek to use standard materials wherever possible; classification and coding of all materials used will help to this end. Careful thought must be given to quality. High quality materials are expensive but may be easier to process, whereas cheaper, low quality materials may cause processing problems. Co-operation is required between designers, engineers, buyers, storekeepers and sales managers to select the best materials. In placing orders, descriptions and codes should be used.

2.2   Purchase requisition

It is important to control the placing of orders with suppliers. This is normally centralised in the purchasing department. Any request for material must therefore be made on a **purchase requisition**. The purchasing manager will verify that requisitions are authorised in accordance with established policy before placing orders.

2.3   Ordering procedure

On receipt of a properly authorised requisition, the purchasing manager will select a supplier and place an order. The selection will be based upon price, delivery promise, quality and past performance.

A copy of the purchase order is sent to the goods receiving department as confirmation of expected delivery.

If a supplier fails to meet a delivery promise, sections of the factory may be brought to a standstill and prevent the company from keeping its delivery promises to its own customers. It is essential that close contact is maintained with suppliers to obtain advance warning of delayed delivery.

2.4   Goods receiving procedure

When goods are received, the goods receiving department will:

(a)   determine what they are, in terms of quantity, apparent quality, the supplier and purchase order number to which they relate;

(b)   check the advice or delivery note accompanying the materials to see that it agrees with the goods sent and then check the order copy to see that the goods are as ordered. Full details of the goods are entered on a **goods received note**.

The goods received note (GRN) is the basis for entering receipts in the stores record.

Certain goods will need to be critically inspected and/or possibly chemically analysed. Normally inspection will be on a sampling basis ie, a number of items selected at random will be investigated and checked against the detailed specification in the purchase order.

2.5   Purchase invoices

A copy of the GRN will be sent to the purchasing department attached to the copy purchase order. When the supplier's invoice is received, the three documents will be passed to the appropriate individual to approve payment of the invoice.

3   STOREKEEPING

3.1   Principles

The storekeeper is responsible for ensuring that materials are accessible for use, protected from deterioration, fire and theft, and handled economically. To those ends an efficient stores layout is essential, the principles of which are:

(a)   Materials should be close to the point where they are most frequently used.

(b)   Racks and gangways should be so arranged that mechanical handling equipment is able to gain easy access to any point.

(c)   Since floor space is expensive, use should be made of the height of the stores.

(d)   Materials should be packed in the normal quantities that are issued eg, a dozen, hundred, gross, etc.

(e)   Use should be made of pallets so that materials can be put into store and removed on the same pallet by fork-lift trucks, etc.

(f)   Racks and bins must be properly labelled to ensure identification of the materials.

(g)   Materials must be put into store in such a way that old stocks are issued first.

(h)   Bulk materials must be stored in such a way that an assessment of the quantity in stock is easy. Thus, instead of putting all the material in a large heap, it should be arranged in a number of smaller containers of known quantity.

(i)   Materials that move relatively slowly can be stored in close-packed racks which are arranged on rails so that those at the front move from side to side to give access to racks at the rear.

Since some of the above principles may in practice conflict, relative benefits need assessment before a given layout is adopted.

3.2   Internal transport and mechanical handling

Handling of materials can be costly and is to be avoided where possible. Gravity feed and conveyor belt production lines will be employed where the nature of the materials and production methods make them appropriate. The location of stores in relation to factory departments will be a vital factor in handling arrangements and careful planning is essential when a factory is first set up. The stores manager is often made responsible for internal transport, but the whole area of material handling is really a specialist subject. When material is moved from point A to point B it is necessary to consider the eventual operation and disposal of material at point B. It is costly to load material in small units onto a truck, move it, work on it and then load it again for further movement. A study of related movement and operations and the use of pallets can lead to great savings.

3.3   Centralised, decentralised and sub-stores

Each business will have factors peculiar to itself that will favour a central store or many sub-stores. In many cases management will decide to keep some materials centrally - probably those of high value - and others on a decentralised basis. Materials of small value but of rapid turnover would probably be kept in sub-stores. The advantages of having departmental sub-stores in additional to the main store are:

(a)   the cost of internal transport is minimised, materials being transported in bulk between the main and sub-stores;

(b)   materials are stored in the department using them: thereby specialist technical knowledge is on hand;

(c)   batching of materials or components for manufacture or assembly may be carried out in advance.

The disadvantages are:

(a)   increased staffing and therefore an increase in indirect labour cost;

(b)   supervision of storekeepers is more difficult;

(c)   larger stocks may be carried because buffer stock of the same item is required in a number of sub-stores, entailing increased storage space, additional working capital, increased administration costs and greater risks;

(d)   a physical stocktake is more complex.

3.4   Use of bin cards

In many businesses store keepers maintain a simple record of receipts, issues and stock in hand, known as the **bin card**. The bin card is a duplication of the quantity information recorded in the stores ledger but storekeepers frequently find that such a ready record is a very useful aid in carrying out their duties.

4   ISSUE OF MATERIALS

Materials issued to production departments (and to other departments for internal use) are controlled by a materials requisition. This document performs two functions - it authorises the storekeeper to release the goods and acts as a posting medium to the stores ledger and bin card.

When unused materials are returned to store, the transaction will be recorded on a document of similar ruling to the materials requisition but printed in a different colour.

Similarly, materials which are transferred from one production order to another (or from one department to another) should be documented for control and accounting purposes.

Items such as nails and screws are in theory direct materials which could be related to specific production orders, but they are usually treated as overhead costs of the production department. A bulk requisition would be placed to cover the requirements for a period.

5   ACCOUNTING FOR DIRECT MATERIALS

5.1   Stores ledger

Accounting for direct materials is carried out in the stores ledger, which contains a detailed record for each class of material handled. The ledger may be in the form of a loose-leaf binder, a card index or, more commonly perhaps, a computer print-out.

Definition   This record of materials is often referred to as a 'perpetual inventory' ie, 'the recording **as they occur** of receipts, issues and the resulting balances of individual items of stock in either quality or quantity and value': CIMA *Official Terminology*.

5.2   Direct materials cost

In theory the cost of materials received is obtained from the supplier's invoice, but the inevitable time-lag between receipt of the goods and paying the invoice would make the stores ledger out of date as a basis for information. Consequently, receipts are posted to the ledger from GRNs; actual prices, if required, are transcribed from purchase orders.

The value of receipts includes any related costs incurred, such as customs duty, carriage and packaging. Where an extra charge covers several items of material, the charge would be apportioned on an equitable basis, probably by weight. If such charges are not significant in relation to the actual cost of materials, they may be treated as indirect costs.

5.3   Example

An invoice of £500 for carriage covers a delivery of Material A (cost £2,000), Material B (cost £3,000) and Material C (cost £5,000); carriage represents 5% of materials cost. The value of the receipts posted to the stores ledger might be:

	Cost		Carriage		Total posted to stores ledger
	£		£		£
Material A	2,000	+	100	=	2,100
Material B	3,000	+	150	=	3,150
Material C	5,000	+	250	=	5,250
	10,000		500		10,500

If, however, the carriage cost was £50 not £500, it would probably be treated not as part of materials cost, but as an overhead cost (see below) of the receiving cost centre.

6   ATTRIBUTING DIRECT MATERIALS COST TO PRODUCTION

6.1   The identification problem

If materials were purchased exactly as required for production, the cost of a particular consignment could be immediately attributed to a specific job or production order. Frequently, however, materials are purchased in large quantities at different prices and issued to production in small lots. In attempting to ascertain unit costs of output, therefore, the cost accountant is faced with the problem of identifying the material cost of a particular issue.

6.2   Example

In November 1,000 tonnes of 'Grotti' were purchased in three lots:

3 November	400 tonnes at £60 per tonne
11 November	300 tonnes at £70 per tonne
21 November	300 tonnes at £80 per tonne

During the same period four materials requisitions were completed for 200 tonnes each, on 5, 14, 22 and 27 November.

In order to calculate the actual material cost of each requisition the cost accountant would need to identify physically from which consignment(s) each issued batch of 200 was drawn. Such precision is uneconomic as well as impractical, so a conventional method of pricing materials issues is adopted.

Methods of pricing issues are:

(a)   first in first out (FIFO) price;
(b)   last in first out (LIFO) price;
(c)   weighted average price;
(d)   next in first out (NIFO) price;
(e)   standard cost.

6.3   Solution

(a)   **First in first out (FIFO) price**

Each issue is valued at the price paid for the material first taken into the stocks from which the issue could have been drawn.

The stores ledger account (in abbreviated form) would appear as below:

GROTTI

Date	Quantity	Receipts (issues) Price £	Value £	@ £60	Quantity @ £70	@ £80
3 Nov	400	60	24,000	400		
5 Nov	(200)	60	(12,000)	(200)		
11 Nov	300	70	21,000		300	
14 Nov	(200)	60	(12,000)	(200)		
21 Nov	300	80	24,000			300
22 Nov	(200)	70	(14,000)		(200)	
27 Nov	(200)	75(W1)	(15,000)		(100)	(100)
30 Nov (bal)	200	80	16,000	-	-	200

Note that the value of the stock at 30 November is at the latest price. Note also that the balance at any time requires analysis by purchase price so that each consignment is exhausted before charging issues at the next price.

(W1)

The 200 units comprise 100 units @ £70 and 100 units @ £80, the £75 shown is thus the average unit cost of the 200 units:

$$\frac{(100 \times £70) + (100 \times £80)}{200} = £75$$

(b)   **Last in first out (LIFO) price**

Each issue is valued at the price paid for the material last taken into the stock from which the issue could have been drawn.

GROTTI

Date	Quantity	Receipts (issues) Price £	Value £	@ £60	Quantity @ £70	@ £80
3 Nov	400	60	24,000	400		
5 Nov	(200)	60	(12,000)	(200)		
11 Nov	300	70	21,000		300	
14 Nov	(200)	70	(14,000)		(200)	
21 Nov	300	80	24,000			300
22 Nov	(200)	80	(16,000)			(200)
27 Nov	(200)	75(W1)	(15,000)		(100)	(100)
30 Nov (bal)	200	60	12,000	200	-	-

Under LIFO the closing stock is now valued at £60 per tonne, the earliest price. The issue on 27 November exhausts the latest receipt (at £80) so that the previous latest is used to price the remaining 100 tonnes issued.

(c)   **Weighted average price**

Each time a consignment is received a weighted average price is calculated as:

$$\frac{\text{Stock value} + \text{Receipt value}}{\text{Quantity in stock} + \text{Quantity received}}$$

The price so calculated is used to value subsequent issues until the next consignment is received.

GROTTI

Date	Quantity	Receipts (issues) Price £	Value £	Weighted average
3 Nov	400	60	24,000	
5 Nov	(200)	60	(12,000)	
11 Nov	300	70	21,000	
Balance	500		33,000	66 (£33,000/500)
14 Nov	(200)	66	(13,200)	
21 Nov	300	80	24,000	
Balance	600		43,800	73 (£43,800/600)
22 Nov	(200)	73	(14,600)	
27 Nov	(200)	73	(14,600)	
30 Nov (bal)	200	73	14,600	

A fresh calculation is required after each receipt but analysis of the balance is unnecessary.

In a computer system, where data is stored for, say, a month and then processed all at once, an average price for the month could be calculated and used to value all issues during the month, irrespective of sequence.

This average can be based on either of the following:

- **Periodic simple average.** Average of all the prices of the period irrespective of quantity delivered (only used where prices do not fluctuate significantly).

- **Periodic weighted average.** Average of all the prices of the period weighted by quantity delivered at each price.

For both alternatives, opening stock is treated as the first delivery of the month.

Illustration

- Periodic simple average $\quad = \dfrac{£(60+70+80)}{3}$

  $= £70$ per tonne.

- Periodic weighted average $= \dfrac{£(24,000+21,000+24,000)}{(400+300+300)}$

  $= £69$ per tonne

The closing balance, 200 tonnes at £70 or at £69, would be treated as the first receipt in the following month to be included in that month's average.

(d)   **Next in first out**

Under this method, each issue is priced at the anticipated cost of the next consignment. Adjustments will be required to equate the issue values with the actual price paid when goods are next received. Differences are adjusted in the costing ledger through a stock adjustment account.

Next order cost for period November 26–30 was £90.

		£	£
Cost of receipts:			
3 November	400 @ £60	24,000	
11 November	300 @ £70	21,000	
21 November	300 @ £80	24,000	
			69,000
Value of issues:			
5 November	200 @ £70	14,000	
14 November	200 @ £80	16,000	
22 November	200 @ £80	16,000	
27 November	200 @ £90	18,000	
Stock:			
30 November	200 @ £90	18,000	
			82,000
Credit stock revaluation reserve			13,000

Note that next in first out is similar to **replacement cost accounting**. In replacement cost accounting each issue is valued at the cost which would be incurred to replace the materials at the **date** it is **issued to production**. If stock is reordered at frequent intervals this price will be the same as the next order price.

(e)   **Standard price**

Definition   The price expected to be paid per unit of the material for a future period of time.

Issues to production and stock balances would be valued at standard price. Differences between the actual price and the standard price of purchases are accumulated in a separate **variance** account for action outside the stores ledger system.

The method avoids the fluctuations in costs caused by timing and provides the considerable benefit of obviating the need to maintain value records in the stores ledger.

Standard cost is £70 per unit.

		£	£
Cost of receipts:			
3 November	400 @ £60	24,000	
11 November	300 @ £70	21,000	
21 November	300 @ £80	24,000	
			69,000
Value of issues:	800 @ £70	56,000	
Stock	200 @ £70	14,000	
			70,000
Credit materials price variance account			1,000

The effect of timing on units costs can be seen from the example. If the issues in November are for identical jobs, cost per unit of output may be different. Under standard costing, each job is equally profitable.

6.4   Comparison of methods

It will be obvious that the method adopted will affect:

(a)   the ascertained actual costs of particular production orders or jobs - the issue on 14 November in the example is attributed with a different material cost in each case;

(b)   the book value of materials stock - it will differ according to the method of pricing used;

(c)   the volume of clerical work or data process involved in maintaining the stores ledger.

The relative advantages and disadvantages of each system are discussed below, particularly in relation to inflationary situations which are now accepted as being normality.

6.5   FIFO

(a)   Advantage:

Produces realistic stock values.

(b)   Disadvantages:

- Produces out of date production costs and therefore potentially overstates profits.
- Complicates stock records as stock must be analysed by delivery.

6.6   LIFO

(a)   Advantage:

Produces realistic production costs and therefore more realistic/prudent profit figures.

(b)   Disadvantages:

- Produces unrealistically low stock values.
- Complicates stock records as stock must be analysed by delivery.

6.7   Weighted average price

(a)   Advantage:

Simple to operate - calculations within the stock records are minimised.

(b)   Disadvantage:

Produces both stock values and production costs which are below current values.

6.8   NIFO

(a)   Advantage:

Produces stock values and production costs which are realistic.

(b)   Disadvantages:

- The complexity and effort of estimating next order prices for each issue.
- Adjustments to equate issue values with receipt values are required continuously.

6.9   Standard price

(a)   Advantage:

Simplifies stock records as no values need to be maintained.

(b)   Disadvantage:

Standards may not reflect current values: if so, stock values and production costs may be unrealistic.

[Conclusion]   Whichever method is adopted it should be applied consistently from period to period and its limitations should be recognised when material cost information is being used. For example, if FIFO is in use and a business is tendering for a special order, it may be dangerous to estimate on the basis of past costs. Such costs probably include the cost of materials purchased some time ago. Additionally, if selling prices are based on ascertained costs, the use of FIFO or weighted average price could lead to under-pricing, since costs may reflect out of date material prices.

Note that for financial accounting purposes, SSAP 9 restricts the range of possible methods to FIFO, weighted average, and standard cost as long as it approximates to one of the first two methods.

In view of the fact that this topic is a frequent subject for examination questions, students should work through the following illustration ensuring that they understand the calculation and implications of the various methods adopted.

6.10   Activity

The stores ledger account for a certain material for the month of October includes the data given below.

You are to assume the following alternative methods are being considered and **you are required** to calculate the values of:

(a)   the stores loss at 31 October using the FIFO system;

(b)   the following issues:

(i)   27 October using LIFO system;

(ii)   14 October using NIFO;

(iii)   9 October using weighted average system;

(iv)   5 October using periodic weighted average system.

Date	Ordered			Received			Issued			Balances in stock		
	Q	*P* £	*A*	*Q*	*P* £	*A*	*Q*	*P* £	*A*	*Q*	*P* £	*A*
1 October										420	1.20	
2 October	500	1.25										
5 October							200					
7 October				300	1.25							
9 October							400					
10 October				200	1.25							
12 October	500	1.20										
14 October							200					
15 October	500	1.30										
16 October				400	1.20							
19 October							300					
20 October				100	1.20							
21 October				200	1.30							
22 October							300					
23 October	500	1.35										
24 October				300	1.30							
26 October				200	1.35							
27 October							400					
28 October				300	1.35							
29 October	500	1.25										
30 October							200					
31 October	Actual stock in hand									380		

Q = Quantity; P = Price; A = Amount

6.11   Activity solution

(a)   **FIFO**

	Quantity
Opening balance	420
Add: Receipts	2,000
	2,420
Less: Issues	2,000
Stock per ledger account	420
Actual stock	380
Stores loss	40

Value = 40 × £1.35 = £54

Note: under FIFO stock balance must represent latest receipts ie, 300 received on 28 October plus 120 of 200 received on 26 October; if the 26 October receipt was at a different price, that price would be used to value the stores loss.

(b)

			Quantity	Price £	Amount £
(i)	**LIFO: 27 October**				
			200	× 1.35	270
			200	× 1.30	260
			400		530

(ii)   **NIFO: 14 October**

Price of next receipt (ie, 16 October)

		Quantity	Price	Amount
		200	× 1.20	240

(iii)   **Weighted average**

		Quantity	Price	Amount
Balance	1 October	420		
Less: Issue	5 October	200		
		220	× 1.20	264
Add: Receipt	7 October	300	× 1.25	375
		520		639
Average = £1.23 each	9 October	400	× 1.23	492

(iv)   **Periodic weighted average price**

		£
420 × £1.20	=	504
500 × £1.25	=	625
500 × £1.20	=	600
500 × £1.30	=	650
500 × £1.35	=	675
2,420		3,054

		Quantity	Price	Amount
Average = £1.26 each	5 October	200	× 1.26	252

7   VALUATION OF STOCK

7.1   SSAP 9 - Stock and work in progress

Although SSAP 9 is a standard for financial reporting, rather than cost accounting, its rules for valuing stock for financial reporting must influence the cost accountant. It is desirable, other things being equal, for the same basis to be used for both internal and external reporting. This section summarises the main points of SSAP 9 in relation to the valuation of stocks and work in progress (excluding long-term contracts).

7.2   Applying SSAP 9

The basic principle of SSAP 9 is that stock should be valued at the lower of cost and net realisable value.

The concept of net realisable value is likely to be of only limited concern to the cost accountant. Where NRV is applied it must be on an individual item or group of items basis, and is defined as follows:

Definition   **Net realisable value** is the actual or estimated selling price (net of trade but before settlement discounts) less:

    (a)   all further costs to completion; and

    (b)   all costs to be incurred in marketing, selling and distributing.

Definition   **Cost** - the cost of bringing the product or service to its present location and condition . . . it includes the costs of purchase and conversion.

Definition   **Cost of purchase** = Purchase price + Import duties + Transport + Handling costs + Other directly attributable costs – Trade discounts, rebates and subsidies.

Definition   **Cost of conversion** = Costs specifically attributable to units of production + Production overheads + Other overheads attributable in the particular circumstances of the business to bringing the product to its present location and condition.

Definition   **Production overheads** = overheads incurred in respect of materials, labour or services for production, based on the normal level of activity.

The inclusion of production and, possibly, other overheads in stock valuation is noteworthy in that it requires an absorption costing system for stock valuation in financial reporting.

Conclusion   The body of SSAP 9 does not lay down any rules for relating varying purchase costs to inventory and output. However, these are contained in the appendix to SSAP 9. They are as follows:

    (a)   FIFO and average cost approaches are acceptable;

    (b)   standard cost is acceptable provided it approximates to actual;

    (c)   LIFO, NIFO, and replacement cost are not generally acceptable for historical cost accounting purposes.

As indicated, SSAP 9 has no mandatory effect on the cost accounts. It may be that management decide to adopt principles for their internal reporting different from those adopted for external reporting purposes. However, the cost accountant must be familiar with financial accounting rules for stock valuation.

8   CHAPTER SUMMARY

This chapter has distinguished between different types of material, and explained the procedures and documents used in purchasing storing and issuing materials.

It has considered the problems of valuing stock and the implications of alternative valuation methods.

9   SELF-TEST QUESTIONS

9.1   What is a purchase requisition? (2.2)

9.2   What is a purchase order? (2.3)

9.3   What is a goods received note? (2.4)

9.4   List the principles of storekeeping. (3.1)

9.5   What are the advantages and disadvantages of using decentralised sub-stores? (3.3)

9.6   What is a materials requisition? (4)

10   EXAMINATION TYPE QUESTION

10.1   Multiple choice questions

For the six months ended 31 October, an importer and distributor of one type of washing machine has the following transactions in his records. There was an opening balance of 100 units which had a value of £3,900.

	Bought	
Date	Quantity in units	Cost per unit £
May	100	41
June	200	50
August	400	51.875

The price of £51.875 each for the August receipt was £6.125 per unit less than the normal price because of the large quantity ordered.

	Sold	
Date	Quantity in units	Cost per unit £
July	250	64
September	350	70
October	100	74

The stock valuation under each of the methods indicated is:

(1)   Weighted average
            £

      (A)   5,187
      (B)   5,000
      (C)   3,900
      (D)   None of these.

(2)   FIFO
            £

      (A)   5,187.50
      (B)   5,000
      (C)   3,900.50
      (D)   None of these.

(3)   LIFO

£

(A)   5,187
(B)   5,000
(C)   3,900
(D)   None of these.

The gross profit under each of the three methods is:

(4)   Weighted average

£

(A)   14,337
(B)   14,150
(C)   13,050
(D)   None of these.

(5)   FIFO

£

(A)   14,337
(B)   14,150
(C)   13,050
(D)   None of these.

(6)   LIFO

£

(A)   14,337
(B)   14,150
(C)   13,050
(D)   None of these.

11   ANSWER TO EXAMINATION TYPE QUESTION

11.1   Multiple choice questions

		£
Sales	250 × £64	16,000
	350 × £70	24,500
	100 × £74	7,400
		47,900

Cost of sales and stock valuation

Weighted average

	Receipts (issues) Units	Receipts £	Issues £	Balance £
Opening balance	100			3,900
May	100	4,100		8,000
June	200	10,000		18,000
July	(250)		11,250	6,750
	150			
August	400	20,750		27,500
September	(350)		17,500	10,000
	200			
October	(100)		5,000	5,000
	100		33,750	

(1)   B

(4)   B   47,900 – 33,750 = 14,150

FIFO

Units in stock	100
Latest purchase at	£51.875
Stock valuation	£5,187.50

(2)   A

Cost of sales	£
Opening stock	3,900
Purchases	4,100
	10,000
	20,750
Closing stock	(5,187)
	33,563
Sales	47,900
Profit	14,337

(5)   A

LIFO		Receipts (issues) Units	Receipts £	Issues £	Balance £
Opening balance		100			3,900
May		100	4,100		8,000
June		200	10,000		18,000
July	(from June)	(200)		10,000	
	(from May)	(50)		2,050	5,950
August		400	20,750		
September (from Aug)		(350)		18,156	8,544
October	(from Aug)	(50)		2,594	5,950
	(from May)	(50)		2,050	3,900
		100		34,850	

(3)   C

(6)   C   47,900 – 34,850 = 13,050

3 ACCOUNTING FOR MATERIALS (2)

INTRODUCTION & LEARNING OBJECTIVES

Syllabus area 6a. Cost accounting appropriate to service and production based organisations. (Ability required 3).

This chapter is concerned with the purchasing, storage and usage of materials and the methods used to control these activities.

When you have studied this chapter you should be able to do the following:

- Explain different inventory control systems.

- Calculate and explain control levels used in inventory control systems.

- Explain the principles and calculation of economic order quantities.

- Distinguish between situations requiring the use of economic order quantity and economic batch quantity models and make appropriate calculations.

- Explain the relationship between stockouts and buffer stocks.

- Calculate the optimum level of buffer stocks.

- Explain the meaning of just-in-time techniques.

- Explain material resource planning.

1 INVENTORY CONTROL

1.1 Inventory control systems

It is important that inventory levels are maintained at a high enough level to service the production facility while at the same time minimising the working capital tied up in inventory. The following sections look at both the physical aspects of different control systems and the mathematical techniques supporting control.

1.2 Two-bin system

Under this system the existence of two bins is assumed, say A and B. Stock is taken from A until A is empty. A is then replenished with the order quantity. During the lead-time (the time taken between ordering goods and receiving them) stock is used from B. The standard stock for B is the expected demand in the lead-time, plus any buffer stock. When the new order arrives, B is filled up to its standard level and the rest placed in A. Stock is then drawn as required from A, and the process repeated.

In considering the costs of stock control, the actual costs of operating the system must be recognised. The costs of a continual review as implied by the two-bin system may be excessive, and it may be more economic to operate a **periodic review system**.

1.3 Periodic review system

Under this system the stock levels are reviewed at fixed intervals eg, every four weeks. The stock in hand is then made up to a predetermined level, which takes account of likely demand before the next review and during the lead-time. Thus, a four-weekly review in a system where the lead-time was two weeks would demand that stock be made up to the likely maximum demand for the next six weeks.

This system is described in some textbooks as the **constant order cycle system**.

| Conclusion |

Advantages of two-bin system	*Advantages of periodic review system*
Stock can be kept at a lower level because of the ability to order whenever stocks fall to a low level, rather than having to wait for the next re-order date.	Order office load is more evenly spread and easier to plan. For this reason the system is popular with suppliers.

1.4 Physical stocks and recorded stocks

The systems described above assume that physical stock counts are taken to arrive at re-order levels. Under the two-bin system this may be so, but increasing reliance is placed on stock records such as bin cards to show when the re-order point is reached. It is frequently found during physical stock checks that recorded stocks bear no relation to stocks actually held. The reasons for differences include:

(a)   breaking of bulk;
(b)   pilferage;
(c)   poor record-keeping.

The consequence of differences between physical and recorded stocks will be that the use of stock records for re-order purposes will be inadequate. Every effort must therefore be made to ensure that stock records are as accurate as possible, otherwise the stock control model will be rendered unreliable. However, more frequent stock counts will raise the cost of stockholding and the model will require further review.

The use of computers in business has resulted in increasing reliance on stock records as opposed to physical stock counts.

1.5 ABC inventory analysis

This is a technique which divides stocks into sub-classifications based on an annual usage value and involves using different control systems for each classification.

It is based on **pareto** analysis which states that approximately 20% of the total quantity of stock lines may account for about 80% of the total value of stock.

The idea is to gear the quality of stock control procedures to the value of the stock and therefore to help ensure that the stock control methods adopted are cost effective.

1.6   Illustration

An example of ABC analysis is the classification of stock as follows:

	No of days' supply held in stock
Class A	2 days
Class B	5 days
Class C	10 days
Class D	20 days or more

Stock levels of high value category A items are kept low in order to save on holding costs.

The priority with category D items is to avoid stockouts, hence much higher stocks are held. The company could use the 'two bin system' for this category of items.

2   INVESTMENT IN INVENTORY

2.1   The benefits and costs of holding stocks

The object of holding stocks is to increase sales and thereby increase profit. If stocks are held, a wider variety of products is offered and customer demand is more immediately satisfied because the product is available which should prevent prospective customers from going elsewhere.

Also, stockholding of materials and components will prevent hold-ups in production.

Holding stock is an expensive business - it has been estimated that the cost of holding stock each year is one-third of its cost. Holding costs include interest on capital, storage space and equipment, administration costs and leases.

But, running out of stock (known as a stock-out) incurs a cost. If, for example, a shop is persistently out of stock on some lines, customers will start going elsewhere. Stock-out cost is difficult to estimate, but it is an essential factor in inventory control.

Finally, set-up or handling costs are incurred each time a batch is ordered. Administrative costs and, where production is internal, costs of setting up machinery will be affected in total by the frequency of orders.

The two major quantitative problems of re-order levels and order quantities are essentially problems of striking the optimum balance between two of the three costs categories above; holding costs, stock out costs and order costs.

Essentially, three inventory problems need to be answered under either of two assumptions:

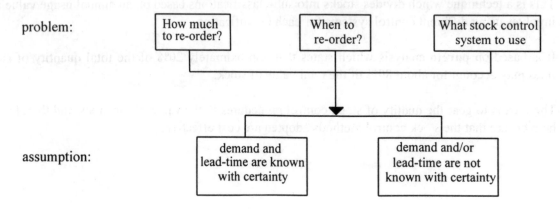

The questions asked are:

(a)   **How much to re-order?**

Large order quantities cut ordering and set-up costs each year. On the other hand, stock volumes will on average be higher, and so holding costs increase. The problem is balancing one against the other. The order quantity that minimises total annual cost is the economic order quantity.

(b)   **When to re-order?**

A gap (known as the lead-time) inevitably occurs between placing an order and its delivery. Where both that gap and the rate of demand are known with certainty, an exact decision on when to re-order can be made. In the real world both will fluctuate randomly and so the order must be placed so as to leave some buffer stock if demand and lead-time follow the average pattern. The problem is again the balancing of increased holding costs if the buffer stock is high, against increased stock-out costs if the buffer stock is low. The quantity of stock at the time of placing the order is the re-order quantity.

3   THE ECONOMIC ORDER QUANTITY

3.1   Calculation of Economic Order Quantity

Consider the following situation. Watallington Ltd is a retailer of beer barrels. The company has an annual demand of 30,000 barrels. The barrels are purchased for stock in lots of 5,000 and cost £12 each. Fresh supplies can be obtained immediately (ie, nil lead time) ordering and transport costs amounting to £200 per order. The annual cost of holding one barrel in stock is estimated to be 10% of the price of a barrel ie, £12 × 0.1 = £1.20.

The stock level situation could be represented graphically as follows:

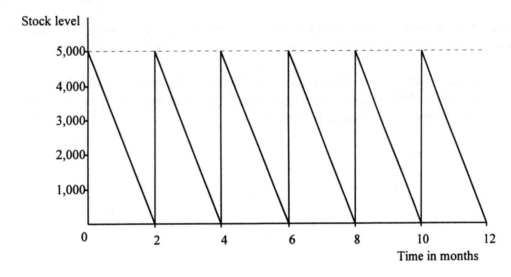

Thus, Watallington Ltd orders 5,000 barrels at a time and these are used from stock at a uniform rate.

Every two months stock is zero and a new order is made and received. The average stock level is $\frac{5,000}{2}$ barrels ie, half the replenishment level.

Watallington's total annual inventory costs are made up as follows:

		£
Ordering costs	$\dfrac{30,000}{5,000} \times £200$	1,200
Cost of holding stock	$\dfrac{5,000}{2} \times £1.20$	3,000
Total inventory costs		4,200

30,000 barrels are purchased annually in lots of 5,000. If each order costs £200, the total ordering costs are £1,200. The cost of holding each barrel in stock was estimated at £1.20. With the average stock being half the replenishment level, the annual stockholding costs are £3,000.

Compare these costs with those of ordering four, six, eight, ten and fifteen times a year.

A	B	C	D	E	F
No of orders per year	Annual ordering costs $£(A \times 200)$	Order size $30,000 \div A$	Average stock $C \div 2$	Stockholding costs per annum $£(D \times £1.20)$	Total inventory $£(B + E)$
	£	barrels	barrels	£	£
4	800	7,500	3,750	4,500	5,300
6	1,200	5,000	2,500	3,000	4,200
8	1,600	3,750	1,875	2,250	3,850
10	2,000	3,000	1,500	1,800	3,800
15	3,000	2,000	1,000	1,200	4,200

To minimise total inventory costs (column F), make between eight and fifteen orders a year ie, order size should be between 3,750 and 2,000 barrels a time. A more explicit solution could be achieved by calculating costs at nine, ten, eleven, twelve, thirteen and fourteen orders per year.

However, rather than continue with the trial and error process, the results from the table could be shown graphically, plotting actual cost against size of order. Three curves result:

(a)   annual ordering costs curve (column B); falling as the order quantity rises
(b)   annual stockholding costs curve (column E); rising as the order quantity rises
(c)   total inventory costs curve (column F).

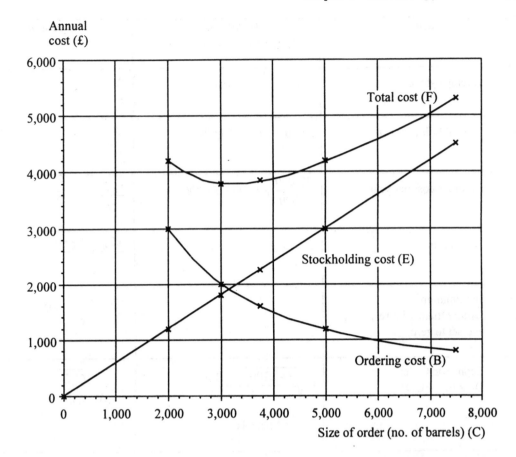

Annual cost (£)

Size of order (no. of barrels) (C)

From the graph the order quantity which gives the lowest total cost is somewhere between 3,000 and 3,200 barrels. It is difficult, however, to be much more accurate than this by reading the graph.

3.2   Economic Order Quantity formula

It is possible to draw general conclusions from a typical situation, such as Watallington, applicable to all inventory problems. The following notation will be used:

x   = batch size
C_0 = fixed costs per batch or order
D   = expected annual sales volume
C_h = cost of holding one unit in stock for one year.

Item	Watallington When order quantity was 5,000	The general model
(a) Average stock	$5,000 \times \dfrac{1}{2} = 2,500$	$\dfrac{x}{2}$
(b) Annual holding cost	$2,500 \times £1.2 = £3,000$	$\dfrac{xC_h}{2}$
(c) Re-order cost per year	$\dfrac{30,000}{5,000} \times £200 = £1,200$	$\dfrac{C_0D}{x}$
(d) Total costs	$£3,000 + £1,200 = £4,200$	$\dfrac{xC_h}{2} + \dfrac{C_0D}{x}$
To find the minimum (e) Differentiate with respect to x and set to zero		$\dfrac{C_h}{2} - \dfrac{C_0D}{x^2} = 0$
(f) Economic Order, Quantity (EOQ).	$= \sqrt{\dfrac{2 \times £200 \times 30,000}{1.2}}$ $= 3,162$ barrels.	$x = \sqrt{\dfrac{2C_0D}{C_h}}$

Using the expression given for total cost above, and the EOQ of 3162 barrels

$$
\begin{aligned}
\text{Total cost} \quad &= \quad £(\frac{30,000}{3,162} \times 200) \quad + \quad £(\frac{3,162}{2} \times 1.20) \\[2mm]
&= \quad £(9.488 \times 200) \quad + \quad 1,581 \times 1.20 \\[2mm]
&= \quad £1,897.6 \quad + \quad £1,897.2 \\[2mm]
&= \quad £3,795 \text{ to the nearest £ when 3,162 barrels are ordered at a time.}
\end{aligned}
$$

(In practice, this would mean taking 9.488 orders a year, which is nonsense. Orders would be in lots of 3,000 barrels at a total inventory cost of £3,800 per annum (see table) which is only £5 more than the theoretical minimum cost.)

3.3   Activity

Calculate the economic order quantity given the following data:

Annual demand	5,000 units
Ordering cost	£150 per order
Annual holding cost	£2 per unit

3.4   Activity solution

$$\sqrt{\frac{2 \times £150 \times 5,000}{£2}}$$

= **866 units** (to nearest unit).

3.5   Economic Batch Quantity

In situations where stock is produced internally, a significant time-lag will elapse between the beginning and end of production of a batch. During this time units will be sold, thus the 'saw-tooth' diagram becomes:

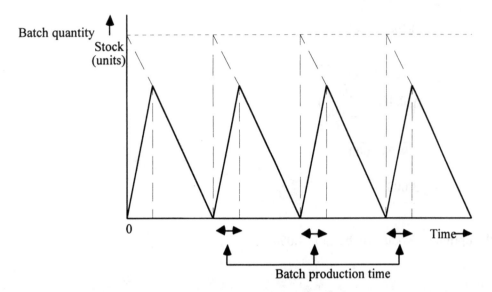

The result is that stock never reaches the level of buffer stock plus order quantity. The average stock is, as a result, less. This difference is a function of the rates of demand and production.

Maximum stock is now (ignoring buffer stock):

$$x(1-\frac{D}{R})$$ where R is annual production rate.

The economic order quantity formula is modified to:

$$\sqrt{\frac{2C_0D}{C_h(1-\frac{D}{R})}}$$

The solution is then referred to as the economic batch quantity (EBQ).

Notes:

(1)   R is the annual production rate on the assumption that the product is produced continuously over the year.

(2)   when R is very large in relation to D, then $(1-\frac{D}{R})\approx 1$ ie, the original formula.

3.6   Example

Smoothy, who manufactures silk ties, asks you to estimate the size of the production run which will give him the lowest cost. You ascertain the following information.

Estimated demand = 9,000 pa (D).

Set-up costs of each production run = £50 (C_0).

Cost of each tie = £4.

Cost of holding one tie in stock for one year = 40p (C_h).

Current rate of production = 1,000 ties per month or 12,000 ties per annum (R)

$$x = \sqrt{\frac{2C_0 D}{C_h(1 - \dfrac{D}{R})}}$$

$$= \sqrt{\frac{2 \times 9,000 \times 50}{0.4(1 - \dfrac{9,000}{12,000})}}$$

$$= \sqrt{9,000,000}$$

$$= \underline{3,000}$$

ie, the optimum production batch is 3,000 ties.

3.7   Activity

Calculate the economic batch quantity from the following data:

Annual demand	10,000 units
Machine set-up costs	£250 per production run
Production rate	1,500 units per month
Stockholding costs	£0.60 per unit per annum.

3.8   Activity solution

$$\sqrt{\frac{2 \times 10,000 \times £250}{0.60(1 - (10,000 / 18,000))}}$$

= 4,330 units.

3.9   Large order discounts

Frequently, discounts will be offered for ordering in large quantities. The problem is: if the order quantity to obtain discount is above what would otherwise be the EOQ, is the discount still worth taking? The problem may be solved by the following procedure:

Step 1   Calculate the EOQ ignoring discounts.

Step 2   If this is below the level for discounts, calculate total annual stock costs.

Step 3   Recalculate total annual stock costs using the order size required to just obtain the discount.

Step 4   Compare the cost of steps 2 and 3 with saving from the discount, and select the minimum cost alternative.

Step 5   Repeat for all discount levels.

3.10 Example

In the Watallington illustration, suppose additionally that a 2% discount is available on orders of at least 5,000 barrels and that a 2.5% discount is available if the order quantity is 7,500 barrels or above. With this information, would the economic order quantity still be 3,000?

£

$\boxed{\textit{Step 1}}$ and $\boxed{\textit{Step 2}}$ have already been carried out, and it is known
that total annual cost at EOQ = 3,795

$\boxed{\textit{Step 3}}$ At order quantity 5,000, total cost

$$= \frac{xC_h}{2} + \frac{C_0 D}{x}$$

$$\frac{5,000 \times 12 \times 0.98 \times 0.1}{2} + \frac{30,000 \times £200}{5,000} = \qquad 4,140$$

Extra costs of ordering in batches of 5,000	(345)
Less: Savings on discount 2% × £12 × 30,000	7,200

$\boxed{\textit{Step 4}}$ Net cost saving   6,855

Hence batches of 5,000 are worthwhile.

Similarly purchasing in batches of 7,500 results in:

£

Total costs	5,187.5
Costs at 5,000	4,125
Extra costs	1,062.5
Savings on extra discount	
(2½ – 2)% × £12 × 30,000	1,800
Net cost saving	737.5

It is concluded that a further saving can be made by ordering in batches of 7,500.

3.11 Sensitivity of result

It is important to be aware not only of the optimum order quantity, but also of the sensitivity of this result to factors such as changes in demand and in fixed costs.

Note in particular that one result of the square root formula is that the order quantity only increases as the square root of any increase in demand.

3.12 Example - sensitivity to demand

In Watallington Ltd suppose actual demand is 45,000 beer barrels per year. What is the cost of basing EOQ on 30,000 barrels per year?

£

(a)   Inventory costs at order level 3,000 units are

$$\frac{45,000 \times 200}{3,000} + \frac{3,000 \times 1.2}{2} = \qquad 4,800$$

(b)   EOQ at demand 45,000 $= \sqrt{\dfrac{2C_0D}{C_h}}$

$$= \sqrt{\dfrac{2 \times 45,000 \times 200}{1.2}}$$

$$= \ 3,873 \text{ (round to 3,750)}$$

cost at order level 3,750 is

$$\dfrac{45,000 \times 200}{3,750} + \dfrac{3,750 \times 1.2}{2} \ = \qquad\qquad 4,650$$

extra cost incurred   £150

It is concluded that the extra costs incurred are only £150 pa ie, EOQ is insensitive to a change in demand of as much as 50%.

3.13   Example - sensitivity to ordering costs

Reverting to the original Watallington data, but assuming fixed costs per order are actually £350. What is the cost of basing EOQ on cost of £200?

                                                                          £

(a)   Inventory costs at order level 3,000 units

$$\dfrac{30,000 \times 350}{3,000} + \dfrac{3,000 \times 1.2}{2} \ = \qquad\qquad 5,300$$

(b)   EOQ at fixed order cost £350

$$\sqrt{\dfrac{2 \times 30,000 \times 350}{1.2}} \ = \ 4,183 \text{ (round to 4,000)}$$

Costs at order level 4,000

$$= \dfrac{30,000 \times 350}{4,000} + \dfrac{4,000 \times 1.2}{2} \ = \qquad\qquad 5,025$$

extra cost incurred   £275

It is concluded that the extra costs incurred are only £275 pa ie EOQ is relatively insensitive to a change in fixed order cost of as much as 75%.

4   RE-ORDER QUANTITY

4.1   When to re-order

The second problem in inventory control is when to re-order. When demand and lead-time are known with certainty this may be calculated exactly.

Re-order level is when lead-time × demand exactly equals units in stock. On this basis, as the next delivery is made the last unit of stock is being sold. However, in the real world this ideal cannot be achieved. Demand will vary from period to period, and re-order points must allow some buffer, or safety, stock.

The size of the buffer stock is a function of three factors:

(a)   Variability of demand.
(b)   Cost of holding stocks.
(c)   Cost of stock-outs (this is the cost of being asked for an item which is out of stock)

The problem may be solved by calculating costs at various levels, by the following procedure:

Step 1   Estimate cost of holding one extra unit of stock for one year.

Step 2   Estimate cost of each stock-out.

Step 3   Calculate expected number of stock-outs associated with each level of stock.

Step 4   Calculate EOQ, and hence number of orders per annum

Step 5   Calculate total expected costs (stock-outs plus holding) per annum associated with each level of buffer stock, and select minimum cost of options.

4.2   Example

Autobits Ltd is one of the few suppliers of an electronic ignition system for cars, and it sells 100 units each year. Each unit costs £40 from the manufacturer, it is estimated that each order costs £10 to handle and that the cost of holding one unit in stock for one year is 25% of the cost price. The lead time is always exactly one week. The weekly demand for units follows a Poisson distribution with a mean of 2, as follows.

Demand	Probability of demand
0	0.14
1	0.27
2	0.27
3	0.18
4	0.09
5	0.04
6	0.01

Autobits estimates that the stock-out cost, the cost of not being able to meet an order, is £20 per unit.

Autobits must estimate both how many units should be ordered at a time and when the orders should be placed.

Step 1   Cost of holding one unit: £10 (£40 × 25%).

Step 2   Cost of stock-out: £20

Step 3   Distribution of demand in lead-time is as shown above:

Hence, the **normal** or expected level of demand in the lead-time is 2, and if buffer stock were zero, reordering would take place when stock fell to 2 ie, Buffer stock is defined as (actual re-order level – expected demand in lead time).

Buffer stock of 4 (6 – 2) would mean that, on the basis of the observations, a stock-out would never occur. Thus, the range of buffer stock options is between 0 and 4 units ie, re-order levels between 2 and 6.

A table can be prepared showing the relationship between buffer stock and actual demand in terms of stock outs.

Pay-off table in terms of stock-outs
(ie, no. of stock-outs per lead-time)

Re-order level	2	3	4	5	6
Actual demand during lead-time					
2 or less	0	0	0	0	0
3	1	0	0	0	0
4	2	1	0	0	0
5	3	2	1	0	0
6	4	3	2	1	0

Multiplying, then, by the probability of that level of demand occurring, the expected number of stock-outs is:

Expected number of stock-outs

Re-order level		2	3	4	5	6
Demand	*Probability*					
2 or less	0.68	0	0	0	0	0
3	0.18	0.18	0	0	0	0
4	0.09	0.18	0.09	0	0	0
5	0.04	0.12	0.08	0.04	0	0
6	0.01	0.04	0.03	0.02	0.01	0
Total = Expected stock-outs per order		0.52	0.20	0.06	0.01	Nil

Step 4

$$\text{EOQ} \sqrt{\frac{2C_0D}{C_h}} = \sqrt{\frac{2 \times 10 \times 100}{10}} = \sqrt{200}$$

$$= \quad 14.142$$

$$= \quad 14 \text{ to nearest whole number}$$

$$\text{Orders per annum} = \frac{100}{14} = 7.142$$

Step 5

(i)	Re-order level	2	3	4	5	6
(ii)	Buffer stocks ((i) – 2)	0	1	2	3	4
(iii)	Annual cost of holding buffer stock ((ii) × £10)	0	£10	£20	£30	£40
(iv)	Stock-outs per order (per step 3)	0.52	0.20	0.06	0.01	Nil
(v)	Annual cost of stock-outs ((iv) × 7.142 × £20)	£74.28	£28.57	£8.57	£1.43	Nil
(vi)	Total buffer stock cost ((iii) + (v))	£74.28	£38.57	£28.57	£31.43	£40

It is concluded that the minimum cost solution is to hold a buffer stock of 2 ie re-order when stocks fall to 4.

Conclusion   From the above analysis, it is apparent that increasing buffer stock is worthwhile if:

Reduction in annual stock-outs costs   >   Unit holding cost

or

Stock-out cost × Orders per annum × Decrease   >   Unit holding cost
in expected number of stock-outs per order

4.3   Alternative method of calculating buffer stock

The method of calculation used above is applicable to any form of distribution of lead-time demand. However, where the demand during the lead-time is described by a Poisson distribution, as was the case with Autobits Ltd, an alternative method may be used to calculate the buffer stock by finding that quantity of stock which minimises the probability of stock-out.

Note: the student may expect to be provided with the probabilities associated with events for any question requiring the use of Poisson distributions.

Because it can be shown that the optimum level of buffer stock is the minimum which satisfies the inequation:

$$\text{Probability of a stock-out} \leq \frac{\text{Cost of holding an extra item which is not required}}{\text{Stock - out cost}}$$

The problem can again be solved by a series of steps:

Step 1   Estimate the probability of at least one stock-out occurring for each re-order level.

Step 2   Calculate EOQ and, hence, the number of orders per annum.

Step 3   Calculate the cost of holding one extra unit from one re-order period to the next.

Step 4   Find the buffer stock level which satisfies the inequation:

Probability of at least one stock-out

$$\leq \frac{\text{Cost of holding one unit which is not required}}{\text{Cost of Stock - out}}$$

4.4   Activity

Given probabilities of demand as follows, what is the expected number of stock-outs if a reorder level of 4 is used?

Demand	Probability of demand
1	0.10
2	0.25
3	0.35
4	0.15
5	0.10
6	0.05

4.5   Activity solution

Expected number of stock-outs is given by:

Demand	Number of stock-outs	Probability	Expected numbers
1-4	Nil	0.85	Nil
5	1	0.10	0.10
6	2	0.05	0.10
			0.20

4.6   Example

Same facts as in example Autobits Ltd above:

Step 1

Demand (D)	Safety stock	Probability of (D) being demanded (given)	Probability of (D) (or more) being demanded	Probability of at least one stock-out (4-3)
(1)	(2)	(3)	(4)	(5)
0	N/A	0.14	1.00	N/A
1	N/A	0.27	0.86	N/A
2	0	0.27	0.59	0.32
3	1	0.18	0.32	0.14
4	2	0.09	0.14	0.05
5	3	0.04	0.05	0.01
6	4	0.01	0.01	Nil

Step 2   EOQ $\sqrt{\dfrac{2C_0 D}{C_h}}$ $=$ $\sqrt{\dfrac{2 \times 10 \times 100}{10}}$ $=$ $\sqrt{200}$

$$= \quad 14.142$$

$$= \quad 14 \text{ to nearest whole number}$$

$$\text{Orders per annum} = \frac{100}{14} = 7.142$$

Step 3   Cost of holding one extra unit from one re-order period to the next

$$= \frac{\text{Annual holding cost}}{\text{No of orders per year}} = \frac{£10}{7.142} = £1.40$$

Step 4   Buffer stock level = level where:

$$\text{Probability of stock-out} \quad \leq \frac{\text{Cost of holding unrequired unit (step 3)}}{\text{Stock - out cost}}$$

$$\leq \frac{£1.4}{£20}$$

$$= 0.07$$

By inspection of column 4 of the table in Step 1, the minimum re-order level which satisfies this inequality is 4 units where probability of stock-out = 0.05.

This equates to the answer obtained in the previous example.

5   INVENTORY CONTROL

5.1   Feedback control - exponential smoothing

It is important that a stock control system should have some mechanism whereby re-order levels and re-order quantities are adjusted according to changes in demand. Consequently, a stock control system should incorporate a feedback system to make new rules for obtaining more effective control in the future.

Some feedback control systems are based on what is known as **exponential smoothing**, whereby the forecast for the next period is based on the forecast for the preceding period, as modified by the actual demand which occurred in that period, ie

New forecast = Old forecast + α (Actual demand – Old forecast)

where α is a fraction between 0 and 1. Where conditions are relatively stable, the new forecast will be based on the old forecast, and thus impute a fairly low value to α (0.1 – 0.2). When conditions are more volatile, a higher value of α (0.5 – 0.7) will be used to emphasis more strongly the divergence of the old forecast from the actual demand.

More sophisticated stock control methods are possible through computerisation. As was pointed out earlier, if stock records are inaccurate, the stock control method will also be inaccurate.

5.2   Control levels

In a system where order quantities are constant, it is important to identify alterations to the estimates on which the EOQ was based. Thus, a reporting mechanism is incorporated whereby the stock controller is notified when the stock level exceeds a maximum or falls below a minimum.

Maximum stock level would represent the normal peak holding ie, buffer stocks plus the re-order quantity. If the maximum is exceeded, a review of estimated demand in lead-time is implied.

Minimum stock level usually corresponds with buffer stock. If stock falls below that level, emergency action to replenish may be required.

The foregoing levels would be subject to modification according to the relative importance/cost of a particular stock item.

5.3   The minimum level

The minimum level has been described above as being equal to the buffer stock. An alternative explanation is to describe it as the level below which stocks would not normally be expected to fall. This is equal to:

Re-order level – (Average usage per day × Average lead time (days))

5.4   Example

ABC Limited uses an average of 90 litres of oil per day. Delivery times vary between 2-4 days. It has set its reorder level at 500 litres.

The minimum level is:

$500 - (90 \times 3)$

$= 230$ litres

5.5   Activity

Calculate the minimum stock level from the following data:

Re-order level	2,400 units
Average lead time	5 days
Maximum usage	600 units per day
Minimum usage	200 units per day

5.6   Activity solution

$2,400 - (400 \times 5)$

$= 400$ units.

5.7   The maximum level

The maximum level may be referred to as the level above which stock should not normally rise, it is given by:

$$\text{Re-order level} + \text{order quantity} - \left(\frac{\text{Minimum usage} \times \text{Minimum lead}}{\text{per day} \quad \text{time (days)}} \right)$$

5.8   Example

Z Limited places an order of 500 units, to replenish its stock of a particular component whenever the stock balance is reduced to 300 units. The order takes at least 4 days to be delivered and Z Limited uses at least 50 components each day.

The maximum level is:

$$300 + 500 - (50 \times 4)$$

$$= 600 \text{ units}$$

5.9   Activity

The following data relates to an item of raw material:

Cost of the raw material	£10 per unit
Usage per day	100 units
Minimum lead time	20 days
Maximum lead time	30 days
Cost of ordering material	£400 per order
Carrying costs	10% per annum

Note: assume that each year consists of 48 working weeks of five days per week.

You are required to calculate

(i)   the order level;
(ii)   the re-order quantity;
(iii)   the maximum level;
(iv)   the minimum level.

5.10   Activity solution

(i)   3,000 units
(ii)   4,382 units
(iii)   5,382 units
(iv)   500 units.

5.11   Slow-moving stocks

Certain items may have a high individual value, but subject to infrequent demands. Slow-moving items may be ordered only when required, unless a minimum order quantity were imposed by the supplier.

A regular report of slow-moving items is useful so that management is made aware of changes in demand and of possible obsolescence. Arrangements may then be made to reduce or eliminate stock levels or, on confirmation of obsolescence, for disposal.

5.12   Stock control systems - summary

It is often assumed in stock control questions that the usage is known precisely and that fresh supplies would be received as soon as stock ran out. In practice, both usage and delivery time are subject to fluctuation and changes in circumstances.

To keep stock levels under control, therefore, management must recognise the existence of uncertainty and will need a regular flow of information on stock levels to act upon. For economy the stock control system is frequently restricted to the most important items. It has been estimated that in many businesses, about 20% of the items comprise about 80% of total materials cost.

A stock control system will contain the following features:

(a)   Prediction of likely usage and delivery period (lead time); expressed as maximum, minimum and average.

(b)   Calculation of order quantity.

(c)   Establishment of control levels - minimum stock, re-order point and maximum level.

(d)   Regular reports.

5.13   Turnover ratio

Stock turnover is the ratio of the average value of stores to annual value of materials consumed. The turnover rate indicates the period for which the working capital investment (represented by the average value of stock) is required.

Turnover ratios need to be closely controlled as a low rate implies excessive stockholding costs; a high rate may, however, reflect an undesirable risk of running out of stock.

For really useful information, turnover ratios should be analysed by type of material. An acceptable rate for one type may be undesirable for another because special factors, such as deterioration, risk and quantity discounts, may affect particular items.

5.14   Calculating the ratio

Stores turnover ratio is usually expressed as a percentage, representing:

$$\frac{\text{Cost of materials used in a period}}{\text{Value of average stock of materials in a period}} \times 100$$

An overall business ratio may be derived from the final accounts by adjusting purchases for stock movements and estimating average stock value as:

$$\frac{\text{Opening stock} + \text{Closing stock}}{2}$$

The business ratio is, however, superficial and inadequate for control purposes. For internal management use ratios may be:

(a)   classified by types of materials stocked;
(b)   compared with previous period or a target/budget;
(c)   related to quantity as well as, or instead of, to value.

5.15   Calculation problems

It is important to recognise the limitations and problems involved in calculating stock turnover ratios:

(a)   If many ratios are calculated at frequent intervals, the work involved may not justify the benefit derived.

(b)   The term 'average' is subject to different interpretations and methods of calculation.

(c)   Comparison of average stock value with the value of purchases over a period may be distorted by fluctuations in prices; ratios based on quantity would obviate this problem but additional analysis work may be required to obtain data covering stock and purchase quantities.

6   CONCLUSIONS

Holding stocks is an investment and thus should only be undertaken if the advantages are greater than the costs involved. In many firms stocks of non-standard and expensive goods are held to satisfy a special customer: how many such firms have ever considered whether the cost of holding these stocks might not be greater than the contribution derived from sales to that customer?

The techniques described earlier relate to single stock items, implying an assumption that if every item is held at an economic level, then total stockholding will be at the optimum. This assumption is valid only if adequate resources (space, personnel and finance) are available to maintain the total optimum level. It is possible that mathematical programming techniques could be used to modify individual levels within overall constraints, but a number of practical approaches to reducing total investment in inventory are appropriate:

(a)   rationalisation of the variety of stock items held;

(b)   reduction in the level of customer services offered, either in general or selectively;

(c)   identifying less profitable items stocked, in relation to some measure which represents a limiting factor in stockholding;

(d)   using long-term contracts with suppliers, whereby deliveries are made according to a schedule which benefits the purchaser in relation to inventory carrying costs.

7   MODERN TECHNIQUES

7.1   Just-in-time scheduling/Kanban

Over the past few years firms (particularly in Japan) have been trying to reduce their stock levels by adopting a 'just in time' system.

At first sight the term 'just-in-time' stock policy would seem to be precisely what an 'ideal stock control system' sets out to achieve: a reorder level selected so that, just as the last unit of stock is used up, a fresh consignment arrives. As such, this is not inconsistent with the use of economic quantity policies. However 'just-in-time' has another interpretation.

A just-in-time production (and stock) system consists of a series of small factory units each delivering to one another in successive stages of production and eventually to the final assembly plant. Each factory unit might work to a lead time of one day ie, each unit delivers to the next unit the exact quantity it needs for the following day's production. It is used widely in the Japanese automobile industry where it is referred to as 'Kanban'.

The system was developed by Toyota who managed to achieve very low stock levels by relying on 'dedicated' suppliers who would deliver on time, as often as two or three times a day, defect-free components. The system has been tried in Britain with mixed results.

In order that such a system can be successfully adopted, the following are required:

(a)   stable, high volume.

(b)   co-ordination of the daily production programmes of the supplier and the consumer.

(c)   co-operation of the supplier who will ensure that the staff will make up for any problems of machine breakdowns or unforeseen defects in components.

(d)   suitably designed factory layout for the consumer (each production line needs its own delivery bay rather than the factory having a single warehouse delivery area).

(e)   a convenient, reliable transport system or the supplier being in close proximity to the consumer.

(f)   part ownership of the supplier by the consumer will help, particularly in fostering a suitable attitude to the job in hand.

The relative costs and benefits of such a policy are:

(a)   warehousing costs have been almost eliminated, sub-contracted to the supplier.

(b)   the quality control function has been made the responsibility of the supplier.

(c)   problems of obsolescence, deterioration, theft, cost of capital tied up and all other costs associated with holding stock have been avoided. (However, the production and unloading facilities may have to be specially designed or redesigned.)

In Britain it might not be possible to obtain suppliers as reliable as can be found in Japan. The accounting effects of JIT are discussed later in the text.

7.2   Material requirements planning (MRP)

This is a rather grand title given to the idea of basing inventory levels on the budget for the period. The ideal firstly is to derive the production budget from the sales budget. Stock requirements are then ascertained from the production budget. The stock requirements are then compared with any inventory on hand to determine the quantities it is necessary to purchase in the period. It is then possible to determine the re-order quantity which should be adopted for that period.

8   SELF-TEST QUESTIONS

8.1   Explain the meaning of the two-bin system of inventory control. (1.2)

8.2   Why may there be differences between physical stocks and recorded stocks? (1.4)

8.3   What is pareto analysis as related to stock control? (1.5)

8.4   Explain the objective of using the EOQ model. (3.1)

9   EXAMINATION TYPE QUESTION

9.1   Computer bureau order quantity

It has been estimated that a computer bureau will need 1,000 boxes of line printer paper next year. The purchasing officer of the bureau plans to arrange regular deliveries from a supplier, who charges £15 per delivery.

The bureau's accountant advises the purchasing officer that the cost of storing a box of line printer paper for a year is £2.70. Over a year, the average number of boxes in storage is half the order quantity (that is the number of boxes per delivery).

The ordering cost is defined as the delivery cost plus the storage cost, where the annual costs for an order quantity of x boxes will be:

Delivery cost:

$$\text{Number of deliveries} \times \text{Cost per delivery} = £\frac{100}{x} \times 15$$

Storage stock:

$$\text{Average stock level} \times \text{Storage cost per box} = £\frac{x}{2} \times 2.70$$

You are required:

(a)   to calculate the delivery cost, storage cost and ordering cost for order quantities of 50, 100, 150, 200 and 250 boxes;

                                                                                                 (3 marks)

(b)   to sketch these values for delivery cost, storage cost and ordering cost on the same graph; and

                                                                                                 (5 marks)

(c)   to estimate the order quantity which will minimise cost.

                                                                                                 (2 marks)

                                                                                        (Total: 10 marks)

10   ANSWER TO EXAMINATION TYPE QUESTION

10.1   Computer bureau order quantity

(a)   **Calculation of cost associated with particular order quantities**

Order Quantity	Delivery cost $\dfrac{1,000}{x} \times 15$ £	Storage cost $\dfrac{x}{2} \times 2.70$ £	Ordering cost Delivery cost + Storage cost £
50	$\dfrac{1,000}{50} \times 15 = 300$	$\dfrac{50}{2} \times 2.70 = 67.50$	367.50
100	$\dfrac{1,000}{100} \times 15 = 150$	$\dfrac{100}{2} \times 2.70 = 135.00$	285.00
150	$\dfrac{1,000}{150} \times 15 = 100$	$\dfrac{150}{2} \times 2.70 = 202.50$	302.50
200	$\dfrac{1,000}{200} \times 15 = 75$	$\dfrac{200}{2} \times 2.70 = 270.00$	345.00
250	$\dfrac{1,000}{250} \times 15 = 60$	$\dfrac{250}{2} \times 2.70 = 337.50$	397.50

(b)   For graph see next page.

(c)   From the graph, the optimum order quantity is approximately **106 units**.

(ie, the graph enables us to obtain a more accurate solution.)

Note: from the figures calculated in (a) we can see that the order quantity of 100 units results in the lowest cost.

This would be the answer to give if we had not been required to prepare a graph.

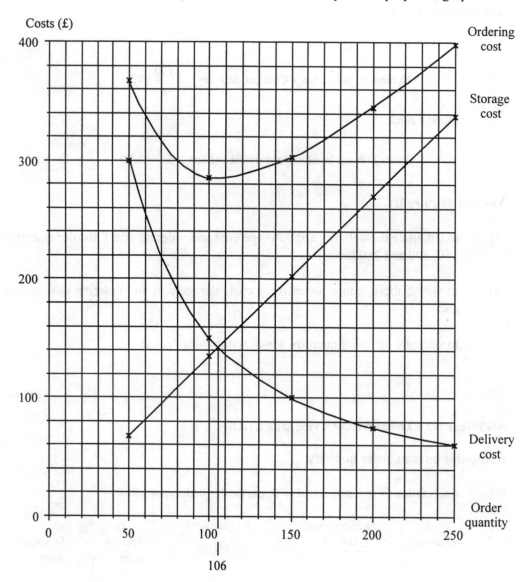

4 ACCOUNTING FOR LABOUR

INTRODUCTION & LEARNING OBJECTIVES

Syllabus area 6a. Cost accounting appropriate to service and production based organisations. (Ability required 3).

This chapter considers the different remuneration methods which may be used to determine the wages of employees together with the procedures and documentation used to record and account for labour costs.

When you have studied this chapter you should be able to do the following:

- Explain the difference between time rate and piece rate remuneration methods.

- Calculate the wage cost of employees including any bonuses.

- Explain the documentation used to attribute labour costs to cost centres and cost units.

---

1 LABOUR COSTS

1.1 Personal history

The personnel department will maintain a history record for each employee. The record will include such details as:

(a) full name and address;
(b) previous employment;
(c) clock number issued;
(d) date engaged;
(e) department, job title and pay rate upon engagement;
(f) amendments to (e) above, recorded as and when the occur;
(g) on the termination of employment, the date and reason for leaving.

1.2 Time recording

Time recording is required both for payment purposes, and also for determining costs to be charged to specific jobs. These may be described diagrammatically:

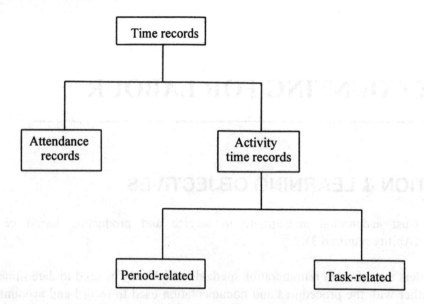

Wages cost represents payments for **direct** and **indirect** labour. Both types of workers will be supplied with **time cards** (gate or clock cards) or other records on which to record their time of arrival and departure from the factory. Such records will provide the basis for wages calculation at time rates. For direct workers **job cards** may also be maintained to record the time spent on particular orders as a basis for cost accounting.

Where possible, time recording clocks should be used to ensure the accuracy of time records.

The precise arrangements for job-time recording should be adapted to the nature and organisation of production, and so will vary from one factory to another. In some cases a card for each job may accompany that job through the factory, each worker involved noting or 'clocking' the time spent on the one card. Alternatively a separate job card or ticket may be issued to each worker for each job.

(a)   **Attendance records**

These are usually either a register, or mechanical/electronic time recorder. The most sophisticated time recorders use plastic identity cards and are directly linked to a central computer.

(b)   **Period related activity time records**

These may be for daily, weekly, or sometimes longer periods. An example of a weekly time sheet is given below:

Weekly Time Sheet				Dept:		
Employees No				**Name**		**Wk Edg**
To be completed by employee				*For Office Use*		
Day	*Start*	*Finish*	*Job*	*Code*	*Hrs*	*Amounts* £ p
Foreman's Signatures:				**Gross Wages**		

(c)   **Task related activity time records**

Known variously as job sheets, operations charts or piecework tickets. They are generally more accurate and reliable than time-related activity time records, and are essential for use with incentive schemes. An example is given below:

Time Sheet					
Employee name:			**No:**		
Start date:			**Finish date:**		
Department:			**Operation:**		
Day	*Start*	*Finish*	*Time*	*Production*	*Foreman's Signature*
1					
2					
3					
4					
5					
Total					
Time allowed					
Time saved					

	Hours	*Rate* £ P	*Paid* £ P
Time wages			
Bonus			
Total wages			

(d)   **Reconciliation of activity time and attendance time**

This is essential to ensure the accuracy of the information.

2   PAYROLL

2.1   Payroll preparation

Because of the sums of money involved, security control is necessary at all stages of the task of payroll preparation and payment. One major area of risk is the introduction of fictitious employees ('dummies' or 'ghosting') in the payroll.

The payroll preparation involves:

(a)   calculating gross wages from time and activity records;

(b)   calculating net wages after PAYE and other deductions, and properly recording the deductions; and

(c)   preparing a cash analysis of total cash required for payment.

2.2   Making up pay-packets

The cash is made up into pay-packets for each employee, together with a pay-slip.

2.3   Paying out wages

This is an area where physical security is very important. Another problem is unclaimed wages (eg, if the employee is sick). Procedures are required for proper control and alternative means of distributing such unclaimed wages.

2.4   Summary

The payroll provides supplementary analysis for entries in the financial accounts and the gross wage total is a control figure for cost analysis.

3   FUNCTIONAL ANALYSIS OF WAGES

Under a costing system, it will be necessary to functionally analyse the gross wages and post these to the cost accounts. This is done from the activity time records:

(a)   Weekly time sheets - no problem.

(b)   Daily time sheets - usually posted from daily sheets, any discrepancy with payroll being charged to an adjustment account.

(c)   Job sheets - again these may lead to small differences, because jobs overlap pay weeks. These are also usually written off to an adjustment account.

Indirect wages are usually analysed according to activity - supervision, inspection, etc.

4   REMUNERATION METHODS

4.1   Time rates

The most common method of payment is time rate, whereby employees are paid a basic rate per hour, day, or week irrespective of production achieved. Basic time rate provides no incentive to improve productivity and close supervision is necessary.

A variation is known as 'higher time rates', where rates above the basic level are offered and paid, to attract more enthusiastic and skilled employees.

4.2   Piece-work

The direct alternative to time rate is piece-work, whereby a fixed amount is paid per unit of output achieved, irrespective of time spent. Rigid inspection procedures are required to ensure work is of an adequate standard.

Straight piece-work is almost extinct today as a result of employment legislation and trade union resistance.

Piece-workers are usually required to keep time records for disciplinary and security purposes.

A variation is 'differential piece rates'. This is almost a penal system, with a low piece rate for the first units of production, and a high piece rate for subsequent units.

4.3   Incentive schemes

These have developed from the piece rate approach, but attempt to avoid the crudities of the system described above.

The variety of approaches are described by the diagram below:

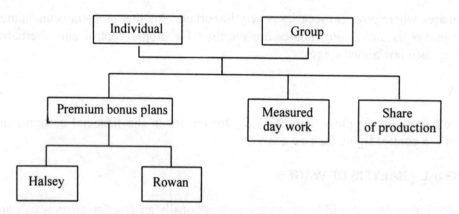

These are all explained in the sections below:

As a general rule, any incentive scheme should satisfy the following requirements:

(a)   Related closely to effort.
(b)   Agreed by prior consultation between employer and employees.
(c)   Understandable and simple to operate.
(d)   Capable of being beneficial to the average worker.

4.4   Premium bonus plans

The basic idea of all premium bonus plans is to pay a basic time rate, plus a portion of the time saved as compared to some agreed allowed time. Examples of such schemes are Halsey and Rowan.

(a)   **Halsey** - The employee receives 50% of the time saving ie,

$$\text{Bonus} = \frac{\text{Time allowed} - \text{Time taken}}{2} \times \text{Time rate}$$

Example

Employee's basic rate	=	£4.80 per hour
Allowed time for Job A	=	1 hour
Time taken for Job A	=	36 minutes

$$\text{Bonus} = \frac{60-36}{2}\times\frac{£4.80}{60} \qquad 0.96$$

$$\text{Basic rate} = \frac{36}{60}\times£4.80 \qquad 2.88$$

Total payment for Job A   3.84

(b) **Rowan** - The proportion paid to the employee is based on the ratio of time taken to time allowed ie,

$$\text{Bonus} = \frac{\text{Time allowed} - \text{Time taken}}{\text{Time allowed}}\times\text{Time rate}$$

Example

Using the facts in (a) above.

$$\text{Bonus} = \frac{36}{60}\times\frac{£4.80}{60}\times 24 \qquad 1.15$$

$$\text{Basic rate} = \frac{36}{60}\times£4.80 \qquad 2.88$$

Total payment for Job A   4.03

Note that if the time taken in the example had been 18 minutes instead of 36, the bonus under Halsey would be £1.68 compared with £1.00 under Rowan. The sliding scale operation of Rowan safeguards the employer against errors in fixing the allowance.

Premium bonus schemes of the type described are really appropriate only for skilled craftsmen. In continuous production the output of the individual worker is largely governed by the speed of the flow line, although such schemes may be suitable for special jobs eg, fitting radios in motor car assembly. As with straight piece-work, production under bonus for time-saving requires strict inspection to prevent poor quality work.

4.5 Measured day work

The concept of this approach is to pay a high time rate, but this rate is based on an analysis of past performance. Initially, work measurement is used to calculate the allowed time per unit. This allowed time is compared to the time actually taken in the past by the employee, and if this is better than the allowed time an incentive is agreed.

Example

Allowed time - 1 hour.

Average time taken by employee over last three months - 50 minutes.

Normal rate - £4.80/hour.

Agreed incentive rate (say) - £5.00/hour.

Note: the incentive rate will be a matter of negotiation, but in the above example is 50% of the time saved.

This incentive wage rate will be reviewed periodically in the light of the employee's actual performance.

4.6   Share of production plans

In order to understand this plan, it is necessary to introduce the concept of added value. This is explained below:

	£
Sales	X
Less: Cost of external inputs (ie, all costs except payroll)	X
Value added	X

Generally, wages tends to maintain a constant relationship to value added, usually about 40%.

Share of production plans are based on acceptance by both management and labour representatives of a constant share of value added for payroll. Thus, any gains in value added - whether by improved production performance or cost savings - are shared by employees in this ratio.

4.7   Example

	£
Sales	100,000
Less: External inputs	55,000
Value added	45,000
Agreed wages share 40% value added	18,000
Wages paid	15,000
Balance paid as bonus	3,000

4.8   Group incentive schemes

All of the schemes discussed above can be operated as group incentive schemes. This more closely relates to reality, in that improved performance is the result of group rather than individual effort.

4.9   Example

Ten men work as a group. When production of the group exceeds the standard - 200 pieces per hour - each man in the group is paid a bonus for the excess production in addition to his wages at hourly rates.

The bonus is computed thus: the percentage of production in excess of the standard quantity is found, and one half of the percentage is regarded as the men's share. Each man in the group is paid as a bonus this percentage of a wage rate of £5.20 per hour. There is no relationship between the individual workman's hourly rate and the bonus rate.

The following is one week's record:

	Hours worked	Production
Monday	90	24,500
Tuesday	88	20,600
Wednesday	90	24,200
Thursday	84	20,100
Friday	88	20,400
Saturday	40	10,200
	480	120,000

You are required:

(a)   to compute the rate and amount of bonus for the week;

(b)   calculate the total pay of Jones, who worked 42 hours and was paid £3.00 per hour basic; and that of Smith, who worked 44 hours and was paid £3.75 per hour basic.

4.10   Solution

(a)
Standard production for the week = 480 hours × 200	=	96,000 pieces
Actual production for the week	=	120,000 pieces

$$\text{Bonus rate} = \frac{24,000}{96,000} \times 0.5 \times £5.20$$

$$= \text{65p per hour}$$

$$\text{Total bonus} = 480 \text{ hours} \times 65p$$

$$= £312$$

(b)

		Jones £		Smith £
Basic	42 × £3.00	126.00	44 × £3.75	165.00
Bonus	42 × £0.65	27.30	44 × £0.65	28.60
Total pay		153.30		193.60

4.11   Activity

Calculate the bonus payable under the Halsey scheme using the following data

Employee's basic rate	£3.60 per hour
Time allowed for job	40 minutes
Time taken for job	25 minutes

4.12   Activity solution

$$\text{Bonus} = \frac{(40-25)}{2} \times \frac{£3.60}{60} = £0.45$$

5   TECHNIQUES OF INCENTIVE SCHEMES

5.1   Work study

The function of work study is to analyse, measure and value operations and processes. The results of work study are the basis for operating incentive schemes, but will also assist in planning and control of production methods and labour efficiency.

Work study comprises three elements:

(a)   Method study - observation and analysis of existing and suggested methods of operation to find the most efficient ways.

(b)   Motion study - development of improvement in work by reducing effort and fatigue, and by relating human effort to the availability and use of mechanical aids.

(c)   Time study - using the results of method and motion study to determine a standard time for each operation.

5.2   Job evaluation

Job evaluation is an attempt to provide a logical basis for paying employees by assessing the characteristics of a job in comparison with other jobs. The system's main application is in large organisations to develop a consistent grading structure, but it can also be of benefit to the personnel department in finding suitable employees and ensuring that they are employed in jobs which fit their individual capabilities.

Job evaluation is not a system of payment by results but may be used to introduce a wage differential based on the characteristics of the job being done.

Example

Job characteristic	Total points	Job XYZ
Training	40	30
Skill	50	40
Physical effort	40	10
Mental effort	60	50
Responsibility	80	40
Working conditions	50	10
Danger	80	20
Total	400	200

Wage differentials: points	Hourly rate increase £
50 - 99	0.10
100 - 149	0.20
150 - 199	0.30
200 - 249	0.40
250 - 299	0.50
300 - 349	0.60
350 - 399	0.70

Increased hourly rate for job XYZ = +£0.40.

5.3   Merit rating

Whereas job evaluation evaluates the **job** irrespective of who does it, merit rating evaluates the **employee** doing the job. The scheme operates in a similar manner to that described for job evaluation but the characteristics will be such things as:

(a)   Initiative;
(b)   Reliability;
(c)   Attendance;
(d)   Punctuality;
(e)   Accuracy;
(f)   Thoroughness;
(g)   Safety;
(h)   Behaviour.

5.4   Incentives to non-production workers

The main incentive schemes are only appropriate where production can be measured in saleable output. However, job evaluation/merit rating and co-partnership/profit sharing can be valuable incentives to service and administration employees.

The principle of relating reward to achievement, however, is capable of adaptation to many activities; for example, typists in a pool could be paid a group bonus based on the number of acceptable pages typed in a period.

Alternatively, managerial and skilled technical employees may be given objectives for achievement in the period ahead and, if they agree that the objectives are attainable, their rewards, in terms of bonus of increased salary, would be related to success in meeting the objectives.

6   LABOUR COST ACCOUNTING AND REPORTS

6.1   Direct and indirect wages

The distinction between direct and indirect costs has previously been explained. Indirect wages represent:

(a)   the cost of time spent by direct labour on non-productive work eg, cleaning machines or waiting for materials;

(b)   the gross wage of factory personnel not actually engaged in production eg, maintenance men, fork-lift truck operators, supervisors.

It was noted above that the gross wages total provided from the payroll represents a control figure for cost analysis and it was seen that gross wages comprise basic pay, overtime, bonuses and allowances. For cost ascertainment purposes, direct wages will be charged to cost units and indirect wages will be charged to cost centres for later allotment to cost units.

The accounting treatment for cost ascertainment purposes sometimes conflicts with the need to provide information for control, but examination of the differences in approach is left to a later chapter.

One further point may require clarification. CIMA defines 'wages cost' as the **cost of employees' remuneration**, which may be interpreted as including salaries of managers and administrators. In fact, the distinction between wages and salaries is meaningless for cost accounting purposes; what is important is whether the payment can be regarded as direct or indirect.

6.2   Accounting treatment of overtime premium

The treatment of the overtime **premium** depends on the reason for the overtime being worked. If the overtime is worked at the specific request of a customer the **premium** should be charged to the customer and therefore to work in progress control.

If the overtime arises as a result of company policy to increase production generally, then the premium should be charged to production overhead along with other indirect wage costs and charged to the product via the overhead recovery rate.

6.3   Productivity

One of the major responsibilities of production management is to improve productivity. To assist in this, regular reports analysed by process, machine group or department are required, showing:

(a)   numbers of employees (direct and indirect);
(b)   labour costs (analysed into basic, premium and bonuses);
(c)   production achieved (in standard hours where a variety of products is made);
(d)   hours worked, hours lost and hours spent on non-productive work;
(e)   ratios to show trends.

Such reports are most effective when a comparison plan is incorporated. A central feature of such a comparison is the **productivity index**. This expresses the actual number of units produced as a percentage of the standard or budgeted production for the period eg, actual production in June was 1,100 units, standard production was 1,000 units. The productivity index is 110%.

Note the difference between **production** and **productivity**. Production is output in terms of units eg, 1,000 units per month. Productivity is this output expressed relative to a vital resource eg, 10 cars per man per year, or 12 tons of steel per man per month.

6.4   Idle time

Idle time is a cost which represents waste and warrants close control. To assist control, time booking procedures should permit analysis of idle time by cause, and analysis should disclose whether idle time was capable of being avoided by action within the business.

The three main causes of idle time are:

(a)   **Production disruption** - due to machine breakdown, shortage of materials, inefficient scheduling etc.

(b)   **Policy decisions** - run-down of stocks, changes in product specification, retraining schemes, etc.

(c)   **Outside influences** - sudden fall in demand due to VAT changes, a strike affecting vital supplies, etc.

6.5   The cost of strikes

It is sometimes necessary to identify the costs of strikes. These may include:

(a)   lost production (to the extent it cannot subsequently be made good);
(b)   loss of customer goodwill;
(c)   penalty clauses in suppliers' contracts if goods are not purchased;
(d)   overtime in post-strike period making good lost production;
(e)   problem of financing the business during the period of the strike.

These costs must be balanced against the savings the company hopes to make by resisting employee demands.

6.6   Labour turnover

The main objective of the personnel department is to minimise turnover of labour. It is evident that each time an employee is replaced, the business incurs direct costs of:

(a)   advertising and selection;
(b)   administering departure and replacement;
(c)   training;
(d)   reduced efficiency until the new employee reaches the required skill.

Furthermore, a high rate of turnover tends to lower the performance of continuing employees, who may become restless and resentful of the extra burden of training new members and of additional temporary duties imposed upon them.

To assist control of labour turnover, the personnel department will maintain records of employees leaving, analysed to show:

(a)   personnel details - sex, age groups etc;
(b)   department or section in which employed;
(c)   length of service;
(d)   reason for leaving.

Analysis in respect of (d) would be useful to disclose whether a particular cause is recurring, especially if the cause can be avoided by action within the business. Such statistics should, however, be regarded with caution, as employees frequently hide, or neglect to explain clearly, the true reason.

6.7   Control of labour costs

It is essential that labour costs are controlled but in modern manufacturing systems labour costs are frequently a small element of the overall costs. The control procedures need to be tailored to each specific situation. If labour costs are, say, 50% of total costs then detailed control procedures can be implemented, if however labour only forms a small, say, 5% of total cost then the control procedures will be less important.

6.8   Direct/indirect wages and control bills

Within any company, and with consistent classification, this ratio should stay fairly constant.

Example

	This week £	Last week £
Direct wages	4,700	4,500
Indirect wages	2,600	2,700
Total	7,300	7,200
Ratio	1.81	1.67

This provides a very crude control over indirect wages.

7   CHAPTER SUMMARY

This chapter has considered the remuneration methods available together with appropriate incentive schemes to improve productivity.

The collection of costs has been explained by reference to the appropriate documentation and labour cost reporting considered.

8   SELF TEST QUESTIONS

8.1   Distinguish between attendance records and activity time records. (1.2)

8.2   List the steps involved in payroll preparation. (2.1)

8.3   Explain work study. (5.1)

8.4   Distinguish between job evaluation and merit rating. (5.2/5.3)

8.5   Explain the difference between direct and indirect wages cost. (6.1)

8.6   Explain the treatment of overtime premium when preparing cost accounts. (6.2)

8.7   Why is it important to control labour turnover? (6.6)

9   EXAMINATION TYPE QUESTIONS

9.1   Control of labour costs

How can the cost accountant help to control labour costs in an organisation?

(15 marks)

9.2   Components A, B and C

A factory manufactures three components A, B and C.

During week 26, the following was recorded:

Labour grade	Number of employees	Rate per hour £	Individuals hours worked
I	6	4.00	40
II	18	3.20	42
III	4	2.80	40
IV	1	1.60	44

Output and standard times during the same week were:

Component	Output	Standard minutes (each) £
A	444	30
B	900	54
C	480	66

The normal working week is 38 hours, overtime is paid at a premium of 50% of the normal hourly rate.

A group incentive scheme is in operation. The time saved is expressed as a percentage of hours worked and is shared between the group as a proportion of the hours worked by each grade.

The rate paid is 75% of the normal hourly rate.

You are required:

(a) To calculate the total payroll showing the basic pay, overtime premium and bonus pay as separate totals for each grade of labour.

(18 marks)

(b) To journalise the payroll assuming: income tax deducted is £884.00; national insurance payable by employee is 6% of gross pay; national insurance payable by employer is 5% of gross pay; 12 employees are members of the Social Club whose weekly subscription is 25 pence.

(6 marks)

(c) To summarise two advantages and two disadvantages of group incentive schemes.

(4 marks)

(Total: 28 marks)

10   **ANSWERS TO EXAMINATION TYPE QUESTIONS**

10.1   **Control of labour costs**

In cost and management accounting the word 'control' has many different meanings. The overall aim of control is to ensure that, for a given level of sales, costs are kept as low as possible and hence that profit is as high as possible.

In this question the examiner is focusing on the ways in which information prepared by the cost accountant or systems implemented by the cost accountant can assist in the control of labour related costs. These may be summarised as follows:

(a) **Labour turnover**

$$\frac{\text{Number of people who leave who require replacement}}{\text{Average number employed}} \times 100$$

This provides an indication of whether an unacceptably high number of people are leaving the company. This can cause costs of recruitment and training to be unnecessarily high.

(b) **Incentive schemes**

A way of improving efficiency and reducing the need for supervision is to use some form of incentive scheme. The cost accountant would be needed to quantify the costs and benefits of schemes.

(c) **Payroll preparation and wage payment procedures**

The cost accountant is in a position to implement control procedures to minimise the risk of fraud or errors in the payroll department.

(d)   **Wage analysis**

When analysing wage costs care should be taken to ensure all costs are accounted for eg, charged to the appropriate job. Any controllable idle time which arises should be analysed into causes and reported to management.

(e)   **Standard costing**

Three major benefits of implementing a standard costing system are:

(i)   In the process of preparing standard costs production methods should be reviewed to try to achieve reductions in cost eg, to make use of newly available technology which may reduce the amount of labour time required.

(ii)   The standard provides a target for the production manager to work to.

(iii)   The standard provides a basis for comparison with actual results. This enables the cost accountant to calculate labour efficiency, rate and idle time variances, providing management with valuable feedback.

(f)   **Clock cards**

Employees' attendance times may be recorded using a properly supervised clock card system. This will facilitate recording lateness and absenteeism of employees.

(g)   **Authorisation**

Procedures should be implemented to ensure that:

(i)   Overtime is only worked when authorised by the appropriate manager.

(ii)   Output of employees on piece-rates is recorded and checked. Arrangements whether employees are paid for any rejects should be built into any scheme.

When setting up any system, procedure or report, consideration should be given as to whether it is cost effective ie, do the potential savings exceed the cost of operating the system/procedure or the cost of preparing the report?

10.2   Components A, B and C

(a)   **Calculation of total payroll cost**

	Grade of labour				
	I	II	III	IV	Total
	£	£	£	£	£
Basic pay:					
I 6 × £4.00 × 40	960.00				
II 18 × £3.20 × 42		2,419.20			
III 4 × £2.80 × 40			448.00		
IV 1 × £1.60 × 44				70.40	
	960.00	2,419.20	448.00	70.40	3,897.60

	£	£	£	£	£
Overtime premium:					
I $5 \times £2.00 \times (40 - 38)$	24.00				
II $18 \times £1.60 \times (42 - 38)$		115.20			
III $4 \times £1.40 \times (40 - 38)$			11.20		
IV $1 \times £0.80 \times (44 - 38)$				4.80	
	24.00	115.20	11.20	4.80	155.20

Bonus payable (see working):

	Grade of labour				
	I	II	III	IV	Total
	£	£	£	£	£
I $\dfrac{6 \times 40}{1,200} \times 360 \times (75\% \times £4)$	216.00				
II $\dfrac{18 \times 42}{1,200} \times 360 \times (75\% \times £3.20)$		544.32			
III $\dfrac{4 \times 40}{1,200} \times 360 \times (75\% \times £2.80)$			100.80		
IV $\dfrac{1 \times 44}{1,200} \times 360 \times (75\% \times £1.60)$				15.84	
	216.00	544.32	100.80	15.84	876.96
Total gross pay	1,200.00	3,078.72	560.00	91.04	4,929.76

WORKING

Standard time for actual output:

Component		Std hrs
A	$444 \times 0.5 =$	222
B	$900 \times 0.9 =$	810
C	$480 \times 1.1 =$	528
Total standard hours		1,560

Actual time:

Grade		
I	6×40	240
II	18×42	756
III	4×40	160
IV	1×44	44
Total standard hours		1,200
Total hours saved		360

(b)   **Journal**

	£	£
Wages	4,929.76	
National insurance (paid by company): 5% × £4,929.76	246.48	
Income tax payable		884.00
National insurance payable £246.48 + 6% × £4,929.76		542.26
Social club (12 × £0.25)		3.00
Bank		3,746.98
	5,176.24	5,176.24

Being the payroll with deductions and national insurance for Week 26.

(c)   Advantages of a group incentive scheme:

(i)   Emphasises the need for worker co-operation to achieve required targets for the company.

(ii)   Applicable when a production line exists or when operatives work in crews or gangs.

Disadvantages of a group incentive scheme:

(i)   The more conscientious members of the group create the benefit that has to be shared with the less efficient members of the group. This can have a demotivational effect on the former.

(ii)   Where there are different degrees of skill required by members of the group it may be difficult to recognise this easily and objectively in allocating the bonus between the group members.

5 ACCOUNTING FOR OVERHEAD COSTS

INTRODUCTION & LEARNING OBJECTIVES

Syllabus area 6a. Cost accounting appropriate to service and production based organisations. (Ability required 3).

Classification and coding of costs. (Ability required 3).

This chapter is concerned with the collection of indirect costs and the attribution of those related to the production function to cost units.

This is achieved using allocation, apportionment and absorption techniques using pre-determined absorption rates based on budgets.

When you have studied this chapter you should be able to do the following:

- Analyse overhead costs by function.

- Explain the need for functional analysis of overhead costs in the context of stock valuation for financial accounts

- Distinguish between costs which can be allocated to a single cost centre and those which must be apportioned.

- Select appropriate bases of apportionment for different overhead costs.

- Select appropriate measures of output as the basis of overhead absorption.

- Calculate absorption rates based on budgets.

- Compare the amount absorbed using pre-determined absorption rates with actual expenditure to calculate the extent of any under or over absorption.

- Explain and evaluate the causes of any under or over absorption.

- Account for any under or over absorption.

- Explain the difference between traditional absorption methods and the use of activity based costing.

---

1 OVERHEADS

1.1 Objectives

Overheads represent the third cost element. Overheads may be classified into direct and indirect, according to whether or not they are directly related to the production process. In many businesses overheads represent a large element of cost; they also present the biggest problems in terms of accounting treatment, as will become apparent.

The objectives of accounting for overheads are:

(a) to identify costs in relation to output products and services;
(b) to identify costs in relation to activities and divisions of the organisation;
(c) to control overhead costs.

The procedures described in the rest of this section are largely concerned with objective (a) above; their relationship to objectives (b) and (c) are discussed subsequently. The steps involved are directed at establishing an **overhead absorption rate**. This rate is used to relate overheads to cost units.

Whilst such an overhead absorption rate may be a blanket rate for the whole enterprise, normally departmental absorption rates will be established for application to cost units passing through all the production cost centres.

1.2 Production overhead

Overhead represents indirect materials, indirect wages and indirect expenses attributable to production and the service activities associated with production. Marketing, general administration, research and development costs which are not associated with production are not usually treated as overheads for this purpose; consequently, the term 'overhead' may be assumed to mean **production overhead**.

Indirect production costs are incurred in three main ways:

(a) **Production activities** - costs arising in production departments such as fuel, protective clothing, depreciation and supervision.

(b) **Service activities** - the cost of operating non-producing departments or sections within the factory eg, materials handling, production control, canteen.

(c) **Establishment costs** - general production overhead such as factory rent/rates, heating and lighting and production management salaries.

It is important to note that analysis of overhead may be used for two purposes:

(a) To facilitate allotment to cost units.
(b) To relate costs to responsibility as an aid to control.

The following section attempts to explain the principle of absorption costing in general. Detailed procedures, however, may be different depending on the costing method used.

2   COST ALLOTMENT PROCEDURES

2.1 Overview

One of the purposes of cost accounting is to provide a basis for valuing work in progress and finished stocks. SSAP 9 states that the financial accounts should reflect a stock value including a share of indirect costs. The main objective of absorption costing is to arrive at such stock valuations.

So far the allocation of direct costs to cost units has been discussed. Now it is necessary to examine the sharing (or allotment) of indirect costs to cost units. A sequence of procedures is undertaken:

Step 1   Collecting production overhead costs by item.

Step 2   Establishing cost centres.

Step 3   Allocating and apportioning overhead costs to cost centres.

Step 4   Apportioning service cost centre costs to production cost centres.

Step 5   Absorbing production cost centre costs in cost units.

The procedure may be illustrated diagrammatically:

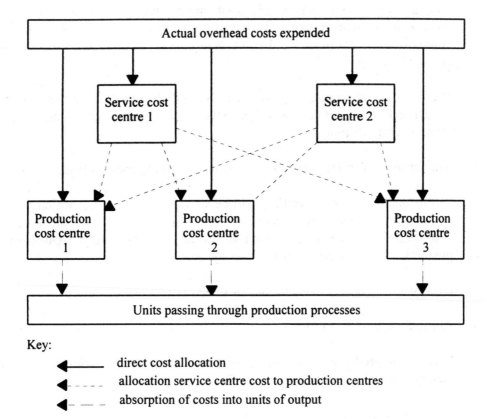

Key:

        ⟵————   direct cost allocation

        ⟵- - - -   allocation service centre cost to production centres

        ⟵- — —   absorption of costs into units of output

The procedures are explained below.

Step 1   **Collecting costs by item**

It has been seen that indirect materials costs were obtained by analysing materials requisitions and that indirect wages cost was derived from an analysis of the payroll. Indirect expenses are recorded from invoices, petty cash vouchers and journal entries (eg, for depreciation) and classified firstly by nature (subjective).

Step 2   **Establishment of cost centres**

In analysing the production activity, the twofold purpose to cost centres and allocation of responsibility for costs should be recognised. Thus, the cost centres established should ideally combine an identifiable activity with a specific person responsible. For example, if Department A comprises three machine groups - I, II and III - under the overall supervision of a departmental supervisor, then it would help responsibility accounting to have only one cost centre for Department A. The three machine groups may, however, perform entirely different production activities, in which case three separate cost centres may be necessary for cost allotment purposes. The cost accountant must decide which alternative to implement.

Service cost centres are usually set up to represent individual service departments eg, stores; but in a large factory a department may combine a number of cost centres related to the responsibility of section heads within the department eg, each sub-store would be a separate cost centre.

| Step 3 | Allocation and apportionment |

The total cost of production overhead needs to be distributed **among** specific cost centres. Some items can be **allocated** immediately eg, the salary of a cost centre supervisor or indirect materials issued to a cost centre; other items need to be **apportioned** between a number of centres eg, factory rent/rates or the factory manager's salary.

The basis for apportioning a total amount will be selected so that the charge to a specific centre will reflect, with reasonable accuracy, the benefit obtained by that centre from the cost incurred.

| Step 4 | Apportioning service cost centre costs to producing cost centres |

Part of the total factory overhead will be allotted to cost centres which do not actually produce the saleable output. In order to reflect the cost of services in unit costs, service cost centre costs must be allotted to producing cost centres (remember these are production services only ie, not marketing, etc).

Once again the basis of apportionment should reflect benefit derived.

| Step 5 | Absorption into cost units |

Finally, the producing cost centres will have been allotted with the total amount of factory overhead, representing:

(a)   allocated costs;
(b)   apportioned costs;
(c)   share of service department costs.

The overhead to be absorbed by a particular cost unit will be calculated by dividing the producing cost centre overhead for a period by the cost units produced by that centre in the period.

When a cost centre produces dissimilar units eg, jobs to customer order, the volume of production must be expressed in a common measurement eg, direct labour hours. When a cost unit passes through several centres, the overhead absorbed should be calculated separately for each centre.

2.2   Illustration of overhead allotment

The ABC Washing Machine Co produces a standard washing machine in three production departments (Machining, Assembling and Finishing) and two service departments (Materials handling and Production control).

Costs for last year, when 2,000 machines were produced, were as follows:

Materials:
Machine shop	£240,000
Assembly	£160,000
Finishing	£40,000
Materials handling	£4,000

Wages:

Machining	10,000 hours at £3.72
Assembly	5,000 hours at £2.88
Finishing	3,000 hours at £3.60
Materials handling	£8,000
Production control	£11,200

Other costs:

Machine shop	£41,920
Assembly	£12,960
Finishing	£7,920
Materials handling	£8,000
Production control	£2,400

It is estimated that the benefit derived from the service departments is as follows:

Materials handling:

Machine shop	60%
Assembly	30%
Finishing	10%

Production control:

Machine shop	40%
Assembly	30%
Finishing	20%
Materials handling	10%

You are required:

(a) to prepare a statement showing the overhead allotted to each of the production departments;

(b) to calculate the unit cost of a washing machine.

2.3 Solution

(a) Overhead allotment

Materials and wages incurred by the production departments may be assumed to be direct costs and therefore excluded from the overhead distribution.

	Total	Machining	Assembly	Finishing	Production control	Materials handling
	£	£	£	£	£	£
Indirect materials (S1)	4,000	-	-	-	-	4,000
Indirect wages (S1)	19,200	-	-	-	11,200	8,000
Other (S1)	73,200	41,920	12,960	7,920	2,400	8,000
(S2)	96,400	41,920	12,960	7,920	13,600	20,000
Production control (S3)	-	5,440	4,080	2,720	(13,600)	1,360
Materials handling (S4)	-	12,816	6,408	2,136	-	(21,360)
(S5)	96,400	60,176	23,448	12,776	-	-

Service department costs have been apportioned to production departments using the percentage benefit shown in the question.

(b)   **Unit cost**

	Machining £	Assembly £	Finishing £	Total £
Direct materials (S1)	240,000	160,000	40,000	440,000
Direct wages (S2)	37,200	14,400	10,800	62,400
Production overheads (S3)	60,176	23,448	12,776	96,400
(S4)	337,376	197,848	63,576	598,800
Units produced				2,000
Cost per unit (S5)				£299.40

2.4   Problems in overhead allotment

The student may reasonably ask 'Why is it necessary to allot overhead expenses if unit costs can be calculated by dividing the total cost by units produced and obtain the same result?' The answer is that the above illustration is an over-simplification of a real life situation and the following aspects of cost ascertainment have been ignored:

(a)   cost units produced are not identical, most businesses produce more than 1 type of good or service;

(b)   work in progress needs to be valued;
(c)   management reports need to be prepared currently;
(d)   cost information is also used to assist control and efficient use of resources.

The above illustration will be used to explain some of the problems of overhead allotment discussed later in this chapter.

2.5   Overhead distribution summary

The illustration above showed a total amount of production overhead of £96,400, which had been allotted to the five cost centres in the production function.

The usual way of recording the details of overhead allotment is to prepare a tabulated overhead distribution summary in the following format:

Overhead item	Total £	Basis of distribution	Cost centres A £	B £	C £	D £	E £
Indirect wages		Payroll					
Indirect materials		Requisition					
Rent		Floor area					
Depreciation		Plant register					
Power		Meters					

The guiding principle is that the total charge for an item should be shared to reflect, with reasonable accuracy, the relative benefit derived by particular cost centres.

Generally, allocation will be more accurate than apportionment but absolute accuracy must often be sacrificed in the interests of economy.   For example, an employer's National Insurance contributions should be analysed according to employee to obtain the exact amounts attributed to each cost centre; the amount involved would probably not justify such analysis and the total charge would be apportioned on the basis of the number of employees in each centre.

2.6   Bases for apportioning costs

In selecting a basis for apportioning an overhead item, the cost of obtaining a high degree of accuracy must be considered.   For example, the charge for heat and light could be shared on the basis of a complex formula incorporating power points, light bulbs and wattage but the student should be aware that the end-result will still be open to question.   When answering examination questions, the student will have to use his own judgement in relation to the information given as it is impracticable to provide a comprehensive list of bases to cover every situation.

2.7   Example

The overhead budget for the month together with data relating to cost centres is as follows:

	£
Supervision	7,525
Indirect workers	6,000
Holiday pay and National Insurance	6,200
Tooling cost	9,400
Machine maintenance labour cost	4,500
Power	1,944
Small tools and supplies	1,171
Insurance of machinery	185
Insurance of building	150
Rent and rates	2,500
Depreciation of machinery	9,250
	48,825

		Machine groups			
	Q	R	S	T	Total
	£	£	£	£	£
Floor space (sq ft)	1,800	1,500	800	900	5,000
Kilowatt hours	270,000	66,000	85,000	65,000	486,000
Capital cost of machines (£)	30,000	20,000	8,000	16,000	74,000
Indirect workers (persons)	3	3	1	1	8
Total workers (persons)	19	24	12	7	62
Machine maintenance hours	3,000	2,000	3,000	1,000	9,000
Tooling costs (£)	3,500	4,300	1,000	600	9,400
Supervision costs (£)	2,050	2,200	1,775	1,500	7,525
Small tools and supplies (£)	491	441	66	173	1,171
Machine running hours	30,000	36,000	19,000	8,000	93,000

Calculate a machine hour rate for each of the four groups of machines.

2.8   Solution

		Machine hour rates				
	Basis	*Q* £	*R* £	*S* £	*T* £	*Total* £
Supervision	A	2,050	2,200	1,775	1,500	7,525
Indirect workers	4	2,250	2,250	750	750	6,000
Holiday pay and NI	5	1,900	2,400	1,200	700	6,200
Tooling cost	A	3,500	4,300	1,000	600	9,400
Machine maintenance labour	6	1,500	1,000	1,500	500	4,500
Power	2	1,080	264	340	260	1,944
Small tools, etc	A	491	441	66	173	1,171
Insurance of machines	3	75	50	20	40	185
Insurance of buildings	1	54	45	24	27	150
Rent and rates	1	900	750	400	450	2,500
Depreciation of machinery	3	3,750	2,500	1,000	2,000	9,250
		17,550	16,200	8,075	7,000	48,825
Machine running hours		30,000	36,000	19,000	8,000	93,000
Machine hour rate		£0.585	£0.450	£0.425	£0.875	£0.525

Bases of apportionment:

1	Floor space	5	Total workers
2	Kilowatt hours	6	Machine maintenance hours
3	Capital cost of		
	machines	A	Direct-allocated
4	No of indirect		
	workers		

Note that depreciation is apportioned on the basis of capital cost. The usage of machines will be reflected in the machine hour rate.

2.9   Activity

Speed Manufacturing Co Ltd

Speed Manufacturing Co Ltd has three production departments (two machine shops and one assembly shop) and three service departments, one of which - the Engineering Service Department - serves the machine shops only.

The annual budgeted overhead costs for the year are:

	Indirect wages £	Consumable supplies £
Machine shop A	23,260	6,300
Machine shop B	20,670	9,100
Assembly	8,110	2,100
Stores	4,100	1,400
Engineering service	2,670	2,100
General service	3,760	1,600
	62,570	22,600

	£
Depreciation of machinery	22,000
Insurance of machinery	4,000
Insurance of building	1,800 (Note 1)
Power	3,600
Light and heat	3,000
Rent and rates	7,050 (Note 2)

Notes:

(1)   Because of special fire risks, Machine shop A is responsible for a special loading of insurance on the building. This results in a total building insurance cost for Machine shop A of one-third of the annual premium.

(2)   The general services department is located in a building owned by the company. It is valued at £6,000 and is charged into costs at a notional value of 8% pa. This cost is additional to the rent and rates shown above.

(3)   The values of issues of materials to the production departments are in the same proportions as shown above for consumable supplies.

The following data is also available:

Departments	Book value of machinery £	Area (sq ft)	Effective HP hours %	Production capacity Direct labour hours	Production capacity Machine hours
Productive:					
Machine shop A	60,000	5,000	50	200,000	40,000
Machine shop B	45,000	6,000	33 1/3	160,000	50,000
Assembly	15,000	8,000	4 1/6	300,000	-
Service:					
Stores	6,000	2,000	-		
Engineering service	18,000	2,500	12 ½		
General service	6,000	1,500	-		
	150,000	25,000	100		

You are required to prepare an overhead analysis sheet showing the bases of any apportionments of overhead to departments.

2.10   Activity solution

Speed Manufacturing Co Ltd

(a)   **Overhead analysis sheet**

	Total	Machine shop A	B	Assem-bly	Stores	Engin-eering service	General service
	£	£	£	£	£	£	£
Indirect wages	62,570	23,260	20,670	8,110	4,100	2,670	3,760
Consumable supplies	22,600	6,300	9,100	2,100	1,400	2,100	1,600
Depreciation of machinery	22,000	8,800	6,600	2,200	880	2,640	880
Insurance of machinery	4,000	1,600	1,200	400	160	480	160
Insurance of building	1,800	600	360	480	120	150	90
Power	3,600	1,800	1,200	150	-	450	-
Light and heat	3,000	600	720	960	240	300	180
Rent and rates	7,050	1,500	1,800	2,400	600	750	-
Notional rent	480	-	-	-	-	-	480
	127,100	44,460	41,650	16,800	7,500	9,540	7,150

Bases of apportionment:

Depreciation and insurance of machinery	:	Book value of machinery
Insurance of building	:	One-third to machine shop A,
	:	balance apportioned on area
Power	:	Effective HP hours
Light and heat	:	Area
Rent and rates	:	Area excluding general service

(b)   **Production departments**

	Machine shop A	B	Assembly	Total
	£	£	£	£
Total from overhead analysis sheet	44,460	41,650	16,800	102,910
Apportionment of service departments:				
Stores (consumable supplies)	2,700	3,900	900	7,500
Engineering service (machine hours)	4,240	5,300	-	9,540
General service (direct labour hours)	2,200	1,650	3,300	7,150
	53,600	52,500	21,000	127,100

2.11   Responsibility criterion

Overhead allotment has so far been looked at from the point of view of benefit obtained. Much of the information is irrelevant, however, for cost control purposes, by segregating those cost centre costs which are controllable by the centre manager.

The above overhead distribution could be adapted to achieve that object by adding a **general** cost centre; items which cannot be controlled by machine group supervisors (such as rent and insurance) would be charged to the general centre as the responsibility of, say, the factory manager. Cost centres would then be allotted overhead in two stages:

(a)   allocation of controllable costs;
(b)   apportioned costs transferred from the general cost centre.

The sub-total of allocated costs would be suitable for control information and the grand total would be used for absorption purposes.

2.12   Reciprocal costs between service centres

A particular problem arises when service centres provide reciprocal services to each other, eg:

In this situation, a secondary allocation of costs arise. There are several methods of dealing with this, the most accurate of which is the algebraic method.

This involves the use of simultaneous equations. If more than three cost centres are involved, a computer is required.

Example

	Production			*Service*	
Department	*A*	*B*	*C*	*P*	*Q*
Costs	£3,000	£4,000	£2,000	£2,500	£2,700
Proportion P	20	30	25	-	25
Proportion Q	25	25	30	20	-

Solution

Let p be total costs P after apportionment Q
Let q be total costs Q after apportionment P

Then
$$p = 2{,}500 + 0.2q \quad (1)$$
$$q = 2{,}700 + 0.25p \quad (2)$$

So
$$p - 0.2q = 2{,}500 \quad (3)$$
$$q - 0.25p = 2{,}700 \quad (4)$$

$(3) \times 5$
$$5p - q = 12{,}500 \quad (5)$$
$$0.25p - q = -2{,}700$$

$$4.75p = 15{,}200$$
$$p = 3{,}200$$

Substituted in (2)
$$q = 2{,}700 + (0.25 \times 3{,}200)$$
$$= 3{,}500$$

2.13   Activity

A company has three production departments: A, B, and C and two production service departments X and Y.

Overhead costs have been attributed to these departments as follows:

Department	£'000
A	120
B	80
C	65
X	24
Y	15

An analysis of the services provided by each service department shows the following percentages of total time spent for the benefit of each department:

Service department	A	B	C	X	Y
X	30%	30%	20%	-	20%
Y	50%	10%	30%	10%	-

Show the apportionment of production service department costs to production departments using the algebraic method.

2.14   Activity solution

(1) $X = £24,000 + 0.1Y$
(2) $Y = £15,000 + 0.2X$

Step 1   (1) becomes:

$X = £24,000 + 0.1 (£15,000 + 0.2X)$

Step 2 $X = £24,000 + £1,500 + 0.02X$

Step 3 $0.98X = £25,500$

Step 4 $X = £26,020$

Step 5 $Y = £15,000 + (0.2 \times £26,020)$

Step 6 $Y = £20,204$

Step 7

	A	B	C	X	Y
Costs allocated	120	80	65	24	15
Apportion X	8	8	5	(26)	5
Apportion Y	10	2	6	2	(20)
	138	90	76	Nil	Nil

2.15   Measuring activity

The overhead absorption rate is the fraction:

$$\frac{\text{Cost centre overhead in £s}}{\text{Cost centre volume in units}}$$

and in the ABC illustration the number of washing machines used was the measure of volume. This was acceptable because the question stated that a standard machine was produced. As all the machines were of the same type it is fair that each one should bear the same share of the costs of operating the departments which produced them.

If, however, the ABC Washing Machine Co produced three types of machine (say regular, super and de-luxe), then the amount of work (and therefore the cost) would be different for each type. The difference in direct cost can be measured; more or less materials would be requisitioned and more or less labour hours would be spent. It would now be unreasonable to use units as the basis for absorbing overheads. It may take longer to produce a de-luxe machine than a regular model and, therefore, the de-luxe machine uses more of the production resources represented by overhead costs.

Thus, volume is usually expressed in terms of a **time** measure, viz:

(a)   direct labour hours; or
(b)   machine hours;

for the purposes of overhead absorption.

Overhead can be absorbed in cost units by means of:

(a)   Rate per unit.
(b)   Percentage of prime cost (direct labour, direct material and direct expenses).
(c)   Percentage of direct wages.
(d)   Direct labour hour rate.
(e)   Machine hour rate.

2.16   Example

Facts as in the ABC illustration. A separate absorption rate for each cost centre is to be calculated as follows:

(a)   Machining: machine hour rate (each machine is manned by four operatives).
(b)   Assembly: direct labour hour rate.
(c)   Finishing: percentage of direct wages.

Absorption rates

$$\text{Machining} = \frac{\text{Cost centre overhead}}{\text{Machine hours}} = \frac{£60,176}{10,000 \div 4} = \text{£24.07 per machine hour}$$

$$\text{Assembly} = \frac{\text{Cost centre overhead}}{\text{Direct labour hours}} = \frac{£23,448}{5,000} = \text{£4.69 per labour hour}$$

$$\text{Finishing} = \frac{\text{Cost centre overhead} \times 100}{\text{Direct wages}} = \frac{£12,776 \times 100}{£10,800} = \text{118.3\% of direct wages}$$

The overhead absorbed by a particular washing machine could then be accumulated.

Assume that a regular machine takes 1 hour machining, 2 hours assembly and 1 hour finishing.

Overhead absorbed

		£
Machining	1 hours × £24.07	24.07
Assembly	2 hours × £4.69	9.38
Finishing	118.3% of (1 × £3.60)	4.25
		37.70

2.17   Predetermined absorption rates

The washing machine illustration implies that absorption rates were calculated after the event ie, when overhead and volume for the period had been ascertained. This is not so. Unit costs are a continuous requirement for management information and will invariably reflect overhead absorption on a predetermined basis, viz:

$$\text{Absorption rate} = \frac{\text{Budgeted overhead}}{\text{Budgeted volume}}$$

Generally, the rate is derived from the annual budget to avoid distortion caused by seasonal fluctuation and to provide a consistent basis for measuring variations.

Actual overhead and/or volume will rarely coincide exactly with budget and therefore a difference between overhead absorbed and overhead incurred will arise.

2.18   Example

In year 9 the budget for a machine shop shows:

Overhead	£60,000
Volume	12,000 machine hours

In January, year 9, the machine shop incurred £5,400 of overhead and 1,050 machine hours were worked.

Calculate the predetermined absorption rate and the overhead under-or over-absorbed in January.

$$\text{Absorption rate} = \frac{\text{Budgeted overhead}}{\text{Budgeted volume}} = \frac{£60,000}{12,000 \text{ machine hours}} = £5.00 \text{ per machine hour}$$

	£
Overhead incurred	5,400
Overhead absorbed (1,050 hours × £5.00)	5,250
Under absorbed overhead	150

The under absorption arises from a combination of two factors:

(a)   overhead costs were higher than budget ($\frac{£60,000}{12}$) for the month;

(b)   volume was greater than budget ($\frac{12,000 \text{ hours}}{12}$) for the month.

In practice a separate absorption rate may be calculated for fixed and variable overhead to enable the effect of cost and volume changes to be shown more clearly. Analysis of over/under absorbed overhead is perhaps covered more appropriately under **standard costing**.

Note that overhead absorbed (sometimes called **recovered**) represents:

Actual production (machine hours in this instance)	×	Predetermined rate per unit (machine hours)

2.19   Activity - using the data from 2.9 above.

    (a)   Calculate suitable overhead absorption rates for the production departments; ignoring the apportionment of service department costs amongst service departments;

    (b)   calculate the overhead to be absorbed by two products, SPK and SGM, with cost sheets showing the following times spent in different departments:

	SPK	SGM
Machine shop A	6 machine hours	3 machine hours
Machine shop B	2 machine hours	8 machine hours
Assembly	5 direct labour hours	7 direct labour hours

2.20   Activity solution

		Machine shop A	Machine shop B	Assembly
	Total costs	£53,600	£52,500	£21,000
(a)	Absorption basis (hours)	40,000 (M/C)	50,000 (M/C)	300,000 (D Lab)
	Overhead absorption rates	£1.34	£1.05	£0.07

(b)   **Absorption of production overhead**

		Product SPK £	Product SGM £
Machine shop A:			
SPK	6 machine hours @ £1.34	8.04	
SGM	3 machine hours @ £1.34		4.02
Machine shop B:			
SPK	2 machine hours @ £1.05	2.10	
SGM	8 machine hours @ £1.05		8.40
Assembly:			
SPK	5 direct labour hours @ £0.07	0.35	
SGM	7 direct labour hours @ £0.07		0.49
Overhead absorbed		10.49	12.91

2.21   Accounting for overhead absorption

The unit cost of production will include overhead at the predetermined rate and, generally, overhead under or over-absorbed will be shown as a separate item in the costing profit and loss account, viz:

Costing profit and loss account

	£
Sales	100
Cost of sales (units sold × unit cost including overheads)	70
Margin	30
Under/(over) absorption	(5)
Operating profit	25

A large balance in the over/under-absorbed account indicates that unit costs are inaccurate and management should be made aware that such costs must be used with care.

The following example will illustrate the cost accounting entries relating to overhead absorbed.

2.22   Example

From the following data relating to four departments of a factory you are required to:

(a)   journalise departmental overheads incurred;
(b)   journalise departmental overheads recovered;
(c)   give the journal entry recording under or over absorbed overhead expenditure.

	Actual expenses £	Absorption rates (based on pre-determined annual estimates)
Department A	1,000	£0.10 per machine hour
Department B	4,000	£0.75 per direct labour hour
Department C	7,000	100% on direct wages
Department D	3,500	£0.25 per unit

	Machine hours worked	Direct labour hours worked	Direct wages £	Units produced
Department A	10,000	11,000	6,000	100,000
Department B	3,000	5,300	6,000	48,900
Department C	6,000	18,000	6,800	52,000
Department D	14,000	30,000	10,000	13,800

2.23   Solution

		Dr £	Cr £
(a)	Department A overhead account	1,000	
	Department B overhead account	4,000	
	Department C overhead account	7,000	
	Department D overhead account	3,500	
	Factory overhead control account		15,500
	Transfer of actual departmental expenses for period	15,500	15,500
(b)	Work in progress account	15,225	
	Department A overhead account		1,000
	Department B overhead account		3,975
	Department C overhead account		6,800
	Department D overhead account		3,450
	Transfer of absorbed departmental expenses for period	15,225	15,225

(c) Profit and loss account   275

       Department B overhead account   25
       Department C overhead account   200
       Department D overhead account   50

Transfer of under absorbed departmental
    expenses for period   275   275

Note: absorbed expenses:

		£
Department A	10,000 machine hours × £0.10	1,000
Department B	5,300 labour hours × £0.75	3,975
Department C	100% of £6,800	6,800
Department D	13,800 units × £0.25	3,450

3 PROBLEMS IN ABSORPTION COSTING

3.1 Problematic cost items

It will be difficult to arrive at an accurate method of allotting certain overhead costs to centres because of their general nature or because of the way they are incurred or merely because the amount does not warrant complicated calculation. The following are suggestions for dealing with problematic items:

(a) **Remuneration of executive directors** - directors' remuneration may be apportioned between factory, administration and marketing according to the estimated proportion of total time devoted to each aspect.

(b) **National insurance and pensions** - it may be convenient to treat employer's contributions for direct workers as overhead expenditure.

(c) **Insurance of factory buildings and plant** - the precise nature of the insurance must be considered as a direct expenses or as factory overhead.

(d) **Research expenditure** - in some cases it may be considered appropriate to treat certain expenditure as a direct expense or as factory overhead. Research into new products or directed towards new discoveries would normally be excluded from costs.

(e) **Estimating expenses and cost of drawing office** - where there are a large number of draughtsmen, they may be required to analyse their time and the jobs on which they have been engaged will be charged accordingly. Estimating expenses are normally treated as general expenses.

(f) **Depreciation of buildings** - this item may be apportioned between functions on the basis of area of cubic capacity. Where there is a substantial difference in the value of certain sections of the whole building (eg, where the offices are located in a more costly structure) it may be necessary to apportion part of the total charge on the basis of value.

(g) **Royalties** - these may be classified as direct production costs or as selling expenses according to whether the royalty is payable on units produced or units sold.

(h) **Accident and employer's liability insurance** - premiums paid should be apportioned according to the total wages of each department. Where, however, there is greater risk of accident in some departments, it may be necessary to weight the charge.

3.2 Volume of activity

It is generally considered that the production budget will be the basis for activity volume used in calculating pre-determined overhead absorption rates, thereby ensuring that unit costs reflect a share of the resources used in manufacture which is based on careful evaluation of the circumstances which will apply at the time such costs are prepared. Other bases are:

(a)   **Average past output** - this basis would be simple to calculate but would be inaccurate when output fluctuates.

(b)   **Normal capacity** - this basis should result in consistency of stock values but may cause misleading conclusions to be drawn from cost information and hide the effect on costs of under-utilisation of capacity.

3.3   Example

Discuss the arguments for and against calculating an overhead absorption rate on the basis of 80,000 direct labour hours, which is the level of activity which is expected to operate next year, instead of a basis of 100,000 direct labour hours, which is the normal level of operations. (No calculations are required in this answer).

3.4   Suggested answer

By using the expected level of activity of 80,000 to calculate the overhead absorption rate, the company is more likely to recover all the production overhead and avoid a large under-recover of fixed costs which will have to be written off. In consequence, product costs will reflect 'actual' incurred costs so that stock values can be said to be more realistic. If selling prices are based upon these costs, it will safeguard the profitability of the company.

The danger, however, of using the lower level of working is that by increasing the cost, and in consequence increasing selling prices, sales may further decline because prices become less competitive. Thus, in the following year the volume of business may be reduced to the equivalent of 60,000 direct labour hours, and the company would be tempted to increase overhead rates and selling prices yet again.

The recommended treatment is for 'normal costs' to be absorbed by 'normal volume'. It provides a reasonable basis for selling prices and gives a product cost which is more meaningful for management.

3.5   Idle time and idle facilities

A substantial proportion of total costs is incurred as a result of time eg, wages and salaries, rent, rates and depreciation. It is vital that the business gets the maximum benefit from the expenditure on costs, which means that employees must be provided with work, and machines, equipment and factory space must be fully utilised. The economic utilisation of resources involves two aspects: the provision of sufficient work for the resources to work on, and ensuring that resources are used efficiently ie, that the maximum output is obtained from a given input of resources.

The cost accountant is, therefore, concerned to measure the use of available time. To do this it is necessary to record when employees are idle and to report these facts, including the cost of idle time, to management. The cost accountant also needs to take into account normal idle time and normal under-utilisation of facilities, especially when setting cost rates for use in estimating. If it is unlikely that a machine will be engaged in productive work twenty-four hours in each day, it is misleading to assume fully capacity in setting overhead rates.

3.6   Example

A factory contains a rework department consisting of two men to whom all completed reject units go for correction. If the volume of rejects becomes larger than they can handle, then one or more assemblers are transferred to assist the two rework men.

You are required to advise whether the cost of rework labour should be treated as direct or indirect wages.

3.7   Suggested answer

The decision as to whether rework labour is treated as a direct or as an indirect cost will largely depend upon whether rework is an infrequent occurrence or may be considered to be a normal production cost.

In the situation described, the existence of a rework department plus occasional assistance implies that rework is frequent and, therefore, it may be advantageous to treat the rework department as a service cost centre. In that way, rework labour plus associated costs can be collected to facilitate control and then charged to specific jobs by means of a predetermined hourly rate.

The above procedure will result in rework costs being treated as a direct expense to jobs and may be inequitable in that rework caused by inefficiency will be treated in the same way as rework arising from the requirements of a particular job. The alternative would be to allocate rework costs to jobs or to departmental overhead depending on the reason for rectification.

3.8   Example

A machine has a potential capacity per annum of 48 weeks at 40 hours per week. It is forecast, however, that the machine will have an actual capacity usage of only 90% because of normal idle time. When the machine is in operation, two operatives who are paid on a time basis of £1.20 per hour each are required. Fixed expenses directly associated with the use of the machine, such as depreciation and maintenance etc, are £3,840 and general factory overhead totals £30,000. General overhead is allocated to machines on the basis of normal capacity which for the factory as a whole is 25,920 machine hours. During the year the machine was actually in operation for 1,650 hours. The abnormal idle time records indicate that time lost was as follows:

Shortage of materials	10 hours
Excess repairs	50 hours
Labour dispute	5 hours
Re-runs	20 hours

From the above information you are required to prepare a statement analysing the cost of abnormal idle time.

3.9   Solution

Cost of abnormal idle time

	Hours lost		Machine idle time @ £3.38 per hour		Labour idle time (@ £2.40 per hour)		Total idle time	
	Hrs	Hrs	£	£	£	£	£	£
Normal (10% × 1,920) (W1)		192		-				-
Abnormal:								
Shortage of materials (W2)	10		34				34	
Excess repairs (W2)	50		169				169	
Labour dispute (W2)	5		17		12		29	
Re-runs (W2)	20		68		48		116	
Unaccounted losses (W2)	13		44				44	
Total abnormal		98		332		60		392

Note: it is assumed:

(a)   that the operatives were employed on another machine during the times when the machine was not in operation, with the exception of the five hours lost owing to the labour dispute;

(b)   that the operatives were paid during the hours of the labour dispute; and

(c)   that the operatives were not in attendance during the hours of unaccounted losses.

WORKINGS

		Hours	Hours
(W1)	**Analysis of capacity utilisation**		
	Potential capacity, 48 weeks @ 40 hours per week		1,920
	Total operated hours	1,650	
	Less: Re-run hours	20	
	Productive operating hours		1,630
	Total idle time (including non-productive operating hours)		290

		Hours
(W2)	**Analysis of idle time**	
	Normal (10%)	192
	Abnormal:	
	Shortage of materials	10
	Excess repairs	50
	Labour dispute	5
	Re-runs	20
	Unaccounted losses (bal fig)	13
	Total abnormal	98
	Total idle time	290

		£
(W3)	**Overhead rate on basis of potential capacity**	
	Fixed expenses:	
	Direct allocation	3,840
	General apportionment $\dfrac{1,728}{25,920} \times £30,000$	2,000
	Total fixed expenses	5,840
	Normal capacity (hours)	1,728
	Rate per hour	£3.38 approx

This rate has been applied to the hours in (ii) above to arrive at the cost of idle time. Operatives' wages have been added for the hours of labour dispute and re-runs as follows:

Labour dispute	5 hours @ £2.40	= £12
Re-runs	20 hours @ £2.40	= £48

4 ACTIVITY BASED COSTING

4.1 Introduction

The traditional method of product costing can be illustrated as follows:

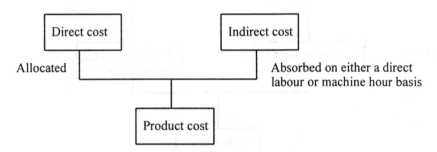

This method of costing is adequate when fixed, indirect costs are low and variable, and direct costs (particularly labour where a direct labour hour absorption rate is used) are high. However, in today's changed manufacturing environment this position does not exist. Direct labour costs per unit of product has significantly decreased, while the fixed, indirect costs of the modern manufacturer have increased.

An American university professor, Robert Kaplan, of the Harvard Business School, was one of the original critics of the traditional method of absorbing indirect costs into product costs. Professor Kaplan has subsequently put forward an alternative approach to product costing. This alternative approach is based on linking overheads to the products which cause them and absorbing on the basis of the activities that 'drive' costs (the cost drivers). This approach is usually referred to as **activity based costing** (ABC).

The ABC system recognises that activities consume resources and products consume activities. In addition, direct labour and machine hours are **not** meaningful cost drivers for many overheads in modern manufacturing environments.

4.2 Definitions

The following terms are often used in an ABC system:

Activity : Discrete services of related tasks, carried out repeatedly.

Cost driver : The event or factor which causes an activity to occur.

Cost pool : All the costs incurred when an activity takes place.

4.3 Uses of ABC

ABC provides cost information which can be used in understanding what drives overhead costs for meaningful performance measurement, product costing and profitability analysis. These are achieved while producing more relevant product costs as follows:

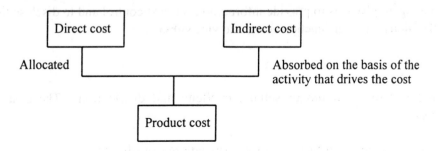

The following is an illustration of the ABC approach:

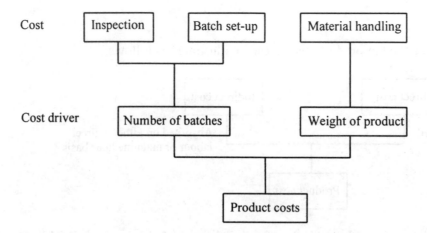

Therefore, the product that is produced in the smallest batches and has a relatively high weight, is deemed to be the most expensive. The number of batches and the weight of the product are the characteristics that drive costs, and are therefore used to absorb indirect costs into the cost of a product.

The use of an appropriate absorption base will not produce 'exact' measures of product cost but they will produce meaningful 'estimates'. With the evolution of manufacturing changing the structure of product cost from primarily variable to predominantly fixed costs and increasing the importance of overhead functions, the recognition of the shortfalls of traditional costing is essential, and the use of a more meaningful system such as ABC should be promoted.

Typical overheads which are not driven by production volume are:

(a)   **Set-up costs** - driven by the number of manufacturing set-ups.
(b)   **Order processing costs** - driven by the number of receiving orders raised.
(c)   **Packing department costs** - driven by the number of packing orders.
(d)   **Engineering department costs** - driven by the number of production orders.

5   COSTS OF NON-PRODUCTION FUNCTIONS

5.1   Absorption of non-production costs

In the past many businesses attempted to ensure that unit costs included a charge for the administration, selling and distribution costs, usually calculated as a fixed percentage of production costs.

The practice has largely been discontinued but that is not to say that such costs should be ignored. The cost of administration, marketing, research and development has a great impact on the fortunes of a business.

The cost accounting emphasis is to provide information for cost control and to disclose the effect of management decisions on other function costs, and **vice versa**.

5.2   Marketing

Marketing comprises the activities of selling, publicity and distribution. The cost accounting system should show:

(a)   suitable cost centre analysis to identify costs with responsibility;

(b)   analysis between fixed and variable, especially for distribution costs eg, packaging and delivery;

(c)   statistical bases to measure and compare costs eg, salemen's calls, number of orders.

5.3   General administration

This function represents the costs of general management, secretarial, accounting and administrative services, except for any such costs which can be directly related to production, marketing, research or development.

Once again the cost accounting emphasis will be on analysis by cost centre for control.

5.4   Research and development

Research costs are those incurred in seeking new or improved products or methods. Development costs are those incurred by those stages from decision implementation to production. Cost analysis will usually relate to natural classification, such as materials or laboratory services and will accumulate costs by specific project.

6   CHAPTER SUMMARY

This chapter has considered the remaining area of cost collection, namely overhead costs, and their attribution to cost units.

It has explained the techniques of allocation, apportionment and absorption of costs and the reasons for attributing costs to cost units using pre-determined absorption rates. Accounting for any consequent under or over absorption has been dealt with together with an analysis of its causes.

Finally traditional methods of accounting for overheads have been compared with the activity based approach.

7   SELF TEST QUESTIONS

7.1   List the objectives of accounting for overhead cost (1.1)

7.2   Explain clearly the differences between the techniques of allocation, apportionment and absorption. (2.1)

7.3   Explain clearly the reciprocal servicing problem of overhead accounting. (2.12)

7.4   Why are pre-determined absorption rates used? (2.17)

7.5   Explain the causes of over/under absorption of overhead cost. (2.18)

7.6   Explain 'activity based costing'. (4.1)

8   EXAMINATION TYPE QUESTIONS

8.1   ABC Manufacturing Company

One of the budget centres of the ABC Manufacturing Company is the boiler house, which raises and supplies steam for all manufacturing budget centres in the company.

The foreman of one of the manufacturing budget centres has complained to the works manager that in his accounts he is charged at different rates each month per lb of steam used. The highest rates have been as much as 20% above the lowest.

You are required to explain in a report to the works manager:

(a)   how such different rates per lb of steam can be incurred in the boiler house;

(b)   why being charged at different rates should present a difficulty to the foreman of the manufacturing budget centre;

(c)   what procedure, as cost accountant of the ABC Manufacturing Company, you would propose to install to remedy this position.

8.2   Fibrex Ltd

Shown below are next year's budgeted operating costs for Fibrex Ltd, a company with three production and two service departments.

	Production departments			Service departments		
	Weaving dept	*Proofing dept*	*Finishing dept*	*Personnel services*	*Equipment maintenance*	*Total*
	£'000	£'000	£'000	£'000	£'000	£'000
Direct materials	7,000	2,000	1,500	-	-	10,500
Direct wages	2,500	5,500	2,000	-	-	10,000
Indirect materials and wages	1,100	900	300	1,500	3,800	7,600
Power	5,200	1,000	200	100	800	7,300
Rent and rates						8,000
Factory administration and supervision						10,000
Machine insurance						2,400

Additional data extracted from next year's budget is shown below:

	Weaving dept	*Proofing dept*	*Finishing dept*	*Personnel services*	*Equip-ment maint-enance*	*Total*
Floor area, square metres	12,000	27,000	6,000	12,000	3,000	60,000
Machine hours	1,600,000	400,000	400,000	-	-	2,400,000
Direct labour hours	1,200,000	1,800,000	600,000	-	-	3,600,000
Number of employees	600	1,000	400	100	400	2,500
Gross book value of equipment	£4.0m	£1.0m	£1.0m	-	-	£6.0m

You are required:

(a)   Calculate the budgeted overhead absorption rates for each production department using the following methods:

   (i)   a machine hour rate in the weaving department;
   (ii)   a direct labour hour rate in the proofing department; and
   (iii)   another suitable method in the finishing department.

It may be assumed that the equipment maintenance department does not service the personnel services department.

All workings should be clearly shown.

(17 marks)

(b)   It has been suggested that, instead of calculating department overhead absorption rates, one blanket rate for a factory may be adequate. Identify the circumstances where such a blanket rate may be suitable.

(5 marks)

(Total: 22 marks)

9   ANSWERS TO EXAMINATION TYPE QUESTIONS

9.1   ABC Manufacturing Co

REPORT

To: Works Manager

From: Cost Accountant

Date: X-X-19XX

Subject: Steam Costs

(a)   The complaint that the cost per lb of steam charged to manufacturing budget centres fluctuates probably arises because the rate is calculated by dividing the month's cost of the boiler house by the total steam raised during the month. Therefore, if either the cost or demand for steam varies each month, the cost per lb will vary. Due to the heavy incidence of fixed costs in the boiler house, in a month when total demand is low, the cost per lb will be higher even though total boiler house costs remain the same.

Consequently the rate charged to a specific manufacturing budget centre will be affected by the use of steam in other centres as well as by boiler house cost fluctuations.

(b)   The problem encountered by the foreman of the budget centre is that he is held accountable for the level of costs incurred in his centre. The unit cost of steam, however, is beyond his control and even though he makes a determined attempt to economise in the use of steam, it may not be reflected in the charge to his centre cause the cost per lb may have increased. Any excess spending by the boiler house foreman is automatically passed on to the manufacturing departments.

(c)   The charge for steam must be based upon a budgeted rate. To calculate the rate, the budgeted annual expenditure of the boiler house is divided by the budgeted demand for steam during this year. The charge to cost centres would then be calculated by multiplying the actual steam used by each centre by the budgeted rate.

The expenditure incurred in the boiler house is thus controlled against a budget and any difference between the actual cost and the amounts charged to manufacturing centres would be analysed between cost increases/savings and under/over-utilisation of steam by the manufacturing centres. Such differences would be charged or credited to profit and loss and serve as useful control information.

SIGNATURE

10.2   Fibrex Ltd

(a)   *Note:* overheads are **indirect** costs so take care to ensure the direct materials and wages are **not** included in the overhead calculations.)

The first step is to allocate the apportion total overheads to the cost centres:

Overhead item	Basis of apportionment	Weaving dept	Proofing dept	Finishing dept	Personnel services	Maint- enance	Total
Indirect materials and wages	Given	1,100	900	300	1,500	3,800	7,600
Power	Given	5,200	1,000	200	100	800	7,300
Rent and rates	Floor area	1,600	3,600	800	1,600	400	8,000
Factory admin & supervision	Number of employees	2,400	4,000	1,600	400	1,600	10,000
Machine insurance	Gross book value	1,600	400	400	-	-	2,400
		11,900	9,900	3,300	3,600	6,600	35,300
Reapportionments: Personnel	(see tutorial note) Number of employees 6:10:4:4	900	1,500	600	(3,600)	600	
						7,200	
Equipment maintenance	Gross book value (or machine hours) 4:1:1	4,800	1,200	1,200		(7,200)	
		17,600	12,600	5,100			

	Weaving Dept	Proofing Dept	Finishing Dept
=	$\dfrac{\text{Budgeted overhead}}{\text{Budgeted machine hours}}$	$\dfrac{\text{Budgeted overhead}}{\text{Budgeted labour hours}}$	$\dfrac{\text{Budgeted overhead}}{\text{Budgeted wage cost}} \times 100$
=	$\dfrac{17,600}{1,600}$	$\dfrac{12,600}{1,800}$	$\dfrac{5,100}{2,000} \times 100$
Overhead absorption rate	£11 per machine hour	£7 per direct labour hour	255% of direct wage cost

Note:

Reapportionment of service cost centres

As personnel provides a service to another service department (equipment maintenance) the quickest approach is first to reapportion the service cost centre which services other service cost centres ie, in this case personnel. Otherwise the apportionment for equipment maintenance would be slightly longer.

(b)   The circumstances under which a blanket overhead rate may be suitable include the following:

   (i)   Where the company offers only a single product or service which must, therefore absorb all overheads irrespective of where they are incurred. This does not obviate the need for charging overheads to functional cost centres for cost control purposes.

   (ii)   Where all products are similar in nature and use approximately the same amount of the services provided by each department.

   (iii)   Where overhead costs are relatively insignificant and the costs of calculating more detailed absorption rates would exceed the benefits resulting from the exercise (eg, under contract costing the majority of costs are direct).

6 COST BEHAVIOUR

INTRODUCTION & LEARNING OBJECTIVES

Syllabus area 6a. Cost behaviour. (Ability required 3).

              6b. Marginal costing compared with absorption costing. (Ability required 3).

This chapter is concerned with the classification of costs by behaviour. Some costs change when activity levels change, whilst others do not. This distinction may be used to provide an alternative method of stock valuation and profit reporting compared to absorption costing. It is widely used in the provision of information to management.

When you have studied this chapter you should be able to do the following:

- Distinguish between fixed and variable costs.

- Understand and explain the meaning of contribution.

- Reconcile the use of linear approximations of cost behaviour with reality using the relevant range argument.

- Separate the fixed and variable elements of a semi-variable cost.

---

1 ANALYSIS OF COSTS

1.1 Total cost

It has been shown that production cost comprises three elements - materials, wages and overheads. It is useful to look at the way costs behave in response to changes in production volume.

1.2 Example

	Production 500 units £	Production 1,000 units £
Sales (@ £3 per unit)	1,500	3,000
Total costs	1,000	1,500
Profit	500	1,500
Average unit cost	£2.00	£1.50
Average unit profit	£1.00	£1.50

Total costs have increased by only 50% although production has doubled. This is because some costs will not rise in relation to the increase in volume.

1.3   The two cost components

[Definition]   A **fixed** cost is a cost which is unaffected by the level of activity.

[Definition]   A **variable** cost is a cost which varys with the level of activity.

Suppose in the example above the product is widgets and the only costs are:

(a)   rental of a fully equipped factory, £500 pa;
(b)   raw materials, £1 per widget.

Then the way these two costs react to producing varying numbers of widgets is as follows:

(a)   **Factory rental - a fixed cost**

Although production rises, the same rent is payable.

Graph showing relationship between total fixed cost and output

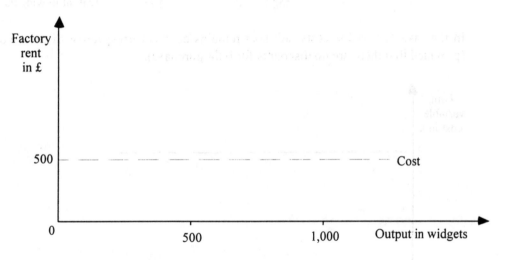

This may be shown by plotting the average fixed cost per unit on a graph.

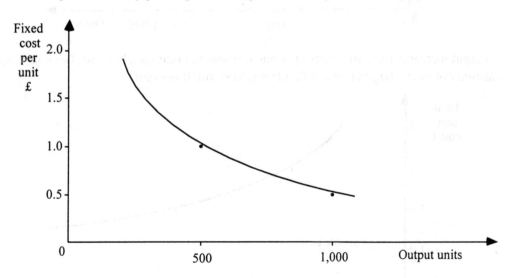

As output increases, unit fixed costs decline. This only changes if a new or larger factory is rented.

(b)   **Raw materials - a variable cost**

Every widget has a raw material cost of £1; therefore, the cost varies directly with the level of production.

Graph showing relationship between total variable cost and output

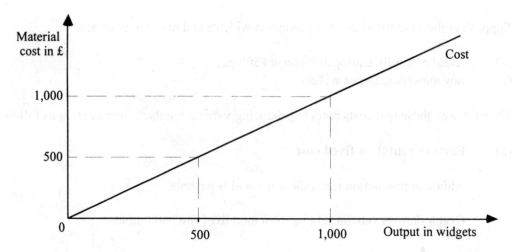

In the case of variable costs unit cost remains constant irrespective of the level of output (provided that there are no discounts for bulk purchase).

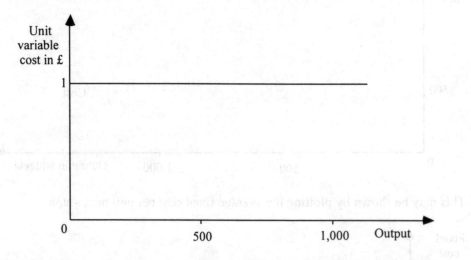

As output increases total unit costs gravitate towards the unit variable cost, because when fixed cost is shared out over a large number of units it is very small per unit.

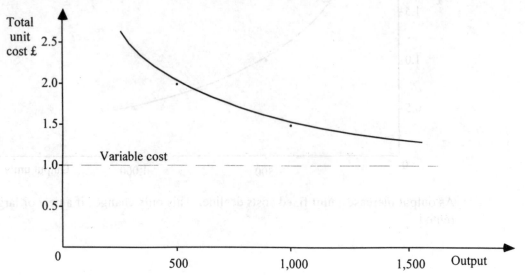

1.4   Contribution

If the two types of cost are segregated, the operating statement can be presented in a different way:

	Production of widgets		
	1 unit	*500 units*	*1,000 units*
	£	£	£
Sales	3	1,500	3,000
Variable costs - Raw materials	1	500	1,000
Contribution	2	1,000	2,000
Fixed costs - Factory rent	500	500	500
Profit/(loss)	(498)	500	1,500

The revised presentation is based on the concept that each unit sold **contributes** a selling price less the variable cost per unit. Total contribution provides a fund to cover fixed costs and net profit.

| **Conclusion** | Sales – Variable cost of sales | = | Contribution |
| | Contribution – Fixed costs | = | Net profit |

Note that unit contribution is a constant number unless prices or the specification for variable costs change.

1.5   Relevant range of activity

The analysis of cost behaviour into fixed and variable is only appropriate when considering a limited range of activity.

(a)   Variable costs are unlikely to be constant per unit. When buying materials, it is normal to obtain discounts for larger orders. Thus, the more eg, tyres ordered, the lower the price paid for each tyre.

Graph showing relationship between the total cost of tyres and the output of cars

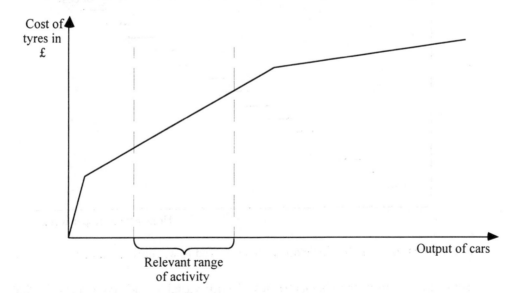

However, in practice it is likely that only relatively limited changes in the level of production will be considered. This is described as the **relevant range of activity**, and within that range unit prices are likely to be constant.

(b)   **Step costs**

Some costs rise in a series of steps. Large steps (renting a second factory) or small steps (renting a typewriter) may occur.

- If the steps are large, the concept of the relevant range of activity usually applies ie, only occasionally is a new factory considered and therefore one can assume the cost to be fixed for the relevant range.

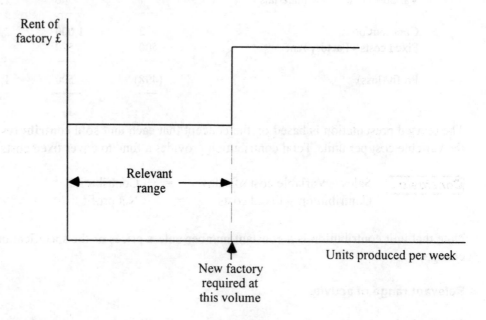

- If the steps are small they may be ignored ie, the cost may be treated as a variable cost.

Graph showing relationship between total rent of typewriters and output

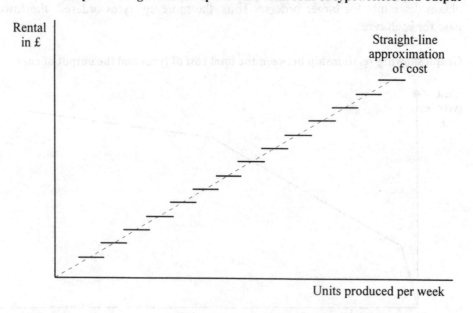

(c)   **Semi-variable costs** (unfortunately also referred to as semi-fixed costs)

Some costs exhibit the characteristics of both variable and fixed costs, in that while they increase with output they never fall to zero, even at zero output.

An example is maintenance costs: even at zero output **standby** maintenance costs are incurred. As output rises so do maintenance costs.

Graph showing relationship between machine maintenance costs and output

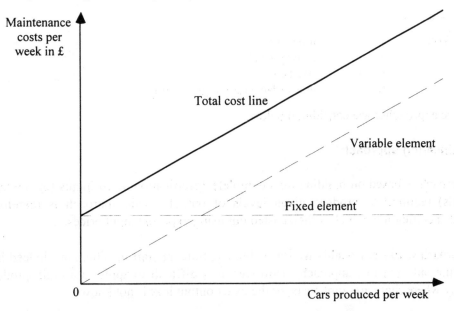

This problem can be dealt with within the basic analysis by saying that the item consists of two components, a fixed cost and a variable cost, and by treating these separately.

1.6   Activity

Make a list of your personal expenditure items each month, classifying them into fixed, variable and semi-variable items.

1.7   Activity solution

Rent - fixed
Rates - fixed
Bank loan - fixed
Petrol - variable
Electricity - semi-variable
Telephone -semi-variable

2   COST PREDICTION

2.1   Introduction

The use of cost behaviour described in the previous sections rests on being able to predict costs associated with a given level of activity. Such data is not available from traditional cost analysis, and alternative approaches must be used. In this process historical information provides valuable guidance, but it must be recognised that the environment is not static, and what was relevant in the past may not be relevant in the future.

Five main approaches may be identified:

(a)   the engineering approach;
(b)   the account analysis approach;
(c)   the high-low method;
(d)   scatter charts; and
(e)   regression analysis.

In all of these approaches the assumption is made that the linear model of cost behaviour is valid, and therefore the relation between costs, y, and activity, x, is the form:

y = a + bx

Where   y   =   total costs
           x   =   activity level
           a   =   fixed costs
           b   =   unit variable (or marginal) cost

These five approaches are considered below.

2.2   The engineering approach

This approach is based on building up a complete specification of all inputs (eg, materials, labour, overheads) required to produce given levels of output.   This approach is therefore based on technical specification, which is then costed out using expected input prices.

This approach works reasonably well in a single product or start-up situation - indeed in the latter it may be the only feasible approach.   However, it is difficult to apply in a multi-product situation, especially where there are joint costs, or the exact output mix is not known.

2.3   The account analysis approach

Rather than using the technical information, this approach uses the information contained in the ledger accounts.   These are analysed and categorised as either fixed or variable (or semi-fixed or semi-variable).   Thus, for example, material purchase accounts would represent variable costs, office salaries fixed cost.   Since the ledger accounts are not designed for use in this way, some reorganisation and reclassification of accounts may be required.

Students should note that this is the approach implicit in many examination questions.

The problems with this approach are several:

(a)   Inspection does not always indicate the true nature of costs.   For example, today factory wages would normally be a fixed cost, with only overtime and/or bonuses as the variable element.

(b)   Accounts are by their nature summaries, and often contain transactions of different categories.

(c)   It rests on historic information with the problems noted above.

2.4   High low (or range) method

This and the next two methods that follow are based on an analysis of historic information on costs at different activity levels.   To illustrate the methods the data below will be used as an example.

Example

The data for the six months to 31 December 19X8 is as follows:

Month	Units	Cost
		£
July	340	2,260
August	300	2,160
September	380	2,320
October	420	2,400
November	400	2,300
December	360	2,266

The variable element of a cost item may be estimated by calculating the unit cost between high and low volumes during a period.

Six months to 31/12/X8	*Units produced*	*Inspection costs*
		£
Highest month	420	2,400
Lowest month	300	2,160
Range	120	240

The additional cost per unit between high and low is $\dfrac{£240}{120\text{ units}}$ = £2 per unit

which is used as an estimate of the variable content of inspection costs. Fixed inspection costs are, therefore:

$$£2,400 - (420 \times £2) = £1,560 \text{ per month}$$
$$\text{or} \quad £2,160 - (300 \times £2) = £1,560 \text{ per month.}$$

ie, the relationship is of the form y = £(1,560 + 2x).

The limitations of the high low method are:

(a)   Its reliance on historic data, assuming that (i) activity is the only factor affecting costs and (ii) historic costs reliably predict future costs.

(b)   The use of only two values, the highest and the lowest, means that the results may be distorted due to random variations in these values.

2.5   Activity

Use the high-low points method to calculate the fixed and variable elements of the following cost:

	Activity	£
January	400	1,050
February	600	1,700
March	550	1,600
April	800	2,100
May	750	2,000
June	900	2,300

2.6   Activity solution

		£
High	900	2,300
Low	(400)	(1,050)
	500	1,250

Variable cost = £1,250/500 = £2.50/unit

Fixed cost = £1,050 − (400 × £2.50) = £50.

2.7   Scatter charts

If the data from the example was plotted on a graph, the result would be a scatter-chart of inspections costs.

Scatter chart showing the relationship between total inspection costs and output

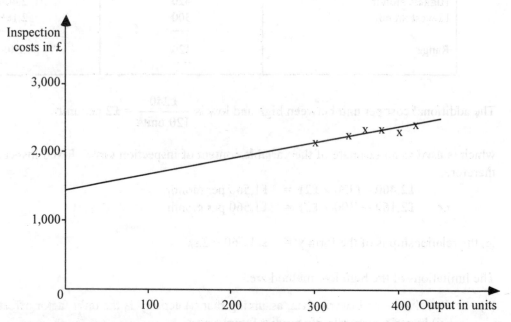

The **line of best fit** (a line which passes through the plotted points to equalise the number of points on each side and the aggregate distance from the line) may be drawn as accurately as possible by inspection. The point at which that line cuts the vertical axis indicates the fixed cost (about £1,460 in the illustration).

Scatter charts suffer from the general limitations of using historic data referred to above. In addition, their problem is that the estimate of the best linear relationship between the data is subjective. Finally, it should be noted that this can only be converted into a mathematical relationship by actual measurement.

2.8   Activity

Plot the data points from the previous activity on a scatter graph and draw a line of best fit to find the fixed cost. Measure the gradient of the line to determine the variable cost.

2.9   Activity solution

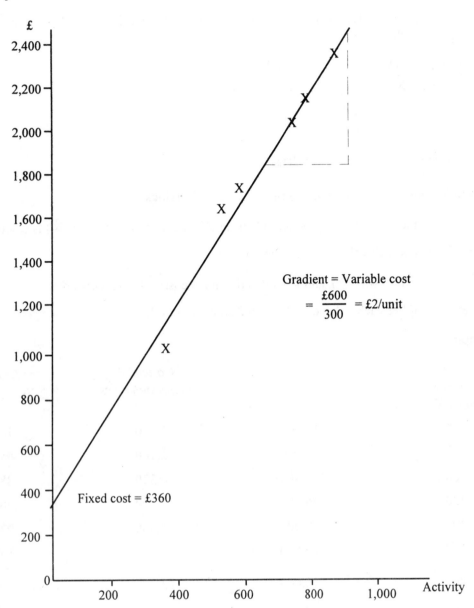

3   REGRESSION ANALYSIS

3.1   Introduction

Regression analysis is a technique for estimating the line of best fit, given a series of data of the type in the example above. It is essentially a statistical technique, and the description that follows is only a working guide for application of the technique to cost prediction.

Regression analysis is based on the concept of drawing the line that minimises the sum of the squares of the deviations of the line from the observed data (hence it is sometimes referred to as the least squares method). The regression line of y on x is used when an estimate of y is required for a given value of x. (This line minimises the sum of the squares of the vertical distances of the points from the line. In most cost accounting circumstances it is the cost (y) which is being predicted from a given output value (x). Thus the regression of line of y on x is calculated.)

The regression line will be of the form $y = a + bx$

where a is fixed cost and b is the variable cost.

3.2   Calculating the regression line

There are various formulae used to calculate the values of a and b; all are equally valid. The first formula given in the exam is

$$b = \frac{\text{Covariance (XY)}}{\text{Variance X}} = \frac{n\sum XY - (\sum X)(\sum Y)}{n\sum XY^2 - (\sum X)^2}$$

$$a = \overline{Y} - b\overline{X}$$

where, n is the number of pieces of data.

The simplest approach is to think in terms of column headings:

Column 1 lists the values of X (production); from this the mean production ($\overline{X}$) is calculated;

Column 2 squares each value of X and sums them.

Column 3 shows the costs (Y), and from this the mean cost ($\overline{Y}$) is calculated;

Column 4 multiplies each value of X by Y and sums the result.

3.3   Example

Column 1 Production units X	Column 2 X	Column 3 Inspection costs Y	Column 4 XY
340	115,600	2,260	768,400
300	90,000	2,160	648,000
380	144,400	2,320	881,600
420	176,400	2,400	1,008,000
400	160,000	2,300	920,000
360	129,600	2,320	835,200
$\sum X$ 2,200	$\sum X^2$ = 816,000	$\sum Y$ = 13,760	$\sum XY$ 5,061,200

$$\overline{X} = \frac{2,200}{6} \qquad\qquad \overline{Y} = \frac{13,760}{6}$$

$$\overline{X} = 367 \qquad\qquad\qquad \overline{Y} = 2,293$$

$$b = \frac{n\sum XY - (\sum X)(\sum Y)}{n\sum X^2 - (\sum X)^2}$$

$$= \frac{6 \times 5,061,200 - 2,200 \times 13,760}{6 \times 816,000 - (2,200)^2} = \frac{30,367,200 - 30,272,000}{489,600 - 4,840,000}$$

$$= \frac{95,200}{56,000} = 1.7$$

ie, variable cost is £1.70 per unit

$$\begin{aligned}
a &= \overline{Y} - b\overline{X} \\
&= 2,293 - 1.7 \times 367 \\
&= 2,293 - 623.9 \\
&= 1,669
\end{aligned}$$

ie, fixed costs are £1,669 and the regression line is y = 1,669 + 1.7X.

3.4 Activity

Using the data from the previous activity, calculate the fixed variable costs using regression analysis and basic algebra

3.5 Activity solution

Production activity (X)	(X²)	Costs (Y)	(XY)
400	160,000	1,050	420,000
600	360,000	1,700	1,020,000
550	302,500	1,600	880,000
800	640,000	2,100	1,680,000
750	562,500	2,000	1,500,000
900	810,000	2,300	2,070,000
4,000	2,835,000	10,750	7,570,000

$\bar{x} = 666.66$ $\qquad\qquad\qquad$ $\bar{y} = 1,791.66$

$$\text{Variable cost} = b = \frac{6 \times 7,570,000 - 4,000 \times 10,750}{6 \times 2,835,000 - (4,000)^2}$$

$$= \frac{45,420,000 - 43,000,000}{17,010,000 - 16,000,000}$$

$$= \frac{2,420,000}{1,010,000} = 2.40$$

$$\text{Fixed cost} = 1,791.66 - (666.66 \times £2.40)$$
$$= £192.$$

3.6 Interpolation and extrapolation

As has been shown, regression lines can be used to calculate intermediate values of the variables. This is known as **interpolation** and it is one of the main uses of regression lines.

It is also possible to extend regression lines beyond the range of values used in their calculation. It is now possible to calculate values of the variables that are outside the limits of the original data, this is known as **extrapolation**.

eg,

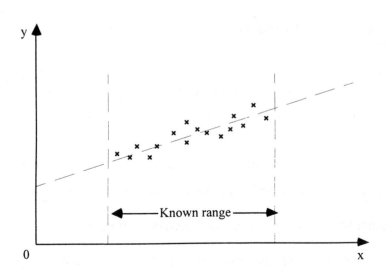

The problem with extrapolation is that it assumes that the linear relationship already calculated is still valid. This may or may not be so.

For example, in the production and cost example, it is quite possible that if the amount of production was increased outside the given range there would come a point where the fixed or variable cost changes.

The resultant diagram could be of this form:

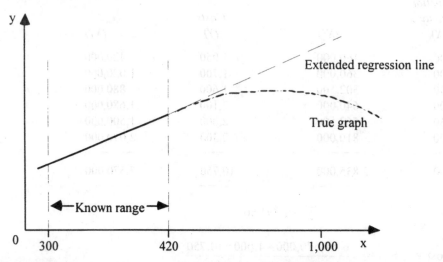

Therefore, the cost of producing 1,000 units as estimated from the regression line may be very different from that actually achieved in practice.

Generally speaking, extrapolation must be treated with caution since outside the range of known values other factors may influence the situation and the linear relationship may not still hold true.

Regression analysis overcomes the limitations of both the high low method and scatter graphs, in that it provides the best estimates of costs from the historic data. However, it suffers from the general limitations of the validity of using historic data, and the assumption of linearity.

3.7   Limitations of using historic costs

The cost accountant must be careful when using analysis of historical costs as a basis for predicting future costs. This is true even if he is fully satisfied with the accuracy of the analysis. The reasons are:

(a)   It is difficult and costly to obtain sufficient data to be confident that a representative sample is used.

(b)   Prediction implies a continuing relationship of costs to volume. In practice, methods and efficiency change.

(c)   The relationship between costs and volume may be obscured by time-lags eg, recruiting trainee labour in anticipation of increased production.

(d)   Factors other than volume of production can influence costs eg, purchasing in small lots could increase handling and incidental material costs.

(e)   Prices of the input factors may change eg, due to inflation or technical change.

(f)   The analysis is based on the assumption that the cost/activity relationship is linear.

3.8   Comparison of accountant's and economist's cost behaviour models

The analysis above has been based on the accountant's model of cost behaviour patterns. This assumes that unit variable cost equals marginal cost. Indeed the CIMA thus defines marginal cost - 'the cost of one unit of a product or service which would be avoided if that unit were not produced or provided'. Thus, the unit marginal cost is a constant, and unit marginal and total costs can be presented thus:

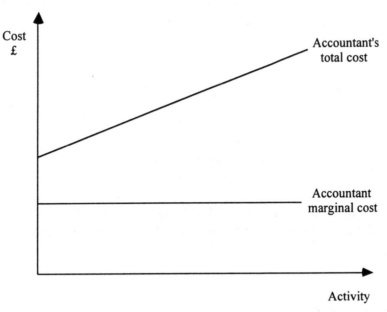

This contrasts with traditional economist's model, where economies of scale mean that marginal cost per unit falls as production increases, and thus total cost is not a straight line

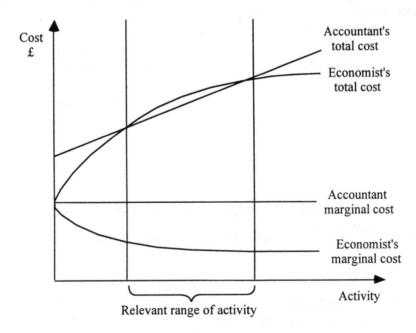

It is apparent that though these represent cost behaviour patterns in different ways, over the 'relevant range' of activity they are substantially similar. The concept of the relevant range is intended to represent the range of activity levels within which management decisions are normally made. Therefore for practical management decision making the accountant's approximation may be regarded as a working approximation to actual cost behaviour patterns.

4   MARGINAL COSTING

4.1   Alternative to absorption costing

Under marginal costing only variable costs are charged to cost units; fixed costs for a period are fully written off in the profit and loss account of the period in which they are incurred.

[Definition]   An accounting system in which variable costs are charged to cost units and fixed costs of the period are written off in full against the aggregate contribution.

The fundamental difference between marginal and absorption costing is therefore one of timing. In marginal costing fixed costs are written off in the period incurred. In absorption costing fixed costs are absorbed into units and written off in the period in which the units are sold.

4.2   Example

Company A produces a single product with the following budget:

Selling price	£10
Direct materials	£3 per unit
Direct wages	£2 per unit
Variable overhead	£1 per unit
Fixed overhead	£10,000 per month.

The fixed overhead absorption rate is based on volume of 5,000 units per month. Show the operating statement for the month, when 4,800 units were produced and sold under:

(a)   absorption costing;

(b)   marginal costing.

Assume that costs were as budget.

4.3   Solution

(a)   **Absorption costing**

	£
Sales (4,800 units)	48,000
Cost of sales (4,800 × £8) (W1)	38,400
Operating margin	9,600
Under absorbed overhead (W2)	(400)
Operating profit	9,200

WORKINGS

(W1)   Unit cost is materials (£3) + wages (£2) + variable overhead (£1) + fixed Overhead absorbed $(\frac{£10,000}{5,000})$ = £2 per unit, giving a cost per unit of £8.

		£
(W2)	Fixed overhead incurred	10,000
	Fixed overhead absorbed (4,800 × £2)	9,600
	Under absorption	400

(b)   **Marginal costing**

	£
Sales (4,800 × £10)	48,000
Variable cost of sales (4,800 × £6)	28,800
Contribution	19,200
Fixed costs	10,000
Operating profit	9,200

In the example operating profit is the same under both methods. That will not be so, however, when production is more or less than sales, ie, if stocks increase or decrease.

In the example if production had been 6,000 units, with sales of 4,800 units, the absorption costing statement would show:

	£	£
Sales (4,800 × £10)		48,000
Cost of sales:		
Production 6,000 × £8	48,000	
Less: Closing stock 1,200 × £8	9,600	
		38,400
Operating margin		9,600
Over absorbed fixed overhead (W1)		2,000
Operating profit		11,600

WORKINGS

	£
(W1) Fixed overheads incurred	10,000
Fixed overheads absorbed (6,000 × £2)	12,000
Over absorption	2,000

The marginal costing statement would show.

	£	£
Sales 4,800 × £10		48,000
Cost of sales		
Production 6,000 × £6	36,000	
Less: Closing stock 1,200 × £6	7,200	
		28,800
Contribution		19,200
Fixed costs		10,000
Operating profit		£9,200

The difference in profit is due to the different stock valuations.

	£	£
Profit MC		9,200
Stock valuation (TAC) (1,200 × £8)	9,600	
Stock valuation (MC) (1,200 × £6)	7,200	
Difference in stock valuation (1,200 × £2)		2,400
Profit under TAC		11,600

4.4   Example

A company sells a product for £10, and incurs £4 of variable costs in its manufacture. The fixed costs are £900 per year and are absorbed on the basis of the normal production volume of 250 units per year. The results for the last four years, when no expenditure variances arose, (ie, all costs were as budgeted) were as follows:

Item	1st year units	2nd year units	3rd year units	4th year units	Total units
Opening stock	-	200	300	300	-
Production	300	250	200	200	950
	300	450	500	500	950
Closing stock	200	300	300	200	200
Sales	100	150	200	300	750

Show the operating statements for each month under

(a)   absorption costing

(b)   marginal costing

4.5   Solution

(a)   Absorption costing

	1st year £	2nd year £	3rd year £	4th year £	Total £
Sales value	1,000	1,500	2,000	3,000	7,500
Opening stock @ £7.60 (W1)	-	1,520	2,280	2,280	-
Costs of production @ £7.60	2,280	1,900	1,520	1,520	7,220
	2,280	3,420	3,800	3,800	7,220
Less: Closing stock @ £7.60	1,520	2,280	2,280	1,520	1,520
Cost of sales	(760)	(1,140)	(1,520)	(2,280)	(5,700)
(Under)/over absorption (W2)	180	Nil	(180)	(180)	(180)
Net profit	420	360	300	540	1,620

(W1)   Unit cost is variable cost £4 + fixed overhead absorbed $\dfrac{£900}{250}$ = £3.60. Giving a cost per unit of £7.60.

(W2)   **Calculation of over/under absorption**

Fixed cost control account

	£		£
Incurred:		Absorbed:	
Year 1	900	300 × £3.60	1,080
Over absorption	180		
	1,080		1,080
Year 2	900	250 × £3.60	900
Year 3	900	200 × £3.60	720
		Under absorption	180
	900		900
Year 4	900	200 × £3.60	720
		Under absorption	180
	900		900

(b)   If marginal costing had been used instead of absorption, the results would have been

	1st year £	*2nd year* £	*3rd year* £	*4th year* £	*Total* £
Sales	1,000	1,500	2,000	3,000	7,500
Opening stock @ £4	-	800	1,200	1,200	-
Cost of production @ £4	1,200	1,000	800	800	3,800
	1,200	1,800	2,000	2,000	3,800
Less: Closing stock @ £4	800	1,200	1,200	800	800
Cost of sales	(400)	(600)	(800)	(1,200)	(3,000)
Contribution	600	900	1,200	1,800	4,500
Less: Fixed costs	900	900	900	900	3,600
Net profit/(loss)	(300)	-	300	900	900

The marginal presentation indicates clearly that the business must sell at least 150 units per year to break even, ie, £900 ÷ (10 – 4) whereas it appeared, using absorption costing, that even at 100 units it was making a healthy profit. The total profit for the four years is less under the marginal principle because the stocks are valued at £800 (£4 × 200) instead of £1,520, ie, £720 of the fixed costs are being carried forward under the absorption principle, but have been charged to profit under marginal costing.

The profit figures shown may be reconciled as follows:

	Year 1 £	Year 2 £	Year 3 £	Year 4 £	Total £
Profit/(loss) under marginal costing	(300)	Nil	300	900	900
Add: Distortion from stock increase					
(200 × £30.60) =	720	(100 × £3.60) =360	-		(200 × £3.60) =720
Less: Distortion from stock decrease			-	(100 × £3.60) =360	
Profit under absorption costing	420	360	300	540	1,620

Note: The under/over absorption figures have nothing to do with the difference in the profit figures, they are caused by production not being at the budgeted level.

4.6 Activity

A company that manufactures one product has calculated its cost on a quarterly production budget of 10,000 units. The selling price was £5 per unit.

Sales in the four successive quarters of the last year were:

Quarter 1	10,000 units
Quarter 2	9,000 units
Quarter 3	7,000 units
Quarter 4	5,500 units

The level of stock at the beginning of the year was 1,000 units and the company maintained its stock of finished products at the same level at the end of each of the four quarters.

Based on its quarterly production budget, the cost per unit was:

	£
Prime cost	3.50
Production overhead (variable and fixed)	0.75
Selling and administration overhead	0.30
Total	4.55

Fixed production overhead, which has been taken into account in calculating the above figures, was £5,000 per quarter. Selling and administration overhead was treated as fixed, and was charged against sales in the period in which it was incurred.

You are required to present a tabular statement to show net profit of the four quarters:

(a)   under absorption costing;
(b)   under marginal costing

(Remember only production costs can be absorbed into stock values, selling and administration fixed overheads must always be charged to profit in the period incurred.)

4.7   **Activity solution**

(a)   **Net profit statement (fixed overhead absorbed)**

	1st quarter	2nd quarter	3rd quarter	4th quarter
Sales units	10,000	9,000	7,000	5,500
Production units	10,000	9,000	7,000	5,500
	£	£	£	£
Sales value (£5 per unit)	50,000	45,000	35,000	27,500
Cost of sales:				
Opening stock at £4.25	4,250	4,250	4,250	4,250
Production at £4.25	42,500	38,250	29,750	23,375
Less: Closing stock at £4.25	4,250	4,250	4,250	4,250
Cost of sales	42,500	38,250	29,750	23,375
Under absorbed production overhead (W)	-	500	1,500	2,250
	42,500	38,750	31,250	25,625
Gross profit	7,500	6,250	3,750	1,875
Less: Selling and administration overhead (10,000 × 0.30)	3,000	3,000	3,000	3,000
Net profit/(loss)	4,500	3,250	750	(1,125)

WORKING   Fixed production overhead absorption rate:

$$\frac{\text{Fixed production overhead}}{\text{Budgeted production}} = \frac{£5,000}{10,000 \text{ units}} = £0.50 \text{ per unit}$$

As finished stock is maintained at 1,000 units, production each quarter must be the same as sales and thus:

	1st quarter	2nd quarter	3rd quarter	4th quarter
Overhead incurred	5,000	5,000	5,000	5,000
Overhead absorbed at 50p per unit				
10,000 × 50p	5,000			
9,000 × 50		4,500		
7,000 × 50p			3,500	
5,500 × 50p				2,750
Under absorption	-	500	1,500	2,250

(b)   **Net profit statement (fixed overhead charged against period sales)**

	1st quarter	2nd quarter	3rd quarter	4th quarter
Sales units	10,000	9,000	7,000	5,500
	£	£	£	£
Sales value	50,000	45,000	35,000	27,500
Less: Variable cost of sales				
(£3.75 per unit)	37,500	33,750	26,250	20,625
Contribution	12,500	11,250	8,750	6,875
Less: Fixed production selling and				
administration overhead	8,000	8,000	8,000	8,000
Net profit/(loss)	4,500	3,250	750	(1,125)

4.8   Effect of fixed overhead in stock values

If marginal costing is adopted, then stocks of works in progress and finished products will be valued at variable costs only. Where production and sales levels are not the same and stock levels are fluctuating, the net profit will be different from that disclosed by an absorption method of costing.

4.9   Criticisms of absorption costing

Preparation of routine operating statements using absorption costing is considered less informative because:

(a)   Profit per unit is a misleading figure: in the example the operating margin of £2 per unit arises because fixed overhead per unit is based on 5,000 units. If another basis were used, margin per unit would differ even though fixed overhead was the same amount in total.

(b)   Build-up or run-down of stocks of finished goods can distort comparison of period operating statements and obscure the effect of increasing or decreasing sales.

(c)   Comparison between products can be misleading because of the effect of arbitrary apportionment of fixed costs.

4.10   Defence of absorption costing

Absorption costing is widely used and the student should understand both principles. Defenders of the absorption principle point out that:

(a)   it is necessary to include fixed overhead in stock values for financial statements; routine cost accounting using absorption costing produces stock values which include a share of fixed overhead;

(b)   for small business, using job costing overhead allotment is the only practicable way of obtaining job costs for estimating and profit analysis;

(c)   analysis of under/over absorbed overhead is useful to identify inefficient utilisation of production resources.

5   **SELF TEST QUESTIONS**

5.1   Distinguish between a fixed and variable cost. (1.3)

5.2   What is contribution? (1.4)

5.3   What is a step-cost? (1.5)

5.4   Why is it necessary to separate the fixed and variable elements of a semi-variable cost? (2.1)

5.5   What is the difference between interpolation and extrapolation? (3.6)

5.6   State the limitations of using historic costs as the basis of predicting future costs. (3.7)

6   **EXAMINATION TYPE QUESTION**

6.1   **D & E Ltd**

D & E Ltd produces brakes for the motor industry. Its management accountant is investigating the relationship between electricity costs and volume of production. The following data for the last ten quarters has been derived, the cost figures having been adjusted (ie, deflated) to take into account price changes.

Quarter	1	2	3	4	5	6	7	8	9	10
Production, X, ('000 units)	30	20	10	60	40	25	13	50	44	28
Electricity costs, Y, (£'000)	10	11	6	18	13	10	10	20	17	15

(Source: Internal company records of D & E Ltd.)

$$\sum X^2 = 12,614, \qquad \sum Y^2 = 1,864, \quad \sum XY = 4,728$$

You are required

(a)   to draw a scatter diagram of the data on squared paper;

(4 marks)

(b)   to find the least squares regression line for electricity costs on production and explain this result;

(8 marks)

(c)   to predict the electricity costs of D & E Ltd for the next two quarters (time periods 11 and 12) in which production is planned to be 15,000 and 55,000 standard units respectively;

(4 marks)

(d)   to assess the likely reliability of these forecasts.

(4 marks)

(Total: 20 marks)

7   ANSWER TO EXAMINATION TYPE QUESTION

7.1   D & E Ltd

(a)   **Scatter graph of electricity cost against production**

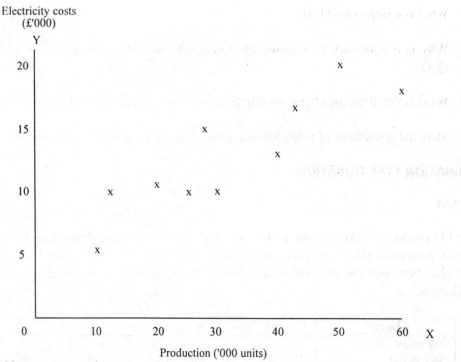

Notes:

(i)   Do not confuse this with a time series graph.

(ii)   Choose the scales so that the graph fits the graph paper.

(iii)   Do not attempt to draw a line through the scatter graph unless the question requires it.

(iv)   Label the axes and state the units.

(b)   The regression line of Y on X is Y = a + bX where

$$b = \frac{n\,\Sigma\,xy - \Sigma\,x\,\Sigma\,y}{\Sigma\,x^2 - (\Sigma x)^2} \qquad \text{and } a = \frac{\Sigma Y - b\Sigma\,x}{n}$$

$$\Sigma X = 320$$

$$\Sigma Y = 130$$

$$n = 10$$

$$b = \frac{10 \times 4,728 - 320 \times 130}{10 \times 12,614 - (320)^2} = \frac{5,680}{23,740}$$

$$= 0.239$$

$$a = \frac{130 - 0.239 \times 320}{10}$$

$$= 5.34$$

The least squares regression line of electricity costs (Y) on production (X) is therefore

$$Y = 5.34 + 0.239X$$

where Y is in £'000 and X in '000 units.

Explanation

Assuming there is an approximately linear relationship between production and electricity costs, which is shown to be reasonable by the scatter graph, the electricity costs are made up of two parts, a fixed cost (independent of the volume of production) of £5,340 and a variable cost per unit of production of £239 per 1,000 units or 23.9p per unit).

(c)   For quarter 11, X = 15, hence

$$Y = 5.34 + 0.239 \times 15$$
$$= 8.93$$

The predicted electricity cost for quarter 11 is therefore £8,930.

For quarter 12, X = 55, hence

$$Y = 5.34 + 0.239 \times 55$$
$$= 18.5$$

The predicted electricity cost for quarter 12 is therefore £18,500.

(d)   There are two main sources of error in the forecasts:

(i)   The assumed relationship between Y and X.

The scatter graph shows that there can be fairly wide variations in Y for a given X. Also the forecast assumes that the same conditions will prevail over the next two quarters as in the last ten quarters.

(ii)   The predicted production for quarters 11 and 12.

No indication is given as to how these planned production values were arrived at, so that it is not possible to assess how reliable they are. If they are based on extrapolation of a time series for production over the past ten quarters, they will be subject to the errors inherent in such extrapolations.

Provided conditions remain similar to the past ten quarters, it can be concluded that the forecasts would be fairly reliable but subject to some variation.

Note: methods for calculation of confidence limits for forecasts are available, but are outside the scope of this syllabus. At this level it is impossible to quantify the reliability, so that comments can only be in general terms, although a correlation coefficient would be worth calculating **if time allowed.**

7 COST ACCOUNTING SYSTEMS

INTRODUCTION & LEARNING OBJECTIVES

Syllabus area 6a. Cost accounting appropriate to service and production based organisations. (Ability required 3).

Design of computerised systems. (Ability required 3).

November 1996 students

This chapter should be studied in full, as it covers these two syllabus areas.

May 1997 students

The wording of this syllabus area changes slightly from May 1997. It removes the phrase 'Design of computerised systems' and replaces it with 'specification, design and operation of databases for the collection of and storage of cost accounting data; use of relevant applications software to extract data and prepare management information'.

The impact of this amendment is to provide more detail of the syllabus area, all of which is fully covered within this chapter. You must therefore study this chapter in full.

This chapter identifies the needs of management in various organisations and the role of the cost accounting department and cost accounting systems in providing that information.

In providing this information, presentation can be most important, different presentation methods are illustrated and their benefits considered.

When you have studied this chapter you should be able to do the following:

- Explain the purposes of information systems.
- Identify the problems associated with information needs.
- Prepare reports using graphs and charts.
- Explain the role of the cost accounting department.
- Explain the cost information needs of different services and functions within an organisation.
- Explain the costing methods used in a range of different industries/organisations.
- Identify and explain the use of non-financial performance indicators.
- Explain the principles of designing computerised systems.

1   COST ACCOUNTING SYSTEMS AND INFORMATION

1.1   Introduction

Information systems have been a necessary part of the business world from the day when people were first brought together for the production of goods and services. In the small business the proprietor is the system designer and controller. He issues orders which are obeyed by his employees and the way these instructions are given and carried out forms part of the system.

In the larger businesses the system is obviously more complex, since individual managers are responsible for performing specific functions eg, personnel, marketing etc, and changes in the overall organisation structure are also evident. Instead of all decisions being taken by one person, there has to be a certain degree of decentralisation eg, many decisions are taken by lower levels of management, provided they are made within the overall company policy dictated by the board of directors.

1.2   Cost accounting systems

Systems of cost accounting exist to provide information to the managers of a business and thus cost accounting systems form part of management information systems. Cost accounting systems may be computerised or they may be operated manually, this choice is often dependent on the size of the organisation and the nature of its operations. In either case data must be collected, processed into information and reported to management.

1.3   Data and information

Definition **Data** is the name given to the basic facts relating to the activities of a business eg, the hours worked by individuals; materials used on a particular job; number of items delivered or returned, etc. In order to manage, operate and control the business the management must ensure that the data is **processed** into **information** ie, assembled into a more meaningful form such as a payroll, job reports, sales analyses, etc.

1.4   Management information systems

Definition A management information system (MIS) is a combination of planned procedures, suitably designed forms, an appropriate organisation structure and managers who are capable of utilising the output which is produced, to assist them in the administration and use of available resources.

1.5   Purpose of information systems

A MIS should exist to enable the individual manager to perform his three main activities:

(a)   **Decision-making**

Certain decisions are based on the ability and experience of the manager but others are based on the availability of up-to-date information. The type of information system used would depend upon:

•   the frequency of decisions to be made; and

•   the time available for selecting and processing the data.

(b)   **Planning and control**

In order to exercise control, the manager must perform the following:

- formulate a plan based on the decision in (a) eg, planned production requirements (this will normally be done by means of a budget);

- record the plan eg, details of quantity and quality of materials to be used in production;

- implement the plan – either personally or by delegation;

- compare the actual results with the planned (budgeted) results; and

- evaluate this comparison in order to determine whether further action is necessary.

(c)   **Co-ordination**

The various sections of the business must operate in harmony. This is especially true in the case of a multi-product enterprise which operates at many geographical locations with each factory or branch having many subsections.

2   ROLE OF THE COST ACCOUNTING DEPARTMENT

2.1   Department organisation

The organisation of the cost department will be governed by the availability of personnel and facilities, the complexity of manufacture and the supply of information required from the cost accounting service. Generally, cost accounting may be divided into two main activities, ascertainment and presentation. The department may well embrace certain other related activities such as stock control or sales analysis.

2.2   Presentation of cost statements

The costing department will produce a wide variety of statements to meet the information needs of management at various levels. These should assist management in its planning, control and decision-making activities. It would be impossible to specify how a particular statement should be presented but certain general principles need to be followed:

(a)   The needs of the recipient must be of paramount consideration. The statement should highlight the important aspects, avoid a debit/credit format of presentation and be tailored in the depth of detail relevant to the status of the recipient.

(b)   Make the statement understandable and unambiguous. This can be achieved by grouping items, by relegating detailed analysis to supporting statements or appendices and by expressing values in round pounds or thousands of pounds, as appropriate.

(c)   A statement should incorporate some form of comparison. Where a budget or standard is appropriate, that will represent the basis for comparison; but in the absence of standards/budgets the comparable results for the previous period could be used.

(d)   Money values on their own may well be meaningless eg, a statement of labour costs without any indication of the number of hours involved, or the value of rejected products without reference to the number of units involved.

(e)   The need for a descriptive title, clear column headings and an indication of the period covered by the statement must be borne in mind.

Students will encounter many examples of cost statements during their study and at work and they are advised to appraise such examples critically. By so doing they will develop the ability to translate cost data in a wealth of detail into cost statements providing useful information to management.

2.3   Reporting to management

In addition to the regular information provided via cost statements, the cost accountant will be asked to provide **ad hoc** reports to management on the evaluation of specific proposals or problems and possibly to advise thereon. The general principles to be followed in the preparation of such a report are:

(a)   **Conciseness** – detailed statements and tables should form appendices to the report rather than be interspersed in the main body of it. If such statements are numerous they should be clearly numbered for ease of reference. The main conclusions and recommendations, if any, should be summarised and highlighted separately in the report.

(b)   **Structure** – the report should be broken down into logical sections with headings for each section. These should be numbered for easy reference, particularly if the report is lengthy.

(c)   **Style** – short sentences expressed in clear language are preferable. The aim is to communicate quickly and unambiguously, not to entertain. Opinion must be clearly separated from facts.

(d)   **Presentation** – the report should contain a descriptive title, indicate the addressee and any other recipients of copies and be dated and signed. Any terms of reference should be included in the report.

2.4   Problems associated with information

(a)   **Too much information**

Vital facts may be overlooked and the quality of decision-making may suffer if too much information is made available to the manager.

(b)   **Responsibility**

Only those persons who are in a position to make decisions should receive the information.

(c)   **Data falls into two categories**

- Costs/revenues which may be controlled; and
- Costs/revenues which cannot be controlled.

These two categories should be clearly segregated.

(d)   **Accuracy**

The information should be as accurate as is necessary for the particular purpose for which it is required. However, there is often a trade-off between accuracy and timeliness (see below).

(e)   **Up-to-date**

Information is of little value if there is an unacceptable time-lag between the actual event and the receipt of information relating to that event. It is often better to give approximate information quickly than to wait until more precise data is available.

(f)   **Relevance**

Information must be put into its correct perspective so that immaterial amounts will not prejudice decision-making.

(g)   **For its own sake**

Often information is produced because it is thought to be worthwhile for its own sake rather than because it is necessary. This is a waste of valuable resources.

(h)   **Exception principle**

Managers are generally very busy so it is helpful for them to have information about problems highlighted. This is achieved by reporting only on events which are unusual or require investigation. No report is needed on matters proceeding according to plan. This principle is known as **exception reporting.** An example is the listing of suppliers' invoices over, say, £1,000, so that the manager can check the high value invoices but need not spend unnecessary time on smaller invoices. A system of budgetary control with variance analysis applies the same principle, the presence of a variance indicating a departure from plan and the need for remedial action.

3   PRESENTATION OF INFORMATION

3.1   Report writing

Accountants are used to dealing with figures, but they must also learn to express themselves clearly in words. This is important not only for the passing of examinations, but also in professional work. Accountants are (or should be!) well prepared for the degree of precision and organisation required in report writing, but may need practice to improve their written style.

The following guidelines for report writing should be observed both in examinations and in practical situations:

(a)   **Reporting objectives**

Every report has several objectives. Generally these will be to:

- define the problem;
- consider the alternatives; and
- make a reasoned recommendation for a specific alternative.

(b)   **Recipient**

The writer should consider the position of the recipient and design the report accordingly. Some recipients will require detailed calculations; others will have little time to study a lengthy report and should therefore be given one of minimum length consistent with providing the required information.

In the examination you should write in a professional report style, pretending that you are writing to a client or to a senior manager.

(c)   **Heading**

Each report should be headed to show who it is from and to, the subject and the date.

(d) **Paragraph point system – each paragraph should make a point; each point should have a paragraph**

This simple rule should always be observed. Important points may be underlined.

(e) **Jargon and technical terms**

The use of jargon should be avoided at all times. If it is necessary to use technical terms, these should be fully explained, as should any techniques with which the recipient may be unfamiliar eg, decision trees, linear programming, marginal costing, etc.

(f) **Conclusion**

A report should always reach a conclusion. This should be clearly stated at the end of the report, not in the middle. The report should make it clear why you have arrived at the stated conclusion: it is not enough merely to state all the alternatives and then to recommend one of them without supportive reasoning.

(g) **Planning**

The report must be properly planned so that all the points appear in the most logical order. In practice a report can be prepared in draft form and then amended. In the examination there is not enough time for this, so the initial planning is of paramount importance. Witness this extract from an examiner's report:

... if only candidates had their hands tied behind their backs for five minutes before being permitted to start writing, in many cases the marks that they might then have obtained could well be significantly higher.

(h) **Figures**

All detailed figures and calculations should be relegated to appendices, only the main results appearing in the body of the report. Remember that comparative figures will often be useful. The report should be made as visually stimulating as possible, for instance by the use of graphs and charts instead of, or to supplement, figures.

3.2 Graphs and charts

The aim of including graphs and charts is to present information in a clear and concise manner. Any graph or chart which does not meet this objective should be excluded. On the other hand, graphs and charts often hold the attention and can illustrate a point much more clearly than can the written word.

Useful graphs and charts include:

(a) break-even charts; (see chapter 14)
(b) graphs showing trends in sales, costs etc; (see chapter 6)
(c) decision trees; (see chapter 15)
(d) linear programming graphs; (see chapter 16)
(e) statistical graphs eg, bar chart, histograms and pie charts.

3.3   Bar chart

Central heating fuels used by Midlands' households: 19X4 to 19X6

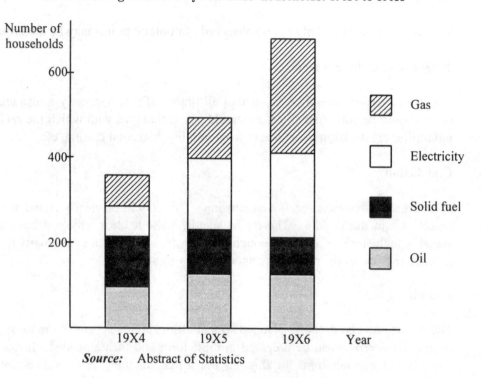

Source: Abstract of Statistics

3.4   Pie chart

Central heating fuels used by Midlands' households in 19X6

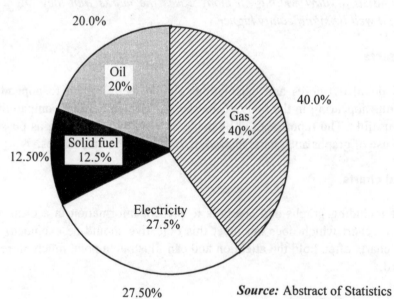

Source: Abstract of Statistics

3.5   Histogram

Weekly income of qualified accountants

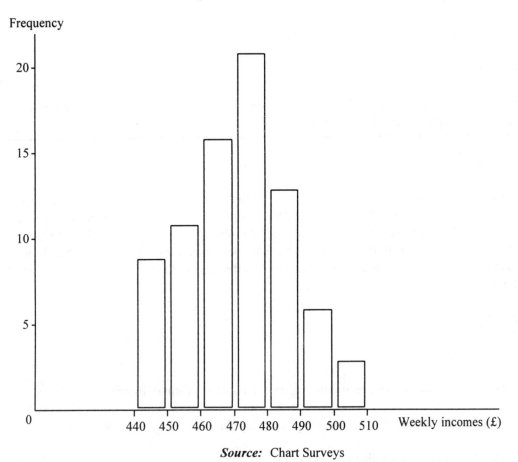

Source: Chart Surveys

3.6   Computer output reports

In a computer system many routine reports will take the form of continuous stationery produced directly by the computer and distributed to the appropriate manager. The great danger with this is the tendency to ignore such reports because of:

(a)   the frequency and quantity of the output;
(b)   lack of understanding of the report's significance.

To overcome these problems it is necessary to:

(a)   Adopt a strict principle of exception reporting.

(b)   Educate and involve managers in computerisation of a system by:

  • requesting their advice on the relevant information to be included; and
  • explaining and translating the computer output.

(c)   Adopt a flexible approach over the discarding of obsolete forms of report and the introduction of new forms. Sufficient flexibility in the systems design will be required to allow this to take place.

There is no reason why forms of output other than continuous stationery should not be considered eg, graph plotters or visual display units, although the additional expense of such equipment must be justified in terms of improvement in information.

4   DESIGN OF COMPUTERISED SYSTEMS

November 1996 students

This section is specifically included in syllabus area 6a.

May 1997 students

This heading in the syllabus is replaced by the more detailed specification explained on page 118. You must still study this part of the syllabus in full.

4.1   Introduction

Before a computer system is produced, it must be designed. The design of a system requires a detailed and critical examination of the system's composition and operation. Design is a creative activity. It must be done methodically: first of all the objective must be considered; then possible solutions; and finally the selection of appropriate solutions must be made. The design stage succeeds the definition stage, and the system which is the result of the design stage is the one which is implemented.

4.2   Design activities

These will include:

(a)   Definition of output requirements: volume, frequency, format, distribution.

(b)   Specification of inputs: volume, frequency, layout.

(c)   Development of overall system logic.

(d)   Determination of control/audit procedures.

(e)   Identification of information flow: data elements, output requirements and data relationships.

(f)   File identification: master and work files, data volumes, frequency of access, retention periods.

(g)   Selection of storage media; type of access, required response time, database considerations.

(h)   Determination of file organisation and record layout.

(i)   Identification of programs and required manual procedures.

(j)   Identification of computer runs (division of computer-based activities).

(k)   Creation of program specifications.

(l)   Test controls and information needs.

(m)   Preparation of detailed implementation plan.

(n)   Cost estimate revisions (if necessary).

(o)   Report preparation for user and system management; design stage documentation.

5   DESIGN OF THE DATA PROCESSING SYSTEM

5.1   Introduction

To illustrate the more practical aspects of system design, we will now take the design of a data processing system based simply upon the idea that we must consider three aspects - inputs, file structures, and output.

5.2   The system objectives

In designing a system, we must try to achieve the following:

(a)   **Simplicity**. The system should be as simple as possible. Unnecessary complications in both planning and operation should be avoided.

(b)   **Flexibility**. The system should be capable of being amended to meet changes in requirements with the minimum of difficulty and delay.

(c)   **Reliability**. The system should not be liable to excessive breakdown, and must meet defined reliability criteria.

(d)   **Accuracy**. The system should detect errors or omissions in its inputs, and should not generate any errors.

(e)   **Acceptability**. The system should be designed to meet the needs of users, and not to minimise systems and programming problems at their expense.

(f)   **Economy**. Costs should be reduced as much as possible.

(g)   **Implementation**. This should be done as easily and economically as possible.

5.3   Components of a data processing system

Data processing systems consist of three basic subsystems:

(a)   output;
(b)   data storage;
(c)   input.

The design of the DP system centres around these three subsystems; provided they are properly catered for, the system should be effective.

5.4   Output subsystem

All output is derived from some combination of three sources – input data, file records and computations. We are concerned therefore with:

(a)   the combination of these three sources for each output;
(b)   the frequency with which the output is required; and
(c)   the format of the output.

All output needs to be analysed carefully; the output analysis chart provides a format which answers the following questions:

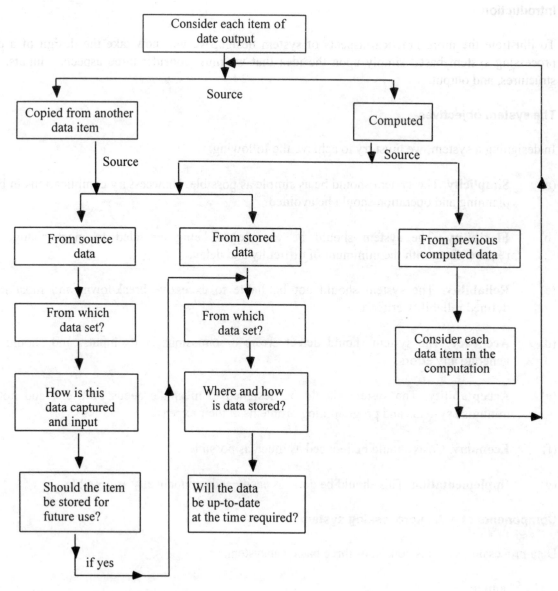

5.5   Phasing and sequence of output

All output needs to be scheduled as to where it falls in relation to:

(a)   the sequence on the output document;
(b)   the input of data;
(c)   file updating;
(d)   previous computer runs.

5.6   Output formats

Careful consideration needs to be given to the physical form of output, eg, printed, VDU or microfilm. Also the design of the output needs careful attention. Much computer output is badly designed and almost unintelligible except to the initiated.

Computer output, whatever its form, should be clear and unambiguous. Its meaning should be obvious to all intended users. Document and code design will be looked at in detail in the following section.

5.7   File storage subsystem

File details need to be specified:

(a)   to ensure that no data is omitted from the file;

(b)   to balance space requirements against processing efficiency;

(c)   to estimate the required storage space; and

(d)   to obtain a picture of the record size.

It is important to estimate the disc storage space required to hold the required files on-line at the same time.

Also the decision must be taken whether to use fixed or variable length records. Variable length records are more economic on storage space, but may require more processing.

5.8   Input subsystem

(a)   **Data capture**

The mode and method of data capture must be determined – telephone, post, personal callers, etc.

(b)   **Batching/on-line entry**

It should be decided whether to batch input documents, or to enter them on line. If the source documents are to be batched, then the frequency and controls must be determined.

(c)   **Entry of code numbers**

Wherever possible code numbers should be preprinted on documents. Where this is possible, the code should be kept as simple as possible. Also checks (eg, check digits) should be built into the input system as far as is practicable.

(d)   **Error messages**

Where errors are detected, error messages should be printed or displayed. The recipients of error messages should understand their meaning.

Procedures must be established for error correction and re-inputting.

5.9   System architecture

The system architecture is the overall structure of input, files, processing and output. The total system is normally divided into a number of routines or runs, eg:

Application	*Routines*
Payroll	Gross wage computation (weekly)
	Payslip printing (weekly)
	Payroll analysis (quarterly)

A routine usually comprises several processing runs. A typical set of processing runs would comprise:

(a)   data validation;

(b)   sorting of input data;

(c)   access master files, eg, pay rates;

(d)   update master file records;

(e)   printing of analysis data;

(f)   document printing.

5.10 Processing terminology

Data needs to be managed so that processing can take place quickly and efficiently. The system should allow the following types of data manipulation.

(a)   **Sorting of data**

All data management systems can sort the data held in their files into a different order. This is called sorting on a key field, eg, sorting all the records in a sales ledger into customer order is sorting on the field 'customer name'.

(b)   **Merging of files**

Merging combines the records in two or more files to provide a single new file, and is often used for the maintenance of cumulative transaction files such as outstanding purchase orders.

(c)   **Amending of data**

A good system should be able to do the following jobs:

(i)   add new records;

(ii)   amend records already in the file;

(iii)   delete records on the file;

(iv)   provide a summary of all the records in an existing file;

(v)   show how each file is built up regarding the number of records in the file and the number of characters in each record; and

(vi)   allow the number of characters per record to be changed (advanced systems only).

(d)   **Updating of data**

Updating adjusts the contents of a record on a file to take account on the latest transactions or changes in reference data. For example a stock balance would be updated by the amount of any receipts or issues contained in the transaction records being processed.

(e)   **Retrieval of data**

The system will be able to retrieve data from the files, either by accessing and printing the whole file or by printing selected parts of that file. Printing will take place after any functions required in parts (b) and (d) above have taken place.

(f)   **Referencing of data**

Referencing describes the interrogation of file data to enable processing to be carried out. No change is made to the data accessed. As an example, employee pay could be calculated by reference to a separate pay rate master file.

(g)   **Restructuring of data**

In addition to the functions listed above, the system will allow the user to write small programs himself, to reanalyse the data in the way he requires. Thus, although basic functions will always be provided in any system, this additional facility now allows the user to define exactly how his data should be amended and displayed.

The result of this is that better control is given to the users of the data, because the information is presented in the best way for them. This allows the limitations of the system menu to be overcome.

5.11   Computer work scheduling

It is important to schedule the tasks to be carried out by the computer within the operational hours. The factors to be taken into account are:

(a)   when source data is available;
(b)   time needed for data entry;
(c)   time for each routine;
(d)   handling of special stationery;
(e)   deadlines for output; and
(f)   priorities.

5.12   Systems specification

This will contain full details of all clerical and computer procedures involved:

(a)   system objectives;

(b)   system description and flowchart;

(c)   file specifications;

(d)   document specifications :

    (i)   samples of forms;
    (ii)   samples of reports;

(e)   program specifications:

    (i)   flowcharts;
    (ii)   test data;
    (iii)   controls;
    (iv)   computer runs;

(f)   implementation procedures:

    (i)   timetable;
    (ii)   changeover procedures;

(g)   equipment;

(h)   user department instructions.

5.13   Reporting to management

The systems analyst then prepares a report for management, which should include the following:

(a)   introduction, including terms of reference;

(b)   description of the proposed system;

(c)   summary of its advantages and disadvantages;

(d)   description of its effect on the organisation, eg, improved performance anticipated, reorganisation necessary, etc;

(e)   resources needed for the system;

(f)   costs;

(g)   method of implementation, and a possible timetable.

Flowcharts and specimen documents should be included to illustrate the text. Charts and graphs should be included when necessary.

There then takes place a process of consultation between the systems analyst and the management who will have to operate the system. Usually, the report gives rise to a number of criticisms or suggestions, which are discussed at meetings between the systems analyst and the managers concerned. The agreements reached are recorded in a final report, copies of which are distributed to those concerned.

6   DOCUMENT AND CODE DESIGN

6.1   Introduction

Input documents have two roles to play. Data is collected onto them, and they are then used as a base for entry onto a computer. There are a number of techniques available for helping to reconcile these sometimes conflicting requirements, but document design is largely a matter of common sense.

The careful design of documents is an essential ingredient of an effective system. Documents should provide an efficient means of transmitting information. There are many costs associated with the use of documentation and inefficient document design will cause additional costs to the business. Costs associated with document design include:

(a)   **Cost of printing**

As a general rule standard size documents are preferred (eg, A4, A5) as they are less expensive than special sizes. Documentation used solely for internal purposes may use lower quality paper and printing than those used for external purposes where the company will wish to use top-quality stationery to impress customers and others. Multi-part stationery is more expensive than single part.

(b)   **Handling costs**

An input form must be easy to complete and to enter into the computer. If a form is inefficiently designed it may not be used properly, eg, a customer sends a cheque for the current month balance only, rather than the total sum due, because a statement does not clearly show the total due. Internal documents may cause delay or additional management time if they do not contain all the information which is needed. A form which is not clearly identified may be mistaken for a different document. Some documents may be handled frequently and so must be capable of standing up to regular use, eg, audit working papers.

6.2   The document description

When an analyst is recording facts about the existing system he will be interested in the documents which are used in the system. The documents will often help to clarify the existing procedures and controls. In a similar way an auditor may well examine documents within a client's accounting system. The analyst may wish to include in his own files copies of documents used in the system, both blank documents and some with specimen data entered.

The documents themselves cannot give a complete picture and to supplement them the analyst may complete a **'document description'** form. An example of such a form is given below with a brief explanation of the data to be included in it.

Notes

(a)   **Title** – gives the form title and number with details of any alternative name commonly used for this document in the company.

(b)   **Purpose** – a brief description of the purpose of the document. This may help to identify unnecessary documents/copies.

(c)   **Originated by** – gives the place and means of origination and may identify the means of combining existing documents.

(d)   **Used by** – this should be related to the purpose of the document to ensure that it is only sent to those who need it. It may indicate the suitability of the layout for the user's needs.

(e)   **Number of copies** – minimum, average and maximum are sometimes for general indication only.

(f)   **Contents** – it is essential for each data item to be clearly indicated on the document. The size column indicates the maximum number of characters making up that field.

(g)   **Sequence** – used where the sequence of field names is different from that in the previous section.

DOCUMENT DESCRIPTION

Title of document		Project Name Date
Purpose		
Originated by		
Used by		

Number of copies		Minimum Average Maximum	} Per

No.	Field Name	Size	Comments

Sequence of data fields
Remarks

6.3   Document design hints

The content and design of a document will be governed largely by its purpose and the system of which it forms part.

There follows some general advice on the design of a document for an examination answer.

(a)   **Determine the purpose of the document**

Read the question carefully and decide what the document is for. You will find that it is created to provide information (eg, to management).   You may conclude that this information (the **output**) should be contained along the bottom row or along the right hand column of the document.

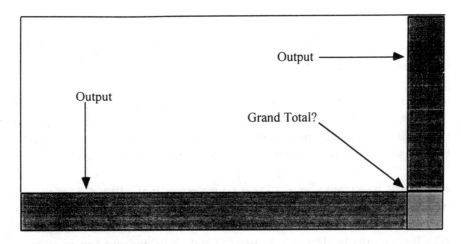

(b)   **Determine the input data required**

Your document will probably have to show the data items which are used to determine the output. For example, to determine the value of an invoice (output) one needs to show what has been sold, the unit price, the price net of VAT, the VAT amount and the gross price (input).

(c)   **Decide the order in which to record the input data**

You should work from left to right across your document or work down from top to bottom (ie, the **process** is left to right or top to bottom).

(d)   **Size of the document**

It was suggested earlier that documents should be a standard size. The document must be big enough to contain all the data and be easily read but not so big as to be difficult to handle and file. The solution in the examination room is normally easy – use one whole sheet of A4 for each document which you have to design. This means that you have a suitably-sized document and you do not have to draw the borders.

(e)   **Title**

The title of a form is important. It should be descriptive and preferably short. If the question in the examination gives the form a title, then use that form in your answer. Write the title of the form IN BLOCK CAPITALS across the top of your answer.

(f)   **Reference numbers**

These are useful for re-ordering purposes. The document number should be placed in a corner of the document so that it can be easily identified when held in a file.

(g)   **Headings**

It is important that as much data as possible is pre-printed on the document so that only variable data needs to be entered when the document is used. Watch out in particular for the need to include:

(i)   dates, eg, DD, MM, YY;

this is important in multi-national systems, since different countries have different standard ways of displaying dates.

(ii)   units, eg, hours, kilos;

       (iii)   instructions, eg, write your name here;

please return this remittance advice with your cheque.

(h)   **Multi-part sets of documents**

It is often effective to print several copies of a document together using carbon between each copy. Remember that it is essential to have the same data at the same position on each copy but that lower copies may have information 'blanked-out' of them, eg, the price of goods is shown on the invoice copy but not on the despatch note copy.

In the examination it is important above all that your answer **looks like a document** which could conceivably **meet the objective described in the question**. You may find it useful with the examination in mind to study documents which you come across at work. Consider the contents and layout. Why has a particular design been used? Could it be improved in any way?

6.4 Code design

Code design is closely linked with the design of documents. The purpose of a code is to identify an item more precisely and concisely than a written description. In a computer-based system a code may also:

(a)   Save storage space. For instance, a product code can be kept on a record which if necessary can be cross-referenced to a more detailed description of the item held as standing data on a master file. There is no need for a detailed description to be included in each record.

(b)   Save input time. The time and cost of data preparation can be reduced. There will need to be some controls to ensure that the code used is correct, eg, by using check digits.

The general features to remember when designing a code system are:

(a)   It should be easy to use. It is particularly important to avoid a situation when a computer generated code is so long that it becomes cumbersome for people to use.

(b)   It must be designed to avoid errors such as the duplication of code numbers for different items.

(c)   It must be flexible to allow for changes in the classification of items which are the subject of the code.

(d)   It must allow for expansion.

(e)   It should preferably be easy for users to remember. In this context descriptive codes are particularly useful.

(f)   It should be easy to validate. Many numbers have an additional digit (check digit) which can be used to assess the feasibility of the number.

6.5 Main types of coding systems

(a)   **Sequence codes**

These entail the allocation of numbers of items in a straightforward numerical sequence. There is no obvious connection between an item and its code; for example:

0001	bolts
0002	washers
0003	screws
0004	nuts

Sequence codes allow for simple file design but they are rarely used when large numbers of items are involved because they do not readily allow for the classification of items.

(b)   **Group classification codes**

These are sometimes known as *block codes* and they extend the simple sequential codes by providing a separate sequence for each group of items; for example:

1000 – 1999	different types of bolts
2000 – 2999	different types of washers
3000 – 3999	different types of screws
4000 – 4999	different types of nuts

In effect the prefix signifies the group to which the item belongs. The code is sequential within each group so that this is only a very limited advance on sequential coding.

(c)   **Faceted codes**

These extend the principle of group classification by having each digit or perhaps several digits representing some facet or characteristic of the item; for example, the first digit is the nature of the item:

1 = bolt
2 = washers
3 = screws

the second digit is the material from which it is made:

1 = steel
2 = brass
3 = zinc

and so on.

(d)   **Significant digits codes**

This extends the concept of faceted codes by using digits in the code which directly represent a feature of the item; for example:

3,203	a brass screw 3 centimetres long
3,204	a brass screw 4 centimetres long

(e)   **Hierarchical codes**

This is a type of faceted code in which each digit represents a classification. The digits to the right represent sub-sets of the digits to the left. Decimal points may be used to break up the code number into its main parts. The best known example is the universal decimal code used by libraries. Another example is the government designed industry classification (SIC code).

(f)   **Mnemonic codes**

These use a mixture of alphabetical and numerical characters to signify characteristics of the items; for example:

MT/FA/HW6/2 stands for

Mid-term course
Financial accounting
Homework question 6
Page 2

Mnemonic codes are often more easily recognisable to people but there is the possibility of numbers being mistaken for letters or vice versa (eg, 1 instead of l). It may be less clear how many items there are in the group than a block code (eg, how many pages make up HW6?).

6.6   Check digits

A common problem in coding systems is that errors may be made in preparing the data. It is relatively easy to make transposition errors when writing down a number. There are several ways in which errors can be reduced:

(a)   Split the code into sub-groups divided by a space or stroke, eg, it is easier to read 23/0570/16 than 23057016.

(b)   Use an alpha-numeric code, eg, it is easier to read and remember OHP 364P than 615 3645.

However, these methods may well escape detection before input to a computer system and so a system of self-checking numbers is often used. The most common is the use of the *check digit.* Check digits are added to the end of a code number to give the whole code (including the check digit) some special mathematical property. Check digits are often used for key field codes. A common model is that where a prime number is used to calculate a check digit which is placed on the right hand side of the code. The check digit is devised so that when the computer performs a processing routine on the whole code, it will yield a number which is exactly divisible by the prime number chosen, ie, there is no remainder. If there is a remainder from the calculation, the code number used is invalid.

As an example we will use the common Modulus 11 system. This means that the prime number used in the calculation is eleven.

We wish to calculate a check digit for the reference number 6312. After we have calculated the check digit the code number will be 6312N where N is the check digit.

Step 1   Assign a weight to each digit using 2 for the digit on the right hand side, ie,

Number	6	3	1	2
Weight	5	4	3	2

Step 2   Multiply each number by the weight and add the totals:

$$6 \times 5 = 30$$
$$3 \times 4 = 12$$
$$1 \times 3 = 3$$
$$2 \times 2 = 4$$
$$\overline{49}$$

Step 3   Divide the total by the modulus:

$$49 \div 11 = 4 \text{ remainder } 5$$

Step 4   The check digit = The modulus – The remainder:

$$11 - 5 = 6$$

Step 5   The full code number becomes 63126

We could now test the code by assuming that the operator accidentally enters the code number 63216:

$$
\begin{aligned}
6 \times 5 &= 30 \\
3 \times 4 &= 12 \\
2 \times 3 &= 6 \\
1 \times 2 &= 2 \\
6 \times 1 &= 6 \\
\hline
&\quad 56 \div 11 = 5 \text{ remainder } 1
\end{aligned}
$$

The fact that there is a remainder shows that the code number is invalid.

This type of check digit has been shown to detect all transposition errors and a high percentage of random errors.

It should be noted that if the check digit works out to be 10 then the Roman Numeral for 10 (X) is sometimes used.

Sometimes different weights and a more complex procedure is used to calculate the check digit. This is often done when there is a need for security or confidentiality.

6.7   Activity

The number 454792 is validated using a modulus 11 check digit. Is this number valid?

6.8   Activity solution

The sequence of weights for a six digit number are 6, 5, 4, 3, 2, 1. The check sum can be calculated using the following formula.

$$
\begin{aligned}
\text{Check sum} &= 6 \times 4 + 5 \times 5 + 4 \times 4 + 3 \times 7 + 2 \times 9 + 1 \times 2 \\
&= 24 + 25 + 16 + 21 + 18 + 2 \\
&= 106
\end{aligned}
$$

This check sum is not exactly divisible by 11 and therefore the number is invalid.

7   COMPUTER APPLICATIONS

7.1   Introduction

A **computer application** is a task which the computer is made to perform. All applications ultimately depend on the processing of data, but they can be sub-divided into three main groups:

(a)   **Commercial**, in which the computer performs administrative data-processing tasks including the maintenance of accounting records. Typically this involves large volumes of data and large file sizes. The main input peripheral is a keyboard, possibly combined with some form of data capture equipment. Large-scale storage devices with rapid access are needed for file handling, and disc-based systems are now the most common.

(b)   **Scientific**, carrying out complex statistical analysis or mathematical manipulation. Relatively small volumes of data may be involved, but they will be subjected to complex processing involving many millions of computer instructions. Specially large processors may be needed for this work to allow more accurate floating-point arithmetic and greater speed of computation.

(c)   **Process control**, in which the computer runs a machine or even a whole factory on the basis of data supplied from the process itself via special sensors and data transmission systems. Examples already implemented range from individual robots to entire steelworks, including automated decision-making processes to optimise the use of raw materials or other resources.

The dividing line between these applications is not always clear, and a computer in use in a particular installation may be involved in more than one type, although there is a certain amount of necessary specialisation to fit them for their particular tasks.

7.2   Commercial use of scientific applications

Financial modelling is one important use of applications in business. Similar forecasting and simulation models can be used for other aspects of the organisation, including non-financial data such as production levels. Mathematical techniques such as statistical analysis, linear programming, critical path analysis, etc can be built into these simulations to allow optimisation of plans and various possibilities to be compared.

Many of these analysis techniques are available for use on microcomputers, although large organisations with complex modelling needs may need access to more specialised equipment. In many cases software exists to make relatively complex analysis available to non-specialists, and reports can be produced in a variety of text and graphics formats using appropriate printers (dot matrix or laser) or plotters, so that the implications of the results can be made as clear as possible.

8   INTEGRATED SYSTEMS

8.1   Introduction

The piecemeal approach to systems development results in a number of separate special-purpose files. It also results in a number of special-purpose systems, each with its own inputs, outputs and programs. This approach has the advantage of simplicity, because systems are developed one at a time, and it is probably the wisest course to adopt when computers are being used for the first time. It also has disadvantages, which are:

(a)   Duplication of data.

(b)   Increased maintenance work.

(c)   Management information is only supplied from one file and may be incomplete.

(d)   Inputs and outputs may be duplicated. The output of one system may have to be converted into an input for another system.

(e)   Systems do not reflect the way in which the organisation works, as a complex set of interlocking and interactive systems.

(f)   Systems and program development work may be duplicated.

It is now considered desirable to develop **integrated systems**.

8.2   Concept of an integrated system

The essential concept is that systems communicate with each other inside the computer instead of outside it.

(a)   The single input principle is used. Input of a transaction results in **all** relevant files being updated.

(b)   Output is produced only for communication to the user. It is not produced to communicate with another system.

(c)   All files can be accessed by programs as needed; a program is not limited to access to a single file.

Integrated systems are usually, but not inevitably, associated with the use of databases.

8.3   Illustration

Three systems which are often integrated are order processing, sales accounting and stock control.

(a)   A customer order is input, and is checked against the customer file (for credit) and the stock file (for availability).

(b)   The stock file is updated. If meeting the order causes the stock to fall below reorder level, an exception report is produced.

(c)   Prices are obtained from the stock file and details of discounts from the customer file, which is then updated with details of the invoice.

It should be noted that a single input (customer order) has caused two files (customer and stock) to be updated and that the outputs produced (exception report, invoice set) are for communication to users and not between systems.

Further systems may be added to the integrated system, eg,:

(a)   If the order could not be met from stock, but had to be manufactured, the production planning system could be activated to schedule the manufacturing processes.

(b)   The production planning system would update the stock file as materials were allocated for the manufacture. The stock control system would in turn be activated to replenish stocks if necessary.

(c)   The order would at the proper time be placed in a work-in-progress file, and processed by the production control system.

8.4   Fully integrated accounting systems

Many commercial packages now exist which provide for the maintenance of all accounting records in one integrated system. These usually work on the three-ledger basis, maintaining Sales, Purchase and Nominal ledgers in such a way that all transactions automatically complete their own double entry. A wide range of these packages exists, and some include detailed stock control and payroll options, together with integrated word processors and spreadsheets so that information can be used anywhere in the system and incorporated into financial modelling routines and reports or letters as required. Most of this software is available for IBM-compatible 16-bit microcomputers, although it is also compatible with many of the faster 32-bit machines based on the 80386 and 80486 microprocessors.

The main disadvantage of this type of software is the fact that it is developed as a package and so may not meet the organisation's information needs exactly. To some extent this problem is outweighed by the flexibility of the packages, many of which can be customised to the user's own requirements, and the large number of different products available.

8.5   Integrated packages

Many integrated packages now exist. Many organisations will use an integrated applications package as an alternative to buying in a number of dedicated application packages.

An integrated package has a number of different modules which usually consist of a:

    spreadsheet,
    word-processor,
    communications package,
    graphics package, and
    database.

Often the price of an integrated package is the same as that of a dedicated package. Integrated packages have certain advantages and disadvantages.

Advantages:

Compatibility between the separate modules.

Efficiency – there is no need to quit one application to access another.

User friendly – there is only one set of Function Keys to learn as they would have the same function in each of the modules.

Disadvantages:

The memory size required might be more than that required by a dedicated package.

The modules contained in the package would not have as many features as in a dedicated application.

There may be more modules contained in it than those required by the user.

9   DATABASES AND DATABASE MANAGEMENT SYSTEMS

9.1   Introduction

Databases are collections of information which may not be computer based. A database can be defined as:

> **Definition**   A structured set of information about a series of individual entities, together with a system for efficient retrieval of that information.

Telephone directories and card index systems are both databases that are not computer based, but the availability of computers has led to a great improvement in the ability to store and retrieve information.

9.2   Database management system (DBMS)

Many applications can share the same database, which is accessed via a type of software called a database management system. This deals with all aspects of accessing the data, and makes it very much easier (and cheaper) to develop and modify applications.

How a DBMS works can be illustrated diagrammatically:

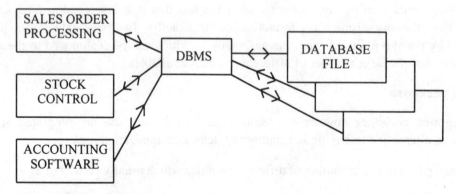

The structure of the database is not relevant to the person programming or modifying the applications. If there is a need to modify the database, then the only piece of software needing modification is the DBMS. Before the advent of database management systems, a change in the structure of the data files would have required each user application to be modified.

9.3   Types of database

There are three basic organisational structures that databases can fall into:

(a)   **Hierarchical databases**

The different items of data are related together like a kind of upside-down tree. Each individual may be related to several items of data below it, but may be related to only on 'parent' item of information.

The invoice data illustrated below is an example of a hierarchical organisation:

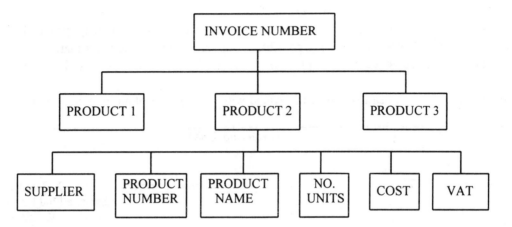

(b)   **Network databases**

A hierarchical structure allows a particular item to have as many items below it as are required, but only one item above it. A network structure eliminates this requirement.

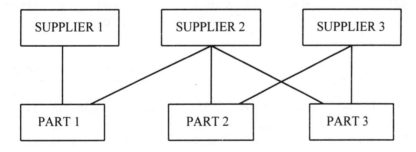

(c)   **Relational databases**

A relational database has a more complex structure. The data is split between a number of different files, which are related using unique keys. The files are two dimensional arrays, with each row representing a record (or tople) and each column representing a field (or domain). Part of a relational database that could be used to control costs in an organisation is seen below. This will show how relational databases work.

	Cost centre	Department no	Cost centre controller	Budget
Budget file				
	0134	1	016480	43100
	0135	1	016480	16300
unique key	0210	1	028311	50000
field →	0686	2	036212	40000

Department file

Department no	Name	Manager	
1	Marketing	016480	
2	Sally	036212	

Personnel file

Personnel no	Name	Address	Salary
016480	J. Smith	43, Acacia Cres	28,000
028311	P Squires	21 Simpson Road	24,000
036212	V Barrett	6 Gornall Drive	35,000

9.4   Data normalisation

The designer of a database will need to decide what data items should be grouped together in a particular table. There will be many possible groupings in any particular situation, but the designer will try to eliminate unnecessary duplication (or redundancy) by normalising the database.

The process of normalisation can be illustrated with an example of an invoice system.

Invoice no 638626

Account no: 1618   *Company name:*   X Balaskas
                                                                    Sandwell Ind Estate
                                                                    Westshire
                                                                    0663 217768

Item	Stock no	No units	Price	VAT	Total
Washers	1033	1,000	£0.10	£17.50	£117.50
Nuts	1211	1,000	£0.20	£35.00	£235.00
Bolts	1212	1,000	£0.20	£35.00	£235.00
Total order value				£87.50	£587.50

This data needs to be split into a series of tables. The first stage is to eliminate data that can be calculated, and therefore does not need to be stored. This would include the item total, the VAT, and the invoice totals. With the allocating of each item into fixed length fields, the data is now said to be in the first normal form.

The main unique key in the invoice is the invoice number. Other keys found on the document are the account number and the stock numbers. The next stages of normalisation is to identify which other items of data on the invoice are dependent on the other key fields.

The company name, address and telephone number will occur on other invoices with the same account number. This information should therefore be split off into a separate file, whose unique key field is the account number.

The item name, stock number and price (but not number of units) depend solely on the stock number. This data can therefore be split off into a stock file.

The invoice data can be represented in three files.

File 1   Invoice file   Invoice no, Account no, Item code 1, No units 1, Item code 2, No units 2, Item code 3, No units 3.

File 2   Customer file   Account no, Name, Address, Telephone no, Outstanding balance.

File 3   Stock file   Stock no, Item name, Stock level, Price, Re-order level, Lead time.

You will note that the outstanding balance for a particular customer is held on the customer file even though it could be calculated from the invoice file. This file is therefore redundant. Because one of the regular analyses produced from the system is a list of all companies owing money, it is more efficient to hold this redundant data item on file than to recalculate it. There will often be a trade off between minimising the amount of data stored and the amount of processing required.

9.5   Data dictionary

With a complex database structure, it is vital that it is documented properly. This is done using a data dictionary, which is defined as:

[Definition]   'An index of the data held in a database, used to assist in maintenance and any other access to the data' (British Computer Society).

The data dictionary will record each item of data held in a database, its characteristics (field width, type of field etc), validation criteria, which file it is held in, its position in that file, the person responsible for maintaining the validity of the data (its owner), and the associated data flows.

9.6   Database administration

A database is designed to fit the needs of a number of users. This brings a number of problems:

(a)   The needs and priorities of the different users must be balanced.
(b)   Data may be modified without the authorisation of the owner of the data.
(c)   The database may need to be modified with the minimum of inconvenience.

To cope with the problems, there will usually be a database administrator (DBA) employed by an organisation. This is an important role, which is often carried out by a senior and experienced person.

[Conclusion]   A database is a structured collection of data, which is accessed using a DBMS (database management system). There are several ways in which the database may be structured, ranging through a simple hierarchical system, via a network organisation to a full relational database. A relational database will be designed to minimise duplication using a process called **normalisation**.

Details of the data held and the flow of data will be recorded in a **data dictionary**.

10   CHAPTER SUMMARY

This chapter has considered the information needs of management, and how these needs are satisfied by the operation and design of a cost accounting system.

Many varied organisations were considered and their needs and information systems compared with those found in more traditional industries.

11   SELF TEST QUESTIONS

11.1   What is a management information system? (1.4)

11.2   What are the purposes of information systems? (1.5)

11.3   List the problems associated with information (2.4)

11.4   What are the basic subsystems of a data processing system? (5.3)

11.5   Name three different types of data manipulation. (5.10)

11.6   What are the following types of code?

Faceted codes.
Hierarchical codes.
Mnemonic codes. (6.5)

11.7   What is the purpose of a check digit? (6.6)

11.8   Name two advantages of an integrated package. (8.5)

11.9   What do the initials DBMS and DBA stand for? (9.2, 9.6)

11.10   Name three types of database. (9.3)

11.11   Define what a data dictionary is. (9.5)

12   EXAMINATION TYPE QUESTION

12.1   Retail organisation

An expanding retailing organisation which currently has ninety shops selling shirts, sweaters, suits and shoes for both males and females in the age range of fifteen to thirty years, has asked you to recommend a user oriented cost/management accounting information system which will assist management in the control of the business.

You are required, as the assistant management accountant:

(a)   to suggest how you would approach the task;

(4 marks)

(b)   to recommend an appropriate information system including performance indicators;

(10 marks)

(c)   to draft a suitable form of weekly profit statement which could be used for each shop;

(7 marks)

(d)   to indicate in what way computers would be used for the system recommended in your answers to (b) above,

(4 marks)

(Total: 25 marks)

13   ANSWER TO EXAMINATION TYPE QUESTION

13.1   Retail organisation

(a)   The first task would be to visit a selected number of shops, to familiarise oneself with the organisation at the retail level. An organisation chart would be drawn up, to clarify the levels of management and their precise functions and responsibilities. Management would be consulted, to determine, if possible, what information was required.

A number of systems suppliers would be approached, to determine what suitable systems eg, hardware and software were available.

A feasibility study would be undertaken, investigating the viability of such a system, and its anticipated costs and benefits.

(b)   An appropriate information system for a retail organisation would heip in the following areas:

(i)   **Stock control**

This is essential for two reasons. Firstly to ensure that materials are delivered to the shops when required, and secondly to control 'slippage', (loss due to shoplifting and theft by staff).

(ii)   **Cash control**

Most retail organisations sell mainly for cash. This should be tightly controlled and not be allowed to lie idle.

(iii)   **Credit control**

Credit sales (if any) should be closely monitored. Limits regarding cheques and credit cards should be clarified.

(iv)   **Internal audit**

An internal audit team should be installed, making frequent, but irregular checks on branches.

(v)   **Staff records**

Records should be maintained of all staff, not only for wages, overtime, bonuses, PAYE, NI etc, but for finding possible promotion prospects and details of labour turnover.

(vi)   **Performance evaluation**

Performance of different shops and managers can be monitored. Sales volume, sales per square foot, ROCE, profit/sales and sales/capital employed are important indicators.

(c)

Weekly profit statement

	Shirts	*Sweaters*	*Suits*	*Shoes*	*Total*

Sales
Cost of sales
Gross profit

Direct shop costs:
        Salaries including NIC
        Bonus and overtime
        Telephone
        Rates
        Insurance
        Sundries

Apportioned head office costs:
        Head office
        Advertising
        Warehousing
        Transport

Net profit

(d)   In an expanding organisation which already has ninety shops there is ample scope for the use of computers.

The obvious areas where computers could be applied are in stock control, cash control and payroll procedures.   The use of electronic tills with code numbers for all goods, and frequent integration into a central computer could facilitate both stock and cash control. Properly constructed, the system could provide the data input for the preparation of both management and financial accounts.

8 JOB AND CONTRACT COSTING

INTRODUCTION & LEARNING OBJECTIVES

Syllabus area 6a. Job, batch, contract costing, including work in progress. (Ability required 3).

This chapter is concerned with the type of costing sometimes known as specific order costing. As its name suggests, this is used where the unit(s) produced can be related to a specific production order as opposed to a continuous production process where items are made for stock.

Specific order costing comprises three costing methods:- job costing, batch costing and contract costing. This chapter considers each of these methods and identifies the differences between them, thus illustrating when each method should be used.

When you have studied this chapter you should be able to do the following:

- Explain when it is appropriate to use job costing.
- Explain how a job costing system operates.
- Explain when it is appropriate to use batch costing.
- Discuss the similarities and differences of job costing and batch costing.
- Explain when it is appropriate to use contract costing.
- Value work-in-progress in accordance with SSAP 9 under systems of job costing, batch costing and contract costing.
- Calculate and explain the need to recognise profits (or losses) on long term contracts.

---

1 APPLICATIONS OF SPECIFIC ORDER COSTING

1.1 Specific order costing

> **Definition** **Specific order costing** is a collective term for **job, batch** and **contract costing.** The distinguishing features are:
> (a) work is separated as opposed to a continuous flow;
> (b) work can be identified with a particular customer's order or contract.

1.2 Introduction to job costing

Job costing is used when firms are engaged in 'one-off' products of a specialist nature such as tools, machines, replacement parts, etc.

The jobbing firm, probably has only a small amount of work of a repetitive nature which means that production plans may be prepared for just a few weeks or months ahead, and have to be flexible to meet urgent orders.

1.3   Introduction to batch costing

Businesses which manufacture a variety of products eg, household electrical goods, to be held in stock prior to sale, will operate **batch costing.** Jobbing methods are still used and the costing system is practically the same as for job costing. The only difference is that instead of charging costs to each separate cost unit, they are charged to the one production order which covers a quantity of cost units. When the order is completed the unit cost is found by dividing the quantity into the total batch cost.

1.4   Introduction to contract costing

The difference between a contract and a job is one of size and time-span. Contract costing is used by businesses undertaking building or other constructional contracts which take months or years to complete. In many cases the work will be done on site and not in the contractor's own works. Each contract is treated as a separate cost unit since management will want to know the profit or loss on each. For major contracts it may be necessary to designate sub-units for each stage of work either to facilitate control or to enable the invoicing of progress claims and the calculation of profit to date.

1.5   Costing principles

Either marginal or absorption costing can be applied in job, batch, and contract costing. Again the decision is influenced by **SSAP 9**, which requires absorption costing for stock valuation purposes, and therefore encourages its application for all costing. The assumption made in the following sections is that absorption costing is to be applied. This is the more complex situation, in that it involves the use of pre-determined overhead rates, and the problems of over-or under-absorption. If marginal costing is applied, then only variable overheads are charged to the production units; other costs are expensed on a time basis.

2   JOB COSTING

2.1   Job cost sheet (or card)

The focal point of a job costing system is the cost sheet (or card). A separate sheet will be opened for each customer's order, on which will be recorded:

(a)   materials purchased specifically for the job (from GRNs or suppliers' invoices);
(b)   materials drawn from stock (from requisitions);
(c)   direct wages (from time sheet/job cards);
(d)   direct expenses (from invoices, etc).

When the job is finished, the cost sheet gives the total direct cost, and overhead can be calculated and entered using one of the accepted methods. If the job is unfinished at the end of an accounting period the total cost recorded to date on the cost sheets will give the work in progress figure. The job cost can be compared with the estimate to analyse the difference between actual and estimated cost. Where the product contains a number of components it is advisable to check that the costs of all the components have been recorded.

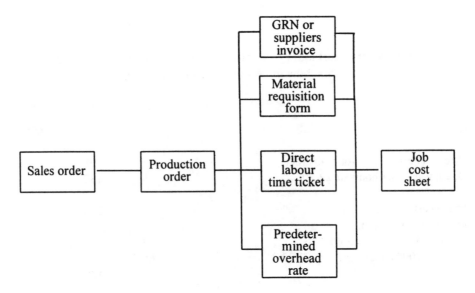

2.2   Example of a job cost

Jobbers Ltd undertakes jobbing engineering work. Among the requests for quotations received in December was one from A for a small machine to be manufactured according to the customer's drawings supplied. Jobbers Ltd prepared an estimate of the material and labour content based on the drawings, and amounts were added for overhead and profit. The estimate indicated a price of £600 and this price was quoted to, and accepted by, A.

The work on A's order was started in January on the authority of Production Order No. 1001 signed by the works manager and was completed in that month. The abstract of stores requisitions issued in January showed the following against Production Order No. 1001:

Stores requisition	£
D57	48
D61	24
D70	26
Total	98

Two operatives paid at £2.20 per hour each had been employed in separate cost centres on Production Order No. 1001 during January and their time-sheets showed that each had worked for thirty hours on that order. The overhead rates for the cost centres in which the operatives are employed are in one centre £2.00 per direct labour hour and 100% on direct wages in the other. Administration and other overhead is recovered at the rate of 30% on production cost.

You are required to prepare a statement showing the cost and profitability of the order from A.

2.3   Solution

Statement of cost and profitability - production order number 1001
machine for A per customer's drawing

	£	£	£
Selling price per estimate			600
Costs:			
Direct materials, per stores abstract		98	
Direct wages, 60 hours @ £2.20		132	
Prime cost		230	
Production overhead:			
30 hours @ £2.00	60		
100% of 30 hours @ £2.20	66		
	—	126	
Production cost		356	
Administration and other overhead, 30% of production cost		107	
Total cost of sales			463
Net profit			137

Note: actual and estimated profit on the order would be compared and any significant difference reported to management. The estimate should have been compiled on the same lines as the actual cost in the above statement to assist in locating the particular costs which were not as estimated.

2.4   Effect of inaccurate overhead absorption rates

The above illustration shows that selling prices can reflect estimates and that the major uncertainty in estimating is calculation of an accurate figure for overhead recovery. Inaccurate estimating can seriously harm the business because:

(a)   if jobs are over-priced, customers will go elsewhere;

(b)   if jobs are under-priced, sales revenue will fail to cover costs and/or provide an adequate return.

2.5   Inaccurate estimate of volume

Predetermined overhead rates are based on a volume estimate. If actual volume is significantly higher or lower than expected, then estimates, and consequently selling prices, will be inaccurate.

2.6   Example

Company A's budget for the year is as follows:

	£
Prime costs	50,000
Overhead	30,000
	80,000
Profit (40% on cost)	32,000
Sales	112,000
Volume	3,000 labour hours

If volume is half budget ie, 1,500 hours, actual results would show:

	£
Prime costs (half budget)	25,000
Overhead absorbed	15,000 (1,500 hours $\times \dfrac{£30,000}{3,000}$)
	40,000
Profit (40% on cost)	16,000
Sales	56,000

Actual overhead incurred would not fall to half the budget, however, because of the fixed element. It may fall to, perhaps, £24,000 but job costs would reflect overhead at the predetermined rate of £10 per hour, leaving £9,000 under-absorbed.

Actual profit would therefore be £(16,000 – 9,000) = £7,000.

2.7   Inaccurate absorption basis

Estimated costs should reflect overhead in relation to the way it is incurred, so that selling prices are competitive but profitable.

2.8   Example

Company B bases its estimates on the following formulae:

Total cost	=	Prime cost plus 40% for overhead
Selling price	=	Total cost plus 25% for profit

Estimates for two jobs show:

Item	Job X £	Job Y £
Direct materials	200	100
Direct wages @ £2 per hour	200	300
Prime cost	400	400
Overhead absorbed (40%)	160	160
Total cost	560	560
Profit (25%)	140	140
Selling price	700	700

Thus both jobs will be priced the same even though it would appear from the direct wages estimate that Job Y takes 50% more time to complete and therefore uses much more of the factory's resources.

Job X may be over-priced in relation to competitors whereas Job Y is under-priced and the business would lose its Job X customers and get more orders for Job Y.

Consider what would happen if 1,500 hours were available. The factory could produce 10 of Job Y or to 15 of Job X.

2.9   Insufficient analysis by cost centre

A similar effect could arise if overhead rates do not recognise use of more or less expensive resources.

2.10   Example

Company C uses a 'blanket' overhead rate calculated as follows:

	Overhead cost £	Labour hours
Cost centre Y	40,000	4,000
Cost centre Z	80,000	4,000
	120,000	8,000

$$\text{Absorption rate} = \frac{£120,000}{8,000}$$

$$= \text{£15 per labour hour}$$

Thus a job which takes one hour in Y will be charged the same amount for overhead as a job which takes an hour in Z even though the latter centre costs twice as much per hour to operate.

Once again, estimates would not reflect a realistic charge for the use of resources and over or under-pricing may result.

2.11   Reconciling job costs with profit and loss account

In many small businesses job costing is carried on in a seemingly haphazard way and little attempt is made to relate the work of estimating and price-fixing to accounting principles. Consequently it may be difficult to reconcile the profit shown by the accounts with that shown by job cards.

2.12   Example

The Industrial Refurbishing Company undertakes repair and reconditioning work on agricultural machinery and it is the practice to charge out each job at a profit of 15% of the invoice value. Cost cards relating to complete jobs for the year ended 31 May 19X4 have been summarised as follows:

	£	£
Materials issued		46,400
Direct labour		34,000
Overhead:		
20% on material	9,280	
100% on direct labour	34,000	
		43,280
Carriage		1,270
Profit		22,050
Sales		147,000

The firm's accountants have summarised the financial accounts for the year as follows:

	£	£	£
Sales			147,000
Less: Stocks and work in progress 1 June 19X3	18,000		
Purchase of materials	51,300		
	69,300		
Less: Stocks and work in progress 31 May 19X4	20,100		
		49,200	
Factory wages		51,000	
Factory expenses		20,000	
			120,200
Gross profit			26,800
Less: General office expenses		8,400	
Estimating and selling expenses		3,600	
Carriage on completed jobs		1,200	
			13,200
Net profit			13,600

You have been asked to explain the difference between the profit shown by the completed jobs summary and that shown by the annual accounts. To assist you the accountants have provided the following analyses:

(a)   The composition of the stocks and work in progress figures is as follows:

	1 June 19X3 £	31 May 19X4 £
Stocks of materials	6,000	6,200
Work in progress:		
Material	9,000	9,100
Labour	3,000	4,800

(b)   Factory wages consist of £38,800 for direct labour and £12,200 for indirect labour.

2.13 Solution

Item	Financial accounts £	£	Cost cards £	Differences £
Opening stock of materials	6,000			
Work in progress	9,000			
	15,000			
Purchases	51,300			
	66,300			
Less: Closing stocks	15,300			
Materials issued		51,000	46,400	4,600 (1)
Opening work in progress wages	3,000			
Direct labour paid	38,800			
	41,800			
Less: Closing work in progress wages	4,800			
Direct labour		37,000	34,000	3,000 (2)
Indirect labour	12,200			
Factory expenses	20,000			
General office	8,400			
Estimating/selling	3,600			
Overhead		44,200	43,280	920 (3)
Carriage		1,200	1,270	(70) (4)

Reconciliation:

	£	£
Profit per cost cards		22,050
Less: Materials not booked (1)	4,600	
Wages not allocated (2)	3,000	
Overhead not absorbed (3)	920	
		8,520
		13,530
Add: Carriage over-recovered (4)		70
Profit per financial accounts		13,600

2.14 Activity

List some causes of discrepancies summarised in the above reconciliation.

2.15 Activity solution

Examples are:

(a)   materials requisition not recorded;

(b)   direct labour shown as indirect;

(c)   over/under-absorption of overhead from various causes.

2.16 Treatment as direct or indirect costs

Instances may arise when analyses for cost ascertainment can conflict with the analyses required for control.

2.17 Example

Jones is paid £4 per hour for a basic week of 40 hours. In one week he worked four hours overtime at double rates and received £28 under a group bonus scheme. His time sheet for that week shows:

	Hours
Job A	20
Job B	10
Job C	8
Training	6
	44

Jones' gross wage may be allocated in two ways:

(a) As an average direct wage per hour ie:

	£
Basic 40 × £4	160
Overtime 4 × £8	32
Bonus	28
	220

$$\text{Hourly rate} = \frac{£220}{44 \text{ hours}}$$

$$= £5.00 \text{ per hour}$$

(b) Basic rate used for costing and overtime premium/bonus treated as indirect wages.

Different allocations would result as follows:

	Method (a)	£	Method (b)	£
Job A	20 × £5.00	100	20 × £4.00	80
Job B	10 × £5.00	50	10 × £4.00	40
Job C	8 × £5.00	40	8 × £4.00	32
		190		152
Overhead:				
Training	6 × £5.00	30	6 × £4.00	24
Overtime		-	4 × £4.00	16
Bonus		-		28
		220		220

Method (a) should give more accurate job costs but the total costs of overtime and bonus will be more difficult to identify for management information purposes.

In answering examination questions concerning problematic items, the student should recognise the different requirements for cost information as well as the practical implications of the suggested treatment.

2.18   Activity

Discuss how a company manufacturing products on a jobbing basis should deal with the following cost accounting problems.

(a)   It employs a draughtsman from whose drawings templates are produced which are used in the production process. These drawings are only made against firm orders. Hitherto the salary and other costs of the draughtsman have been included in factory overhead and absorbed into the cost of the job as part of total factory overhead.

   Discuss whether this method of dealing with the draughtsman's costs is satisfactory and suggest what alternative approach might be taken.

(b)   The company is at present operating a day and evening shift. It now proposes a night shift whose average wage rate would involve a premium. This night shift would concentrate on one particular contract which would continue over a period of two to three years.

   Discuss how the company should deal with the night shift premium in calculating the costs of its products.

(c)   One of the major production cost centres involves a chemical process which is very complex. The time required to produce any particular quantity of output depends rather unpredictably on a wide range of factors, some of which are outside the control of the operator.

   As a result, a subsidiary smaller machine to do 'touching up' work as and when products require it has been installed in that cost centre.

   Discuss the case for treating the wages of the operator of the subsidiary machine as an overhead of the cost centre rather than as direct wages.

2.19   Activity solution

(a)   As drawings are only made against firm orders, the cost of producing the drawings may be considered as a direct cost rather than as a production overhead. More accurate information, at little expense, could be obtained by an analysis of time spent by the draughtsman; an hourly rate, including associated costs, could be developed for charging to jobs. The hourly rate could incorporate normal idle time or, alternatively, hours not attributable to a specific order could be charged to drawing office overhead at the rate developed.

(b)   It appears that the night shift will be operated to fulfil the one particular long-term contract. Consequently, there would be no justification for including the night-shift premium in factory overhead as that would unfairly burden jobs completed during the day and evening shift. In fact it could be appropriate to separate this particular contract from the normal costing routine and treat it as a marginal contract by only charging costs directly incurred.

(c)   The alternative methods for dealing with the wages of the operator of the subsidiary machine are:

(i)   **Charge as direct wages**

This method implies that the operator's time can conveniently be analysed between products.   In addition, the machine operating costs should be charged in conjunction with the operator's wages ie, a composite machine hour rate will be developed.

(ii)   **Charge as overhead of the production cost centre**

Machine operating costs would be charged similarly.

The first method would achieve greater accuracy of product costs and provide useful information on the cost of the 'touching up' machine but would involve additional clerical work analysing the operator's time and developing a machine hour rate.

2.20   Cost control

When production is related to a specification or to customers' orders, the costing system will be interlocked with estimating so that the estimate can be used as a standard to locate excessive usage of materials and time.

Control will be assisted by:

(a)   **Detailed production orders**

These should be subject to serial number control.   The production order is the authority to obtain or allocate specific resources in the form of materials, labour and machines.

(b)   **Excess material requisitions**

Additional requirements for material would be supplied only on presentation of a properly authorised document which would show the reason for additional need.

(c)   **Route cards**

Each production order can be supported by route cards which specify the sequence of operations and the estimated time for each operation or stage.   Actual time would be recorded and causes of excess time noted where appropriate.

(d)   **Regular reports**

The above documents will form the basis of a report to show the incidence of excess usage together with an analysis of main causes.   The aim would be to prevent recurrence, where possible by appropriate action, eg:

* amendment of existing methods of estimating usages;
* change of supplier;
* increased labour training;
* introduction of incentive payment to all grades of works labour;
* improved system of preventive plant maintenance.

2.21   Job profitability and pricing

Management of a jobbing firm would be very interested in comparing the profitability of different types of work to assist:

(a)   selection of the most profitable mix, possibly by rejection of some jobs, giving priority to others and by sub-contracting;

(b)   identification of work where prices could be shaded or where increases may be necessary.

One of the major obstacles to accurate job cost ascertainment is the calculation of a reasonable proportion of fixed overhead to be recovered. Accurate estimation of volumes and costs is difficult and the diversity of production methods in a jobbing business complicates any attempt to establish an equitable basis for apportionment and absorption of costs. It may be more realistic for price fixing purposes, therefore, to ignore indirect costs and to base selling prices on direct cost plus contribution; control of fixed costs will, of course, still be a vital area.

An inherent danger when prices are based on contribution is the tendency to under-price because 'any contribution is better than losing the order'. That approach may be justifiable in exceptional circumstances but in the long run selling prices must cover all costs and provide an acceptable return.

2.22   Defective work and rectification

A business may incur extra cost by producing replacements for units scrapped as defective, or by rectifying the units. Two main objectives must be considered when accounting for the cost of defective output:

(a)   control of the level of defective work and rectification;

(b)   ensuring that selling prices cover, among other factors, the production cost including normal defective work and rectification.

For the first objective it is important to determine the costs already incurred, or additional costs spent in rectifying sub-standard units. The decision regarding whether units are to be scrapped or reworked is normally taken by the production manager on notification by the inspection department by means of a **rejection note.** The decision will be affected by the costs of the raw material and the setting-up costs of machines. It may be simpler and cheaper to scrap sub-standard units and increase the size of a later batch of units rather than arrange for a small rectification order to be processed separately through the factory. The cost of defective work can be isolated by using special job numbers to which the costs are charged. If units are scrapped and not replaced on the original order, the rejection note can be used by the cost department as a voucher with which to credit the job cost account and debit the defective work account. If the units are to be replaced on the original order by processing a small replacement batch, theoretically it is this replacement order which should be charged to the defective work account to give a more accurate figure of the cost of defectives. If units are to be rectified, the costs of rectification will be charged to the rectified account.

In connection with selling prices, it is important for the cost accountant to appreciate the estimating system. The estimator may anticipate a certain level of scrap for a particular job but the cost accountant may have already allowed for normal scrap in setting overhead rates. Thus, it is possible that an excessive allowance for scrap may be built into the estimated cost.

The cost accountant is likely to express the overhead rate for defectives in terms of a rate per machine or labour hour. This assumes, therefore, that the cost of scrap is related to the number of hours worked on a job. This is inaccurate because the cost of scrap is more likely to be related to the total value of material handled. It is better, therefore, to exclude scrap from the overhead rate and calculate a separate scrap allowance to be included in the direct cost estimates.

If the scrap has any realisable value either by sale or by re-use as a raw material substitutive, the sale proceeds or the normal cost of the raw material should be credited to the defective work account.

2.23   Setting up costs

When a business makes a variety of products in batches, the costs of clearing and re-setting machines are likely to be significant and worthy of comprehensive analysis and control. The costing procedure should be aimed to reflect, as accurately as possible, such costs in individual product costs without incurring excessive clerical expense to attain accuracy. Methods available are:

(a)   **Include setting up costs with direct labour costs**

Setting up costs for a period will thus be apportioned over products on the basis of units produced in the period. This method is simple to operate but will ignore effect on cost of different lengths of production run.

(b)   **Treat setting up costs as a production overhead**

The apportionment will be the same as in (a) above if overhead is absorbed in relation to direct labour. If, however, overhead is recovered in a machine hour rate, the charge will reflect the varying incidence of setting up costs between machines.

(c)   **Cost each batch separately**

Actual set up time will be booked to particular batches from time sheets. This method will result in accurate product costs but may cause clerical work when a large number of batches pass through a process.

(d)   **Analyse set-up time by product, accumulate for a period and apply product costs**

Accurate product costs will be provided which will tend to fluctuate from period to period depending on the incidence of long or short production runs. In addition, this method will require special time recording and analysis.

(e)   **Develop standard set up costs for each product and apply the standard as a cost per batch processed**

The set up cost per unit will vary according to the batch size which will disclose the cost effect of long or short runs. In addition, actual set up costs can be compared with standard to measure efficiency. Use of a standard, however, will leave a balance of over or under-absorbed cost to be dealt with in the accounts.

3   BATCH COSTING

3.1   Combined job and batch costing

Many businesses combine job costing with batch costing. This occurs where the business assembles a product to meet a customer's specification, but the assembly contains a number of components that can also be used in other assemblies. The components will be produced in batches and a batch cost sheet will record the costs. When the components are finished the order will be closed and the components will be transferred into a finished parts store at, say, the average cost of the batch. When the customer orders his particular assembly, a new order number will be raised and the required components drawn from store and charged against the assembly order.

3.2   Economic batch quantity

Where products are made in batches for stock to await sale or use in assemblies, the quantity to be produced in any one batch is a recurring and major problem, which involves consideration of:

(a)   Rate of consumption.

(b)   Storage costs and availability.

(c)   Time required to set up and take down production facilities.

(d)   Capacity available in terms of machines, labour and services in relation to requirements for other products.

The **Economic batch quantity** (EBQ) can be estimated by:

(a)   Tabulated analysis; calculating unit costs for a range of batch quantities to select the batch with the lowest unit cost.

(b)   Graphical analysis: plotting storage costs against production costs.

(c)   Formula:

$$EBQ = \sqrt{\frac{2CoD}{Ch\left(1-\frac{D}{R}\right)}}$$

where   D = annual demand
Co = setting up/taking down costs
Ch = annual storage costs
R   = annual production rate.

Note that this is the same as the EOQ formula for stock holding if R is large in relation to D.

3.3   Product line information

Batch costing is typically employed where a wide variety of products are held in stock. The cost accountant will be called upon for detailed information on product costs to satisfy the following needs:

(a)   **Production planning/control**

Scheduling to maintain stock levels and to meet demand fluctuations could be a major problem requiring continuous information on set up costs, machine utilisation and stock movements.

(b)   **Product profitability pricing**

Management are likely to require regular analyses of product costs and profits; maintenance or improvement of margins will be a recurring problem. The information will also assist in directing sales effort and formulating sales policy.

(c)   **Research**

Cost information, perhaps on an **ad hoc** basis, will be required in the development of new products or in improving operations.

4   CONTRACT COSTING

4.1   Contract ledger entries

In contract costing each contract is a separately identifiable **cost unit,** so that costs will be accumulated in a separate ledger account for **each** contract. The various elements of cost are dealt with as follows:

(a)   **Direct materials**

Materials charged to the contract may include both materials purchased specially and materials issued from the contractor's store. The appropriate costs are debited to the contract account. Control of materials at the site can be impaired by the difficulty of organising effective procedures for recording receipts and for returns from site to store of materials surplus to contract requirements.

(b)   **Direct wages**

Labour charges to the contract may include design and drawing office work (involving a time-booking procedure for salaried staff), manufacturing operations in the factory, and work on the site. All labour employed at the site of a contract will be direct. Time sheets may be necessary to disclose the time spent by workers at different sites. All such labour costs are debited to the contract account.

(c)   **Direct expenses**

Direct contract costs other than materials and labour are often very significant. The two major items falling within this category are **plant** and **sub-contracted work.**

   •   **Plant**

Plant or equipment may be purchased specifically for a contract, in which case the contract account is debited with the cost. Alternatively, plant may be transferred from another contract, in which case it is the written down value that is debited to this contract and credited to the contract from which it has been moved. At the end of each financial period the depreciated value of any plant owned is shown as a credit entry in the contract account (ie, as a balance carried down on the account to the next period). The net effect of the bookkeeping entries is that depreciation on the plant is automatically debited to the contract. Plant may be hired for use on a particular contract. As the business does not own such plant, the only ledger entries are the hire charges which are debited to the contract account. It is also possible to charge the contract account with a notional hire charge for plant owned by the business, thus treating the plant hire department as a separate entity.

   •   **Sub-contracted work**

In the case of a large contract or one involving specialist activities, the business may engage sub-contractors in certain aspects of the work. The cost of any sub-contracted work is a direct expense of a contract and is debited to the contract account.

(d)   **Indirect costs**

Many contractors do not attempt to apportion such costs to specific contracts as they are often negligible compared with direct costs. However, if such apportionment of indirect costs is carried out, the resultant amount is debited to the contract account.

4.2   Architects' certificates and retention monies

For each contract a price is agreed between the business and the client. This is known as the contract price. In the case of large contracts, where the work involved may spread over many months or even years, the contractor will expect interim payments from the client in respect of the contract price. Such payments will be related to the work done so far on the contract. The procedure involved is as follows:

(a)   **Architects' certificates**

As the work on a contract proceeds, the client's architects (or surveyors) will issue certificates indicating that so much of the contract price is now due to the contractor in respect of the work completed. In most cases at this stage the contractor will invoice the contractee with a progress payment.

(b)   **Retention monies**

The contractor normally receives only a proportion of the value shown on the architects' certificates while the contract is still in progress. The amounts held back by the client are known as retention monies. Such retention monies would only be paid over to the contractor some time after the completion of the contract when any faulty work has been rectified.

(c)   **Bookkeeping**

The architects' certificates received by the contractor could be used to make a memorandum record only until the completion of the contract when the contract price would be credited to the contract account. Alternatively, the value of the certificates could be credited to the contract account and debited to the personal account of the client as they are received.

Progress payments received by the contractor from the client are credited to the personal account of the client. Such payments must be deducted from the value placed upon the work performed to date for presentation in the balance sheet.

4.3   Attributable profit on uncompleted contracts

Where a contract extends over a long period **SSAP 9 (Stocks and long-term contracts)** allows the contractor to take credit for part of the profit **attributable** to the contract in each year's accounts. This percentage of completion method avoids the inconsistency of having a number of years with no profit from a particular contract and then suddenly making a profit in the year when it is completed. In deciding to what extent profit can be taken on uncompleted contracts the following matters are important considerations:

(a)   the successful outcome of the contract should be certain before any interim profit is taken;

(b)   any profit should only be taken in proportion to the work completed to date on the contract; and

(c)   any anticipated overall loss on the contract should be provided for as soon as it is recognised.

4.4   Calculation of interim profit

The calculation of the profit to be taken on an uncompleted contract involves five steps:

Step 1   Determine the total sales value of the contract (for a fixed price contract this will be the contract price). Call this (a)

Step 2   Compute the total expected costs to complete the contract. Call this (b); it consists of two elements:

    (i)   the actual costs incurred to date on the contract; plus

    (ii)   the estimated future costs necessary to complete the contract.

Step 3   The expected overall profit on the contract is given by (a) minus (b).

Step 4   The attributable profit to date on the contract should reflect the amount of work that has been completed so far. It is calculated as follows:

Attributable profit to date =

$$\frac{\text{Value of work certified to date}}{\text{Total sales value of contract}} \times \text{Expected overall profit}$$

It is important to realise that the attributable profit thus calculated is the **cumulative** figure to date.

Step 5   The profit to be taken **this year** (ie, debited to the contract account this year) is the cumulative attributable profit calculated at step 4 less the profit on the contract already recognised in previous years (debited to the contract account and credited to profit and loss account).

Unfortunately, some examination questions do not provide sufficient information to use this approach. If not told the estimated future costs, it is necessary to use the following procedure:

	£	£
Profit to date:		
Value of work certified		200,000
Less: Cost to date	80,000	
Less: Cost of work not yet certified	15,000	
		65,000
Profit to date		135,000

Sometimes this figure is reduced by an arbitrary amount (eg, one-third) to allow for the fact that the contract is incomplete and therefore the outcome is not certain.

The profit to be taken **this year** (ie, debited to the contract account this year) is the profit to date (reduced if necessary) less the profit on the contract already recognised in previous years (debited to the contract account and credited to profit and loss account).

Notes:

(1)   It is always necessary to calculate profit to ensure that losses are identified and provided for.

(2)   Attention must be paid to the cost of work not yet certified. This arises where some work has been done but not checked/certified by the architects. Hence the costs will be included in the ledger but the selling price of this work is excluded from the value of work certified. The idea is, therefore, to calculate only profit on work that has been certified.

4.5   Valuation of contracts in progress

Accurate valuation of work in progress, represented by uncompleted contracts, is vital for preparing realistic financial statements for a contracting business.   The following suggestions may merit consideration:

(a)   **Contract analysis**

Divide the contract into identifiable sections to aid cost control and comparison of the cost of completed work with certified work. Allocation of codes to sections and sub sections of contracts will help to locate excess expenditure.

(b)   **Prefabricated units**

Where these are held in central store and issued to sites on request, standard costs may be established so that purchase or manufacture of prefabricated units is controlled centrally.

(c)   **Plant**

Where items of plant are transferred from one site to another, it may be beneficial to treat plant handling as a service department ie, by developing standard hire charges and by controlling plant utilisation against budget.

4.6   A worked example

Contract No. 412 commenced during 19X1 and has a fixed contract price of £200,000. The costs incurred during the year 19X1 for materials, wages and sub-contractors' charges totalled £90,000. Plant costing £20,000 was purchased during 19X1 specifically for Contract No. 412.

At the end of 19X1:

(a)   the plant was valued at £15,000;

(b)   unused materials on the site were valued at £19,000;

(c)   architects' certificates had been issued showing that the value of work completed was £100,000.

It is estimated that further costs totalling £74,000 would be incurred in order to complete the contract. The figure includes the appropriate cost of plant and sub-contractors in the future.

Retention money representing 20% of the certified value of the work completed has been held back by the client. The balance of the money due has been paid. The contractor credits the contract account with the full value of the architects' certificates as they are received.

You are required to prepare:

(a)   a calculation of the profit to be taken to the profit and loss account for 19X1;

(b)   a calculation of the valuation of work in progress that would appear in the balance sheet as at the end of 19X1;

(c)   the entries for this year in the contract account and the client (contractee) account.

4.7   Solution

(a)   **Profit taken on contract for 19X1**

		£
Actual costs incurred to date:		
	Materials, labour and sub-contractors' costs	90,000
	Less: Materials on site at end of 19X1	19,000
		71,000
	Add: Plant depreciation £(20,000 – 15,000)	5,000
	Contract costs incurred to end of 19X1	76,000
	Contract costs incurred to end of 19X1	76,000
	Add: Estimated future costs to complete the contract	74,000
	Total estimated contract costs	150,000
Contract profit:		
	Contract price (fixed)	200,000
	Less: Contract costs (as above)	150,000
	Contract profit (estimated)	50,000

$$\text{Profit taken in 19X1} = \frac{\text{Work certified}}{\text{Contract price}} \times \text{Estimated contract profit}$$

$$= \frac{£100,000}{£200,000} \times £50,000$$

$$= £25,000$$

Note: as contract number 412 commenced during 19X1, this cumulative attributable profit is debited to the contract account in 19X1. No profit had been taken on this contract in earlier years.

(b)

	£
Contract costs incurred to end of 19X1	76,000
Add: Profit taken in 19X1 (as in (a) above)	25,000
	101,000
Less: Progress payments received and receivable (see note below)	100,000
Value of work in progress at end of 19X1	1,000

Note: 'progress payments received and receivable' is the total value of the architects' certificates that have been invoiced to the client. The £100,000 is made up of:

	£
Payment by client	80,000
Retention monies (20%)	20,000
	100,000

(c)   **Ledger accounts**

Contract number 412

	£		£
Materials, wages and sub-contractors' costs	90,000	Client account (certified work)	100,000
		Materials c/d	19,000
Plant (at cost)	20,000	Plant c/d	15,000
Profit and loss account	25,000	Work in progress c/d	1,000
	135,000		135,000
Work in progress b/d	1,000		
Materials b/d	19,000		
Plant b/d	15,000		

Client (contractee) account

	£		£
Contract account (certified work)	100,000	Cash received (progress payment)	80,000
		Balance c/d	20,000
	100,000		100,000
Balance c/d	20,000		

4.8   Activity

Watch-It-Go-Up Ltd has a contract for an office and leisure complex. Work is part complete at the year end on 30 June 19X3. The following information is available:

	£'000
Contract price	2,500
Direct materials:	
Issued	680
Returned to suppliers	30
Transferred to other contracts	30
On site at 30 June	40
Direct wages:	
Paid	440
Accrued	20
Direct expenses:	
Paid	50
Accrued	10
Value of work certified to date	1,500
Received from contractee	1,200
Plant installed on site:	
Cost	200
Valuation 30 June	150
Estimated cost to completion	700

Progress payments are based on architects' certificates less 20% retention.

You are required to:

(a)   calculate attributable profit for the year to 30 June 19X3;

(b)   calculate contract work in progress on 30 June 19X3;

(c)   prepare the contract and client ledger accounts.

4.9   Activity solution

(a)   **Costs incurred to date**

	£'000	£'000
Actual costs incurred to date:		
Materials issued		680
Less: Returns	30	
Transfers	30	
On site 30 June	40	
	—	100
		580
Wages - paid and accrued		460
Direct expenses - paid and accrued		60
Plant depreciation £(200,000 − 150,000)		50
Contract costs incurred to date		1,150

	£'000
Contract costs to completion	
Incurred (above)	1,150
Estimated further costs	700
Total estimated contract costs	1,850
Estimated contract profit	
Fixed contract price	2,500
Total estimated costs	1,850
Estimated profit	650

Attributable profit

Profit taken in year to 30 June 19X3 $= \dfrac{\text{Work certified}}{\text{Contract price}} \times \text{Contract profit}$

$$= \text{£'000} \left(\frac{1,500}{2,500} \times 650 \right)$$

$$= \text{£390,000}$$

(b)   **Work in progress**

	£'000	£'000
Contract costs to 30 June 19X3		1,150
Add: Profit taken		390
		1,540
Less: Progress payments:		
Received	1,200	
Receivable	300	
	—	1,500
Value of work in progress at 30 June 19X3		40

(c)

Contract account

	£'000		£'000
Material costs	680	Material returns	30
Wages:		Material transfer	30
Cash	440	Client account (work certified)	1,500
Accrued	20	Plant c/d	150
Direct expenses:		Materials c/d	40
Cash	50	Work in progress	40
Accrued	10		
Plant	200		
Profit and loss account	390		
	1,790		1,790

Client (contractee) account

	£'000		£'000
Contract account		Cash received (progress	
(certified work)	1,500	payment)	1,200
		Balance c/d	300
	1,500		1,500

5 CHAPTER SUMMARY

This chapter has considered the three methods of specific order costing and identified when each of them is to be used.

In the case of long-term contracts the recognition of profits (and losses) has been considered in the light of accounting concepts.

6 SELF TEST QUESTIONS

6.1   What is job costing? (1.2)

6.2   What is batch costing? (1.3)

6.3   What is contract costing? (1.4)

6.4   Explain how setting up costs may be incorporated into job costs. (2.23)

6.5   In the context of contract costing, explain the use of architects' certificates. (4.2)

6.6   In the context of contract costing, explain the meaning of 'attributable profit' on uncompleted contracts. (4.3)

6.7   List the steps required to calculate interim profits on uncompleted contracts. (4.4)

6.8   Why is it necessary to calculate interim profits on uncompleted contracts. (4.4)

7 EXAMINATION TYPE QUESTIONS

7.1 Job number 123

In order to identify the costs incurred in carrying out a range of work to customer specification in its factory, a company has a job costing system. This system identifies costs directly with a job where this is possible and reasonable. In addition, production overhead costs are absorbed into the cost of jobs at the end of each month, at an actual rate per direct labour hour for each of the two production departments.

One of the jobs carried out in the factory during the month just ended was Job No. 123. The following information has been collected relating specifically to this job:

(1)   400 kilos of Material Y were issued from stores to Department A.

(2)   76 direct labour hours were worked in Department A at a basic wage of £4.50 per hour. 6 of these hours were classified as overtime at a premium of 50%.

(3)   300 kilos of Material Z were issued from stores to Department B. Department B returned 30 kilos of Material Z to the storeroom being excess to requirements for the job.

(4)   110 direct labour hours were worked in Department B at a basic wage of £4.00 per hour. 30 of these hours were classified as overtime at a premium of 50%. All overtime worked in Department B in the month is a result of the request of a customer for early completion of another job which had been originally scheduled for completion in the month following.

(5)   Department B discovered defects in some of the work, which was returned to Department A for rectification. 3 labour hours were worked in Department A on rectification (these are additional to the 76 direct labour hours in Department A noted above). Such rectification is regarded as a normal part of the work carried out generally in the department.

(6)   Department B damaged 5 kilos of Material Z which then had to be disposed of. Such losses of material are not expected to occur.

Total costs incurred during the month on all jobs in the two production departments were as follows:

	Dept A £	Dept B £
Direct materials issued from stores*	6,500	13,730
Direct materials returned to stores	135	275
Direct labour, at basic wage rate**	9,090	11,200
Indirect labour, at basic wage rate	2,420	2,960
Overtime premium	450	120
Lubricants and cleaning compounds	520	680
Maintenance	720	510
Other	1,200	2,150

Materials are priced at the end of each month on a weighted average basis. Relevant information of material stock movements during the month, for materials Y and Z, is as follows:

	Material Y	Material Z
Opening stock	1,050 kilos (value £529.75)	6,970 kilos (value £9,946.50)
Purchases	600 kilos at £0.50 per kilo	16,000 kilos at £1.46 per kilo
	500 kilos at £0.50 per kilo	
	400 kilos at £0.52 per kilo	
Issues from stores	1,430 kilos	8,100 kilos
Returns to stores	-	30 kilos

*   This includes, in Department B, the scrapped Material Z. This was the only material scrapped in the month.

**   All direct labour in Department A is paid a basic wage of £4.50 per hour, and in Department B £4.00 per hour. Department A direct labour includes a total of 20 hours spent on rectification work.

You are required:

(a)   to prepare a list of the costs that should be assigned to Job No. 123. Provide an explanation of your treatment of each item.

(17 marks)

(b)   to discuss briefly how information concerning the cost of individual jobs can be used.

(5 marks)

(Total: 22 marks)

7.2   Jigantic plc

Jigantic plc is a building company engaged in the construction of hospitals and other major public buildings; most of the contracts undertaken extend over a three or four year period.

Shown below are the expenses incurred for the year ended 31 May 19X1, together with other operating details for three of the contracts in which the company is currently engaged:

	Contract A £'000	Contract B £'000	Contract C £'000
Contract price	4,000	10,200	12,000
Value of work certified by contractees'			
architects	2,350	7,500	11,000
Cash received from contractees	2,000	6,750	9,900
Costs incurred to 1 June 19X0	-	2,400	5,550
Cost incurred during the year:			
Materials	1,100	1,600	1,050
Labour	700	1,150	975
Other expenses, excluding depreciation	350	475	775
Plant and equipment:			
Written down value at 1 June 19X0	300	800	700
Written down value at 31 May 19X1	600	525	175
Purchases during the year	725	400	125
Cost of work not yet certified	75	-	800

The agreed retention rate is 10% of the value of work certified by the contractees' architects.

Contract C is nearing completion and the site manager estimates that costs of £425,000, in addition to those tabulated above, will be incurred in order to complete the contract. He also considers that the plant and equipment on site will be worthless by the time the contract is complete.

The nature of the work undertaken by Jigantic plc is such that it may be regarded as reasonable for the company to include in its annual accounts a prudent estimate for profit attributable to that part of the work on each contract certified as complete at the end of each accounting year.

Profit of £1,150,000 was taken on Contract C in the accounting periods up to and including 31 May 19X0. No profit had been taken on contract B as, at the 31 May 19X0, work on the project had only recently commenced.

The directors of Jigantic plc propose to incorporate into the company's profit and loss account for the year ended 31 May 19X1, the following amounts of profit/(loss) for each contract:

Contract A	Nil
Contract B	£720,000
Contract C	£2,400,000

Making whatever calculations you consider necessary, **you are required** to carefully explain whether you agree with the proposed profit/(loss) figures for the above contracts. If you consider any of the proposed amounts are inappropriate suggest, with supporting explanations and calculations a more suitable figure.

(20 marks)

8 ANSWERS TO EXAMINATION TYPE QUESTIONS

8.1 Job number 123

Notes:

(1) One point to note is that overhead is absorbed at an **actual** rate. The normal approach is to use a pre-determined rate.

(2) The examiner has presented the information in three sections:

    (a) quantities specifically related to Job 123
    (b) actual costs of Departments A and B;
    (c) information concerning Materials Y and Z.

The approach in answering is to go through the items in (a) above one at a time and select the relevant information from the other parts of the question as needed.

(3) The weighted average used here is a periodic average ie, calculated monthly as opposed to continuous - valuing each issue as it occurs during the month. The latter approach is normally used in questions concerning valuation of issues.

(4) There does not appear to be any reason for the examiner stating the value of direct materials issued from stores - £6,500 and £13,730. Note that this must include materials other than Y and Z because the value of issues of Y is: £0.505 × 1,430 = £722.15 and Z is £1.45 × 8,100 = £11,745.

(a) **List of costs which should be assigned to job number 123**

(1)

	Kilos	£
Material Y:		
Opening stock	1,050	529.75
Purchases	600	300.00
	500	250.00
	400	208.00
	2,550	1,287.75

$$\text{Weighted average price} = \frac{1,287.75}{2,550} = 0.505$$

		£
Value of material issued to this job: 400 kilos @ £0.505	=	202.00

(2)   Department A labour: 76 hours @ £4.50   =   342.00

It is assumed that the overtime is not worked at the specific request of the customer for Job 123 and hence the premium has been excluded from direct cost and therefore included in production overhead.

Rectification work:

As this is regarded as a normal part of the work carried out **generally** by the department, it is assumed to be non-controllable and should therefore be included in the cost of jobs. It is assumed most equitable to do this, not by charging each specific job with rectification costs but to charge this cost to jobs via the overhead absorption rate.

(3)

	Kilos	Value £
Material Z	6,970	9,946.50
	16,000	23,360.00
	22,970	33,306.50

Weighted average price $= \dfrac{33,306.50}{22,970} = 1.45$

Value of material issued to this job: $(300 - 30 - 5) \times £1.45$ =   384.25

Material damaged:

As this loss is not expected to occur, it is controllable/abnormal.
The cost should, therefore, be charged to the profit and loss
account and excluded from the cost of jobs.

(4)   Department B labour: 110 hours @ £4   =   440.00

The cost of the overtime premium should be charged to the other customer's jobs.

(5)   Production overhead:

	Dept A £	Dept B £
Amount incurred:		
Rectification labour cost:		
20 × 4.50	90	-
Indirect labour	2,420	2,960
Overtime premium	450	-
Lubricants and cleaning		
compounds	520	680
Maintenance	720	510
Other	1,200	2,150
	5,400	6,300

                                        Carried forward   1,368.25

	£
Brought forward	1,368.25

Actual labour
hours $\quad \dfrac{9,090}{4.50}=2,020 \qquad \dfrac{11,200}{4}=2,800$

Less: Rectification hours	20	
	2,000	2,800

Overhead recovery rate:

$\dfrac{\text{Actual overhead}}{\text{Actual labour hours}}=\qquad \dfrac{5,400}{2,000} \qquad \dfrac{6,300}{2,800}$

$\qquad\qquad\qquad = £2.70 \text{ per} \qquad = £2.25 \text{ per}$
$\qquad\qquad\qquad \text{labour hour} \qquad \text{labour hour}$

Production overhead absorbed by Job number 123:
	£
Department A: 76 hours @ £2.70	205.20
Department B: 110 hours @ £2.25	247.50
Cost of Job No. 123	1,820.95

(b)   The cost of individual jobs may be used in the following ways:

(i)   the estimated cost can be calculated in advance in order to provide a basis for fixing the selling price. In this case it would be necessary to use a pre-determined overhead absorption rate.

(ii)   The estimated budgeted cost can be used as a guideline while the work is being carried out so as to try to ensure that actual costs are kept within the original estimate.

(iii)   The actual cost of jobs can be used for valuing work-in-progress stock if the job is on hand at the end of the accounting period.

(iv)   Actual cost can be compared with the estimated cost in order to identify variances on individual cost items. This should help to control costs and to improve the quality of future estimates.

(v)   Actual cost can be compared with the selling price of the job in order to assess profitability of the job.

8.2   Jigantic plc

Note:

The key to dealing with the profit calculation is to try to use the SSAP 9 approach by calculating total profit (contract price - [costs to date + estimated costs to completion]).

If there is insufficient information (ie, estimated costs to completion not given), then calculate profit to date based on value of work certified ie, profit should always be calculated so as to identify any losses - in this case on Contract A.

It is then necessary to consider whether the contracts are sufficiently far advanced for it to be

'prudent' to recognise profit.

For Contract B the contract is, based on 'sale value', ($\frac{7,500}{10,200} \times 100\%$) approximately 75% completed.

It is therefore assumed reasonable to take profit.

It is also reasonable to take profit on Contract C as it is 'nearing completion'.

(i)   **Cost of contracts as at 31 May 19X1**

	Contract A £'000	Contract B £'000	Contract C £'000
Cost to 1 June 19X0		2,400	5,550
Costs incurred during the year:			
Materials	1,100	1,600	1,050
Labour	700	1,150	975
Other expenses	350	475	775
Depreciation (ii)	425	675	650
Total cost to 31 May 19X1	2,575	6,300	9,000

(ii)   **Depreciation of plant and equipment**

	Contract A £'000	Contract B £'000	Contract C £'000
Written down value, 1 June 19X0	300	800	700
Purchases	725	400	125
	1,025	1,200	825
Written down value, 31 May 19X1	600	525	175
Depreciation for the year	425	675	650

Contract A

	£'000	£'000
Value of work certified		2,350
Cost as at 31 May 19X1 (i)	2,575	
Less: Cost of work not yet certified	75	
		2,500
Loss to date		(150)

To include a 'nil' profit in the accounts would be inappropriate since clearly the contract has incurred a loss of £150,000 to date. In accordance with the prudence concept of **SSAP 2** and the requirements of **SSAP 9** relating to long-term contract work-in-progress, this loss should be incorporated into the year's accounts. Strictly speaking the loss expected to arise on the whole of the contract should be provided for but insufficient information has been given to do this. (ie, estimated completion costs not given).

Contract B

	£'000
Value of work certified	7,500
Cost as at 31 May 19X1 (i)	6,300
Profit to date	1,200

The proposed profit figure of £720,000 is well below the profit which has been earned to date. However, because of the uncertainty surrounding long-term contracts, considerable caution should be exercised when allocating profits over the life of a contract. Hence a figure lower than £1,200, presumably reduced in accordance with the accounting policy of the company, is acceptable.

Note: it would appear that the examiner used the following formula for estimating the amount of profit to incorporate into the profit and loss account:

$$\frac{2}{3} \times \frac{\text{Cash received}}{\text{Value of work certified}} \times \text{Profit to date} = \frac{2}{3} \times \frac{6,750}{7,500} \times 1,200 = 720$$

This formula is recognised in many textbooks but represents only one possible way of prudently reducing profits to take account of the uncertainty surrounding uncompleted contracts.

Contract C

	£'000	£'000
Contract price		12,000
Cost as at May 19X1 (i)	9,000	
Estimated completion costs (425 + 175)	600	
		9,600
Estimated total profit		2,400

The proposal to incorporate a profit of £2,400,000 in the profit and loss account for the year ended 31 May 19X1 is not allowable for three reasons:

(i)   an estimated profit of £1,150,000 for Contract C has already been included in previous years' accounts;

(ii)   some provision should be made for expenses which have not been anticipated but which may well arise, for example, the cost of rectification work; and

(iii)   part of the work is yet to be carried out. Profit should only prudently be taken on work completed by the end of the accounting period.

Hence the figure of £2,400,000 needs to be reduced in two respects: firstly to reflect the work done to date - by using the formula:

$$\text{Total profit} \times \frac{\text{Value of work certified}}{\text{Contract price}}$$

and secondly by the profit incorporated in previous years' profit and loss accounts.

	£'000
Profit on contract to date $2,400 \times \dfrac{11,000}{12,000}$	2,200
Less: Profit already taken	1,150
Profit applicable to this year's accounts	1,050

9 SERVICE COSTING

INTRODUCTION & LEARNING OBJECTIVES

Syllabus area 6a. Service costing, including work in progress. (Ability required 3).

Service costing poses particular problems because there is often not an immediately recognisable unit of output.

When you have studied this chapter you should be able to do the following:

- Recognise the application of composite cost units in service organisations.

- Classify costs in service organisations so that meaningful management reports may be produced.

1 SERVICE COSTING

1.1 Service costing

Definition   Service costing is the cost accounting method that can be applied when the business provides a service, or to a service activity within a manufacturing business. Examples are:

         (a)   transport;
         (b)   power generation;
         (c)   hotels.

1.2 Application of service costing

Some of the principles explained in the previous section are appropriate to service costing in that costs are charged to activities and averaged over the units of service provided.

The method is appropriate when the service can be expressed in a standardised unit of measurement eg, an accountant provides an individual service to each client, but the service could be measured in man-hour units.

1.3 Identification of cost units

A major problem in service industries is the selection of a suitable unit for measuring the service ie, in deciding what service is actually being provided and what measures of performance are most appropriate to the control of costs. Some cost units used in different activities are:

Service	Cost unit
Electricity generation	Kilowatt hours
Canteens and restaurants	Meals served
Carriers	Miles travelled: ton-miles
Hospitals	Patient-days
Passenger transport	Passenger-miles: seat-miles

A service undertaking may use several different units to measure the various kinds of service provided eg, an hotel may use:

Service	*Cost unit*
Restaurant	Meals served
Hotel services	Guest-days
Function facilities	Hours

When appropriate cost units have been determined for a particular service, provision will need to be made for the collection of the appropriate statistical data. In a transport organisation this may involve the recording of mileages day-to-day for each vehicle in the fleet. For this each driver would be required to complete a log sheet. Fuel usage per vehicle and loads or weight carried may be appropriate for the business.

1.4   Collection, classification and ascertainment of costs

Costs will be classified under appropriate headings for the particular service. This will involve the issue of suitable cost codes to be used in the recording and, therefore, the collection of costs. For a transport undertaking the main cost classification may be based on the following activities:

(a)   operating and running the fleet;
(b)   repairs and maintenance;
(c)   fixed charges;
(d)   administration.

Within each of these there would need to be a sub-classification of costs, each with its own code, so that under (c) fixed charges, there might appear the following breakdown:

(a)   road fund licences;
(b)   insurances;
(c)   depreciation;
(d)   vehicle testing fees; and
(e)   others.

In service costing it is often important to classify costs into their fixed and variable elements. Many service applications involve high fixed costs and the higher the number of cost units the lower the fixed costs per unit. The variable cost per unit will indicate to management the additional cost involved in the provision of one extra unit of service. In the context of a transport undertaking, fixed and variable costs are often referred to as standing and running costs respectively.

1.5   Cost sheets

At appropriate intervals (usually weekly or monthly) cost sheets will be prepared by the costing department to provide information about the appropriate service to management. A typical cost sheet for a service would incorporate the following for the current period and the cumulative year to date:

(a)   Cost information over the appropriate expense or activity headings.

(b)   Cost units statistics.

(c)   Cost per unit calculations using the data in (a) and dividing by the data in (b). Different cost units may be used for different elements of costs and the same cost or group of costs may be related to different cost unit bases to provide additional control information to management. In the transport organisation, for example, the operating and running costs may be expressed in per mile and per day terms.

(d)   Analyses based on the physical cost units.

On a transport cost sheet, the following non-cost statistics may be shown:

- average miles covered per day;
- average miles per gallon of fuel.

2   COST INFORMATION FOR SERVICES AND FUNCTIONS

2.1   Information objectives

Cost information relating to service activities is likely to be directed at three main areas:

(a)   cost control;

(b)   optimum utilisation of services;

(c)   relationship to products and users.

Analysis of service activity costs and presentation of information must be tailored to specific requirements. The following notes attempt to provide guidance which can be used in a practical situation.

2.2   Marketing

The marketing function is generally considered to embrace the activities of assessing demand, promoting sales and distributing the product. For cost ascertainment, these activities need to be clearly separated as the cost structure of each will possess different characteristics.

Control of marketing costs will be exercised through budgets. The following factors merit consideration when budgets are established:

(a)   Budget centres should be clearly related to executive responsibility. The sales function may be divided into geographical area, for example, whereas distribution may be on a product or activity basis of responsibility.

(b)   Costs may need to be classified in accordance with factors which influence them eg:

- Establishment – will include salaries of marketing management and central administration expenses which will be affected only by price changes or by major policy decisions.

- Sales force – remuneration and expenses of salesmen which will be affected by planned sales effort.

- Variable with sales – the level of commission, delivery and packing can be set in relation to the sales budget.

- Appropriations – market research, advertising and promotion are likely to be budget appropriations which can be controlled by analysing the total budget into specific projects.

(c)   Where appropriate, a flexible budgeting approach should be adopted.

(d)   Presentation of reports will be improved by incorporation of units for cost measurement eg, miles travelled for salesmen's expenses and number of orders for order processing costs. In addition, those cost units can be used for apportionment of marketing costs between products, areas, classes of trade, etc.

2.3   Research and development

The cost information requirements for the research and development function will be directed to:

(a)   measure the cost effectiveness of the function;

(b)   control expenditure on specific and general projects;

(c)   assist planned allocation of research and development resources.

These objects will be achieved by a sensible analysis of costs coupled with an informative and timely reporting system. In broad terms, costs will be analysed to specific projects and to general research, sub-divided to show major classification of research work. In addition, analysis of costs by nature will be useful to show the relevance of payments to outside organisations, cost of purchased materials, usage of own facilities and fixed departmental costs.

Control and cost effectiveness would be assisted by applying budgetary control to the function. It is likely that the budget for research and development will represent an annual appropriation authorised by management; the appropriation would be allocated between specific projects and general work. Periodic reports can be presented to compare actual with budget by project and sub-project, to identify areas of over spending and to support requests for additional or re-allocated appropriations. The control reports would serve as a basis for audit of projects and for allocation of resources.

SSAP 13 Accounting for research and development

Research and development expenditure means expenditure falling into one or more of the following broad categories (except to the extent that it relates to locating or exploiting mineral deposits or is reimbursable by third parties either directly or under the terms of a firm contract to develop and manufacture at an agreed price which has been calculated to reimburse both elements of expenditure):

(a)   Pure (or basic) research: original investigation undertaken in order to gain new scientific or technical knowledge and understanding. Basic research is not primarily directed towards any specific practical aim or application;

(b)   Applied research: original investigation undertaken in order to gain new scientific or technical knowledge and directed towards a specific practical aim or objective;

(c)   Development; the use of scientific or technical knowledge in order to produce new or substantially improved materials, devices, products, processes, systems or services prior to the commencement of commercial production.

Standard accounting practice

The standard requires that:

The cost of fixed assets acquired or constructed in order to provide facilities for research and development activities over a number of accounting periods should be capitalised and written off over their useful life.

Expenditure on pure and applied research (other than that referred to in the previous paragraph) should be written off in the year of expenditure.

Development expenditure should be written off in the year of expenditure except in the following circumstances when it may be deferred to future periods:

(a)   there is a clearly defined project; and

(b)   the related expenditure is separately identifiable; and

(c)   the outcome of such a project has been assessed with reasonable certainty as to:

    •   its technical feasibility; and

    •   its ultimate commercial viability considered in the light of factors such as likely market conditions (including competing products), public opinion, consumer and environmental legislation; and

(d)   if further development costs are to be incurred on the same project the aggregate of such costs together with related production, selling and administration costs are reasonably expected to be more than covered by related future revenues; and

(e)   adequate resources exist, or are reasonably expected to be available, to enable the project to be completed and to provide any consequential increases in working capital.

In the foregoing circumstances development expenditure may be deferred to the extent that its recovery can reasonably be regarded as assured.

The criteria for determining whether development expenditure may be deferred should be applied consistently.

If development costs are deferred to future periods, their amortisation should commence with the commercial production of the product or process and should be allocated on a systematic basis to each accounting period, by reference to either the sale or use of the product or process or the period over which the product or process is expected to be sold or used.

Deferred development expenditure should be reviewed at the end of each accounting period and where the circumstances which have justified the deferral of the expenditure no longer apply, or are considered doubtful, the expenditure, to the extent to which it is considered to be irrecoverable, should be written off immediately.

Development expenditure once written off should not be reinstated even though the uncertainties which had led to its being written off no longer apply.

In the financial statements there must be disclosed not only the movements on deferred development expenditure, but also the amount carried forward at the beginning and end of the accounting period. Furthermore, deferred development expenditure must not be included in current assets but should be separately disclosed. The accounting policy followed should be clearly explained.

2.4   Purchasing

Control of the purchasing activity will be exercised through:

(a)   **Purchasing budget** – this needs to be divided into broad areas to align with responsibility and developed from production/stock budgets. Regular updating to meet changes in circumstances will be necessary for planning and control.

(b)   **Cost variances** – detailed and timely analysis of material price variances should assist in cost reduction and the influence of purchasing on other variances (eg, idle time) must be considered.

(c)   **Stock reports** – regular reports about stock items which have become slow-moving or obsolete are vital to purchasing efficiency.

Determination of the optimum (or economic) order quantity is a problem which will concern management. The mathematical approach to this problem is dealt with elsewhere but the cost accountant will probably be called upon to provide information on costs at various levels of stockholding and purchasing activity.

2.5   Maintenance

This activity will probably consist of planned preventive maintenance work and minor repair jobs.

The latter kind of work can be controlled by applying traditional job costing methods but maintenance will involve problems of scheduling and resource allocation.

2.6   Power generation

Where a manufacturing undertaking uses power which is generated internally, both the cost of generation and the usage by production activities will require control. Power department costs may be controlled against a budget and a standard unit charge levied against production departments. In that way the production departments would be responsible only for variations in usage compared to their flexible budgets; variations in the cost of providing power and under/over-utilisation against plan would be indicated by under/over-recovery of power department costs.

2.7   Example of cost statement in power supply industry

The following figures were taken from the annual accounts of two electricity supply boards working on uniform costing methods:

Meter reading, billing and collection costs

	Board A £'000	*Board B* £'000
Salaries and wages of:		
Meter readers	150	240
Billing and collection staff	300	480
Transport and travelling	30	40
Collection agency charges	-	20
Bad debts	10	10
General charges	100	200
Miscellaneous	10	10
	600	1,000
Units sold (millions)	2,880	9,600
Number of consumers (thousands)	800	1,600
Sales of electricity (millions)	£18	£50
Size of area (square miles)	4,000	4,000

Prepare a comparative cost statement using suitable units of cost. Brief notes should be added, commenting on likely causes for major differences in unit costs so disclosed.

2.8   Solution

Electricity Boards A and B
Comparative costs – year ending ....

	Board A £'000	*% of total*	*Board B* £'000	*% of total*
Salaries and wages:				
Meter reading	150	25.0	240	24.0
Billing and collection	300	50.0	480	48.0
Transport/travelling	30	5.0	40	4.0
Collection agency	-	-	20	2.0
Bad debts	10	1.7	10	1.0
General charges	100	16.6	200	20.0
Miscellaneous	10	1.7	10	1.0
	600	100.0	1,000	100.0

	£	£
Cost per:		
Millions units sold	208	105
Thousand consumers	750	625
£m of sales	33,333	20,000
Square mile area	150	250

Possible reasons for unit cost differences include:

(a)   **Area density.** B covers the same size of area but has double the number of consumers, indicating that B is a more urban territory.

(b)   **Industrialisation.** Costs per unit are almost twice as high for A but the pattern is not continued for costs in relation to sales value. B, therefore, probably contains a higher proportion of industrial consumers at cheaper rates.

(c)   **Territory covered.** Comparative costs per square mile deviate from the pattern shown by the other measurement units, confirming that the bulk of costs is incurred in relation to consumers and usage.

3   COSTING IN SPECIFIC SITUATIONS

3.1   Introduction

This section is concerned to examine costing problems in specific types of industrial and service organisations. It should be appreciated that whilst the general principles remain constant, various special factors may influence the practice of cost accounting eg:

(a)   any special statutory rules;
(b)   the nature of the product or service;
(c)   the organisational context.

The specific industries identified below do not form a comprehensive list, but they are amongst the more important. The information is primarily derived from a series of CIMA publications, 'Framework Series' about the accounting aspects of various industries.

3.2   Water industry

(a)   **Nature of the industry**

The water industry may be considered as combining all human activities within the water cycle – the process whereby the water which falls naturally is used for man's purposes before disposal to sea. The more significant activities undertaken by bodies with specific responsibilities within the water cycle are:

- water conservation;
- water supply;
- sewerage;
- sewage treatment and disposal;
- land drainage and flood protection;
- fisheries; and
- water quality regulation and pollution alleviation.

(b)   **Functional peculiarities**

The ten Regional Water Authorities (RWAs) were set up by the Water Act 1973 and on 1 April 1974 they took over:

- water undertakings;
- sewerage and sewerage treatment functions;
- river authorities.

In 1990, the Water Authorities were privatised by the Conservative Government.

(c)   **Charging**

RWA's levy a water and sewerage rate, separate to other rates. This is directly collected by the RWA's.

(d)   **Financial regime**

The whole of a water authority's income is derived from charges to its consumers.

As in business generally, capital expenditure may be partly financed internally, by revenue surpluses or depreciation provisions, but is partly financed by borrowing.

(e)   **Accounting problems**

In 1974 RWAs faced the problems of changing from the local government type of accounting operated by their predecessors to a more commercial style.

It was necessary to construct the accounting system in such a way as to enable appropriate charges to be levied to cover the costs incurred on each service, avoiding cross-subsidies between the services.

(f)   **Accounting policies**

The RWAs have developed accounting policies similar in most respects to those in large commercial undertakings. They face, however, difficulties in measuring their outputs in a meaningful way and thus providing unit costs.

It might appear that costs per volume of water supplied or sewage treated could readily be prepared. As, however, the supply to most consumers is not metered at their premises the volume supplied can only be estimated.

Apart from this, high level unit costs are not particularly useful since most costs are fixed and do not vary with throughput. In water supply only power and chemicals vary significantly. Unit costs are more useful in limited areas such as vehicle maintenance and operation.

(g)   **Objectives of the accounting system**

RWA internal accounts, therefore are mainly designed to measure performance against an expenditure budget prepared annually.

(h)   **Cost systems**

The development of effective cost systems has been handicapped, as explained earlier, by the absence of suitable output measures for most of the industry's activities. Very detailed analysis of expenditure is provided but the comparison is normally with expenditure budget rather than on a unit cost basis.

3.3   Insurance industry

(a)   **Objectives**

The objectives of cost attribution are to satisfy information requirements for management and statutory purposes to further the efficient operation of the enterprise and discharge its statutory information disclosure obligations.

This involves determining the costs associated with:

- class of business eg, Motor or Ordinary Life Business;
- line or Risk Group eg, Private Care or Life Endowment policy;
- individual Product eg, Third Party Private Car or With Profits Endowment;
- function eg, claims settlement;
- project eg, new accounting system; and
- broker Agency connection.

(b)   **Difficulties in cost identification**

Costs are readily recorded by cost centre and analysed by type or class of expenditure. This does not provide enough information to satisfy management requirements. To answer these and many other questions it is necessary to further analyse clerical and other costs – allocation and apportionment.

(c)   **Methods of staff cost apportionment/identification**

- Work measurement.
- Policy count.
- Numbers of accounting entries.
- Premium income.
- Staff time record.
- Staff time estimate.

(d)   **Apportionment of other costs**

Generally a system of cost centres will enable expenses to be allocated, at source, direct to user department and subsequently to revenue account on the user departments apportionment basis.

However, sometimes expenses are of a general nature or are more conveniently recorded by an intermediate cost centre prior to being subsequently periodically charged to user department.

(e)   **Cost relationship**

In the context of an Insurance Company the principal area of cost is salary and related expenditure of staff with other significant areas being accommodation and communication services, computer facilities, promotional and marketing expenditure.

The initial factors to be identified are the product lines of business or saleable services which are provided by the insurance company. For a composite office these services will be principally General and Long Term business but it should be remembered that other services are frequently offered by the Company. Examples of such services are computer bureaux facilities, survey and risk management, claims handling, investment, executorship and trust management.

(f)   **The use of total absorption costing in the insurance industry**

Insurance Companies have traditionally used the total absorption costing method both for statutory and management purposes. This was, and is still, necessary for statutory accounts.

(g)   **Functional costing**

The assessment of sales effort would involve the systematic consideration of the activities of each cost centre to identify those related to sales.

The functions relating to the operation of general business might be typically listed as:

Selling or Acquisition – the cost of obtaining new business
Underwriting – the assessment of premiums to be charged
Accounts Control – the collection of premiums
Claims – the servicing of claims
Investment – the most suitable and profitable use of cash resources
Management or Administration – the cost of generally controlling the business.

3.4   Banking

(a)   Nature of the business

Banking covers an enormously wide spectrum from multi-national universal banks at one end to the specialised institutions at the other.

The wider context is referred to only to the extent necessary to focus on one key area, that of domestic retail banking as represented by the British Clearing Banks.

The primary function of banking may be described as taking deposits and borrowing, lending, transmitting, exchanging and investing with the objectives of making profits out of the use of funds and the provision of services. Less obviously, the very heart and essence of the banking industry is the handling of information.

(b)   Functional peculiarities, including funding

'Banking', bankers have always claimed, 'is different'. But this must not be taken to imply that management techniques, developed in other industries have no application in banking, nor indeed that other industries can learn nothing from banking.

- Banks function by seeking to attract funds.

- Funds and funds transfer were used as the main vehicle for the sale of services.

- The importance of the confidence factor.

- A final functional peculiarity is one that banks share with other organisations with similar economic characteristics of 'high volume, repetitive production of joint products, using large fixed investment and subject to uneven workflow'.

(c)   Principal accounting problems

From the accounting viewpoint banks differ from most other industrial organisations in that their business is entirely based on data and information.

Two further differences stem from the bank's product, financial value. The first is the need to maintain security – vital for instilling confidence. The second difference derives from the increasingly onerous reporting requirements of the regulatory authorities.

(d)   Objectives of the accounting system

- **Managerial**

  Information must be continuously available, certainly daily, and at all levels, to enable a mix of assets and liabilities to be managed.

- **Proprietorial and statutory**

    The format and content of financial statements of UK banks is determined by the Companies Acts, SSAPs and custom in the industry.

- **Regulation**

    The supervision of the Banking Sector by the Bank of England.

(e)   **Elements of cost**

Although the principles of costing are generally applicable, some understanding is necessary of cost characteristics, cost behaviour and the cost flow pattern fashioned by factors peculiar to banking.

- Variable work loads.
- High fixed expenses.
- Large fixed investment.
- Production-line type of activities.
- Joint products.
- Predictability of activity.
- Cost traceability.
- Costing for marketing information.

3.5   Accounting for local government

(a)   **Nature of local government**

Since 1974, local government in England and Wales has been for most practical purposes, a dual system based on the administrative areas known as counties and districts.

Financial control by the central government derives from the fact that a large proportion of local finance comes in the form of government grant.

Another distinguishing feature of local government is that the ruling body is of course directly elected. While this democracy is undoubtedly essential to local government, it does impose significant costs. Systems, including accounting systems, are more bureaucratic.

In common with most of the public sector, the objectives of local government are difficult, if not impossible, to define in quantitative terms.

(b)   **Functional peculiarities**

The governing body of a local authority is the County Council (or District Council).

The 'spending' committees (education etc,) are serviced by sub-committees of one sort or another.

The committee structure dictates/reflects the structure of departments ie, the officers of the authority.

One effect of this structure is to emphasise and institutionalise the professionalism that is characteristic of local government.

The following organisation chart is typical.

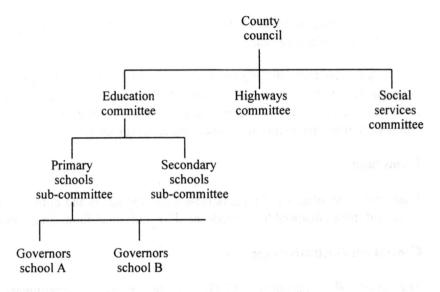

(c)   **Funding**

On average around 50% of revenue expenditure is financed by central government.

After government grants, the biggest proportion of revenue finance is from business rates and the council tax.

The main source of capital finance has traditionally been from borrowing.

(d)   **Principal accounting problems**

There are significant differences (compared with businesses) in local government accounting. These relate to:

• **Fund accounting**

Local government accounts are not a representation of a single homogeneous body. Rather, the authority is seen as a combination of separate 'funds'. For each fund, there is a self-contained set of accounts; each have a revenue account and a balance sheet. The funds have been established over many years, typically by statute.

Therefore, there is not one balance sheet but many, and there are many revenue accounts.

• **Accruals accounting**

Capital expenditure is accounted for on the receipts and payments basis (by convention). Revenue expenditure is ultimately accounted for on the income and expenditure basis. However, not all local authorities use this basis continuously.

• **Capital expenditure vs revenue expenditure**

Capital expenditure is rigidly defined. Usually by way of note to the balance sheet, working capital is divided into that part which is financing capital expenditure and that which is financing revenue. Receipts from the sale of capital assets can only be used for further capital expenditure.

- **Capital accounting**

  A *de minimus* rule, and precedent, allows some capital expenditure to be expensed. Most however, is capitalised.

  The major accounting differences result from the statutory requirement that the principal repayments on any loans raised for capital expenditure **must** be charged to the revenue account. This, of course is in stark contrast to business practice where principal repayments are balance sheet movements.

- **Loans fund**

  Loans funds account for the loans raised and repaid by the authority on the one hand, and loans advanced to and redeemed by individual funds on the other.

- **Central administrative expenses**

  The costs of departments which service spending departments, normally accumulated within the rate fund, are recharged either partially or wholly to receiving accounts on a variety of bases. Examples of bases used are: hours (from timesheets compiled for the purpose), floor space, number of employees, etc.

(e)   **Special terminology**

Definition   **Capital expenditure.** Although the official CIMA definition broadly applies in local government, the actual categories of capital expenditure are specified by the government.

Capital outlay and other long term outlay. Capital outlay refers to fixed assets which are realisable (building land): other long term outlay is fixed assets which are not (roads, bridges).

Deferred charges = deferred expenditure.

Capital discharged. This term can only be fully understood in the context of the later discussion on capital accounting.

Revenue contribution to capital outlay. Arises when expenditure is capitalised but is partially or wholly financed from revenue expenditure.

Capital receipts unapplied. Capital receipts which have not yet been used to finance specific capital expenditure.

Capital fund. A reserve to meet future capital expenditure.

Loans fund. Acts as a broker within the authority. Borrows externally and then lends to individual spending departments.

(f)   **Fundamental accounting concept**

Local authorities adopt accruals accounting to a considerable extent, though not completely.

Capital expenditure is dealt with on the cash basis.

(g)   **Objectives of the accounting system**

Financed stewardship has always been at the heart of local government accounting.

In local government, stewardship has the additional dimension of 'compliance with the budget'.

(h)   **Business rates and council tax accounts**

Business rates are fixed each year. The government sets the rate per pound and the income is calculated is follows:

Business rateable values × rate per pound

The council tax is based on the numbers of residential homes within an area. The government sets upper spending limits for each County or District. The charge for each home is calculated as follows:

$$\frac{\text{Estimated expenditure}}{\text{No. of homes in area}} - \text{Government allowance}$$

(i)   **Capital accounting and loans fund**

There is, of course, no subscribed capital in local authorities. Further, they have no general power to depreciate their assets. Accounting practice in this area is therefore very different from commercial accounting. A broad summary would be:

•   Fixed assets are financed by loan (most often), from Capital Fund, from Capital Grants, from Capital Receipts or from revenue.

•   Regardless of how they are financed, those assets which are depreciable are **not** depreciated.

•   If they are financed by loan, the loan repayments are charged to revenue – they are not balance sheet movements alone.

(j)   **Financial planning**

Throughout the public sector, financial planning revolves around, or is embodied in the government's public expenditure White Papers.

(k)   **Capital budgets**

As with financial accounts, the distinction between capital and revenue is maintained. Capital budgets are based on individual projects.

(l)   **Revenue budgets**

It is no exaggeration to say that revenue budgets are at the heart of the financial management of local authorities. The budgetary process dominates the accountant's year.

(m)   **Budgetary control**

It is clear from the foregoing that the budget determines the rates.

The budget thus becomes a target against which actual performance can be measured. Overspending against the budget is clearly undesirable. Underspending is also, at least theoretically disapproved of because it means that the year's ratepayers have paid too much.

Unavoidable overspendings need to be detected as early as possible so that committee approval can be received for an increased budget.

(n)   **Financial reports**

The law has much to say about local government financial reporting.

All accounts should be made up yearly to 31 March.

These regulations require that as soon as possible after the accounts have been audited, the Local Authority should prepare an abstract of its audited accounts.

A distinction has recently been made between the abstract of accounts and the Annual Report.

The Secretary of State's power was exercised in 1981 when he issued the code of practice, 'Local Authority Annual Reports'. This recommends that they publish an Annual Report to include a wide range of financial and non-financial information.

4   PERFORMANCE INDICATORS

Introduction

Service industries like manufacturers, need performance indicators to appraise the performance of individuals and cost centres.

If materials are used performance indicators could reflect conversion cost of added value.

4.1   Conversion cost and added value

Conversion cost is the sum of the production costs of converting purchased materials. It may be a more useful index for measuring performance than production costs where material prices fluctuate rapidly and/or when comparing different undertakings whose use of materials differs in significance.

Added value is the increase in market value resulting from an alteration in form, excluding the cost of bought out materials and services. Unlike conversion cost, added value includes profit so it is a meaningful basis for assessing the profit earning performance ability of a business by excluding the **passing on** of costs incurred.

Example

	Period I £'000	Period II £'000
Materials	240	120
Conversion cost	120	240
Profit	90	90
Sales	450	450

The ratio of profit to sales is identical for both periods but a comparison of profit to added value discloses a significant change in operating methods.

Added value is sales value - material cost, ie, 210 in period 1 and 330 in period 2.

Thus, the ratio of profit to added value in period 1 is $\frac{90}{210} \times 100\% = 43\%$

period 2 is $\frac{90}{330} \times 100\% = 27\%$.

4.2   Activity indices

Departments or undertakings which do not produce output that can be measured in units of production or in standard hours are nevertheless subject to performance measurement. The cost accountant will, therefore, aim to select a basis for measuring performance which can be meaningfully related to the work performed and costs incurred.

For example:

(a)   **Maintenance**

- Man-hours worked;
- breakdowns repaired.

(b)   **Purchasing**

- Number of employees;
- number of invoices processed.

(c)   **Personnel**

- Total company employees;
- number of engagements/terminations.

(d)   **Salesmen**

- Number of calls;
- miles travelled;
- orders received.

5   CHAPTER SUMMARY

Service costing was explained, together with the problems of identifying a suitable cost unit in such organisations, and possible performance indicators.

6   EXAMINATION QUESTION

6.1   Bus service

A small private company in a town with 190,000 inhabitants has decided to take advantage of the de-regulation of passenger transport services. It is proposing to operate a bus service on six particular routes where, after carrying out market research, it has been identified that there are opportunities to compete with existing services. Currently, the company has five 3 ton trucks which are engaged in light road haulage for regular established customers and has two mini-vans which are used as a courier service for fast delivery of letters and lightweight parcels.

The company has its own garage facilities for the repair and maintenance of its vehicles. The offices are located on the first floor above the garage and an upper floor, currently used for the storage of old records, is being cleared for conversion into office accommodation. At the rear of the garage and offices is a fenced compound where the vehicles are kept overnight. The compound is locked and floodlit during the hours of darkness and a security firm patrols regularly.

A suitably qualified person has been recruited to manage the bus operation and you have been engaged as the accountant for the expanding business. The owner of the company, a former transport manager, looks after selling and control of routing and utilisation of the five trucks and two mini-vans. His wife and a full-time bookkeeper undertake all the administrative work. Seven drivers and two garage mechanics are employed.

Cost accounting records kept have been of a rudimentary nature but the financial accounts, prepared at the end of every quarter by the company's auditors, show the business to be very profitable. The owner is conscious that, with expansion, better records will have to be maintained. From the accounts and in conjunction with the auditors, you ascertain that costs for the following expense headings are available.

> Depreciation
> Drivers' wages
> Employer's National Insurance contributions
> Fuel
> Holiday pay
> Insurance
> Management and staff salaries
> Mechanics' wages
> Oil
> Rent and rates for garage, office and compound
> Replacement parts and spares
> Road fund licences
> Security costs
> Tyre replacements

The newly-engaged passenger transport manager informs you that six minibuses at a total cost of £210,000 are on order. Each bus can seat twenty people and nine people are allowed to stand. The buses will each be operated by one person and the manager is currently interviewing drivers who hold PSV (public service vehicle) driving licences. He indicates that he will need information from you to ascertain the profitability of each route operated.

You are required, bearing in mind the objectives of cost accounting,

(a)   to draft a form for the ascertainment of operating costs for the vehicles currently owned.

(10 marks)

(b)   to draft a form suitable for the proposed passenger service to show income and expenditure.

(10 marks)

(c)   to comment on the allocation and apportionment of overheads now that they have been increased substantially following the recruitment of yourself and the passenger transport manager.

(5 marks)

7   ANSWER TO EXAMINATION TYPE QUESTION

7.1   Bus service

(Tutorial note: this question will give you important practice in using your common sense to deal with an unfamiliar scenario. The examiner often sets questions which require you to do this.*)*

(a)   The expense headings listed show both direct and indirect costs. The form recording operating costs should allow these to be disclosed separately. (Assumption: each driver is assigned to a particular vehicle, so that his/her wages are treated as a direct cost).

	Notes	Vehicle reg no XXX123X ... £	Total £
Direct costs			
Depreciation of vehicle		X	
Driver's wages, NI and holiday pay		X	
Fuel	(2)	X	
Insurance		X	
Oil	(2)	X	
Spares	(2)	X	
Road fund licence		X	
Tyres	(2)	X	
Mechanics' wages	(1)	X	
Total		X	
Indirect costs	(3)		
Depreciation of fixtures etc		X	
Salaries		X	
Rent and rates		X	
Security		X	
Mechanics' wages	(1)	X	
Total		X	

Notes:

(1) Most of the mechanics' time will be spent doing identifiable work on individual vehicles, and this should be charged out on the basis of job cards etc. This enables management to identify any vehicle which requires an unusually high level of work and may be in need of replacement. Idle time or time spent on other activities should be treated as an indirect cost.

(2) It should be possible to record issues of all these items for each vehicle.

(3) A basis of apportionment will have to be devised - eg, mileage - but it should be recognised that these are largely fixed costs, unrelated to the amount of vehicle activity. An allocation can be made, but the profitability of each vehicle should be judged on its contribution to direct costs.

(b)

	Route No. £	Total £
Income		
Passengers		
Full fare	X	
Concessionary		
OAPs	X	
Schoolchildren	X	
Other	X	
Season tickets	X	
	—	—
Total income	X	
	—	—
Direct expenditure		
Drivers' wages, holiday pay and NI	X	
Depreciation of vehicle	X	
Fuel	X	
Oil	X	
Tyres	X	
Spares	X	
Licence	X	
Mechanics' wages	X	
	—	—
Total	X	
	—	—
Contribution	X	
Indirect expenditure		
Salaries	X	
Rent and rates	X	
Depreciation of fixtures etc	X	
Security	X	
	—	
Total	X	—
	—	—
Profit	X	

(c)   As the administrative expenditure increased, the business will carry a higher burden of indirect costs. It must always be remembered that, although such costs may be allocated for purposes of pricing, the most important index of profitability is the difference between income from operations and the direct costs incurred.

The passenger transport manager is presumably engaged entirely in that sector of the company's activities and his salary will be allocated accordingly. But the salary of an accountant will presumably need to be allocated across the three sectors of the business (haulage, courier services and passenger transport). A suitable allocation basis (in theory) would be the amount of time devoted by the accountant to each area; in practice, it would be difficult to establish this with any accuracy.

10 PROCESS COSTING

INTRODUCTION & LEARNING OBJECTIVES

Syllabus area 6a. Process costing: the principle of equivalent units, treatment of normal and abnormal losses and gains, joint products and by-products; problems of common costs. (Ability required 3).

This chapter is concerned with the methods of costing used in situations where the units produced are homogeneous, and the operations used to achieve the final result are continuous.

This type of costing method may be used in situations where the final result is a product (output costing and process costing).

This chapter shows when to use each of these costing methods, and how to use each method to value cost units.

Finally the use of values derived from these methods is considered in the area of decision making and the inherent problems discussed.

When you have studied this chapter you should be able to do the following:

- Distinguish between output costing and process costing.

- Explain the meaning of and differences between normal losses and abnormal losses/gains.

- Account for process costs involving losses.

- Explain and apply the equivalent units concept to opening and closing work in process.

- Explain and use both the FIFO and weighted average methods of dealing with opening work in process (including recognising which method to use when the information provided is limited).

---

1 PROCESS COSTING

1.1 Continuous production

In specific order costing costs were directly allocated to a particular job or batch. When standardised goods or services result from a sequence of repetitive and continuous operations, it is useful to work out the cost of each operation. Then, if unit produced is assumed to have involved the same amount of work, costs for a period are charged to processes or operations, and unit costs are ascertained by dividing process costs by units produced. This is known as **process costing.**

1.2 Output costing

Definition Output costing applies when standardised goods are produced from a single operation eg, mining, quarrying.

1.3   Process costing

> *Definition*   Process costing applies when standardised goods are produced from a series of inter-connected operations eg,

(a)	oil refining;
(b)	breweries;
(c)	canned food.

2   OUTPUT COSTING

2.1   Special features of output costing

The basic physical feature of output costing is that only a single operation is required to obtain the final product. Examples of output costing include the extraction of minerals. Output costing applies where such minerals are sold as the final product immediately after extraction; if they are, instead, further processed within the same organisation; then process costing (see below) should be used.

The finished products, such as the minerals extracted, are homogeneous (that is one tonne of mineral extracted is indistinguishable from another). As a consequence it is assumed that each unit of the product will require the same level of resources to acquire as the next unit. It is therefore not necessary to identify the cost of each tonne, (if this were possible, its cost could not be justified). Instead the total cost of a particular time period is divided by the output of the period and an average cost per unit calculated.

2.2   Calculating the unit cost

Assume that Z Ltd extracts clay from the ground in a single process and sells it to a local pottery.

During June costs incurred amount to £19,500 and output was 6,500 tonnes of clay.

The cost per tonne is:

$$\frac{\text{Cost incurred}}{\text{Output in tonnes}}$$

$$= \frac{£19,500}{6,500}$$

$$= £3 \text{ per tonne.}$$

This would be used to evaluate stock and prepare profit statements.

2.3   Activity

Calculate the cost per tonne given that:-

Costs incurred	=	£46,740
Output	=	16,400 tonnes

2.4   Activity solution

Cost per tonne = £46,740/16,400 = £2.85.

3   PROCESS COSTING

3.1   Special features of process costing

The basic physical feature of a processing system is that as products pass from the raw material input stage to becoming finished products they pass through a number of distinct stages or **processes** of manufacture. In such a situation it is not feasible to link the cost of specific inputs to specific units of output. For example, in the production of paint it would be impossible to isolate one unit of output (a litre can of paint) and determine precisely which inputs have finished up in that particular litre of paint. The nature of a processing business is such that inputs are being added continuously to the manufacturing process, losing their identity, and a continuous output of production is being achieved.

Ascertaining the cost of production involves:

(a)   determination of the costs (direct and indirect) associated with each process;

(b)   calculation of the average process unit cost by dividing the appropriate costs by the appropriate number of units of output;

(c)   valuation of the units of output transferred from one process to the next and any work in process by applying the unit costs;

(d)   the cost of output from the first process becomes the cost of input to the second process and so on until output from the final process has accumulated the cost of all processes.

This procedure is complicated by the following factors:

(a)   output units will not equal input units to the extent that losses are sustained during processing;

(b)   the existence of partially processed units ie, work in process, at the end of the period;

Each of these factors will be considered in this chapter.

3.2   Basic principles

The nature of the processing operation is such that the input volume rarely equals the output volume, the difference, or loss, is analysed between that which is expected (and considered to be unavoidable) and any additional loss (or lack of loss) which actually occurs.

3.3   Normal loss

 Normal loss is the amount of loss expected from the operation of a process. This expectation is based on past experience, and this loss is considered to be unavoidable.

The normal loss is usually expressed as a percentage of the input volume, the cost of its production must be borne by the remaining output.

3.4   Example

The following data relates to process one during March:

Input materials 1,000 kg costing	£9,000
Labour cost	£18,000
Overhead cost	£13,500

A normal loss equal to 10% of input was expected. Actual output was 900 kg.

Solution

Step 1   Calculate the number of normal loss units.

Step 2   Calculate the expected number of output units.

Step 3   Total the process costs.

Step 4   Calculate the cost per unit.

Step 5   Write up the process account and normal loss account.

Step 1   The normal loss equals 10% of 1,000 kg = 100 kg.

Step 2   The expected output units equals the input less the normal loss = 1,000 kg – 100 kg = 900 kg.

Step 3   The total process costs = £40,500.

Step 4   The cost per unit equals:

$$\frac{£40,500}{900} = £45 \text{ per kg}$$

Step 5

Process account

	Kg	£		Kg	£/kg	£
Material input	1,000	9,000	Normal loss	100	-	-
Labour		18,000	Output	900	45	40,500
Overhead		13,500				
	1,000	40,500		1,000		40,500

Note:

(a)   that the process account contains columns to record both quantities and values which are both balanced off.

(b)   that no value is attributed to the normal loss units in this example (next the effect of scrap and similar values will be shown).

3.5   Normal losses having a scrap sales value

When normal losses have a scrap value, reduce the cost of the process by the income anticipated from the normal loss.

3.6   Example

Suppose that the normal loss of 100 kg in the last example could be sold as scrap for £9/kg.

Step three is now amended to recognise the reduction in process costs caused by the income anticipated from the normal loss.

Step 3   becomes: The total process cost is

£40,500 (as before) – (100 kg × £9/kg) (the scrap value of the normal loss).

= £39,600

Step 4   The cost per unit is now:

$$\frac{£39,600}{900}$$

= £44/kg

Step 5

Process account

19XX	Units	£	19XX	Units	£/Units	£
Material input	1,000	9,000	Normal loss	100	9	900
Labour		18,000	Output	900	44	39,600
Overhead		13,500				
	1,000	40,500		1,000		40,500

Note that the normal loss now has a value equal to its scrap value.

Since the process account is part of the cost book-keeping system (see later in this text), a corresponding debit entry must be made for the normal loss:

Normal loss account

19XX	Units	£	19XX	Units	£
Process account	100	900	Cash/bank	100	900

3.7   Activity

Calculate the cost per tonne from the following data:

Input 5,000 tonnes costing	£15,000
Labour cost	£6,000
Overhead cost	£10,025

Normal loss is 10% of input and has a scrap value of £4/tonne.

Write up the process account and the normal loss account.

3.8   Activity solution

Normal loss = 500 tonnes and has a value of £2,000 (500 × £4)

Process costs   = £31,025 – £2,000 = £29,025

Cost per tonne = $\dfrac{£29,025}{4,500}$ = £6.45

Process account

	Tonnes	£		Tonnes	£/ton	£
Materials	5,000	15,000	Normal loss	500	4	2,000
Labour		6,000	Output	4,500	6.45	29,025
Overhead		10,025				
	5,000	31,025		5,000		31,025

Normal loss a/c

	Tonnes	£		Tonnes	£
Process a/c	500	2,000	Cash/bank	500	2,000

4   ABNORMAL LOSSES AND GAINS

4.1   Introduction

Often the operation of processes results in the actual loss being different from that expected. The differences are referred to as abnormal losses and gains.

4.2   Abnormal losses

[Definition]   The extent to which the actual loss exceeds the normal loss is referred to as the abnormal loss. This loss is unexpected and considered to be avoidable consequently the cost of producing abnormal loss units is not treated in the same way as the cost of the normal loss.

Abnormal losses are valued initially as if they had been good output, the loss (reduced by any scrap value) is then debited to the profit and loss account via the abnormal loss account.

The following example shows how to account for abnormal losses

4.3   Example

The following data relates to one process during April:

Input materials 1,000 kg costing	£9,000
Labour cost	£18,000
Overhead cost	£13,500

A normal loss equal to 10% of input was expected.
Actual output was 850 kg.
Losses are sold as scrap for £9/kg.

4.4   Solution

The steps to arrive at cost per unit are the same as in the earlier example.

[Step 1]   The normal loss equals 10% of 1,000 kg = 100 kg.

[Step 2]   The expected output units equals the input less the normal loss
= 1,000 kg – 100 kg = 900 kg.

[Step 3]   The process costs equal
£40,500 – (100 kg × £9) = £39,600.

Step 4   The cost per unit equals

$$\frac{£39,600}{900} = £44$$

Step 5

Process account

	Units	£		Units	£/Units	£
Material input	1,000	9,000	Normal loss	100	9	900
Labour		18,000	Abnormal loss			
			(W1)	50	44	2,200
Overhead		13,500	Output	850	44	37,400
	1,000	40,500		1,000		40,500

WORKINGS

(W1)   The abnormal loss units equals the difference between the actual and expected output. These are valued at the cost per unit calculated in step four.

Normal loss

	Units	£		Units	£
Process account	100	900	Cash/bank	150	1,350
Normal loss					
Abnormal loss account	50	450			
	150	1,350		150	1,350

Abnormal loss

	Units	£		Units	£
Process account	50	2,200	Normal loss account	50	450
Abnormal loss			Profit & Loss		1,750
	50	2,200		50	2,200

(W2)   The distinction between normal and abnormal losses is purely an accounting one, all of the loss may be sold as scrap for £9/kg. All of these proceeds are credited to the normal loss account and any balance on this account is transferred to the abnormal loss account.

Note that the transfer to profit and loss shown in the abnormal loss account is the net cost of producing the unexpected loss (after deducting its scrap value). This is used to control the costs of excess losses ie, 50 units @ (£44 – 9) = £1,750.

4.5   Activity

Calculate the net cost of the abnormal loss from the following data:

Input quantity	5,000 kg
Normal loss	5% of input
Process costs	£16,500
Actual output	4,600 kg

Losses are sold for £2.35 per kg.

4.6 Activity solution

> **Step 1** Normal loss = 5% × 5,000 kg = 250 kg
>
> **Step 2** Scrap value of normal loss = 250 kg @ £2.35 = £587.50
>
> **Step 3** Net process cost = £16,500 – £587.50 = £15,912.50
>
> **Step 4** Cost per unit = $\dfrac{£15,912.50}{4,750 \text{ kg}}$ = £3.35
>
> **Step 5** Net cost of abnormal loss/kg = £3.35 – £2.35 = £1.00
> Volume of abnormal loss = 4,750 kg – 4,600 kg = 150 kg
>
> Answer: net cost of abnormal loss = 150 kg @ £1.00 = £150

4.7 Losses having a disposal cost

Sometimes, instead of having a sale value losses have a disposal cost (this occurs particularly when toxic chemicals are processed). From an accounting viewpoint the treatment is the same as that shown above for losses having a sale value except that the value is negative.

The disposal cost of the normal loss must be entered in the process account either alongside the normal loss quantity as a negative value on the credit side or as a debit (ie, an extra cost). In either case the quantity MUST be entered on the credit side.

4.8 Actual loss is less than normal loss (abnormal gains)

> **Definition** The extent to which the actual loss is less than the normal loss is referred to as an abnormal gain.

The following example shows how to account for abnormal gains.

4.9 Example

The following data relates to one process during May:

Input materials 1,000 kg costing	£9,000
Labour cost	£18,000
Overhead cost	£13,500

A normal loss equal to 10% of input was expected.
Actual output was 920 kg.
Losses are sold as scrap for £9/kg.

4.10 Solution

The steps are the same as was shown earlier:

> **Step 1** The normal loss equals 10% of 1,000 kg = 100 kg.
>
> **Step 2** The expected output units equals the input less the normal loss
> = 1,000 kg – 100 kg = 900 kg
>
> **Step 3** The process costs equal £40,500 – (100 kg × £9) = £39,600.

Step 4   The cost per unit equals $\dfrac{£39,600}{900} = £44$

Step 5

Process account

	Units	£/unit	£		Units	£/unit	£
Material input	1,000		9,000	Normal loss	100	9	900
Labour			18,000	Output	920	44	40,480
Overhead			13,500				
Abnormal gain	20	44	880				
	1,020		41,380		1,020		41,380

WORKINGS

(W1)   The abnormal gain units equals the difference between the actual and expected output. These are then valued at the cost per unit calculated in step four. Note that these entries are made on the debit side of the process account, thus causing it to balance.

Normal loss

	Units	£		Units	£
Process account	100	900	Cash bank	80(W2)	720
Normal loss			Abnormal gain		
			account	20	180
	100	900		100	900

Abnormal loss

	Units	£		Units	£
Normal loss account	20	180	Process account	20	880
Profit and loss (W3)		700	Abnormal gain		
	20	880		20	880

(W2)   This is the actual loss being sold at £9/kg.

(W3)   This represents the net benefit of producing less loss than expected (after deducting the lost income from the anticipated scrap sales). ie, 20 (£44 – £9) = £700.

5   PARTIALLY PROCESSED UNITS

5.1   Introduction

At the end of a period there may be some units which have been started but have not been completed. These are said to be closing work in process units.

Assuming at this stage that there is no opening work in process, the output for a period will consist of:

(a)   units of production that have been started and fully processed within the period;

(b)   units of production that have been started in the period but which are only part-processed at the end of the period; this closing work in process will be completed next period when further costs will be incurred in completing it.

5.2 Equivalent units

Costs in a process costing system are allocated to units of production on the basis of **equivalent units.** The idea behind this concept is that once processing has started on a unit of output, to the extent that it remains in an uncompleted state it can be expressed as a proportion of a completed unit. For example, if 100 units are exactly half-way through the production process in terms of the amount of cost they have absorbed, they are effectively equal to 50 complete units. Therefore, 100 units which are half-complete can be regarded as 50 equivalent units that are complete.

5.3 Example

A manufacturer starts processing on 1 March. In the month of March he starts work on 20,000 units of production. At the end of March there are 1,500 units still in process and it is estimated that each is two thirds complete. Costs for the period total £19,500.

Calculate the value of the completed units and the work in process at 31 March.

5.4 Solution

	Units	Proportion complete	Equivalent units
	(a)	(b)	(c)=(a)×(b)
Started and completed	18,500	1	18,500
Work in process	1,500	⅔	1,000
			19,500

$$\text{Cost per equivalent unit} = \frac{£19,500}{19,500} = £1$$

Valuation

	Equivalent units	Cost £
Finished production	18,500 × £1	18,500
Work in process	1,000 × £1	1,000
Total costs for period		£19,500

The 1,500 physical units in process at the end of the period have a value (based on 1,000 equivalent units) of £1,000.

5.5 Extension of the equivalent units approach

In practice it is unlikely that all inputs to production will take place at the same time, as was suggested in the example above. For instance, materials are frequently added at the beginning of a process, whereas labour may be applied throughout the process. Thus, work in process may be **more complete** as regards one input or cost element than as regards another. Equivalent units must thus be calculated separately for each input and costs applied on that basis.

5.6 Example

As in the example above, except that:

(a)   all materials have been input to the process;
(b)   work in process is only one-third complete as regards labour;
(c)   costs for the period are:

	£
Materials	10,000
Labour	9,500
Total	19,500

5.7 Solution

	Units	Materials		Labour	
		Proportion complete	*Equivalent units*	*Proportion complete*	*Equivalent units*
Started and completed	18,500	1	18,500	1	18,500
Work in process	1,500	1	1,500	⅓	500
Total equivalent units			20,000		19,000

Cost per equivalent unit

$$\frac{£10,000}{20,000} = 50p \qquad \frac{£9,500}{19,000} = 50p$$

Valuation

	Materials	Labour	Total £
Cost of finished production	18,500 × £0.50 = £9,250	18,500 × £0.50 = £9,250	18,500
Cost of work in process	1,500 × £0.50 = £750	500 × £0.50 = £250	1,000
Total costs for period			19,500

5.8 Six-step method for process costing

The approach used in the last two examples can be summarised into a six-step technique which can be generally used in process costing problems:

Step 1   Trace the physical flow of units so that units input to the production process are reconciled with units output or in process at the end of the period.

Step 2   Convert the physical units determined in Step 1 into equivalent units of production for each factor of production (ie, materials, labour, etc.)

Step 3   Calculate the total cost for each factor for the period.

Step 4   Divide the total costs by equivalent units to establish a cost per equivalent unit.

Step 5   Multiply equivalent units by the cost per equivalent unit to cost out finished production and work in process. Reconcile these values to the total costs for the period as calculated in Step 3.

Step 6   Write up the ledger accounts.

5.9 Example

The Excelsior Co Ltd manufactures a single product in two successive processes. The following information is available for the month of July:

Process 1

(a)   No opening work in process on 1 July.

(b)   During the month 815 units costing £2,415 were put into process.

(c)   Labour and overhead incurred amounted to £1,600.

(d)   During the month 600 units were finished and passed to Process 2.

(e)   On 31 July 190 units remained in process, the operations on which were half completed, but the materials for the whole process have been charged to the process.

Process 2

(a)   No opening work in process on 1 July.

(b)   The cost of labour and overhead in this process was £900, and material costing £350 was added at the end of operations.

(c)   On 31 July 400 units had been transferred to finished stock.

(d)   At that date 180 units remained in process, and it was estimated that one-third of the operations had been completed.

You are required to show the process accounts, treating any process losses as a normal loss.

5.10   Solution

Process 1

	Units	£		Units	£
Input	815	2,415	Process 2	600	3,216
Labour and overhead		1,600	Work in process c/d	190	799
			Process loss	25	-
	815	4,015		815	4,015

Process 2

	Units	£		Units	£
Process 1	600	3,216	Finished stock	400	3,351
Labour and overhead		900	Work in process c/d	180	1,115
Material added		350	Process loss	20	-
	600	4,466		600	4,466

WORKINGS

Valuation of work in process

Process 1

Step 1   Opening work in progress + Units started = Units finished + losses + Closing work in progress

0 + 815 = 600 + losses + 190

Thus, losses in the period were 815 − (600 + 190) = 25.

Step 2

	Units	Materials Proportion complete	Materials Equivalent units	Labour and overhead Proportion complete	Labour and overhead Equivalent units
Started and completed	600	1	600	1	600
Work in progress	190	1	190	½	95
Total equivalent units			790		695

Step 3

Costs		£2,415	£1,600

Step 4

Cost per unit $\dfrac{2,415}{790} = £3.057$ $\dfrac{1,600}{695} = £2.302$ £5.359

Step 5

Value of work in process	$190 \times £3.057 = £580$	$95 \times £2.302 = £219$	£799
Value of output		$600 \times £5.359 =$	£3,216

Process 2

Step 1

Opening work in progress	+	Units transferred from process 1	=	Units finished+	losses	+	Closing work in progress
0	+	600	=	400	+	losses +	180

Thus, losses in the period were 600 - (400 + 180) = 20

Step 2   Equivalent units

	Units	Materials from process 1 Proportion complete	Materials from process 1 Equivalent units	Labour and overheads Proportion complete	Labour and overheads Equivalent units	Added materials Proportion complete	Added materials Equivalent units
Started and completed	400	1	400	1	400	1	400
Work in progress	180	1	180	⅓	60	0	0
Total equivalent units			580		460		400

Step 3

Costs		£3,216	£900	£350

Step 4

Cost per unit
$$\frac{£3,216}{580} = £5.54 \qquad \frac{£900}{460} = £1.96 \qquad \frac{£350}{400} = £0.875$$

Step 5

Value of work in progress	$(180 \times £5.54) + (60 \times £1.96) = £1,115$
Value of output	$(400 \times £5.54) + (400 \times £1.96) + (400 \times £0.875) = £3,350$

Notes:

(1)   The cost of normal losses is borne **pro rata** by the effective units.

(2)   As the material costing £350 was added **at the end** of operations in Process 2, none of it relates to the work in process units.

6   OPENING WORK IN PROCESS

6.1   Introduction

In the previous examples it was assumed that there was no opening stock of work in process. In reality, of course, this is unlikely to be the case, and changes in levels of work in process during the period can give rise to problems. There are basically two methods of accounting for such changes, namely:

(a)   the weighted average (or averaging) method;
(b)   the FIFO method.

6.2   Weighted average (or averaging) method

Under this method the opening stock values are added to the current costs to provide an overall average cost per equivalent unit. No distinction is, therefore, made between units in process at the start of the period and those added during it and the costs associated with them.

6.3   Example

FL Manufacturing Co Ltd
Process information for month ended 31 December

Work in process, 1 December (15,000 units, two-fifths complete) £10,250 (work in process value made up of: materials £9,000 plus conversion costs £1,250).

Units started during December	30,000
Units completed during December	40,000
Work in process, 31 December	5,000 (half-completed)
Material cost added in month	£24,750
Conversion cost added in month	£20,000

Materials are wholly added at the start of the process. Conversion takes place evenly throughout the process.

Calculate the values of finished production for December and work in process at 31 December, using the weighted average method.

6.4 Solution

It is easiest to use the six step method, proceeding as follows:

FL Manufacturing Co Ltd
Production cost report for month ended 31 December

Step 1 physical flows

	Units	Units
Work in process at start	15,000	
Added	30,000	
To be accounted for		45,000
Units completed	40,000	
In process at end	5,000	
Units accounted for		45,000

Step 2 equivalent units

	Materials	Conversion
Completed	40,000	40,000
In progress at end (conversion half-complete)	5,000	2,500
	45,000	42,500

Note: at this point the degree of completion of opening work in process is irrelevant under the weighted average method. It would, of course, have been used to value work at 30 November.

	Materials £	Conversion £	Total £
Step 3 costs to be accounted for			
Work in process at 1 December	9,000	1,250	10,250
Add: Costs incurred in December	24,750	20,000	44,750
	33,750	21,250	55,000

Step 4 costs per equivalent unit

$$\frac{£33,750}{45,000} = 75\text{p} \qquad \frac{£21,250}{42,500} = 50\text{p}$$

Step 5 cost of finished

work	40,000 × 75p = £30,000	40,000 × 50p = £20,000	50,000
Cost of work in progress	5,000 × 75p = £3,750	2,500 × 50p = £1,250	5,000
Total costs (agreed with total per Step 3)			55,000

The important feature of this method is that the costs associated with opening work in process are added to the costs arising in the current period and then they all become part of an averaging procedure.

Step 6

Process account

	Units	£		Units	£/unit	£
Opening WIP	15,000	10,250	Output	40,000	1.25	50,000
Materials	30,000	24,750	Closing WIP	5,000	1	5,000
Conversion cost		20,000				
	45,000	55,000		45,000		55,000

Do not proceed until you have re-worked this example correctly without consulting the solution.

6.5   FIFO method

In contrast to the weighted average method, the FIFO method distinguishes between units completed in the period that were in opening work in process and those started **and** completed in the period.

6.6   Example

Process information as stated in example in above.

Calculate values of finished production and work in process using the FIFO method.

Step 1   **physical flows**

	Units
Work in process, 1 December	15,000
Units started	30,000
To account for	45,000
Units completed:	
From opening work in process	15,000
From units started in period	25,000
Work in process at 31 December	5,000
Units accounted for	45,000

Note: the separate identification of units in opening work in process.

Step 2   **equivalent units** (work done in the period)

	Materials £	Conversion £	Total £
Units completed:			
From opening work in process ($\frac{3}{5}$)	-	9,000	
From current production	25,000	25,000	
Work in process at December ($\frac{1}{2}$)	5,000	2,500	
	30,000	36,500	

Step 3   costs to be accounted for

	£	£	£
Work in process at 1 December			10,250
Costs added	24,750	20,000	44,750
			55,000

Step 4   costs per equivalent unit (for work done in the period)

$$\frac{£24,750}{30,000} = £0.825 \qquad \frac{£20,000}{36,500} = £0.548$$

Step 5   cost of finished production

	£	Cost £
From opening work in process:		
Value at 1 December	10,250	
Add: Conversion, 9,000 × £0.548	4,930	
		15,180
Started and completed in period:		
Materials, 25,000 × £0.825	20,625	
Conversion, 25,000 × £0.548	13,700	
		34,325
Total value of work completed		49,505
Value of work in process:		
Materials, 5,000 × £0.825	4,125	
Conversion, 2,500 × £0.548	1,370	
Total value of work in process		5,495
Total costs for period (agreed with total per Step 3)		55,000

Step 6

Process account

	Units	£		Units	£/Unit	£
Opening WIP	15,000	10,250	Output	40,000	1.24	49,505
Materials	30,000	24,750	Closing			
Conversion cost		20,000	WIP	5,000	1.10	5,495
	45,000	55,000		45,000		55,000

Now re-work the above example without looking at the solution.

6.7   Choosing the valuation method - in practice

In practice the FIFO method is little used, for two main reasons:

(a)   It is more complicated to operate.

(b)   In process costing, it seems unrealistic to relate costs for the previous period to the current period of activities.

6.8   Choosing the valuation method - in examinations

In order to use the weighted average or FIFO methods to account for opening work in process different information is needed:

For weighted average:

An analysis of the opening work in process value into cost elements (ie, materials, labour)

For FIFO:

The degree of completion of the opening work in process for each cost element.

If all of the information is available so that either method may be used, the question will specify the required method.

7   LOSSES IN PROCESS - INTERACTION WITH WORK IN PROCESS

7.1   Introduction

In a process, we may have to deal with both losses and work in progress.

7.2   Example

Input to Process A was 1,000 units costing £4,500. Conversion costs were £3,400. The normal process loss is estimated as 10% of input. At the end of the period 780 units were transferred to Process B and 100 units were in process, 50% complete as regards conversion. There was no opening work in process.

Calculate the cost of transfers to process B, abnormal losses and the value of work in process.

Process A - unit costs

	Materials units	*Conversion equivalent units*
Input to Process A	1,000	
Less: Normal loss (10%)	100	
	900	
Transfer to Process B	780	780
Work in process	100	50
Abnormal loss	20	20
Total units/equivalent units	900	850

Step 1   Physical flow

Input   =   output   +   losses   +   closing work in progress

1,000 units =   780   +   losses   +   100

Thus, losses = 120 units of which normal loss is 10% of input ie, 10% × 1,000 = 100 units

Thus, abnormal losses are 20 units.

Step 2   Equivalent units

	Units	Materials Proportion complete	Equivalent units	Conversion costs Proportion complete	Equivalent units
Started and completed	780	1	780	1	780
Started and abnormally lost	20	1	20	1	20
Work in progress	100	1	100	½	50
Total			900		850

Step 3   Costs £   4,500   3,400

Step 4   Cost per unit   £5   £4

Notes:

(1)   The **normal** loss of 100 units is excluded from the output units. By doing so the cost of such a loss is absorbed into the unit cost. The unit cost is thus increased.

(2)   Losses are usually assumed to occur at the end of a process ie, when the units involved are fully processed.

Step 5   Valuation

		£	£
Total costs allocated to:			
Transfer to Process B	780 × £9		7,020
Abnormal loss	20 × £9		180
Work in process carried down:			
Materials	100 × £5	500	
Conversion	50 × £4	200	
			700
Total (agrees with costs incurred)			7,900

7.3   Abnormal gains

If, in the previous example, 820 units had been transferred to Process B, an abnormal gain (ie, a lower than normal loss) would have arisen. Unit cost would, however, be the same because the normal loss of 100 units is absorbed and the abnormal **gain** is valued at normal unit cost as a **credit** to the process.

		£
Input costs (as above)		7,900
Transfer to Process B	820 × £9	7,380
Abnormal gain	−20 × £9	(180)
Work in process (as before)		700
		7,900

Note that unit cost always represents $\dfrac{\text{Normal process cost}}{\text{Normal output}}$

7.4   Scrap recovery (normal or abnormal)

Remember that where the losses (normal or abnormal) are in the form of scrap they may be sold to generate revenue.

The treatment of such revenue is consistent with that of losses:

(a)   revenue from normal losses is **deducted** from process costs;

(b)   revenue from abnormal losses (or forgone if there is an abnormal gain) is deducted from the value debited (or credited) to profit and loss account.

7.5   Example

Data as per example above but the loss is sold as scrap for £1.80 per unit.

Process A - unit costs

	Materials	Conversion
Output in units (as before)	900	850
	£	£
Costs	4,500	3,400
Less: Revenue from scrap sales of normal loss (100 × £1.80)	180	-
	4,320	3,400
Cost per unit	£4.80	£4.00

Note: the recovery is deducted from materials cost since the value of scrap is related to its material content, thus reducing the cost per unit for materials. The cost per unit for conversion remains unchanged.

Process A - cost allocation

		£	£
Input costs net of revenue from scrap sales of normal loss			7,720
Allocated to:			
Transfer to Process B	780 × £8.80		6,864
Abnormal loss	20 × £8.80		176
Work in process:			
Materials	100 × £4.80	480	
Conversion	50 × £4.00	200	
			680
Total (agrees with net costs incurred)			7,720

Revenue from the abnormal loss of 20 units will be credited to profit and loss account, so that the net cost of abnormal losses is £176 − (20 × £1.80) = £140.

7.6   Partially completed losses

The example above assumed that losses occurred at the end of the process and, therefore, were completed units. If a question indicates that losses occur part way through the process, the following procedure can be adopted:

Step 1   calculate the equivalent units for normal and abnormal losses;

Step 2   divide costs by output units (including losses) to find unit costs by cost element;

Step 3   multiply normal losses by the unit cost in step 2;

Step 4   divide step 3 by the total units **excluding** normal losses;

Step 5   now step 2 + step 4 = unit cost including normal loss; step 5 can be used for cost allocation.

7.7   **Example**

Input to Process A was 1,000 units. Process costs for the month were £3,608.

780 units were transferred to Process B in the month and 100 units were in progress at the end of the month (50% complete). Normal loss is estimated as 10% of input and losses occur when the process is 60% complete.

Normal loss is 100 units and abnormal loss is:

$(1,000 - (780 + 100 + 100)) = 20$ units

Unit costs may be calculated:

	Equivalent units
Transfer to B	780
WIP (50%)	50
Normal loss (100 × 60%)	60
Abnormal loss (20 × 60%)	12
	902

	£
Process costs	3,608
Per unit	4.00

The cost value attributable to normal loss is:

60 @ £4   =   £240

and the cost per unit is increased by:

$$\frac{£240}{(902 - 60)} = 28.5\text{p approximately}$$

Process cost is thus allocated:

	£
Transfer to B 780 units × £4.285	3,342.30
WIP 50 equivalent units × £4.285	214.25
Abnormal loss 12 equivalent units × £4.285	51.42
Rounding-off	0.03
	3,608.00

The rounding would normally be added to the output value, thus increasing it to £3,342.33.

It may be suggested that if WIP is less advanced than the point where losses occur, then the valuation should exclude any share of normal loss because

(a)   normal loss may reasonably be anticipated; and

(b)   the difference in valuation is unlikely to be significant enough to warrant cumbersome calculation.

8   ACCOUNTING CONCLUSIONS

8.1   Introduction

The output of a process is sometimes transferred into stock or direct to the next process at a price in excess of cost. This is done so that each process will not benefit from economies effected by, or be penalised by inefficiency of, previous processes. Transfers will be at market prices unless such information is not available when they will be made at prices fixed to give an agreed percentage of profit.

The system would be simpler if there were not stocks on hand at the end of an accounting period as all the internal profits would have been realised. Where, however, process stocks and stocks of finished products are in hand at an accounting date, the book values of such stocks include profit added by transfer processes, which must be deleted for balance sheet purposes. This is done by debiting profit and loss account and crediting a provision account with the amount of the unrealised profit included in valuation of closing stock, less any provision brought forward from the previous period in respect of the opening stock.

It is emphasised that it is only the proportion of the stock which represents the product of a **previous** process that includes profit; processes do not add profit to their own stocks.

8.2   Ledger entries - conclusion

When drawing up process cost accounts it is important to include columns for the appropriate physical units involved in addition to the usual debit and credit value columns. The physical unit columns should be balanced in the same manner as the value columns.

The bookkeeping entries in the ledger accounts to record process costing transactions are as follows:

(a)   Process accounts are debited with all the appropriate costs incurred and the appropriate physical units associated with the material input.

(b)   For any normal loss in process, the process account is credited with the physical units involved. If the loss has a recoverable value (eg, as scrap), the process account is also credited with the appropriate value. The debit is in the normal process loss account.

(c)   Units of production that have finished being processed and have been transferred to the next process (or to finished stock) are credited to the process account they have left and debited to next process account (or finished stock account). The physical units involved are evaluated at the process cost per unit.

(d)   Any closing work in process will be evaluated at the process cost per unit (due recognition having been taken of the equivalent units involved) and the balance carried down in the process account.

(e)   Any abnormal loss in process is credited to the physical units column of the process account. The units are evaluated at the process cost per unit. The debit is to the abnormal loss account. If an abnormal gain is involved the entries are, of course, reversed.

(f)   The accumulated balance of physical units in the abnormal loss account is valued at the recoverable value for losses, if any, and credited to the account. The debit is to the normal process loss account. The physical units columns in the abnormal loss account are thus balanced and the balancing value is transferred to the profit and loss account, thereby finally closing off the abnormal loss account.

(g)   Any sums received from the sale of losses should be credited to the normal loss account along with the physical units involved. Any stock of losses (scrap) deemed to be saleable will be evaluated at its expected recoverable value.

Any balance of value on the normal loss account would represent a difference between the expected and the actual sums recovered, and would be transferred to the profit and loss account. It is the expected recoverable value that is used to credit the original process account (and debit the normal loss account) when losses arise.

9   CHAPTER SUMMARY

This chapter has explained two more methods of costing: output costing and process costing. Each of these are used in organisations whose operations are continuous and are only artificially stopped and re-started by the preparation of monthly cost accounts.

In dealing with process costing the problems of losses and work in process have been illustrated and their solution methods shown.

10   SELF TEST QUESTIONS

10.1   What is output costing? (1.2)

10.2   What is process costing? (1.3)

10.3   Explain the special features of output costing. (2.1)

10.4   What is a normal loss? (3.3)

10.5   What is an abnormal loss? (4.2)

10.6   What is an abnormal gain? (4.8)

10.7   Explain the concept of equivalent units. (5.2)

11   EXAMINATION TYPE QUESTION

11.1   Chemical Compound

A chemical compound is made by raw material being processed through two processes. The output of Process A is passed to Process B where further material is added to the mix. The details of the process costs for the financial period number 10 were as shown below:

Process A
Direct material	2,000 kilograms at £5 per kg
Direct labour	£7,200
Process plant time	140 hours at £60 per hour

Process B

Direct material	1,400 kilograms at £12 per kg
Direct labour	£4,200
Process plant time	80 hours at £72.50 per hour

The departmental overhead for Period 10 was £6,840 and is absorbed into the costs of each process on direct labour cost.

	Process A	Process B
Expected output was	80% of input	90% of input
Actual output was	1,400 kgs	2,620 kgs

Assume no finished stock at the beginning of the period and no work-in-progress at either the beginning or the end of the period.

Normal loss is contaminated material which is sold as scrap for £0.50 per kg from Process A and £1.825 per kg from Process B, for both of which immediate payment is received.

You are required to prepare the accounts for Period 10, for

(i)   Process A,
(ii)   Process B,
(iii)   Normal loss/gain,
(iv)   Abnormal loss/gain,
(v)   Finished goods,
(vi)   Profit and loss (extract).

(15 marks)

12   ANSWER TO EXAMINATION TYPE QUESTION

12.1   Chemical Compound

(i)   **Process A**

$$\text{Cost/kg} = \frac{\text{Total costs - scrap value of normal loss}}{\text{Expected output}}$$

Total costs

	£
Direct material (2,000kg @ £5/kg)	10,000
Direct labour	7,200
Process plant time (140hrs @ £60/hr)	8,400
Departmental overhead (60% × £7,200) (W1)	4,320
	29,920
Scrap value of normal loss (20% × 2,000kg × £0.50/kg)	200
	29,720

$$\text{Cost/kg} = \frac{£29,720}{2,000\text{kg} \times 80\%} = £18.575/\text{kg}$$

Process A

	Kg	£		Kg	£
Direct material	2,000	10,000	Normal loss	400	200
Direct labour		7,200	Process B	1,400	26,005
Process plant hire		8,400	Abnormal loss	200	3,715
Departmental overhead		4,320			
	2,000	29,920		2,000	29,920

(ii)   **Process B**

Total costs £

	£
Transfer from process A	26,005
Direct material (1,400kg @ £12/kg)	16,800
Direct labour	4,200
Process plant time (80hrs @ £72.50/hr)	5,800
Departmental overhead (60% × £4,200)	2,520
	55,325
Scrap value of normal loss (2,800kg × 10% × £1.825)	(511)
	54,814

$$\text{Cost/kg} = \frac{54,814}{2,800\text{kg} \times 90\%} = £21.751587$$

Process B

	Kg	£		Kg	£
Process A	1,400	26,005	Normal loss	280	511
Direct material	1,400	16,800	Finished goods	2,620	56,989
Direct labour		4,200			
Process plant time		5,800			
Departmental overhead		2,520			
Abnormal gain	100	2,175			
	2,900	57,500		2,900	57,500

(iii)

Normal loss/gain

	Kg	£		Kg	£
Process A	400	200	Abnormal gain - B	100	182.5
Abnormal loss - A	200	100	Bank (Bal)	780	628.5
Process B	280	511			
	880	811		880	811

(iv)

Abnormal loss/gain

	Kg	£		Kg	£
Process A	200	3,715	Normal loss/gain	200	100
Normal loss/gain	100	182.5	Process B	100	2,175
			P&L a/c (Bal fig)		1,622.5
	—	—		—	—
	300	3,897.5		300	3,897.5

(v)

Finished goods

	£		£
Process B	56,989		

(vi)

Profit and Loss account (Extract)

	£		£
Abnormal loss/gain	1,622.5		

WORKINGS

(W1)   Departmental overhead absorption rate

$$= \frac{£6,840}{£7,200 + £4,200} = 60\% \text{ of direct labour cost}$$

11 JOINT AND BY-PRODUCTS

INTRODUCTION & LEARNING OBJECTIVES

Syllabus area 6a. Process costing: the principle of equivalent units, treatment of normal and abnormal losses and gains, joint products and by-products; problems of common costs. (Ability required 3).

When you have studied this chapter you should be able to do the following:

- Distinguish between joint and by-products.

- Account for by-products.

- Account for joint products using different apportionment bases for common (pre-separation) costs.

- Critically appraise the use of common cost apportionments in the measurement of product profitability.

- Evaluate the decision whether to further process a product (or products) beyond the separation point.

1 JOINT PRODUCTS AND BY PRODUCTS

1.1 Introduction

The nature of process costing is that the process often produces more than one product. These additional products may be described as either **joint** or **by-products**. The distinction is of great importance, and is a matter of drawing a dividing line. Essentially joint products are both main products whereas by-products are incidental to the main products. Rules as to drawing the dividing line are provided by the CIMA's Terminology (1991). Costs incurred in processing prior to the separation of the products are known as common costs (or joint costs).

1.2 Joint products

Definition Two or more products separated in the course of processing, each having a sufficiently high saleable value to merit recognition as a main product.

1.3 By-product

Definition Output of some value produced incidentally in manufacturing something else (main products).

These definitions still leave scope for subjective judgement, but they provide a basis for such judgement. The distinction is important because the accounting treatment of joint and by products differs.

1.4   Relationship between processes, joint and by products

The following diagram illustrates the relationships:

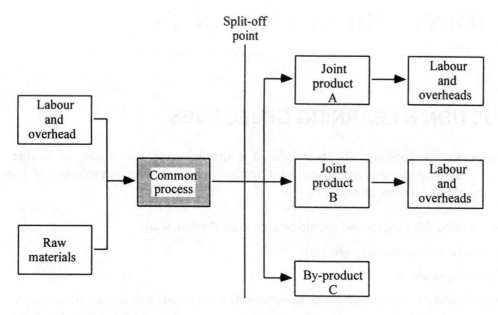

1.5   Accounting for by-products

Either of the following methods may be adopted:

(a)   the proceeds from the sale of the by-product may be treated as pure profit;

(b)   the proceeds from the sale, less any handling and selling expenses, may be applied in reducing the cost of the main products (ie, the treatment given to normal losses in the last chapter).

If a by-product needs further processing to improve its marketability, such cost will be deducted in arriving at net revenue, treated as in (a) or (b) above.

Note that recorded profits will be affected by the method adopted if stocks of the main product are maintained.

1.6   Example

Output from a process was 1,300 kilos of the main product and 100 kilos of a by-product. Sales of the main product were 1,000 kilos realising £6,000; sales of the by-product realised £160 but incurred £30 distribution cost. Process costs were £5,200.

Method (a)

	£	£
Main product sales		6,000
Process costs	5,200	
Less: Closing stock $\frac{300}{1,300} \times £5,200$	1,200	
		4,000
		2,000
Add: Net profit of by-product sales £160 – 30)		130
Net profit		2,130

Method (b)

	£	£
Main product sales		6,000
Process costs	5,200	
Less: By-product revenue	130	
	5,070	
Less: Closing stock $300 \times \dfrac{£5,070}{1,300}$	1,170	
Cost of sales		3,900
Net profit		2,100

Under method (b), a portion of by-product revenue is deferred in the stock value of the main product.

1.7 Accounting for joint products

Joint products are, by definition, subject to individual accounting procedures. Common costs may require apportionment between products if only for joint valuation purposes.

The main bases for apportionment are:

(a) **Physical measurement of joint products**

When the unit of measurement is different eg, litres and kilos, some method should be found of expressing them in a common unit. Some common costs are not incurred strictly equally for all joint products: such costs can be separated and apportioned by introducing weighting factors.

(b) **Market value**

The effect is to make each product appear to be equally profitable. Where certain products are processed after the point of separation, further processing costs must be deducted from the market values before common costs are apportioned.

(c) **Technical estimates of relative use of common resources**

Apportionment is, of necessity, an arbitrary calculation and product costs which include such an apportionment can be misleading if used as a basis for decision making.

1.8 Valuation of joint product stocks

In the following example common costs are apportioned on the following bases:

(a) physical measurement;
(b) market value at point of separation;
(c) net realisable value/net relative sales value;
(d) technical estimates of relative usage.

The methods will result in different stock valuations and, therefore, different recorded profits.

1.9   Example

	Kgs produced	Kgs sold	Selling price per kg	Common cost
Product A	100	80	£5	
				£750
Product B	200	150	£2	

(a)   **Apportionment by physical measurement**

$$\frac{\text{Common cost}}{\text{Kgs produced}} = \frac{£750}{300} = £2.50 \text{ per kg for A + B}$$

Trading results:

	Product A	£	Product B	£	Total £
Sales	80 × £5.00	400	150 × £2.00	300	700
Cost of sales	80 × £2.50	200	150 × £2.50	375	575
Profit/(loss)		200		(75)	125
Value of closing stock	20 × £2.50	50	50 × £2.50	125	

The main point to emphasise about joint products is the production mix. In this case the production ratio is 100 : 200 which means that, in order to obtain 1 kg of A, it is necessary also to produce 2 kgs of B, at least in the short term. (In the longer term it may be possible through research and development work to change the mix.)

In attempting to assess the profitability of the common process it is necessary to assess the overall position as follows:

		£
Sale value of production A	100 × £5	500
Sale value of production B	200 × £2	400
		900
Common cost		750
Profit		150

This profit figure should be used to evaluate the profitability of the common process.

Referring back to the trading results, it is important to appreciate that the 'loss' on B has been created by the common cost apportionment, ie.

	£
Selling price	2.00
Share of common cost	2.50
Loss	0.50

A decision not to produce and sell B is not possible ie, if B were not produced, then neither could A be produced.

A further point to note is that stock of B could not be valued at £2.50 bearing in mind that stock should be valued at the lower of cost and net realisable value.

(b)   **Apportionment by market value at point of separation**

		Sales value of production £	Proportion	Common cost apportionment £	Per kg £
A	100 × £5	500	5/9	417	4.17
B	200 × £2	400	4/9	333	1.67
				750	

Trading results:

	£	£	£
Sales			700
Common cost		750	
Less: Closing stock:			
A 20 × £4.17	83		
B 50 × £1.67	83		
		166	
Cost of sales			584
Profit			116

Notes:

(1)   Apportionment is on the basis of proportionate sales value of production.

(2)   Further processing or marketing costs specifically attributable to one product would be deducted from selling price to arrive at an estimated market value at split-off point.

(3)   This approach provides a more realistic estimate of cost to use for valuing stock of B ie, £1.67.

(c)   **Apportionment by net realisable value**

This approach should be used in situations where the sale value at the split-off point is not known, either because the product is not saleable, or if the examiner does not tell you - or if specifically asked for by the examiner.

Further information needed:

	Further processing costs	*Selling price after further processing*
Product A	£280 + £2.00 per kg	£8.40
Product B	£160 + £1.40 per kg	£4.50

Apportionment of common costs:

	Final sale value of production £	Allocatable further processing cost £	Net realisable value £	Common cost apportionment £	Per kg £
Product A	100 × £8.40 = 840	280 + 100 × £2.00 = 480	360	$\frac{360}{360+460} \times £750 = 329$	3.29
Product B	200 × £4.50 = 900	160 + 200 × £1.40 = 440	460	$\frac{460}{360+460} \times £750 = 421$	2.10

Trading results (for common process only):

	£	£	£
Sales			700
Common cost		750	
Less: Closing stock:			
A 20 × £3.29	66		
B 50 × £2.10	105		
	——	171	
Cost of sales			579
			——
Profit			121
			——

Notes:

(1)   As we **know** sale value of B at the point of separation is £2, we can see that this method results in an unrealistic stock value of £2.10.   Bear in mind that this approach should only be used where the sale value at the split-off point is not known - or if instructed to by the examiner.

(2)   The effect of further processing is considered in more detail below.

(d)   **Using technical apportionment**

The technical apportionment ratios are:

A – 60%
B – 40%

	£	£	£
Sales	400	300	700
	——	——	——
Common costs (apportioned 60 : 40)	450	300	750
Less: Stock value:			
Common costs A $= \dfrac{20}{100} \times £450$	90		90
B $= \dfrac{50}{200} \times £300$		75	75
	——	——	——
Cost of sales	360	225	585
	——	——	——
Net profit	40	75	115
	——	——	——

It is noteworthy that all the methods produce similar, but not identical results.

1.10   Activity

A Process produces two joint products X and Y. During August the process costs attributed to completed output amounted to £122,500. Output of X and Y for the period were:

X   3 tonnes
Y   4 tonnes

Calculate the cost attributed to each joint product using the weight basis of apportionment.

1.11   Activity solution

X   £52,500
Y   £70,000

1.12   Problems of common costs

Even if careful technical estimates are made of relative benefits, common costs apportionment will inevitably be an arbitrary calculation.   When providing information to assist decision making, therefore, the cost accountant will emphasise cost revenue differences arising from the decision.

Examples of decisions involving joint products are:

(a)   withdrawing, or adding, a product;
(b)   special pricing;
(c)   economics of further processing.

Apportioned common costs are **not** relevant to any of the above decisions although a change in marketing strategy may affect total joint costs eg, withdrawing a product may allow capacity of the joint process to be reduced.

In the short or medium term, it is probably impractical and/or uneconomic to alter the processing structure.   The relation benefit derived by joint products is, therefore, irrelevant when considering profitability or marketing opportunities.

1.13   Common costs and decisions

(a)   **Decisions regarding joint process**

The joint process should, as stated above, be evaluated by looking at the **total** revenue and **total** cost for that process.   However, it is important also to note that further processing may well increase profits.   This further processing is only possible **if** the joint process is carried out.

(b)   **Decision regarding further processing of individual products**

For this purpose it is assumed that further processing of products is independent ie, a decision to process one joint product in no way affects the decision to process further the other joint products.   It should also be noted that joint costs are not affected by whether individual products are further processed, and are therefore not relevant.

To evaluate processing of the individual products it is necessary to identify the **incremental** costs and **incremental** revenues relating to that further processing ie, the **additional** costs and revenue brought about directly as a result of that further processing.

1.14   Example

Restating the data from the example above.

	Kgs produced	*Kgs sold*	*Selling price at split-off point*	*Further processing costs*	*Selling price after further processing*
Product A	100	80	£5	£280 + £2.00 per kg	£8.40
Product B	200	150	£2	£160 + £1.40 per kg	£4.50

Evaluation of further processing:

	Product A			Product B	
	£	£		£	£
Incremental revenue	100 × £(8.40 − 5.00)	340	200 × £(4.50 − 2.00)		500
Incremental cost:					
Fixed		280		160	
Variable	100 × £2	200	200 × £1.40	280	
		480			440
Increase/(decrease) in profit		(140)			60

On the basis of these figures the decision to recommend would be:

       A   Sell at split-off point for £5.

       B   Sell after further processing for £4.50.

This would result in overall profits on this **production** volume of:

	£
Common process	150
Further processing of B	60
Profit	210

Note: the timing of recognition of this profit is dependent on the basis used for valuation of stocks, as discussed above.

The recommendation to sell A at the split-off point and B after further processing is based on two assumptions:

(a)   all relevant 'effects' of the decision have been included ie, quantified;

(b)   production volume achieved is A 100 kgs, B 200 kgs.

Before a final decision is made these assumptions must be considered:

(a)   **All effects of decision quantified**

The course of action recommended could have other effects not included above, eg

- Products A and B in their final state may be in some way 'complementary' ie, it may only be possible to sell B for £4.50 if A is also available in a further processed state at a price of £8.40.

- The company may currently be carrying out further processing of A. The decision above could therefore result in having to reduce the workforce employed in this processing. The remaining workforce could, for example, go out on strike, causing a loss of production and sales of A and B. These factors should be carefully assessed before a final decision is made.

(b)   **Production volume**

By looking in more detail at the further processing of A it is possible to see that further processing of 1 kg of A results in an incremental contribution of:

	£
Incremental revenue £(8.40 − 5.00)	3.40
Incremental variable cost	2.00
Incremental contribution	1.40

It is therefore possible to identify the level of activity at which further processing of A becomes worthwhile ie, the 'break-even volume'.

$$\text{Break-even volume} = \frac{\text{Incremental fixed costs}}{\text{Incremental contribution per kg}}$$

$$= \frac{280}{1.40}$$

$$= 200 \text{ kgs}$$

Hence, if the volume of A in the future is greater than 200 kgs, further processing becomes economically worthwhile.

2   CHAPTER SUMMARY

Joint and by-products have been distinguished and the various apportionment methods illustrated and their limitations discussed.

3   SELF TEST QUESTIONS

3.1   What is a joint product? (1.2)

3.2   What is a by-product? (1.3)

4   EXAMINATION TYPE QUESTIONS

4.1   Armor plc

Armor plc operates a process which produces an industrial cleansing chemical, and shown below are the costs incurred by the process during month 7 together with other relevant operating data.

Direct materials transferred into process:	
10,000 kilos at £0.15 per kilo	£1,500
Conversion costs	£1,330
Output:	
Finished production	8,400 kilos
By-product	500 kilos
Toxic waste	800 kilos

The toxic waste is the same chemical as the finished product except that it has been polluted at the final operation. The cost of disposing of the toxic waste is £0.80 per kilo. The by-product is transferred to a subsidiary operation where it is packed at a cost of £0.25 per kilo. These costs are not included in the direct materials and conversion costs tabulated above.

The selling price of the by-product is £0.75 per kilo and the process is credited with the net realisable value of the by-product produced. During month 7, 30 kilos of the by-product were sold.

The normal output from the process per 1,000 kilos of direct material is:

Finished production	850 kilos
By-product	50 kilos
Toxic waste	60 kilos
Loss as a result of evaporation	40 kilos

You are required:

(a)   to prepare the following accounts recording month 7 transactions for the above process:

- Process account
- By-product account
- Normal toxic waste account

- Any relevant abnormal loss/gain accounts.

(15 marks)

(b)   to explain the reasons for your treatment of the toxic waste including an explanation of how the total cost of abnormal toxic waste has been calculated.

(5 marks)

(Total: 20 marks)

4.2   XY Ltd

XY Ltd operates a chemical process which jointly produces four products, A, B, C and D. Product B is sold without further processing, but additional work is necessary on the other three before they can be sold. Budgeted data for the year were as follows:

	Production lb	Closing stock lb	Sales lb
Production:			
Product A	150,000	10,000	140,000
Product B	110,000	15,000	95,000
Product C	60,000	5,000	55,000
Product D	180,000	Nil	180,000

There were no opening stocks of the four products. Closing stocks were ready for sale.

	Selling prices per lb £	Cost of additional work to make product saleable per lb
Product A	0.70	0.10
Product B	0.60	-
Product C	0.60	0.20
Product D	1.35	0.35

	£
Production cost of the joint process	180,000
Other costs:	
Administration (fixed)	45,000
Selling:	
Fixed	35,000
Variable (£0.01 per lb sold)	4,700

An overseas customer has expressed interest in buying from existing production 50,000lb each in one year of any or all of Products A, C and D before they have been further processed by XY Ltd. He has offered to pay the following prices:

	Price per lb £
Product A	0.65
Product C	0.52
Product D	0.90

On such sales, variable selling costs would be only £0.006 per lb. Fixed administration and selling costs would remain as stated above.

The costs of the joint process are to be apportioned to individual products on the following bases:

(a)   weight of products produced;

(b)   sales value of products produced less the cost of additional work incurred to make products saleable.

You are required for each of the above bases to calculate for the year:

(a)   gross profit per product (ie, before deducting administration and selling overhead);
(b)   total gross profit;
(c)   total net profit.

You are also required:

(d)   to state which products you would recommend XY Ltd to sell to the overseas customer before further processing at the prices quoted in order to increase net profit;

(e)   to calculate the increase in the annual net profit of XY Ltd if your advice at (d) above was followed.

5   ANSWERS TO EXAMINATION TYPE QUESTIONS

5.1   Armor plc

Note: the approach is to prepare the process account in the usual way taking the relevant cost and output figures from the question, except for the toxic waste.

The way to deal with the losses is to put in the pre-determined figures first (based on input) ie,

Normal toxic waste: $10,000 \times \dfrac{60}{1,000} =$ 600

Hence, abnormal toxic waste (bal fig)   200

Total toxic waste   800

Normal loss from evaporation: $10,000 \times \dfrac{40}{1,000} =$ 400

The balancing figure in the quantity columns of the process account is the abnormal gain.

The next stage is to prepare the by-product account to find the net realisable value of the by-product; this value is then credited to the process account.

It is then possible to compute the cost per kilo, bearing in the mind that it is necessary to add the disposal cost of the normal waste to total cost. The cost per kilo figure can then be used to complete the value columns in the process account and then complete the entries in the waste/gain accounts.

(a)

Process account - Month 7

	kilos	£		kilos	£
Direct material	10,000	1,500	Finished production	8,400	3,024
Conversion costs		1,330	By-product	500	250
		———	Normal toxic waste	600	-
		2,830	Abnormal toxic waste	200	72
Waste disposal costs			Normal evaporation loss	400	-
(600 @ 0.8)		480			
Abnormal gain	100	36			
	———	———		———	———
	10,100	3,346		10,100	3,346
	———	———		———	———

By-product account

	kilos	£		kilos	£
Packing cost:			Sales	30	22.50
500 @ 0.25		125	Balance c/d	470	352.50
Process account					
(bal fig)	500	250			
	500	375		500	375.00

Normal toxic waste account

	kilos	£		kilos	£
Cash	600	480	Process account	600	480

Abnormal gain account

	kilos	£		kilos	£
Profit and loss account	100	36	Process account	100	36

Abnormal toxic waste account

	kilos	£		kilos	£
Process account	200	72	P&L a/c	200	232
Cash: 200 @ £0.8		160			
	200	232		200	232

WORKING

Calculation of cost per kilo

$$= \frac{\text{Total cost} + \text{Disposal cost of normal toxic waste} - \text{Net realisable value of by-product}}{\text{Input} - \text{Normal toxic waste} - \text{By-product} - \text{Normal evaporation loss}}$$

$$= \frac{2,830 + 480 - 250}{10,000 - 600 - 500 - 400}$$

$$= \frac{3,060}{8,500} = £0.36 \text{ per kilo}$$

(b)   The general principle behind treatment of the toxic waste is whether the waste is considered normal or abnormal.

Normal waste is waste which arises as a result of the nature of the process and is therefore regarded as unavoidable. The cost of this normal waste should therefore be incorporated into the cost of the product - the cleansing chemical. In this case the normal waste increases the normal cost in two ways:

(1)   yield is reduced: this causes a higher unit cost;

(2)   there is an additional cost of disposing of the waste.

The amount by which actual waste exceeds the normal or expected waste is termed 'abnormal' and is assumed to be controllable/avoidable. This waste should not have occurred and the cost is therefore excluded from the cost of output and written off to the profit and loss account. The cost comprises the normal output cost plus the additional disposal cost.

The management of Armor plc should investigate to ascertain the cause of this abnormal waste.

5.2   XY Ltd

(a)   )
(b)   )   Profit statement (see below)
(c)   )

(i)   **Joint costs apportioned on weight of products**

	Product A 000 lb	B 000 lb	C 000 lb	D 000 lb	Total 000 lb
Sales	140	95	55	180	470

	A £	B £	C £	D £	Total £
Sales	98,000	57,000	33,000	243,000	431,000
Less: cost of sales	64,400	34,200	30,800	127,800	257,200
Gross profit	33,600	22,800	2,200	115,200	173,800

				£	
Less: Administration costs				45,000	
Less: Selling costs: Fixed				35,000	
Variable				4,700	
					84,700
Net profit					89,100

WORKINGS

$$\text{Joint cost per lb} = \frac{\text{Costs}}{\text{Weight produced}}$$

$$= \frac{£180,000}{500,000}$$

$$= 0.36$$

As closing stocks are **ready for sales**, cost of sales is valued at joint plus additional costs, ie:

Product	Joint £	Cost per lb additional £	Total	Sales 000 lb	Cost of sales £
A	0.36	0.10	0.46	140	64,400
B	0.36	-	0.36	95	34,200
C	0.36	0.20	0.56	55	30,800
D	0.36	0.35	0.71	180	127,800

(ii)   **Joint costs apportioned on net sales value of production**

	Product A £	B £	C £	D £	Total £
Sales	98,000	57,000	33,000	243,000	431,000
Less: Cost of sales	56,000	28,500	22,000	153,000	259,500
Gross profit	42,000	28,500	11,000	90,000	171,500
Less: Administration and selling costs:					84,700
Net profit					86,800

WORKINGS

	Product				Total
	A	*B*	*C*	*D*	
	000 lb	*000 lb*	*000 lb*	*000 lb*	*000 lb*
Production	150	110	60	180	500
	£	£	£	£	£
Selling prices	0.70	0.60	0.60	1.35	
Sales value of production	105,000	66,000	36,000	243,000	450,000
Less: Additional costs	15,000	-	12,000	63,000	90,000
Net sales value of production	90,000	66,000	24,000	180,000	360,000
Apportioned joint cost (50%)	45,000	33,000	12,000	90,000	180,000
Additional costs	15,000	-	12,000	63,000	90,000
Production costs	60,000	33,000	24,000	153,000	270,000
Closing stock	$(\frac{10}{150})$4,000	$(\frac{15}{110})$4,500	$(\frac{5}{60})$2,000	-	10,500
Cost of sales	56,000	28,500	22,000	153,000	259,500

(d)   **Price comparison**

	Product		
	A	*B*	*C*
	£	£	£
Existing price per lb	0.70	0.60	1.35
Less: Additional costs per lb	0.10	0.20	0.30
Net revenue per lb	0.60	0.40	1.00
Overseas offer	0.65	0.52	0.90
Gain/(loss) per lb	0.05	0.12	(0.10)
Reduction in variable selling costs per lb	0.004	0.004	0.004
Net gain/(loss) per lb	0.054	0.124	(0.096)

Recommendation: sell Products A and B to the overseas customer.

(e)   **Increase in annual net profit**

	£
Additional revenue:	
Product A 50,000 lb @ £0.05	2,500
Product B 50,000 lb @ £0.12	6,000
	8,500
Add: Reduction in variable selling costs 100,000 lb @ £0.004	400
Net profit increase	8,900

Note: all other costs and revenue will be unaffected.

12 COST BOOKKEEPING

INTRODUCTION & LEARNING OBJECTIVES

Syllabus area 6a. Integrated and non-integrated systems, including their reconciliation. (Ability required 3).

The basic principles of double entry and ledger accounts apply to cost accounting as well as to financial accounting. However the detailed application of these principles differs and the cost accounts must provide more detailed information than is normally required for financial accounts.

In this chapter the basic principles of the two main systems of cost accounting bookkeeping will be examined. These two systems are known as interlocking accounts (non-integrated accounting sytems) and integral or integrated accounts.

When you have studied this chapter you should be able to do the following:

• Describe a system of interlocking accounts and integral accounts.

• Detail the differences between financial and costing profit in an interlocking system.

• Understand the ledger account entries in an interlocking system.

• Describe an integral accounts system.

---

1 METHODS OF COST BOOKKEEPING

1.1 Interlocking accounts (non-integrated accounting)

Definition **Interlocking accounts** are a system in which the cost accounts are distinct from the financial accounts; both sets are kept in agreement or are readily reconcilable.

The recording system may be arranged in two ways:

(a) Separate book records without control account: separate costing records are derived independently from the source documents, but are reconciled periodically with the financial records.

(b) Separate cost ledger with control account: a separate costing ledger is maintained under the control of the cost accountant, but integrated with the financial books by means of a cost ledger control account through which all cost and revenue information for re-analysis is transferred.

1.2 Reconciliation of financial and costing profit

Where the cost accounts are maintained independently in an interlocking system it is necessary to reconcile the financial and costing results.

1.3   Activity

List the differences that you think there might be between the financial and costing profits under the following headings:

(a)   Appropriations of profit not dealt with in the costing system.

(b)   Income and expenditure of a purely financial nature (ie, nothing to do with manufacturing).

(c)   Items where financial and costing treatments differ.

1.4   Activity solution

(a)   **Appropriations of profit not dealt with in the costing system**

(i)   Corporation tax;

(ii)   transfers to reserves;

(iii)   dividends paid and proposed;

(iv)   amounts written off intangibles such as goodwill, discount on issue of debentures, expenses of capital issues, etc;

(v)   appropriations to sinking funds for the repayment of loans;

(vi)   charitable donations where no direct benefit is derived by the employees of the company.

(b)   **Income and expenditure of a purely financial nature** (ie, outside the scope of manufacture)

(i)   Interest and dividends received;

(ii)   rents receivable - however, if this arises from part of rented business premises which have been sublet, only the profit element should be excluded, the proportion representing cost being deducted from rents payable to determine the net rent of premises;

(iii)   profits and losses on the sale of fixed assets and investments;

(iv)   interest on bank loans, mortgages and debentures;

(v)   damages payable at law, fines and penalties.

(c)   **Items where financial and costing treatments differ**

(i)   Differences in the valuation of stocks and work in progress. The latter may, for costing purposes, be valued at factory cost (including production overhead), whereas prime cost may be employed in the financial accounts. Likewise, stocks of materials and finished goods may be written down in the financial accounts to net realisable value.

(ii)   Depreciation. In the financial accounts this charge is normally based solely upon the passage of time, whereas in the cost accounts it may be a variable charge based upon machine/man hours worked.

(iii)   Abnormal losses in production and storage. In the financial accounts, materials and wages will include any abnormal losses of material or time. In the cost accounts such losses may be excluded to avoid misleading comparisons.

(iv)   Interest on capital.   Notional interest on capital employed in production is sometimes included in the cost accounts to reflect the nominal cost of employing the capital rather than investing it outside the business.

(v)   Charge in lieu of rent.   Again a notional amount for rent may be included in costs in order to compare costs of production with costs of another business which occupies a rented or leasehold factory.

1.5   Integral accounts

 Integral or integrated accounts are a set of accounting records which provides financial and cost accounts using a common input of data for all accounting purposes.

2   THE COST LEDGER IN AN INTERLOCKING SYSTEM

2.1   Cost ledger contra account

In an interlocking system the cost accounts will only need to record transactions relating to operating revenue and costs; details of capital, debtors and creditors are part of the financial accounting routine.   Frequently, however, such financial accounts are merged into a single account (cost ledger contra) solely to maintain the double entry principle within the cost accounts.

2.2   Control accounts

The cost ledger for a manufacturing business will probably contain control accounts for:

(a)   stores;
(b)   work in progress;
(c)   finished stock;
(d)   production overhead;
(e)   general administration costs;
(f)   marketing costs.

2.3   Subsidiary ledgers

Each control account will be supported by a subsidiary ledger to provide the detail required for financial reporting and/or management information.   Analysis will be by:

(a)   item of material;
(b)   job number (job costing), product (batch costing) or process (process costing);
(c)   job or production;
(d)   cost centres (there will be more than one of these).

2.4   Cost ledger accounts

In addition to the cost ledger contra and the control accounts detailed above, separate accounts will be kept as required, particularly:

(a)   sales;
(b)   cost of sales;
(c)   wages;
(d)   profit and loss.

Subsidiary details in the form of a sub-ledger or analysis columns may be necessary.

2.5   Accounting entries

Entries to the cost ledger follow the sequence of transactions in the manufacturing business:

	Transaction	*Journal entry*	*Document*
(a)	Purchases	Dr Stores Cr Contra	Invoice/GRN
(b)	Gross wages	Dr Wages Cr Contra	Payroll
(c)	Expenses incurred	Dr Production overhead Dr General admin cost Dr Marketing cost Cr Contra	Invoices/ Petty cash/ Journal
(d)	Materials issued	Dr Work in progress (direct) Dr Production overhead (indirect) Cr Stores	Requisitions
(e)	Analysed wages	Dr (as (d) above) Cr Wages	Time sheets, etc
(f)	Overhead absorbed	Dr Work in progress Cr Production overhead	Cost journal
(g)	Completed work	Dr Finished stock Cr Work in progress	Production order
(h)	Goods sold	Dr Cost of sales/contra Cr Finished stock/sales	Delivery note/ Invoice

Notes:

(i)   (d) and (e) could affect general administration and marketing.

(ii)   Overhead absorbed (f) would be debited to finished stock if work in progress is valued at prime cost.

(iii) In a marginal costing system entry (f) would be for variable overhead only.

2.6   Period end procedure

At the end of the reporting period a profit and loss account can be prepared from the cost ledger in the following format:

£

Sales
Less: Cost of sales
____

Gross margin

Add/Less: Over/under-absorbed overhead
Less: General administration costs
    Marketing costs
____

Operating profit
____

Balances in stores, work in progress and finished stock represent stock valuations at cost. At the end of the financial year the costing profit and loss account will be closed by transfer to cost ledger contra and the balances in stock accounts carried forward with an offsetting credit in cost ledger contra.

2.7   Example

The following illustrates the double entry aspect of recording transactions, firstly using an interlocking (non-integrated) system; and then using an integral system.

	£
Incurred direct wages	100,000
Incurred indirect production wages	41,200
Administration salaries paid	12,800
Purchased raw materials	46,500
Paid business rates	4,000
Paid creditor for materials	41,400
Paid wages	98,700
Paid PAYE creditor	40,900
Paid bank charges	420
Sales on credit	480,000
Production overhead costs (other than business rates) paid	81,400
Received from debtors	414,600

Notes: (re: Interlocking system)

(1)   In the cost ledgers production overhead costs are absorbed into cost units using an absorption rate of 100% of direct wage costs. Any under or over absorption is carried forward to the end of the year.

(2)   Stocks of raw material are valued using FIFO in the financial ledgers and LIFO in the cost ledgers. There was no opening stock, closing stock was valued:

   FIFO   £6,300
   LIFO   £4,800

(3)   There is no work-in-progress or stock of finished goods.

(4)   The amount payable to the PAYE creditor in respect of wages and salaries is £43,400.

(5)   Business rates are to be apportioned:

   Production   80%
   Administration   20%

Interlocking system

Financial ledger

Wages and salaries				Wages control			
	£		£			£		£
Wages control	154,000	Profit & loss	154,000	PAYE creditor	43,400	Wages &	
				Bank	98,700	Salaries	154,000

PAYE creditor				Raw material purchases			
	£		£		£		£
Bank	40,900	Wages control	43,400	Creditor	46,500	Profit & loss	46,500

Creditor - Raw materials

	£		£
Bank	41,400	Purchases	46,500

Rates

	£		£
Bank	4,000	Profit & loss	4,000

Bank charges

	£		£
Bank	420	Profit & loss	420

Debtors

	£		£
Sales	480,000	Bank	414,600

Stock

	£		£
Profit & loss	6,300		

Bank

	£		£
Debtors	414,600	Wages control	98,700
		PAYE creditor	40,900
		Creditor	
		- materials	41,400
		Rates	4,000
		Bank charges	420
		Overhead costs	81,400

Sales

	£		£
Profit & loss	480,000	Debtors	480,000

Overhead costs

	£		£
Bank	81,400	Profit & loss	81,400

Profit & loss

	£		£
Raw material	46,500	Sales	480,000
Wages &		Raw material	
salaries	154,000	stock	6,300
Rates	4,000		
Bank charges	420		
Overhead costs	81,400		
Net profit	199,980		
	486,300		486,300

Cost ledger

Raw material control

	£		£
CLC	46,500	WIP	41,700
		Bal c/d	4,800
	46,500		46,500

Work in progress

	£		£
CLC	100,000	Cost of sales	241,700
Raw material	41,700		
Prod Ohd	100,000		
	241,700		241,700

Cost ledger control (CLC)

	£		£
Sales	480,000	Raw material	46,500
		WIP	100,000
		Prod Ohd	41,200
		Admin Ohd	12,800
		Prod Ohd	3,200
		Admin Ohd	800
		Prod Ohd	81,400

Production overhead

	£		£
CLC	41,200	Work in	
CLC	3,200	progress	100,000
CLC	81,400	Bal c/d	25,800
	125,800		125,800

Sales

	£		£
Profit & loss	480,000	CLC	480,000

Administration overhead

	£		£
CLC	12,800	Profit & loss	13,600
CLC	800		
	13,600		13,600

Cost of sales

	£		£
WIP	241,700	Profit & loss	241,700

Profit & loss

	£		£
Cost of sales	241,700	Sales	480,000
Admin Ohd	13,600		
Net profit	224,700		
	480,000		480,000

Profit reconciliation

	£	£
Net profit as per financial ledgers		199,980
Adjust for item not in cost ledger:		
Bank charges		420
Differences in treatment of:		
Production overhead costs	25,800	
Closing stock valuation	(1,500)	
		24,300
Net profit as per cost ledgers		224,700

Integrated system (Note. Stocks are valued on a FIFO basis.)

Raw material control

	£		£
Creditor	46,500	WIP	40,200
		Bal c/d	6,300
	46,500		46,500

Creditor

	£		£
Bank	41,400	Raw materials	46,500

Work in progress

	£		£
Wages control	100,000	Cost of sales	240,200
Raw material	40,200		
Prod'n Ohd	100,000		
	240,200		240,200

Wages control

	£		£
Bank	98,700	Work in	
PAYE creditor	43,400	progress	100,000
		Production Ohd	41,200

Production overhead

	£		£
Wages control	41,200	WIP	100,000
Bank	3,200	Bal c/d	25,800
Bank	81,400		
	125,800		125,800

Administration overhead

	£		£
Bank	12,800	Profit & loss	13,600
Bank	800		
	13,600		13,600

Bank

	£		£
Debtors	414,600	Admin Ohd	12,800
		Admin Ohd	800
		Production Ohd	3,200
		Creditor	41,400
		Wages control	98,700
		PAYE creditor	40,900
		Bank charges	420
		Production Ohd	81,400

PAYE creditor

	£		£
Bank	40,900	Wages control	43,400

Cost of sales

	£		£
WIP	240,200	Profit & loss	240,200

Bank charges

	£		£
Bank	420	Profit & loss	420

Debtors

	£		£
Sales	480,000	Bank	414,600

Sales

	£		£
Profit & loss	480,000	Debtors	480,000

Profit & loss

	£		£
Cost of sales	240,200	Sales	480,000
Admin Ohd	13,600		
Bank charges	420		
Net profit	225,780		
	480,000		480,000

2.8   Interlocking and integrated systems - a comparison

The above example has identified the following differences between these systems:

- Many transactions are recorded twice when an interlocking system is used, once in the cost ledger and once in the financial ledger. This is an additional administrative cost.

- Some transactions are not recorded in the cost ledger when an interlocking system is used.

- Some items (eg, stock) may be valued differently in each set of ledgers when an interlocking system is used.

- An integrated system classifies costs similarly to the classifications used in the cost ledger of an interlocking system. The integrated ledger records all transactions and shows the asset and liability accounts similarly to those in the financial ledger of an interlocking system.

In summarising the above it can be shown that the interlocking system provides more flexibility because it is not constrained (in the cost ledger) by the regulations of financial accounting. However, this flexibility has a cost:

- the administrative burden of recording many transactions twice (referred to above); and

- the need to prepare a statement reconciling the profit shown by the cost and financial ledgers.

2.9 Example

The following illustrates the double entry aspect of cost accounting. The entries relating to notional charges and absorption of non-production cost are unlikely to be encountered in practice, but will test your application of accounting procedure.

Details are given below of the operations during a period of one month of a manufacturing company which makes a single product.

You are required to show the entries in the cost accounts.

Data for a period of one month:

	Opening stock		Closing stock	
	Units	£	Units	£
Raw materials:				
Direct		15,000		20,000
Indirect production		1,700		3,000
Work in progress:				
Direct materials		3,000		3,500
Direct wages		1,000		1,200
Finished goods	7,500	9,000	10,000	12,000
Sales 150,000 units				225,000
Rent of offices				1,500
Advertising				2,000
Stationery				840
Rates on factory				2,700
Salesmen's commission and expenses				1,400
Insurance of offices				80
Depreciation of machinery				6,400
Warehouse rentals				800
Secretarial wages				3,000
Repairs to plant				1,850
Salesmen's salaries				6,000
Insurance of factory				1,100
Accounting staff wages				8,200
Delivery charges				450
Other factory expenses				7,950
Other administration expenses				2,480
Other marketing expenses				6,250
Purchase of materials:				
Direct				65,000
Indirect production				5,000
Direct wages				55,000
Factory indirect wages				15,000
Loan interest received				500
Included in factory expenses are:				
Notional charge for use of own premises				2,800
Notional interest on capital employed in the business				400

'Other marketing expenses' wrongly contains an amount of £4,500 which should be in 'Other factory expenses'.

The cost accounts are kept separately from the financial accounts. In the cost accounts the company absorbs factory overhead at 40% of prime cost of finished units produced, administration overhead at 10p per unit produced and marketing overhead at 9p per unit delivered.

2.10   Solution

The question should be tackled in logical sequence.

Step 1   Open the necessary cost accounts, which are:

>   Direct raw materials
>   Indirect production materials
>   Work in progress
>   Factory overhead
>   Administration overhead
>   Marketing overhead
>   Finished goods
>   Cost of sales
>   Profit and loss
>   Cost contra (memo to maintain double entry)

Step 2   Record the opening balances on the stock accounts, crediting cost contra, and post purchases of materials.

Step 3   Post the issues of material.

Step 4   Charge direct wages to work in progress and indirect wages to factory overhead.

Step 5   Charge the remaining costs for the period to appropriate overhead accounts.

Step 6   Complete the work in progress account. The balance, after posting the closing stock, represents the prime cost of finished units produced.

Step 7   Debit finished goods account with factory and administration overhead at the absorption rates given.

Step 8   Complete the finished goods account. The balance, after posting the closing stock, represents cost of goods sold. The number of units produced (required for Step 7 above) represents Sales + Closing stock − Opening stock, ie, 150,000 + 10,000 − 7,500 = 152,500.

Step 9   Debit cost of sales with absorbed marketing overhead.

Step 10   Compile the profit and loss account by posting sales, cost of sales, and the balances on overhead accounts (under/over-absorption).

Solution (for guidance, the entries have been referenced to the sequence above)

(a)

Direct raw materials

	£		£
Opening stock b/d (2)	15,000	WIP - issued to production (3)	60,000
Cost contra - purchases (2)	65,000	Closing stock c/d	20,000
	80,000		80,000

Indirect production materials

	£		£
Opening stock b/d (2)	1,700	Factory overhead - issues (3)	3,700
Cost contra - purchases (2)	5,000	Closing stock c/d	3,000
	6,700		6,700

Work in progress

	£		£
Opening stock b/d (2)	4,000	Finished goods - prime cost	
Direct raw materials (3)	60,000	of finished units (6) (bal fig)	114,300
Direct wages (4)	55,000	Closing stock c/d	4,700
	119,000		119,000

Factory overhead

	£		£
Indirect materials (3)	3,700	Finished goods - absorbed	
Indirect wages (4)	15,000	overhead @ 40% of £114,300	45,720
Factory rates (5)	2,700		
Depreciation of machinery (5)	6,400		
Repairs to plant (5)	1,850		
Factory insurance (5)	1,100		
Other factory expenses (5)	7,950		
Marketing overhead (error)	4,500		
	43,200		
Profit and loss over-absorbed			
overhead (10)	2,520		
	45,720		45,720

Administration overhead

	£		£
Rent of offices (5)	1,500	Finished goods - absorbed	
Stationery (5)	840	overhead: 152,500 units	
Insurance of offices (5)	80	@ 10p per unit (7)	15,250
Secretarial wages (5)	3,000	Profit and loss -	
Accounting staff wages (5)	8,200	under-absorbed (10)	850
Other admin expenses (5)	2,480		
	16,100		16,100

Marketing overhead

	£		£
Advertising (5)	2,000	Factory overhead (error)	4,500
Salesmen's commission/		Cost of sales - absorbed	
expenses (5)	1,400	overhead @ 9p per unit on	
Warehouse rentals (5)	800	150,000 units delivered (a)	13,500
Salesmen's salaries (5)	6,000		
Delivery charges (5)	450		
Other expenses (5)	6,250		
Profit and loss - over-absorbed			
overhead (10)	1,100		
	18,000		18,000

Finished goods

	Units	£		Units	£
Opening stock (2)	7,500	9,000	Cost of sales (8)		
Work in progress (6)	152,500	114,300	(bal fig)	150,000	172,270
Factory overhead (7)		45,720	Closing stock	10,000	12,000
Admin overhead (7)		15,250			
	160,000	184,270		160,000	184,270

Cost of sales

	£		£
Finished goods (8)	172,270	Profit and loss (10)	185,770
Marketing overhead (9)	13,500		
	185,770		185,770

Profit and loss

	£		£
Cost of sales (10)	185,770	Sales (10)	225,000
Admin overhead (10)	850	Factory overhead (10)	2,520
Balance - costing profit	42,000	Marketing overhead (10)	1,100
	228,620		228,620

Cost contra account

	£	£		£
Sales (10)		225,000	Balance b/d (2)	
Balance c/d:			(15,000 + 1,700 + 4,000	
Raw material	20,000		+ 9,000)	29,700
Indirect material	3,000		Purchases (2) (65,000 + 5,000)	70,000
Work in progress	4,700		Wages (4) (55,000 + 15,000)	70,000
Finished goods	12,000		Factory overhead (5)	20,000
		39,700	Admin overhead (5)	16,100
			Marketing overhead (5)	16,900
			Balance c/d	
			Costing profit (10)	42,000
		264,700		264,700

2.11   Activity

Take the costing profit of £42,000 and prepare a statement showing any additional items necessary in order to give the financial accounting profit.

2.12   Activity solution

	£	£	£
Profit per costing profit and loss account			42,000
Add: Loan interest received (excluded from cost accounts)		500	
Notional charges not included in financial accounts:			
Rent	2,800		
Interest	400		
		3,200	
			3,700
Profit per financial accounts			45,700

3   INTEGRAL ACCOUNTS

3.1   Purpose of integration

Integration of the cost and financial accounts into one comprehensive system offers savings in work by avoiding:

(a)   Duplication of certain accounting entries, for example in an interlocking system, purchases of raw materials would be posted thus.

Financial account	Dr Purchases	Cr Creditors
Cost account	Dr Stores	Cr Cost Contra

In an integral system, a single entry would suffice, ie,

Dr Stores   Cr Creditors

(b)   Reconciliation of costing with financial profit; only one profit and loss account would be prepared.

More importantly perhaps, integration should improve the usefulness of, and promote the reliance upon, the accounting system as an information base. The overall system will be subject to control by external, internal and management audit. Furthermore, the design of accounting procedures will have to co-ordinate the requirements for management and financial information.

3.2   Methods of integration

Various methods of integrating the financial and cost accounts exist and the system must take into account the structure, etc, of the company and the normal information requirements for management and outsiders, eg, shareholders and the Revenue. Some requirements will be met by a two-fold analysis of costs: by natural headings and by cost centres, products, etc.

The organisation of the accounting department can take the same form as if separate cost and financial accounting systems were in use. The cost department will become involved in a detailed analysis of WIP and overhead accounts (and probably sales as well), and will supply details of transfers from WIP to finished goods, of overhead recovery, and, where applicable, an analysis of variances.

Division of work can be incorporated in the accounting system by:

(a)   Creating a cost ledger control account in the main ledger. The account would operate in the same way as a debtors' control account, ie, all entries affecting the cost accounts would be posted to cost ledger control and the cost accountant would be responsible for maintaining all the subsidiary ledgers and accounts.

(b)   Opening cost control and financial control accounts. The accounts would perform a similar function to branch/head office accounts to separate cost and financial accounting. The cost control and financial control accounts would be kept in agreement except that balances would appear on opposite sides.

3.3   Accounting for production overhead

Production overhead costs are those costs incurred in the production function but which cannot be economically identified with the cost unit to which they relate.

The requirements of SSAP 9 for stock valuations used in financial accounting are that stocks should be valued at their total cost including an appropriate proportion of production overhead.

Since work-in-progress is a form of stock this valuation rule must also apply to work-in-progress.

To achieve this valuation production overhead absorption rates are used and applied to cost units as they are being completed (via the work-in-progress account). This ensures that finished units and work-in-progress at the end of a period are valued at their total cost.

3.4   Integrated system example

The following example illustrates the use of an integrated system within a processing organisation.

Note how this system includes accounts for debtors, creditors, bank, capital etc, which differs from the interlocking system example earlier.

From the following informations **you are required**

(a)   to write up the accounts in the cost ledger for June; and

(22 marks)

(b)   to extract a trial balance as at 30 June.

(6 marks)

(Total: 28 marks)

The trial balance of the cost ledger as at 31 May was as follows:

	£	£	£
Stores control		90,400	
Work-in-progress, Process 1:			
Direct materials	8,200		
Direct wages	6,400		
Production overhead	22,400		
		37,000	
Work-in-progress, Process 2:			
Direct materials	31,200		
Direct wages	8,800		
Production overhead	22,000		
		62,000	

	£		£
Finished goods	89,000		
Production overhead, under-/over-absorbed			4,800
Sales			680,000
Cost of sales	529,200		
General ledger control			131,800
Abnormal loss	9,000		
	816,600		816,600

During June the following transactions took place:

	£
Materials returned to suppliers	1,560
Actual cost of materials purchased	42,500
Materials issued to:	
Process 1	21,200
Process 2	10,400
Materials issued to production maintenance department	1,280
Direct wages incurred in:	
Process 1	16,800
Process 2	21,600
Indirect wages and salaries incurred	48,200
Production indirect expenses incurred	72,000
Sales	300,000

Production reports include the following:

	Direct materials £	Direct wages £
Abnormal loss in:		
Process 1	480	400
Process 2	1,400	280
Transfer from:		
Process 1	24,600	19,600
Process 2	110,000	20,520

The value of finished goods in stock at 30 June was £98,200.

Overhead is absorbed by means of direct wages percentage rates.

Production transferred from Process 1 to Process 2 is treated as an item of materials cost in Process 2 accounts.

Stores control

	£		£
Balance, 31 May	90,400	Returns	1,560
Purchases	42,500	Process 1	21,200
		Process 2	10,400
		Production maintenance	1,280
		Balance, 30 June	98,460
	132,900		132,900

Work-in-progress - Process 1

	Material £	Wages £	Overhead £	Total £		Material £	Wages £	Overhead £	Total £
Balance, 31 May	8,200	6,400	22,400	37,000	Abnormal loss	480	400	1,400	2,280
Direct materials	21,200	-	-	21,200	Transfers to				
Direct wages	-	16,800	-	16,800	Process 2	24,600	19,600	68,600	112,800
Production					Balance 30 June	4,320	3,200	11,200	18,720
overhead	-	-	58,800	58,800					
	29,400	23,200	81,200	133,800		29,400	23,200	81,200	133,800

Work-in-progress - Process 2

	Material £	Wages £	Overhead £	Total £		Material £	Wages £	Overhead £	Total £
Balance, 31 May	31,200	8,800	22,000	62,000	Abnormal loss	1,400	280	700	2,380
Transfers in					Transfers to				
(Process 1)	112,800	-	-	112,800	finished goods	110,000	20,520	51,300	181,820
Direct materials	10,400	-	-	10,400	Balance, 30 June	43,000	9,600	24,000	76,600
Direct wages	-	21,600	-	21,600					
Production									
overhead	-	-	54,000	54,000					
	154,400	30,400	76,000	260,800		154,400	30,400	76,000	260,800

Finished goods

	£		£
Balance, 31 May	89,000	Cost of sales (bal. fig.)	172,620
Process 2	181,820	Balance, 30 June	98,200
	270,820		270,820

Production overhead control

	£		£
Indirect wages and salaries	48,200	Balance, 31 May	4,800
Production indirect expenses	72,000	WIP, Process 1	58,800
		WIP, Process 2	54,000
Maintenance	1,280	Balance, 30 June	3,880
	121,480		121,480

Sales

	£		£
Balance, 30 June	980,000	Balance, 31 May	680,000
		General ledger control	300,000
	980,000		980,000

Cost of sales

	£		£
Balance, 31 May	529,200	Balance, 30 June	701,820
Finished goods	172,620		
	———		———
	701,820		701,820
	———		———

General ledger control

	£		£
Returns	1,560	Balance, 31 May	131,800
Sales	300,000	Purchases	42,500
Balance, 30 June	31,340	Direct wages	38,400
		Indirect wages and salaries	48,200
		Production indirect expenses	72,000
	———		———
	332,900		332,900
	———		———

Abnormal loss

	£		£
Balance, 31 May	9,000	Balance, 30 June	13,660
Process 1	2,280		
Process 2	2,380		
	———		———
	13,660		13,660
	———		———

(b) **Trial balance as at 30 June**

	£	£	£
Stores control		98,460	
Work-in-progress, Process 1:			
Direct materials	4,320		
Direct wages	3,200		
Production overhead	11,200		
	———		
		18,720	
Work-in-progress, Process 2:			
Direct materials	43,000		
Direct wages	9,600		
Production overhead	24,000		
	———		
		76,600	
Finished goods		98,200	
Production overhead, under-/over-absorbed		3,880	
Sales			980,000
Cost of sales		701,820	
General ledger control			31,340
Abnormal loss		13,660	
		———	———
		1,011,340	1,011,340
		———	———

4   CHAPTER SUMMARY

The information required in cost accounting is often somewhat different to that required in a financial accounting system. The traditional method of dealing with this is to keep two separate sets of ledgers which are not integrated with each other. This is known as an interlocking system. The alternative is to integrate the two systems and this is known as an integral or integrated system.

5   SELF TEST QUESTIONS

5.1   What is an interlocking system of accounts? (1.1)

5.2   What are the two ways in which an interlocking system can be arranged? (1.1)

5.3   What type of appropriations of profit might there be that are not dealt with in a costing system? (1.4)

5.4   What types of items might be treated differently in financial and costing accounts? (1.4)

5.5   What are integral (or integrated) accounts? (1.5)

5.6   What is the name of the account used in the cost ledger of an interlocking system in order to maintain the double entry? (2.1)

5.7   What types of control accounts are likely to be kept in an interlocking system? (2.2)

5.8   What accounts, other than control accounts and the cost ledger contra, are likely to be kept in an interlocking system? (2.4)

5.9   What are the two main benefits of an integral system of accounting? (3.1)

5.10   In an integral system what would be the double entry for purchase of raw materials? (3.1)

6   EXAMINATION TYPE QUESTION

6.1   Accounting records

A company keeps cost accounting records which are quite separate from its financial accounting records, and prepares a profit and loss account from each of the two sets of records. For the financial year just ended, the figure of 'profit' in the cost accounting records is substantially different from the figure of 'profit' in financial accounting records.

List the items that might cause this difference.

(15 marks)

(CIMA November 1987)

7   ANSWER TO EXAMINATION TYPE QUESTION

7.1   Accounting records

Items included in financial accounts but not in cost accounts

Income:

        Cash, quantity and trade discounts
        Rents receivable
        Profit on sale of assets
        Income from non-trading activities
        Interest on investments
        Dividends on investments

Costs:

> Abnormal losses
> Goodwill written off
> Other intangible assets written down
> Corporation tax
> Donations

Note: dividends paid and proposed do not necessarily cause a 'difference' in the 'profit', only in the balance carried down.

This also applies to transfers to reserves.

Items included in cost accounts but not in financial accounts

Notional charge for rent where premises are owned.

Notional charge for interest on capital employed.

Use of different stock valuation methods (note that this should be reflected in the financial accounts if an efficient stock records system is employed).

Under/over-absorption of overheads.

Depreciation rates/capital allowances for fixed assets.

13 DECISION MAKING - THEORETICAL ASPECTS

INTRODUCTION & LEARNING OBJECTIVES

Syllabus area 6a. Use of relevants, opportunity and notional costs; classification and coding of costs. (Ability required 3).

When you have studied this chapter you should be able to do the following:

- Distinguish between relevant and irrelevant information.

- Identify cost classifications used in decision making.

- Explain the importance of the timing, format and accuracy of information for decision making.

- Explain the decision making cycle.

- Distinguish between different types of problem.

- List typical decision-making situations.

1 RELEVANT AND IRRELEVANT INFORMATION

1.1 Introduction

Decision making requires both quantitative and qualitative information. Such quantitative information comprises costs and revenues which to be of use to the decision maker must be relevant.

1.2 What are relevant costs and revenues?

Relevant costs and revenues are those which are different as a consequence of the decision made or its recommended course of action being taken. Since relevant costs and revenues are those which are different it effectively means costs and revenues which **change** as a result of the decision. Since it is not possible to change the past (because it has already happened), then relevant costs and revenues must be future costs and revenues. Past costs are usually referred to as sunk costs.

1.3 Relevant costs and opportunity costs

Definition Opportunity cost is the value of a benefit sacrificed in favour of an alternative course of action.

An opportunity cost may also be described as the cost of a particular course of action compared to the next best alternative course of action.

Relevant costs may involve incurring a cost or losing a revenue which could be obtained from an alternative course of action. The incurrence of costs is sometimes referred to as cashflow costs whereas the loss of revenue is an opportunity cost. Opportunity cost is an imputed cost, ie, a cost that is not normally recognised in accounting procedures. Opportunity cost has no relevance to financial accounting, but is relevant in decision making.

1.4   Cashflow costs

Cashflow costs are those arising in cash terms as a consequence of the decision. Such costs can never include past costs or costs arising from past transactions or decisions. Costs such as depreciation based on the cost of an asset already acquired can never be relevant, nor can committed costs eg, lease payments in respect of an asset already leased, nor will re-allocations of total costs ever be relevant to the decision. Only costs which change in total because of the decision are relevant costs.

2   COST CLASSIFICATION AND DECISION MAKING

2.1   Introduction

You should recall from your earlier studies that many different classifications of cost may be used depending upon the purpose of the information. For decision making purposes one of the most useful forms of classification is by behaviour, ie, how costs change as the activity level changes. Look back at Chapter 6 to revise fixed costs, variable costs, step-costs and semi-variable costs.

2.2   Cost behaviour and decision making

Some costs are affected by changes in activity to a greater or lesser extent than others. Much of management decision making is concerned with activity, and relevant costs have been described as those which change as a consequence of the decision. Variable costs are those costs which change in proportion to changes in the level of activity. Thus whenever the decision involves increases or decreases in activity it is almost certain that variable costs will be affected and therefore will be relevant to the decision.

Fixed costs are generally regarded as those costs which are **not** affected by changes in the level of activity and therefore are irrelevant to decisions. However, a stepped fixed cost may be relevant.

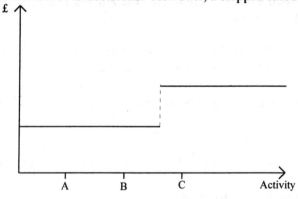

A change in activity from point A to point B does not affect the level of **total** fixed costs because both activity levels lie on the same fixed cost step. For such a decision the fixed cost is irrelevant because it is not changing. However a change in activity from point B to point C does affect the level of total fixed costs. Thus such a decision causes the total fixed costs to change and in such circumstances they are relevant. When fixed costs become relevant to a decision by changing in this way the extra fixed cost is usually referred to as the INCREMENTAL FIXED COST or differential cost.

Semi-variable costs comprise both a fixed and variable element. The variable element is relevant to decision, the fixed element is irrelevant (unless it is a step fixed cost). It is therefore necessary to separate the fixed and variable components of semi-variable costs to isolate the relevant and non-relevant parts of the cost.

3   USING QUANTITATIVE AND QUALITATIVE INFORMATION IN DECISION MAKING

3.1   Introduction

Quantitative information is information expressed in numerical terms. Although in the context of decision making this is often costs and revenues, quantitative information for decision making can also be non-financial information.

Qualitative information is information which cannot be expressed in numerical terms. It is often opinions connected with the effects of a decision.

3.2   Quantitative information

Although often measured in financial terms using costs and revenues measured in monetary units, other forms of quantitative information may be used in a decision making situation. For example the quantity of resources required (materials, labour, machines); or the effects of the decision on percentage market shares could be useful quantitative information.

3.3   Qualitative information

Qualitative information is often in the form of opinions which show the effects of decisions on people and the community within which the entity operates. Interested groups include:

(a)   **Employees** will be affected by certain decisions which may threaten their continued employment, or cause them to need re-training.

(b)   **Customers** will be interested to know about new products, but will want to be assured that service arrangements etc, will continue for existing products;

(c)   **Suppliers** will want to be aware of the entity's plans, especially if smart orders are used within a JIT environment;

(d)   **Competitors** will want to assess their market position following the entity's decision. They may have to make their own decisions as a consequence.

In addition the following other qualitative factors need to be considered when making a decision:

(i)   the effects of inflation

- inflation can seriously affect the validity of cost/revenue estimates.

(ii)   the effects on the environment

- certain decisions may affect emissions and pollution of the environment. The green issue and the entity's responsibility towards the environment may seriously affect its public image.

(iii)   legal effects

- there may be legal implications of a course of action, or a change in law may have been the cause of the decision requirement.

(iv)   political effects

- government policies, both in taxation and other matters may impinge on the decision.

(v)   timing of decision

- the timing of a new product launch may be crucial to its success.

Each of these factors must be considered before making a final decision. Each of these factors is likely to be measured by opinion. Such opinions must be collected and co-ordinated into meaningful information.

4   THE DECISION MAKING CYCLE

4.1   Introduction

The following diagram illustrates the decision making cycle:

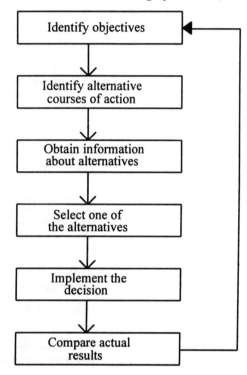

You should note the similarities between this diagram and that of the planning, control and decision making process earlier in this text. The component parts of the decision making cycle are considered in the following paragraphs.

4.2   Identify objectives

The objectives within a decision making context are likely to be to solve a problem although they may be more of a planning nature to improve profitability. You should appreciate that decision making is an integral part of the planning process.

4.3   Alternative courses of action

Once the objectives have been identified the next stage is to determine the courses of action which may be used to meet those objectives and gather information about them. Such information may be quantitative (both monetary and non-monetary) and qualitative. Once the information has been gathered it must be considered and the best course of action chosen.

4.4   Implement the decision

Once the course of action has been chosen the next step is to implement the decision. This may require management to place orders for plant or equipment or other assets, or it may be simply a decision to work overtime or change the product mix. Clearly the timescale in which the decision is implemented will differ depending upon the original objective and the chosen course of action.

4.5   Comparing actual results

This part of the cycle might be described as a post implementation review or audit. Before results can be compared they must be collected using both quantitative and qualitative measures. These results are then compared with the original objectives and where necessary a further decision is made to modify the action being taken.

5   DECISIONS AND QUANTITATIVE TECHNIQUES

5.1   Introduction

Decisions made by management can be divided into different types, which can affect the quantitative techniques used to assist in those decisions. The following chapters explain these decision types in more detail, but the following table identifies the types of decision and the quantitative techniques which may be used.

5.2   Typical decision situations

Type of decision		*Quantitative technique*
(1)	ACCEPT/REJECT eg, opening a new factory, buying an asset	CONTRIBUTION ANALYSIS using marginal costing
(2)	RANKING eg, product mix	CONTRIBUTION PER UNIT OF RESOURCE using marginal costing
(3)	CONTROL	VARIANCE ANALYSIS comparisons between actual and target
(4)	INVESTMENT	INVESTMENT APPRAISAL using discounted cashflow techniques

Each of these decision types may include variables, the value of which is uncertain. Uncertainty may be dealt with using probability, expected values and decision trees.

6   CHAPTER SUMMARY

In this chapter we have considered the principles of decision making, starting with the distinction between relevant and irrelevant information.

We then noted that both quantitative and qualitative information may be relevant to a decision and explained how each of these types of information may be used.

The decision making cycle was then compared to the planning process, and the principles of modelling discussed.

Finally different types of decision were identified and the appropriate quantitative techniques for their solution matched with each decision type.

7   SELF TEST QUESTIONS

    7.1   Define a relevant cost. (1.2)

    7.2   Define an opportunity cost. (1.3)

    7.3   Distinguish between fixed and variable costs. (2.2)

    7.4   Explain the relevance of variable costs. (2.2)

    7.5   Explain the relevance of fixed costs. (2.2)

    7.6   Distinguish between quantitative and qualitative information. (3.2, 3.3)

    7.7   Explain the decision making cycle. (4)

8   EXAMINATION TYPE QUESTION

8.1   Relevant costs in decision making

For decision making it is claimed that the relevant cost to use is *opportunity cost*. In practice, management accountants frequently consider costs such as *marginal costs*, *imputed costs* and *differential costs* as the relevant costs.

You are required

(a)   to explain the terms in italics and to give an example of each;

                                                       (6 marks)

(b)   to reconcile the apparent contradiction in the statement;

                                                       (6 marks)

(c)   to explain in what circumstances, if any, fixed costs may be relevant for decision making.

                                                       (5 marks)

                                              (Total: 17 marks)

9   ANSWER TO EXAMINATION TYPE QUESTION

9.1   Relevant costs in decision making

(a)   **Opportunity cost**

        Opportunity cost is 'the value of a benefit sacrificed in favour of an alternative course of action'. It is a measure of the sacrifice made in addition to the price paid for a resource. If, for example, skilled labour is in short supply, then the opportunity cost of using some of that labour for a contract would be the contribution that could otherwise be earned with that labour.

        Marginal cost

        Marginal cost is 'the cost of one unit of product or service which would be avoided if that unit were not produced or provided'. It is usually the variable cost per unit but could include fixed costs if these are increased as a result of producing one more unit (if 'stepped') and can also include the opportunity cost of scarce resources used to make the product.

Imputed costs

Imputed costs are 'costs recognised in particular situations that are not regularly recognised by usual accounting procedures' (*Horngren*). Imputed costs are not usually recognised because they do not represent actual expenditure incurred by the company. Opportunity cost is an imputed cost. An example is notional rent charged to a division which occupies a factory owned by the company to enable comparison with divisions with rented premises.

Differential cost

Differential cost or incremental cost is 'the difference in total cost between alternatives, calculated to assist decision-making'. For example, if alternative 1 involves a rental of £2,000 and alternative 2 involves a rental of £2,500, then choosing alternative 2 instead of alternative 1 will involve a differential cost of £500.

(b)   The apparent contradiction is partly caused by the overlap between the terms used. As mentioned above opportunity cost is an imputed cost. Opportunity cost is also a differential cost, i.e. if selecting one course of action results in use of scarce resources, then the marginal cost plus the lost contribution is the differential cost of consuming the scarce resource.

(c)   Fixed costs may be relevant when they increase as a result of undertaking a particular course of action. For example, if it is necessary to rent an additional piece of equipment for £6,000 in order to increase production volumes from the current maximum capacity of 5,000 units to a capacity of 9,000 units of a product, then that rent is a relevant cost of increasing production even though it is fixed for the range from 5,001 to 9,000 units. For decisions regarding current capacity (up to 5,000 units) the existing fixed costs are not relevant. Fixed costs of this type are often referred to as 'stepped costs'. In the medium to long-term, fixed costs can be affected by a decision and therefore become relevant.

The marginal cost of using a scarce resource is the opportunity cost of an additional unit of that resource. If there are no alternative uses for a resource which has not yet been acquired, the 'value of the benefit sacrificed' is simply the cash spent in acquiring it.

Marginal, imputed and differential costs can be seen to be different examples of opportunity costs. The original statement in this question is therefore seen to be correct. The main difficulty in terminology arises when 'marginal cost' is taken to be the same as 'variable cost'. Variable cost will only be equal to marginal cost under certain circumstances.

14 DECISION MAKING - CVP ANALYSIS

INTRODUCTION & LEARNING OBJECTIVES

Syllabus area 6b. The concept of contribution; relevant costs. (Ability required 3).
Break-even analysis, break-even and profit volume graphs. (Ability required 3).

In the previous chapter the principles of decision-making information were explained. We will now apply those principles to the decision making technique known as CVP analysis.

When you have studied this chapter you should be able to do the following:

- Explain and calculate the breakeven point from data using graphical or mathematical methods.

- Distinguish between the accountant's and economist's breakeven charts.

- Justify the assumptions concerning linearity.

- Comment on the limitations of CVP analysis.

- Explain avoidable, incremental and opportunity costs.

---

1 WHAT IS CVP ANALYSIS?

1.1 Introduction

Cost-volume-profit (CVP) analysis is a technique which uses cost behaviour theory to identify the activity level at which there is neither a profit nor a loss (the breakeven activity level).

It may also be used to predict profit levels at different volumes of activity based upon the assumptions of cost and revenue linearity.

1.2 Cost and revenue assumptions

CVP analysis assumes that selling prices and variable costs are constant per unit and that fixed costs are constant in total.

1.3 What is contribution?

Contribution is the term used to describe the difference between sales revenues and variable costs. This may be calculated in total, or on a per unit basis using selling prices and variable costs per unit.

The difference between contribution and fixed costs is profit (or loss); thus when contribution equals fixed costs, breakeven occurs. A target profit can be converted into a target contribution to use to calculate the number of units required to achieve the desired target profit.

It is very difficult to use profit in the calculations because if total fixed costs are assumed to be constant, fixed cost per unit, and thus profit per unit is changing everytime the activity level changes; whereas contribution per unit is constant.

1.4   Definitions

(a)   Unit contribution   = Selling price per unit – variable costs per unit.

(b)   Total contribution   = Volume × (Unit contribution).

(c)   Contribution target   = Fixed costs + Profit target.

(d)   Volume target $= \dfrac{\text{Contribution target}}{\text{Unit contribution}}$

1.5   Example

Company   :   Widgets Ltd
Product   :   Widgets
Selling price   :   £3 per unit
Variable costs   :   Raw materials, £1 per unit
Fixed costs   :   Factory rent, £500 pa.

(a)   How many widgets must be sold per annum to break-even?

$$\text{Volume target} = \frac{\text{Contribution target}}{\text{Selling price} - \text{variable costs per unit}}$$

$$= \frac{£500 + £0}{£3 - £1} = 250 \text{ widgets.}$$

At sales volume of 250 units per annum, Widgets Ltd will make nil profit or loss:

		£
Sales	250 × £3	750
Variable costs	250 × £1	250
		500
Fixed costs		500
Profit/(loss)		Nil

(b)   If rent goes up by 10% and Widgets Ltd aims to make £200 pa profit, what annual output is needed?

$$\text{Volume target} = \frac{\text{Contribution target}}{\text{Unit contribution}} = \frac{£500 + £50 + £200}{£3 - £1} = 375 \text{ widgets}$$

(c)   Assuming the maximum possible output of Widgets Ltd is 250 widgets pa, what selling price would achieve the required profit target of £200 (assuming the increased rent)?

Contribution target   =   Fixed costs + Profit target
                            =   £550 + £200 = £750

and

Total contribution   =   Volume × (Selling price per unit – Variable costs per unit)

$$\therefore \ 750 \ = \ 250 \times (SP - 1)$$
$$750 \ = \ 250 \ SP - 250$$
$$1{,}000 \ = \ 250 \ SP$$

The required selling price (SP) is therefore, £4 per unit, giving:

			£
Sales	:	250 widgets × £4 =	1,000
Variable costs	:	250 × £1	250
Contribution			750
Fixed costs:			550
Profit			200

The simple example above illustrates that, given the cost/selling price structure, a range of alternative predictions can be easily calculated. Any change in selling price or variable costs will alter unit contribution; changes in fixed costs or profit required will affect the contribution target.

1.6 Contribution to sales ratio

In the above illustration, it was assumed that Widgets Ltd had sold only one product. If it had produced three products, say widgets, gidgets and shmidgets and the unit contribution of each product was different, then it would be uninformative to assess total volume in terms of units.

If, however, the relative proportion of each product sold could be assumed to remain similar or if each product has the same ratio of contribution to sales value, then similar calculations could be made for the business as a whole. Output would be expressed in terms of sales revenue rather than numbers of units, ie:

$$\text{Contribution to sales ratio (C/S ratio)} = \frac{\text{Contribution in £}}{\text{Sales in £}}$$

Note: students may encounter the term profit to volume (or P/V) ratio, which is synonymous with the contribution to sales ratio. Profit to volume is an inaccurate description, however, and should not be used. The C/S ratio is conveniently written as a percentage.

1.7 Example

Widgets Ltd operating statement for year 3 shows:

	Widgets	*Gidgets*	*Schmidgets*	*Total*
Sales units	100	40	60	200
	£	£	£	£
Sales value	400	240	300	940
Variable costs	220	130	170	520
Contribution	180	110	130	420
Fixed costs				350
Profit				70
C/S ratio	45%	46%	43%	44½%

$$\text{Break-even volume in sales value} = \frac{\text{Fixed costs}}{\text{C / S ratio}}$$

$$= \frac{£350}{44\frac{1}{2}\%} = £786.50$$

Thus, the business must sell about £790 of a mixture of widgets, gidgets and shmidgets before it starts to make a profit. The calculation in this instance would be acceptably accurate because the three products have almost identical C/S ratios. If the ratios were significantly different, however, use of the total C/S ratio would imply that the proportions of widgets, gidgets and schmidgets to total sales remained the same over the range of output considered.

1.8   Margin of safety

The difference between budgeted sales volume and break-even sales volume is known as the **margin of safety**. It indicates the vulnerability of a business to a fall in demand. It is often expressed as a percentage of budgeted sales.

1.9   Example

Budgeted sales	:	80,000 units
Selling price	:	£8
Variable costs	:	£4 per unit
Fixed costs	:	£200,000 pa

$$\text{Break even volume} = \frac{200,000}{8-4}$$

$$= 50,000 \text{ units}$$

$$\therefore \text{ Margin of safety} = 80,000 - 50,000$$

$$= 30,000 \text{ units or } 37\frac{1}{2}\% \text{ of budget.}$$

The margin of safety may also be expressed as a percentage of actual sales or of maximum capacity.

Students should note the relationship between the margin of safety when expressed as a percentage of actual sales and the C/S and profit to sales (P/S) ratio.

$$\text{P/S ratio} = \text{Margin of safety} \times \text{C/S ratio.}$$

1.10   Example

	£
Sales	10,000
Variable costs	6,000
	4,000
Fixed costs	2,500
	1,500

(a)   P/S ratio $= \dfrac{1,500}{10,000}$

    $= 15\%$

(b)   C/S ratio $= \dfrac{4,000}{10,000}$

    $= 40\%$

(c)   Break-even sales $= \dfrac{2,500}{0.4}$

    $= £6,250$

Excess sales $= 3,750$

Margin of safety $= \dfrac{3,750}{10,000}$

    $= 37.5\%$

$\therefore$ P/S ratio $= 37.5\% \times 40\%$

    $= 15\%$

2   THE ACCOUNTANT'S AND ECONOMIST'S BREAKEVEN CHARTS

2.1   The accountant's breakeven chart

The accountant's breakeven chart makes certain assumptions concerning the linearity of costs and revenues:

(i)   that selling price is constant per unit irrespective of the number of units to be sold;

(ii)   that fixed costs are constant in total; and

(iii)   that variable costs are constant per unit irrespective of the number of units produced.

There is also an assumption that if there is any difference between sales and production volumes such stocks are valued at their variable cost.

The accountant's breakeven chart is thus depicted with costs and revenues as straight lines as shown below.

Accountant's break-even chart

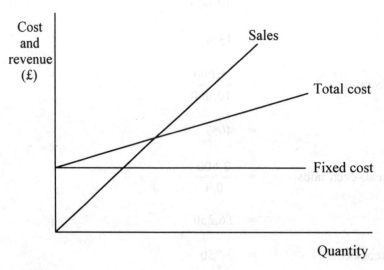

2.2   The economist's breakeven chart

However, most firms would ultimately encounter the conditions generally postulated by the economist:

(a)   it is unlikely the last unit could be sold for the same price as the first; and

(b)   material costs and labour costs rise as output tends upward. The effect of quantity discounts is offset by less efficient production and overtime rates or less skilled labour force.

The economists break-even chart has two break-even points thus:

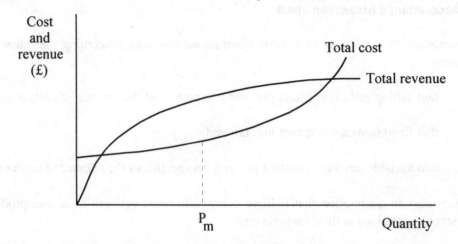

Profit is maximised at the level of output P_m where there is the greatest vertical difference between the total cost and total revenue curves.

3   LINEARITY ASSUMPTIONS AND RELEVANT RANGE

3.1   Introduction

As shown above the economist's model uses curves to represent costs and revenues, because values are not constant per unit.

3.2   Revenue curves

To sell more units demand must be increased, and to do this the price must be reduced. Thus sales revenue may be depicted:

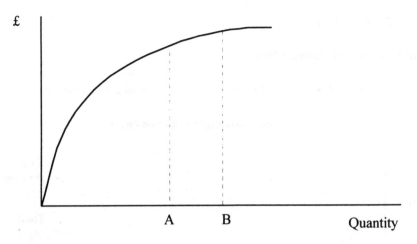

However, in such a chart the range of activity levels depicted is from zero to maximum and this is unlikely to occur in reality. It is more likely that the range of activity will lie between points A and B. It can be seen that between these points the revenue curve is virtually a straight line.

3.3   Curvi-linear variable costs

A similar principle applies to variable costs where it could be argued that the effects of quantity discounts on materials, and overtime/inefficiencies on labour costs cause these to be depicted as curves:

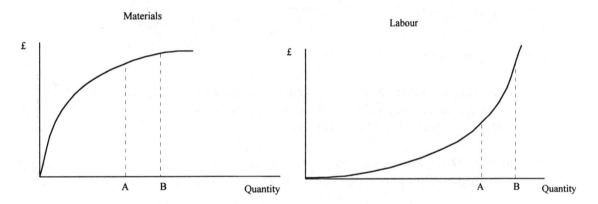

However, two arguments exist to support the accountant's linear model in respect of these costs:

(i)   that if each of these types of cost are added together, their total will approximate to a straight-line; and

(ii)   that within a likely range of activity the curves themselves are virtually linear.

4   BREAK-EVEN CHARTS

4.1   The conventional break-even chart

The conventional break-even chart plots total costs and total revenues at different output levels:

Conventional break-even chart

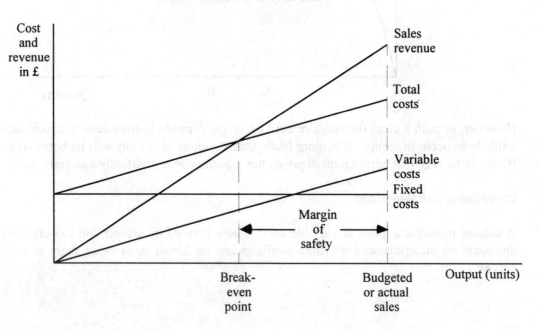

The chart or graph is constructed by:

(a)   plotting fixed costs as a straight line parallel to the horizontal axis;
(b)   plotting sales revenue and variable costs from the origin;
(c)   total costs represent fixed plus variable costs.

The point at which the sales revenue and total cost lines intersect indicates the break-even level of output. The amount of profit or loss at any given output can be read off the chart.

The chart is normally drawn up to the budgeted sales volume.

The difference between the budgeted sales volume and break-even sales volume is referred to as the margin of safety.

4.2   Usefulness of charts

The conventional form of break-even charts was described above. Many variations of such charts exist to illustrate the main relationships of costs, volume and profit. Unclear or complex charts should, however, be avoided as a chart which is not easily understood defeats its own object.

Generally, break-even charts are most useful to:

(a)   Compare products, time periods or actual versus plan.
(b)   Show the effect of changes in circumstances or to plans.
(c)   Give a broad picture of events.

4.3   Contribution break-even charts

A contribution break-even chart may be constructed with the variable costs at the foot of the diagram and the fixed costs shown above the variable cost line.

The total cost line will be in the same position as in the break-even chart illustrated above; but by using the revised layout it is possible to read off the figures of contribution at various volume levels, as shown in the following diagram:

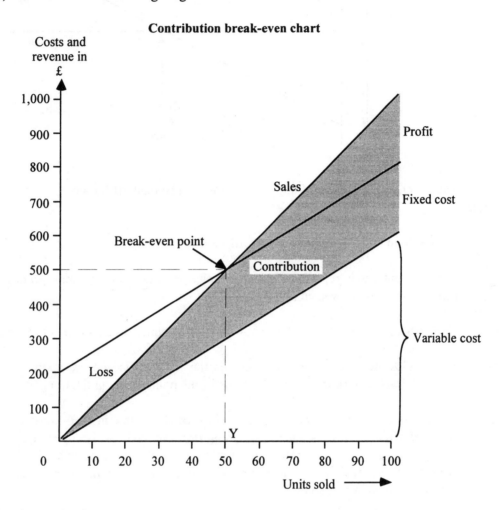

Contribution break-even chart

4.4   Profit-volume chart

Break-even charts usually show both costs and revenues over a given range of activity and they do not highlight directly the amounts of profits or losses at the various levels. A chart which does simply depict the net profit and loss at any given level of activity is called a **profit-volume chart (or graph)**.

Profit-volume chart (1)

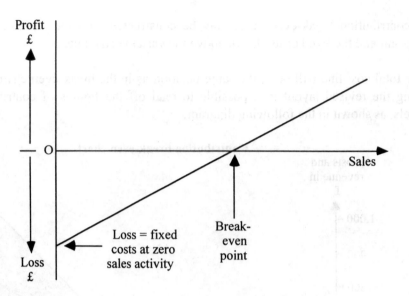

From the above chart the amount of net profit or loss can be read off for any given level of sales activity.

The points to note in the construction of a profit-volume chart are:

(a)   The horizontal axis represents sales (in units or sales value, as appropriate). This is the same as for a break-even chart.

(b)   The vertical axis shows net profit above the horizontal sales axis and net loss below.

(c)   When sales are zero, the net loss equals the fixed costs and one extreme of the 'profit volume' line is determined - therefore this is one point on the graph or chart.

(d)   If variable cost **per unit** and fixed costs **in total** are both constant throughout the relevant range of activity under consideration, the profit-volume chart is depicted by a straight line (as illustrated above). Therefore, to draw that line it is only necessary to know the profit (or loss) at one level of sales. The 'profit-volume' line is then drawn between this point and that determined in (c) and extended as necessary.

(e)   If there are changes in the variable cost per unit or total fixed costs at various activities, it would be necessary to calculate the profit (or loss) at each point where the cost structure changes and to plot these on the chart. The 'profit-volume' line will then be a series of straight lines joining these points together, as simply illustrated as follows:

Profit-volume chart (2)

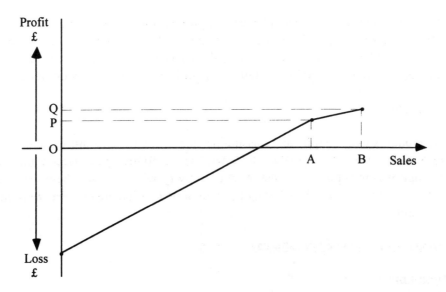

This illustration depicts the situation where the variable cost per unit increases after a certain level of activity (OA) eg, because of overtime premiums that are incurred when production (and sales) exceed a particular level.

Points to note:

(a)   the profit (OP) at sales level OA would be determined and plotted;

(b)   similarly the profit (OQ) at sales level of OB would be determined and plotted;

(c)   the loss at zero sales activity (= fixed costs) can be plotted;

(d)   the 'profit-volume' line is then drawn by joining these points, as illustrated.

4.5   Requirements of break-even analysis model

Break-even analysis is useful insofar as it either meets or approximates to the requirements of the model. These requirements are:

(a)   Cost can be classified as either fixed or variable.

(b)   Over the time scale and activity range under review, unit variable costs remain constant and total fixed costs remain constant.

(c)   Unit sales price remains constant.

(d)   The costs and relationships are known.

Despite the obvious limitations these requirements impose, break-even analysis is of great practical importance. This is not just for itself, but because of the understanding it gives of cost behaviour patterns for decision purposes, considered further below.

5   LIMITATIONS OF CVP ANALYSIS

5.1   Introduction

The requirements of the breakeven model referred to above, limit the usefulness of CVP analysis for planning and decision making. In particular its usefulness is limited in multi-product situations and where uncertainty of input values exists.

5.2   Multi-product situations

When an organisation sells more than one product there is always difficulty in identifying the fixed costs relating to a specific product, and inevitably there will be some fixed costs which are not product specific. Consequently a particular sales mix has to be assumed in order to use the model, and then the breakeven point can only be quantified in terms of sales values.

5.3   Uncertainty

The model is over-simplistic by assuming that variable costs are constant per unit and fixed costs are constant in total. In reality there will be economies and diseconomies of scale which occur, although it is uncertain as to the level of activity which causes them, and the extent to which the costs will be affected. The CVP model cannot be manipulated to deal with these and other forms of uncertainty.

6   AVOIDABLE AND INCREMENTAL COSTS

6.1   Avoidable cost

 An avoidable cost is a cost which will not be incurred if a particular decision is made. It is usually used in the context of a fixed cost. For example if a fixed cost can be identified to the production of a single product, and the production of that product is stopped, then the fixed cost would not be incurred: it is therefore avoided because of the decision.

6.2   Incremental cost

 An incremental cost is the extra cost incurred as a result of a decision. Thus if a decision is made to increase production and to do so an additional machine is to be leased, then the lease cost of the additional machine is an incremental cost.

7   FIXED COSTS AND TIME

7.1   Introduction

A fixed cost is a cost which is assumed in CVP analysis to remain constant irrespective of the level of activity. Such costs are often considered to be uncontrollable, but this is not usually true within the longer term.

7.2   Controllability and time

The controllability of costs must be considered in connection with the powers of the managers concerned. In the context of fixed costs it is common for costs to be uncontrollable because of a contractual agreement or similar long-term arrangement. Thus the cost is uncontrollable within the short-term but outside this timescale the agreement will eventually lapse, or significant changes can be made to production methods. When this occurs costs which were uncontrollable become controllable because of a decision opportunity. However, once the decision has been made, the cost becomes uncontrollable at its new level and therefore fixed once again.

8   RELEVANT COSTS FOR SPECIFIC DECISION SITUATIONS

8.1   Accept or reject decision analysis: an illustration

Spartan plc manufactures a wide range of soft toys. The managers of the business are considering whether to add a new type of toy animal, the Wimble, to the product range. A recent market research survey, undertaken at a cost of £2,000, has indicated that demand for the Wimble would last for only one year, during which time 100,000 of these could be sold at £6 each.

It is assumed that production and sales of the Wimble would take place evenly throughout the year. Manufacturing cost data is available as below.

Raw materials

Each Wimble would require three types of raw material, A, B and C. Material A is used regularly in the business and stocks are replaced as necessary. Material B is currently being held as surplus stock as a result of over-ordering on an earlier contract. This material is not used regularly by Spartan plc and would be sold if not required for the manufacture of the Wimble. Material C would have to be bought in specially for the Wimble, since stocks of this item are not normally held.

Current stock levels and costs of each raw material are shown below:

Raw material	Amount required per Wimble (m)	Current stock level (m)	Original cost (£/m)	Replacement cost (£/m)	Realisable value (£/m)
A	0.8	200,000	1.05	1.25	0.90
B	0.4	30,000	1.65	1.20	0.55
C	0.1	0	-	2.75	2.50

Labour

In producing one Wimble, half an hour of skilled labour and a quarter of an hour of unskilled labour would be required, at wage rates of £3 per hour and £2 per hour respectively. One supervisor would be required full-time at an annual salary of £7,000.

Skilled labour for the production of Wimbles would have to be recruited specially, whilst 25,000 surplus unskilled labour hours are expected to be available during the coming year if Wimbles are not manufactured. However, company policy dictates that no unskilled worker will be made redundant in the foreseeable future.

The supervisor has agreed to delay immediate retirement for one year, and to waive his annual pension of £4,000 in return for his annual salary during this period.

Machinery

Two machines, X and Y, would be required to manufacture Wimbles, details of which are as below:

	X	Y
Original cost	£35,000	£25,000
Accumulated depreciation	£24,000	£18,000
Written down value	£11,000	£7,000
Age	4 years	6 years
Estimated remaining useful life	1 year	2 years
Estimated value at end of useful life	£5,000	£1,000

Details are also available of cash values relating to the two machines at the start and end of the year during which Wimbles would be produced.

		Start of the year £	End of year £
Machine X:	Replacement cost	40,000	45,000
	Resale value	7,000	5,000
Machine Y:	Replacement cost	30,000	33,000
	Resale value	4,000	3,000

If machine X is not used for the manufacture of Wimbles then it would be used to manufacture existing products, the sale of which would result in an estimated £50,000 net receipts.

Machine X is one of a number of identical machine types used regularly on various products by Spartan plc. Each of this type of machine is replaced as soon as it reaches the end of its useful life.

Machine Y is the only one of its type within the firm and if not used in the manufacture of Wimbles would be sold immediately.

Overheads

Variable overhead costs attributable to Wimbles are estimated at £1.50 per item produced. Production fixed overheads are allocated by Spartan plc to products on the basis of labour hours, and the rate for the coming year has been established at £2.50 per labour hour. The manufacture of Wimbles will not result in any additional fixed costs being incurred.

We can now turn our attention to assessing whether, on the basis of the information given the manufacture and sale of Wimbles represents a profitable opportunity to Spartan plc. In doing so, the relevant cost of using each resource required to produce Wimbles must be identified. For each resource, a comparison is required showing the cash flows associated with manufacture and those associated with non-manufacture. The difference between the two represents the incremental cost of applying each resource to the production of Wimbles.

Cash flows

	Manufacture £	Non-manufacture £	Incremental cost £
Raw materials			
A	(100,000)	0	(100,000)
B	(12,000)	16,500	(28,500)
C	(27,500)	0	(27,500)
			(156,000)
Labour			
Skilled	(150,000)	0	(150,000)
Unskilled	(50,000)	(50,000)	0
Supervisor	(7,000)	(4,000)	(3,000)
			(153,000)
Machinery			
X	0	40,000	(40,000)
Y	3,000	4,000	(1,000)
			(41,000)
Overheads			
Variable	(150,000)	0	(150,000)
Fixed	-	-	-
			(150,000)
Total incremental cost			(500,000)
Total sales revenue			600,000
Net cash inflow (contribution)			100,000

Thus, £500,000 is the relevant cost to Spartan plc for producing 100,000 Wimbles during the forthcoming year. Taking the cash generated from sales into consideration a net cash inflow of £100,000 would result from this trading opportunity. At this stage you are advised to review critically the build-up of incremental cost shown above before reading further, in order to establish whether or not the principle of relevance has been fully understood. The basis for establishing the relevant cost of each resource is examined below.

Raw materials

A: since this material is used regularly within the business and stocks are replaced as used, the 80,000 metres required would be replaced for subsequent use on other jobs at the current replacement cost of £1.25 per metre.

B: if Wimbles are manufactured a further 10,000 metres would have to be purchased at £1.20 per metre. The historic cost of the 30,000 metres already in stock is a sunk cost and is therefore not relevant. If Wimbles are not manufactured, the existing stock would be sold off at the realisable value of £0.55 per metre.

C: the only cash flow arising here is that relating to the special purchase of 10,000 metres at £2.75 per metre if Wimbles are produced.

To summarise, the relevant cost of raw materials is identified as being their current replacement cost, unless the material in question is not to be replaced, in which case the relevant cost becomes the higher of current resale value or the value if applied to another product (economic value).

Labour

Skilled: in manufacturing Wimbles additional wage payments of £150,000 would be made ie, 50,000 hours @ £3 per hour. These payments relate to specifically recruited labour.

Unskilled: the cost of 25,000 hours of unskilled labour will be incurred by Spartan plc regardless of whether Wimbles are produced. Company policy has effectively turned this unskilled labour wages element into a fixed cost which cannot be adjusted in the short term and is therefore not relevant to the decision at hand.

Supervisor: the relevant cost of the supervisor is the difference between the wages paid if Wimbles are produced, and the pension cost that would be avoided in this situation.

In assessing the relevant cost of labour the avoidable costs of production have been identified ie, those which will not be incurred unless Wimbles are produced. If any element of the labour resource could be used for some other profitable purpose, then the opportunity cost representing the income forgone would have to be included in the analysis.

Machinery

X: it would cost Spartan plc £40,000 if the company were to lose the use of machine X, if the £50,000 annual net receipts associated with the existing use of the machine are to be restored by immediately replacing the loss of that machine. This is known as the **deprival value** and is represented in the analysis by a cash outflow.

Y: the manufacture of Wimbles would delay the sale of machine Y by one year, during which time the resale value of the machine would have been reduced by £1,000 as shown in the table of machine values above.

In determining the relevant costs associated with the use of plant and machinery, similar considerations apply as to those identified in respect of raw materials. If plant and equipment is to be replaced at the end of its useful life, or would be immediately replaced should the business be deprived of the use of an asset, then current replacement cost is the relevant cost. If the asset is not to be replaced, then the relevant cost becomes the higher of resale value or associated net receipts arising from use of the asset (economic value).

In this analysis of relevant cost, the assumption is made that the use of machine X is profitable for the company. If a situation arises in which an asset is not generating sufficient net receipts to meet a target rate of return the replacement of the asset would presumably not be encouraged since its use is uneconomic, and thus replacement cost is not relevant since it would not represent a viable option.

You should note however, that correctly identifying the true cost of using a particular asset may be difficult in practice, since economic values are not easily identified.

Overheads

Variable costs of £1.50 per Wimble are avoidable, being incurred only if Wimbles are produced. In contrast, fixed overhead may be assumed to be fixed regardless of the product being produced and the level of activity over a given range. Since fixed overhead is unaffected by the opportunity being considered, any apportionment of fixed cost is meaningless and would serve only to distort the profitability of the project.

For decision purposes, only those costs that will vary as a result of the decision taken are relevant.

A form of statement similar to that shown above for the analysis of differential cash flows could be used for presentation to management. In addition, supplementary information should be provided in order to disclose the principles adopted in evaluating the cost of use of each resource. Attention should be drawn to the fact that the surplus cash figure of £100,000 is the anticipated increase in Spartan plc's cash reserves arising from the manufacture of Wimbles rather than applying the required resources to their best alternative use.

Thus from a purely financial viewpoint the production and sale of Wimbles appears to be worthwhile. However, as was noted earlier, there may be other factors of interest to the decision-maker. Non-quantifiable qualitative factors such as the effect on longer term marketing strategy, customer reaction, competitor reaction etc, should be identified and incorporated into the analysis so that a balanced judgement may be made.

[Conclusion]   In the above analysis the principle of relevance was applied in the evaluation of the financial factors surrounding the manufacture of Wimbles. At no time was historic cost suggested as being an appropriate measure of the relevant cost of a resource.

This presents a practical problem since conventional cost accounting records deal with costs already incurred ie, historic cost. It may therefore be difficult to extract replacement costs or opportunity costs from the organisation's information system. Moreover, if the relevant cost approach is to be adopted, the accountant is faced with the task of educating managers, if the correct interpretation is to be placed on the figures presented.

However, despite these obstacles to adopting the correct approach to decision-making, the alternative route of applying conventional cost accounting principles is likely to lead to sub optimal decisions. The dangers inherent in the historic cost accounting approach are discussed below.

Generally, the conventional cost accounting approach involves the identification of the historical or estimated costs of the resources actually used on a project, and these are then related to the revenues arising. The costs as identified often include fixed costs which are assigned on a subjective basis and do not therefore directly relate to the project under consideration. As a result, the worthiness of the particular opportunity may well be under or over-estimated.

Consider the conventional profitability statement set out below in relation to the manufacture of Wimbles:

Trading statement: Wimbles

	£	£	£
Sales			600,000
Less: Costs:			
Raw materials			
A (80,000m @ £1.05)	84,000		
B (30,000m @ £1.65 + 10,000m @ £1.20)	61,500		
C (10,000m @ £2.75)	27,500		
		173,000	
Labour			
Skilled (50,000 hours @ £3)	150,000		
Unskilled (25,000 hours @ £2)	50,000		
Supervisor	7,000		
		207,000	
Depreciation of machinery			
X [(11,000 - 5,000) ÷ 1]	6,000		
Y [(7,000 - 1,000) ÷ 2]	3,000		
		9,000	
Overheads			
Market research survey	2,000		
Variable (100,000 @ £1.50)	150,000		
Fixed (75,000 @ £2.50)	187,500		
		339,500	
Total costs			728,500
Trading loss			(128,500)

In applying conventional cost accounting practice, some specific resources are charged to a project at their original cost. Consider, for example, the costs of raw materials applied to the trading statement above. However, the inclusion of historic cost is incorrect for decision analysis. The crucial question to be answered in evaluating a course of action is: how will the cash flows of the business be affected? Thus, in the case of raw materials in our example, only the costs of the extra 10,000 metres of B and the 10,000 metres of additional material C are relevant costs; the historic costs are not, since they do not have any impact on future cash flows.

A second major difference of approach lies in the treatment of depreciation of assets. The traditional accounting methods of depreciation, such as those on a straight line or reducing balance basis, are an extension of the practice of matching or recovering past costs. Yet for decision purposes what is required is an evaluation of the sacrifice involved in using the asset on the project under consideration.

The third area of difference concerns fixed costs. In the example above, there are unskilled labour wages and fixed overhead costs in respect of the decision to manufacture Wimbles since they cannot be affected by it. Nevertheless, fixed costs such as these are often assigned to available project opportunities under conventional accounting practice.

It has been shown that the differences between conventional accounting practice and differential cash flow analysis may give rise to alarming discrepancies. In our example a conventional trading 'loss' of £128,500 is in fact an incremental cash flow surplus of £100,000. It is therefore not difficult to envisage sub-optimal decisions being taken as a result of advice which is based on conventional accounting practice. The notion of 'different costs for different purposes' should be borne in mind when providing financial information for managers.

9   CHAPTER SUMMARY

This chapter has considered the application of cost behaviour to CVP analysis and the calculation of output levels to achieve target profits using breakeven theory.

We have then seen how the accountant's and economist's breakeven charts differ and explained the concept of the relevant range.

Finally the limitations of CVP analysis were considered and related to avoidable, incremental and controllable costs within the short and long term time horizon.

10   SELF TEST QUESTIONS

10.1   What is CVP analysis? (1.1)

10.2   What is contribution? (1.3)

10.3   What is the contribution to sales ratio? (1.7)

10.4   Explain the term 'Margin of Safety'. (1.9)

10.5   Distinguish between the accountant's and economist's breakeven chart. (2.1, 2.2)

10.6   Explain the concept of the 'relevant range' in the context of CVP analysis. (3)

10.7   Explain the limitations of CVP analysis. (5)

10.8   Explain the term 'avoidable cost'. (6.1)

10.9   Explain the term 'incremental cost'. (6.2)

10.10   Explain the importance of the time horizon in respect of fixed cost classification. (7)

11   EXAMINATION TYPE QUESTION

11.1   Shoe shop

The following details relate to a shop which currently sells 25,000 pairs of shoes annually

Selling price per pair of shoes	£40
Purchase cost per pair of shoes	£25

Total annual fixed costs

	£
Salaries	100,000
Advertising	40,000
Other fixed expenses	100,000

You are required:

Answer each part independently of data contained in other parts of the requirement.

(a)   Calculate the break-even point and margin of safety in number of pairs of shoes sold.

(b)   Assume that 20,000 pairs of shoes were sold in a year.

Accumulate the shop's net income (or loss).

(c)   If a selling commission of £2 per pair of shoes sold was to be introduced, how many pairs of shoes would need to be sold in a year in order to earn a net income of £10,000?

(d)   Assume that for next year an additional advertising campaign costing £20,000 is proposed, whilst at the same time selling prices are to be increased by 12%.

What would be the break-even point in number of pairs of shoes?

12   ANSWER TO EXAMINATION TYPE QUESTION

12.1   Shoe shop

(a)   Break-even point $= \dfrac{\text{Total fixed costs}}{\text{Contribution per pair}}$

Contribution per pair   = Selling price – Variable cost = 40 – 25 = 15

Break-even point $= \dfrac{100,000 + 40,000 + 100,000}{15}$

= 16,000 pairs

Margin of safety   = Current levels of sales – Break-even sales

= 25,000 – 16,000

= 9,000 pairs

(b)   Net income from sale of 20,000 pairs:

	£
Contribution: 20,000 × 15	300,000
Less: Fixed costs	240,000
Net proft	60,000

(c)   Sales volume for a required profit $= \dfrac{\text{Total fixed cost + Required profit}}{\text{Contribution per pair}}$

$= \dfrac{240,000 + 10,000}{15 - 2}$

Sales volume for a net income of £10,000 =   19,231 pairs

Note: Because of the need for a whole number answer, actual net income will be [19,231 × 13 – 240,000] ie, £10,003.

(d)   Break-even point = $\dfrac{240,000 + 20,000}{\left(15 + \left(40 \times \dfrac{12}{100}\right)\right)}$

Break-even point = $\dfrac{260,000}{19.8}$ = 13,132 pairs

Note: again this whole number answer results in just above break-even point being achieved ie,

Contribution: 13,132 × 19.8 =	260,013.6
Less: Fixed costs	260,000.0
Net income	13.6

15 DECISION MAKING - TECHNIQUES

INTRODUCTION & LEARNING OBJECTIVES

Syllabus area 6b. Limiting factors, including problems requiring graphical linear programming solutions. (Ability required 2).
Decisions about alternatives, such as make or buy. (Ability required 3).
Product sales pricing and mix. (Ability required 2).

In this chapter a number of decision making situations are illustrated with examples.

When you have studied this chapter you should be able to do the following:

- Identify different types of decision making situation.

- Explain the technique to be used in different decision making situations.

- Select and use relevant data to solve decision making problems.

---

1 DECISION MAKING AND TIME HORIZONS

1.1 Introduction

Decision making may be applied to solve short-term operating problems or be part of the longer term planning process. In this way decision making may be stated to be short-term or long-term.

1.2 Short term decision making

Short term decision making assumes that decisions previously made concerning fixed plant and equipment cannot be altered. Thus such decisions often involve making the best use of existing resources.

1.3 Long term decision making

In the longer term earlier decisions may be altered, new investment in plant and equipment may be considered, and so such decisions have more variables and are more complex.

Long term decisions require more assumptions about the future and must consider the opportunity cost of investing for a future reward. These aspects of uncertainty and the time value of money are considered later in this text.

2 QUALITATIVE FACTORS IN SOURCING AND PRODUCT LINE DECISIONS

2.1 Introduction

In any decision making situation, the decision made will impact on a number of interested groups, such as employees, customers, suppliers and competitors and may also affect the scarce resource management. Each of these factors is considered below.

2.2   Qualitative factors

The following factors (interested groups) may be affected by a decision:

- employees. Any decision which affects working practices will have a morale effect on employees. Some decisions, such as to close a department, will have a greater effect than others, for example an increase in production, but both will affect employees.

- customers. Customers will be affected by any decision which changes the finished product or its availability. For example, the deletion of a product will force customers to choose an alternative item.

- suppliers. Suppliers will be affected by changes to production which require different raw materials or delivery schedules. For example an increase in production may cause the supplier to increase their production of the raw material.

- competitors. Any decision to change product specification or pricing will affect competitors who will then choose whether or not to respond.

- scarce resource management. A change in production as a result of the decision may alter the demand for individual resources thus changing the resource availability.

3   QUANTITATIVE AND QUALITATIVE FACTORS AND THE DECISION MAKING CYCLE

3.1   The decision making cycle

The decision making cycle was explained earlier in this text; you should remember that it contains three fundamental phases:
- identify objectives and courses of action available;
- select alternative and implement the decision;
- compare actual results.

3.2   Quantitative factors

In each of the three phases identified above numerical data will be collected to establish the objective, to identify the best course of action, and to compare the actual results with the target. Examples of such quantitative factors include:
- percentage market share
- likely demand patterns
- cost of investment
- actual sales volume (units)
- actual sales value
- market sales volume (units).

3.3   Qualitative factors

In each phase there are also qualitative factors to be considered, which may include:
- social and environmental effects of a particular objective;
- the opinions of customers and employees.

4   LIMITING FACTORS

November 1996 students

The syllabus refers to limiting factors, but does not specify further, apart from the requirement to study linear programming. You should study this section in full.

May 1997 students

The syllabus is amended to state 'Limiting factors, single scarce resource problems including situations with demand constraints'. You must still study this section in full.

4.1   Introduction

In most business situations only a limited number of business opportunities may be undertaken. Some factor will limit the ability to undertake all the alternatives. This factor is referred to as the **limiting factor**.

4.2   Production scheduling with one limiting factor

Consider the situation where there is one factor limiting operations and two or more possible products. The management accountant must advise management on how to schedule production so as to maximise profits subject to the constraint.

The essential elements of the problem are as follows:

(a)   The object is to maximise profits. Therefore only costs and revenues that vary according to the decision are considered; since fixed costs do not, they are irrelevant and may be ignored.

(b)   This leaves revenue and variable costs, which together specify the contribution of each product line. The aim is to maximise the total contribution.

(c)   The real cost of producing Product 1 rather than Product 2 is the contribution of Product 2 forgone - the opportunity cost. It must be ensured that the total contribution of Product 1 gained exceeds that of Product 2 lost.

(d)   Total contribution is given by units multiplied by contribution per unit. The number of units is limited by the limiting factor. In the evaluation of alternative products consideration must be given not only to contribution per unit, but also to the number of units that can be produced, subject to the limiting factor.

(e)   To take both of these factors together, total contribution is maximised by concentrating on that product which yields the **highest contribution per unit of limiting factor**.

4.3   Example

A company makes and sells two products - X and Y. It has a shortage of labour, which is limited to 200,000 hours pa. This is insufficient to satisfy the full demand for both products. The unit costs, contributions and labour hours used are as follows:

	Product X	*Product Y*
Labour hours per unit of output	5	10
	£	£
Selling price	80	100
Variable cost	50	50
Contribution per unit	30	50

There are two ways in which the production scheduling problem can be solved.

(a)   Calculate total contribution if each is produced in turn:

Total contribution

$$\text{Product X units} = \frac{200,000}{5} = 40,000$$
$$\text{Contribution} \times \text{units} = £30 \times 40,000 \qquad\qquad £1,200,000$$

$$\text{Product Y units} = \frac{200,000}{10} = 20,000$$
$$\text{Contribution} \times \text{units} = £50 \times 20,000 \qquad\qquad £1,000,000$$

Thus, Product X would be produced since it maximises total contribution.

(b)   The quicker alternative is to find which product has the higher contribution per unit of limiting factor ie, per labour hour:

Contribution per labour hour

$$\text{Product X} = \frac{£30}{5} = \qquad\qquad £6$$
$$\text{Product Y} = \frac{£50}{10} = \qquad\qquad £5$$

This is of course merely a way of short-cutting the calculations in (a) above, and exactly the same conclusion is reached: production should concentrate on Product X.

4.4   Other considerations in the limiting factor situation

(a)   In the long run management must seek to remove the limiting factor. In the above example management should be recruiting and training additional labour. Thus, any one limiting factor should only be a short-term problem. However, as soon as it is removed it will be replaced by another limiting factor.

(b)   Even in the short run management may be able to find ways round the bottleneck eg, overtime working, temporary staff and sub-contracting might all be solutions to the situation described.

(c)   Nor may it always be easy to identify the limiting factor. In practice several limiting factors may operate simultaneously. However, even in examination questions, where there is only one limiting factor, it may be necessary to identify between several possible limiting factors.

(d)   It is also possible that there may be other parameters setting minimum production levels eg, there may be a contract to supply Y so that certain minimum quantities must be produced.

4.5   Example

X Ltd makes three products, A, B and C, of which unit costs, machine hours and selling prices are as follows:

	Product A	Product B	Product C
Machine hours	10	12	14
	£	£	£
Direct materials @ 50p per lb	7 (14 lbs)	6 (12 lbs)	5 (10 lbs)
Direct wages @ 75p per hour	9 (12 hours)	6 (8 hours)	3 (4 hours)
Variable overheads	3	3	3
Marginal cost	19	15	11
Selling price	25	20	15
Contribution	6	5	4

Sales demand for the period is limited as follows:

Product A	4,000
Product B	6,000
Product C	6,000

As a matter of company policy it is decided to produce a minimum of 1,000 units of Product A. The supply of materials in the period is unlimited, but machine hours are limited to 200,000 and direct labour hours to 50,000.

Indicate the production levels that should be adopted for the three products in order to maximise profitability, and state the maximum contribution.

4.6   Solution

First determine which is the limiting factor. At potential sales level:

	Sales potential units	Total machine hours	Total labour hours
Product A	4,000	40,000	48,000
Product B	6,000	72,000	48,000
Product C	6,000	84,000	24,000
		196,000	120,000

Thus, labour hours is the limiting factor. The next stage is to calculate contribution per labour hour:

Product A $\frac{£6}{12}$ = £0.500

Product B $\frac{£5}{8}$ = £0.625

Product C $\frac{£4}{4}$ = £1.000

Thus, production should be concentrated on C, up to the maximum available sales, then B, and finally A.

However, a minimum of 1,000 units of A must be produced. Taking these factors into account, the production schedule becomes:

	Units produced	Labour hours	Cumulative labour hours	Limiting factor
Product A	1,000	12,000	12,000	Policy to produce 1,000 units
Product C	6,000	24,000	36,000	Sales
Product B	1,750	14,000	50,000	Labour hours

5   PROBLEMS INVOLVING PRODUCT MIX AND DISCONTINUANCE

5.1   Introduction

It is considered more informative to present comparison statements on a contribution basis, because where two or more products are manufactured in a factory and share all production facilities, the fixed overhead can only be apportioned on an arbitrary basis, and thus should not influence figures used for decision making.

5.2   Example

A factory manufactures three components – X, Y and Z – and the budgeted production for the year is 1,000 units, 1,500 units and 2,000 units respectively. Fixed overhead amounts to £6,750 and has been apportioned on the basis of budgeted units: £1,500 to X, £2,250 to Y and £3,000 to Z. Sales and variable costs are as follows:

	Component X	Component Y	Component Z
Selling price	£4	£6	£5
Variable cost	£1	£4	£4

The budgeted profit and loss account based on the above is as follows:

	Component X		Component Y		Component Z		Total	
Sales units	1,000		1,500		2,000		4,500	
	£	£	£	£	£	£	£	£
Sales value		4,000		9,000		10,000		23,000
Variable cost	1,000		6,000		8,000		15,000	
Fixed overhead	1,500		2,250		3,000		6,750	
		2,500		8,250		11,000		21,750
Net profit/(loss)		1,500		750		(1,000)		1,250

Clearly there is little value in comparing products in this way. If the fixed overhead is common to all three products, there is no point in apportioning it. A better presentation is as follows:

	Component X	Component Y	Component Z	Total
Sales units	1,000	1,500	2,000	4,500
	£	£	£	£
Sales value	4,000	9,000	10,000	23,000
Variable cost	1,000	6,000	8,000	15,000
Contribution	3,000	3,000	2,000	8,000
Fixed cost				6,750
Net profit				1,250

Analysis may show, however, that certain fixed costs may be associated with a specific product and the statement can be amended to differentiate specific fixed costs (under products) from general fixed costs (under total).

5.3   Closure of a business segment

Part of a business may appear to be unprofitable. The segment may, for example, be a product, a department or a channel of distribution. In evaluating closure the cost accountant should identify:

(a)   loss of contribution from the segment;

(b)   savings in specific fixed costs from closure;

(c)   penalties eg, redundancy, compensation to customers etc;

(d)   alternative use for resources released;

(e)   non-quantifiable effects.

5.4   Example

Harolds department store comprises three departments - Menswear, Ladies' Wear and Unisex. The store budget is as follows:

	Mens £	Ladies £	Unisex £	Total £
Sales	40,000	60,000	20,000	120,000
Direct cost of sales	20,000	36,000	15,000	71,000
Department costs	5,000	10,000	3,000	18,000
Apportioned store costs	5,000	5,000	5,000	15,000
Profit/(loss)	10,000	9,000	(3,000)	16,000

It is suggested that Unisex be closed to increase the size of Mens and Ladies.

What information is relevant or required?

5.5   Solution

Possible answers are:

(a)   Unisex earns £2,000 net contribution (store costs will be re-apportioned to Mens/Ladies).

(b)   Possible increase in Mens/Ladies sales volume.

(c)   Will Unisex staff be dismissed or transferred to Mens/Ladies?

(d)   Reorganisation costs eg, repartitioning, stock disposal.

(e)   Loss of custom because Unisex attracts certain types of customer who will not buy in Mens/Ladies.

5.6   Comparing segment profitability

When presenting information for comparing results or plans for different products, departments etc, it is useful to show gross and net contribution for each segment. The information in the example above would be presented in the following form.

	Menswear	Ladies Wear	Unisex	Total
	£'000	£'000	£'000	£'000
Sales	40	60	20	120
Direct cost of sales	20	36	15	71
Gross contribution	20	24	5	49
Department costs	5	10	3	18
Net contribution	15	14	2	31

Note that the store costs if shown would only appear in the total column. In addition, the statement should include performance indicators relevant to the type of operation. For a department store, such indicators would include:

(a)   C/S ratios (based on **gross** contribution);
(b)   gross and net contribution per unit of floor space;
(c)   gross and net contribution per employee.

For a manufacturing company, more relevant indicators would include:

(a)   contribution per labour/machine hour;
(b)   added value/conversion cost per hour;
(c)   added/value conversion cost per employee.

5.7   Temporary shut-down

When a business has experienced trading difficulties which do not appear likely to improve in the immediate future, consideration may be given to closing down operations temporarily. Factors other than cost which will influence the decision are:

(a)   suspending production and sales of products will result in their **leaving the public eye;**

(b)   dismissal of the labour force will entail bad feeling and possible difficulty in recruitment when operations are restarted;

(c)   danger of plant obsolescence;

(d)   difficulty and cost of closing down and restarting operations in certain industries eg, a blast furnace.

The temporary closure of a business will result in additional expenditure eg, plant will require protective coverings, services will be disconnected. In the same way, additional expenditure will be incurred when the business restarts.

On the other hand, a temporary closure may enable the business to reorganise efficiently to take full advantage of improved trading conditions when they return.

In the short term a business can continue to operate while marginal contribution equals fixed expenses. In periods of trading difficulty, as long as some contribution is made towards fixed expenses, it will generally be worthwhile continuing operations.

5.8   Example

A company is operating at 40% capacity and is considering closing down its factory for one year, after which time the demand for its product is expected to increase substantially. The following data applies:

	£
Sales value at 40% capacity	60,000
Marginal costs of sales at 40% capacity	40,000
Fixed costs	50,000

Fixed costs which will remain if the factory is closed amount to £20,000. The cost of closing down operations will amount to £4,000.

Prepare a statement to show the best course of action.

Statement of profit or loss

Continuing operation	£	*Temporary closure*	£
Sales	60,000	Fixed expenses	20,000
Marginal cost of sales	40,000	Closing down costs	4,000
Contribution to fixed costs	20,000		
Fixed costs	50,000		
Net loss	(30,000)		(24,000)

Ignoring non-cost considerations, the company will minimise its losses by closing down for one year.

Students should note that the marginal contribution of £20,000 does not cover the difference between existing fixed costs and those that remain on closure (ie, £(50,000 − 24,000) = £26,000 compared to £20,000).

6   DIVESTMENT

6.1   Introduction

A company may have to drop existing product-market areas as well as develop new ones. For instance, a product might be nearing the end of its life cycle and it might be better to 'kill it off' once sales have fallen below a certain level rather than let it decline to zero. Advertising expenditure to boost the sale of a declining product is often not worthwhile in terms of the return achieved.

The precise timing of a decision to drop a certain line (or cease selling it in a particular market) is admittedly difficult, but most companies probably tend to leave it too late. Some of the reasons for the reluctance to drop products are:

(a)   The company might have invested large sums of money in the project and does not want to abandon it.   Management accountants will recognise that this is a quite erroneous standpoint – the money already spent is a sunk cost and it is the future not the past which is important. Companies should be prepared to 'cut their losses' – it is no good throwing good money after bad.

(b)   Perhaps the person who designed the product is still with the firm. He and probably many others are 'attached' to the product and want to keep it going. In addition, the marketing director might be an optimist who thinks that sales of the product will suddenly turn up again. This can happen, but is unlikely unless the cause of the fall in demand is the general economic climate – but we are really talking about products which have a history of continuously falling demand.

(c)   Attention is directed towards new products and no-one thinks what should happen to the old ones (until resources are scarce and there is a search for economies).

(d)   There is a feeling that customers should be kept happy and a fear that they will be lost to the firm if the particular product is withdrawn. This fear need have no foundation if a new product is launched as the old one is withdrawn. Anyway, does it matter if some old customers are lost, as long as more new ones are gained?

(e)   A very real problem exists of what to do with the work force who have been running an existing production line if it is suddenly shut down. It may be easier to absorb the work force into other areas if production is run down gradually. There are, however, arguments against this:

   (i)   Morale among those remaining on the product may fall if they know that their job is eventually going to go and they do not know when, or where they will be moved. If this loss of morale is reflected in their work the product may become even more uneconomic.

   (ii)   A sensible programme of retraining can ensure that workers released from an old line will be available for a new process.

   (iii)   It may prove more costly to keep the workers employed on the old process than to pay them for doing nothing until their services are again required elsewhere.

The detailed programming of divestment is of course a matter for the administrative and operating plans, but at the strategic level it is important to emphasise that this is one area for examination.

6.2   Example on shut down and divestment

The annual flexible budget of a company is as follows:

Production capacity	40%	60%	80%	100%
Costs:	£	£	£	£
Direct labour	16,000	24,000	32,000	40,000
Direct material	12,000	18,000	24,000	30,000
Production overhead	11,400	12,600	13,800	15,000
Administration overhead	5,800	6,200	6,600	7,000
Selling and distribution overhead	6,200	6,800	7,400	8,000
	51,400	67,600	83,800	100,000

Owing to trading difficulties the company is operating at 50% capacity. Selling prices have had to be lowered to what the directors maintain is an uneconomic level and they are considering whether or not their single factory should be closed down until the trade recession has passed.

A market research consultant has advised that in about twelve months' time there is every indication that sales will increase to about 75% of normal capacity and that the revenue to be produced in the second year will amount to £90,000. The present revenue from sales at 50% capacity would amount to only £49,500 for a complete year.

If the directors decide to close down the factory for a year it is estimated that:

(a)   the present fixed costs would be reduced to £11,000 per annum;

(b)   closing down costs (redundancy payments, etc) would amount to £7,500;

(c)   necessary maintenance of plant would cost £1,000 per annum; and

(d)   on re-opening the factory, the cost of overhauling plant, training and engagement of new personnel would amount to £4,000.

Prepare a statement for the directors, presenting the information in such a way as to indicate whether or not it is desirable to close the factory.

6.3   Solution

To: the board of directors

From: the management accountant

Date: X-X-19XX

Subject: desirability of closing the factory for a year

In the forthcoming year (19X1) our alternatives are:

(1)   Continue operating

		£
Sales		49,500
Total cost		59,500
Loss		10,000

(2)   Close down for 19X1 and re-open in 19X2.

		£
(a)	Unavoidable fixed cost	11,000
(b)	Redundancy payment	7,500
(c)	Necessary maintenance	1,000
(d)	Re-opening cost	4,000
		23,500

This is more than twice the loss incurred if we continue at 50% capacity and I would suggest continuing production.

(3)   The anticipated result for 19X2 would be

		£
Sales		90,000
Total cost		79,750
Profit		10,250

Finally assuming the consultant's forecast is correct and we carry on producing, the cumulative position at the end of year 19X2 would be a small profit of £250 without the trauma of closing down.

WORKINGS

(W1)   Since direct labour and direct material increase from zero by equal increments of cost for each 20% change in volume they must be entirely variable. The increments for activity changes on production, administration and selling overhead do not account for all the cost and these must therefore include a fixed proportion.

Production capacity	*40%*	*60%*	*Increment for 20%*	*Fixed*
	£	£	£	£
Direct material	16,000	24,000	8,000	-
Direct wages	12,000	18,000	6,000	-
Production overhead	11,400	12,600	1,200	9,000
Administration	5,800	6,200	400	5,000
Selling and distribution	6,200	6,800	600	5,000
Total			16,200	19,000

Allowance for 50% $= \dfrac{50}{20} \times 16,200 + 19,000 = £59,500$

or

				£
Direct material	$= \dfrac{50}{20} \times 8,000$		$=$	20,000
Direct wage	$= \dfrac{50}{20} \times 6,000$		$=$	15,000
Production overhead	$= \left(\dfrac{50}{20} \times 1,200 \right) + 9,000$		$=$	12,000
Administration	$= \left(\dfrac{50}{20} \times 400 \right) + 5,000$		$=$	6,000
Selling	$= \left(\dfrac{50}{20} \times 600 \right) + 5,000$		$=$	6,500
Total cost				59,500
Revenue at 50%				49,500
Loss at 50% activity				(10,000)

(W2)   Second year

$$\text{Total cost} \quad = \quad \left(\frac{75}{20} \times 16{,}200\right) + 19{,}000 \quad = \qquad 79{,}750$$

Revenue at 75% activity   90,000

Profit at 75% activity   10,250

7   MAKE OR BUY DECISIONS

7.1   Types of make or buy decisions

Occasionally a business may have the opportunity to purchase, from another company, a component part or assembly which it currently produces from its own resources.

In examining the choice, management must first consider the following questions:

(a)   Is the alternative source of supply available only temporarily or for the foreseeable future?

(b)   Is there spare production capacity available now and/or in the future?

7.2   Spare capacity

If the business is operating below maximum capacity, production resources will be idle if the component is purchased from outside. The fixed costs of those resources are irrelevant to the decision in the short term as they will be incurred whether the component is made or purchased. Purchase would be recommended, therefore, only if the buying price were less than the variable costs of internal manufacture.

In the long term, however, the business may dispense with or transfer some of its resources and may purchase from outside if it thereby saves more than the extra cost of purchasing.

7.3   Example

A company manufactures an assembly used in the production of one of its product lines. The department in which the assembly is produced incurs fixed costs of £24,000 pa. The variable costs of production are £2.55 per unit. The assembly could be bought outside at a cost of £2.65 per unit.

The current annual requirement is for 80,000 assemblies per year. Should the company continue to manufacture the assembly, or should it be purchased from the outside suppliers?

7.4   Solution

A decision to purchase outside would cost the company £(2.65 - 2.55) = 10p per unit, which for 80,000 assemblies would amount to £8,000 pa. Thus, the fixed costs of £24,000 will require analysis to determine if more than £8,000 would actually be saved if production of the assembly were discontinued.

7.5   Other considerations affecting the decision

Management would need to consider other factors before reaching a decision. Some would be quantifiable and some not:

(a)   **Continuity and control of supply.** Can the outside company be relied upon to meet the requirements in terms of quantity, quality, delivery dates and price stability?

(b)   **Alternative use of resources.** Can the resources used to make this article be transferred to another activity which will save cost or increase revenue?

(c)   **Social/legal.** Will the decision affect contractual or ethical obligations to employees or business connections?

7.6   Capacity exhausted

If a business cannot fulfil orders because it has used up all available capacity, it may be forced to purchase from outside in the short term (unless it is cheaper to refuse sales). In the longer term management may look to other alternatives, such as capital expenditure.

It may be, however, that a variety of components is produced from common resources and management would try to arrange manufacture or purchase to use its available capacity most profitably. In such a situation the limiting factor concept makes it easier to formulate the optimum plans; priority for purchase would be indicated by ranking components in relation to the excess purchasing cost per unit of limiting factor.

7.7   Example

Fidgets Ltd manufactures three components used in its finished product. The component workshop is currently unable to meet the demand for components and the possibility of sub-contracting part of the requirement is being investigated on the basis of the following data:

	Component A	Component B	Component C
	£	£	£
Variable costs of production	3.00	4.00	7.00
Outside purchase price	2.50	6.00	13.00
Excess cost per unit	(0.50)	2.00	6.00
Machine hours per unit	1	0.5	2
Labour hours per unit	2	2	4

You are required:

(a)   to decide which component should be bought out if the company is operating at full capacity

(b)   to decide which component should be bought out if production is limited to 4,000 machine hours per week

(c)   to decide which component should be bought out if production is limited to 4,000 labour hours per week

7.8   Solution

(a)   Component A should always be bought out regardless of any limiting factors, as its variable cost of production is higher than the outside purchase price.

(b)   If machine hours are limited to 4,000 hours:

	Component B	Component C
Excess cost	£2	£6
Machine hours per unit	0.5	2
Excess cost per machine hour	£4	£3

Component C has the lowest excess cost per limiting factor and should, therefore, be bought out.

Proof:

	Component B	Component C
Units produced in 4,000 hours	8,000	2,000
	£	£
Production costs	32,000	14,000
Purchase costs	48,000	26,000
Excess cost of purchase	16,000	12,000

(c)   If labour hours are limited to 4,000 hours:

	Component B	Component C
Excess cost	£2	£6
Labour hours	2	4
Excess cost per labour hour	£1	£1.50

Therefore, component B has the lowest excess cost per limiting factor and should be bought out.

Proof:

	Component B	Component C
Units produced in 4,000 hours	2,000	1,000
	£	£
Production costs	8,000	7,000
Purchase costs	12,000	13,000
Excess cost of purchase	4,000	6,000

8   EVALUATING PROPOSALS

8.1   Volume and cost structure changes

Management will require information to evaluate proposals aimed to increase profit by changing operating strategy. The cost accountant will need to show clearly the effect of the proposals on profit by pin-pointing the changes in costs and revenues and by quantifying the margin of error which will cause the proposal to be unviable.

8.2 Example

A company produces and sells one product and its forecast for the next financial year is as follows:

	£'000	£'000
Sales 100,000 units @ £8		800
Variable costs:		
Material	300	
Labour	200	
	—	500
Contribution (£3 per unit)		300
Fixed costs		150
Net profit		150

As an attempt to increase net profit, two proposals have been put forward:

(a) to launch an advertising campaign costing £14,000. This will increase the sales to 150,000 units, although the price will have to be reduced to £7;

(b) to produce some components at present purchased from suppliers. This will reduce material costs by 20% but will increase fixed costs by £72,000.

Proposal (a) will increase the sales revenue but the increase in costs will be greater:

	£'000
Sales 150,000 × £7	1,050
Variable costs	750
	300
Fixed costs plus advertising	164
Net profit	136

8.3 Solution

Proposal (a) is therefore of no value and sales must be increased by a further 7,000 units to maintain net profit:

Advertising cost	=	£14,000
Contribution per unit	=	£2
∴ Additional volume required	=	7,000 units

Proposal (b) reduces variable costs by £60,000 but increases fixed costs by £72,000 and is therefore not to be recommended unless the total volume increases as a result of the policy (eg, if the supply of the components were previously a limiting factor). The increase in sales needed to maintain profit at £150,000 (assuming the price remains at £8) would be:

Reduced profits at 100,000 units	=	£12,000
Revised contribution per unit	=	£3.60
∴ Additional volume required	=	3,333 units

8.4   Utilisation of spare capacity

Where production is below capacity, opportunities may arise for sales at a specially reduced price, for example, export orders or manufacturing under another brand name (eg, 'St Michael'). Such opportunities are worthwhile if the answer to two key questions is 'Yes':

(a)   Is spare capacity available?

(b)   Does additional revenue (Units × Price) exceed additional costs (Units × Variable cost)?

However, the evaluation should also consider:

(i)   Is there an alternative more profitable way of utilising spare capacity (eg, sales promotion, making an alternative product)?

(ii)   Will fixed costs be unchanged if the order is accepted?

(iii)   Will accepting one order at below normal selling price lead other customers to ask for price cuts?

The longer the time period in question, the more important are these other factors.

8.5   Example

At a production level of 8,000 units per month, which is 80% of capacity, the budget of Export Ltd is:

	Per unit £	8,000 units £
Sales	5.00	40,000
Variable costs:		
Direct labour	1.00	8,000
Raw materials	1.50	12,000
Variable overheads	0.50	4,000
	3.00	24,000
Fixed costs	1.50	12,000
Total	4.50	36,000
Budgeted profit	0.50	4,000

An opportunity arises to export 1,000 units per month at a price of £4 per unit.

Should the contract be accepted?

8.6   Solution

(a)   Is spare capacity available?   Yes

			£
(b)	Additional revenue	1,000 × £4	4,000
	Additional costs	1,000 × £3	3,000
			1,000

Increased profitability

Therefore, the contract should be accepted.

Note that fixed costs are not relevant to the decision and are therefore ignored.

8.7   Calculation of basic selling price

When a business manufactures a limited range of repetitive products, initial estimation of economic selling prices is most useful.

8.8   Example

The Dainty Dolly Co manufactures a single product, the Dainty, which is a life-size doll selling in the high-price toy market through approved dealers.

The standard cost of the doll is as follows:

	£
Direct material	9
Direct labour	7
Variable factory overhead	4
Variable selling overhead	2

Production capacity is 60,000 pa and market research suggests that with an aggressive sales effort this quantity could be sold.

The company expects a return on capital employed of 20% before tax.

Inflation is expected to be as follows for the variable costs:

Direct material	2%
Direct labour	5%
Variable factory overhead	2%

Fixed costs are not affected by inflation and will be:

Production	£80,100
Selling and administration	£63,300

The company's assets involved in the product are as follows:

Land and buildings	£135,000
Plant and equipment	£125,000
Fixtures and fittings	£40,000

In addition, there will be a working capital requirement which the company estimates will be £10 for each unit produced and sold in the year.

Calculate the list selling price for the Dainty which will cover a dealership discount of 20% on list price and enable the company to achieve its profit objective.

8.9   Solution

	£	£ per unit
Variable costs:		
Direct materials £9 + 2%		9.18
Direct labour £7 + 5%		7.35
Factory overhead £4 + 2%		4.08
Selling overhead		2.00
		22.61
Fixed costs:		
Production	80,100	
Selling and administration	63,300	
	143,400	
Units of production	60,000	
Fixed cost per unit		2.39
Total cost		25.00
Profit required (see workings)		3.00
Sales price to dealer		28.00
20% dealer discount $\frac{20}{80} \times £28.00$		7.00
List price		35.00

WORKINGS

The company requires 20% return on capital employed.

	£
Capital employed:	
Land and buildings	135,000
Plant and equipment	125,000
Fixtures and fittings	40,000
Current assets 60,000 units × £10	600,000
	900,000
20% return	180,000
Return per unit of production	£3.00

8.10   Special contract pricing

A business which produces to customer's order may be working to full capacity. Any additional orders must be considered on the basis of the following questions:

(a)   What price must be quoted to make the contract profitable?

(b)   Can other orders be fulfilled if this contract is accepted?

In such a situation the limiting factor needs to be recognised so that the contract price quoted will at least maintain the existing rate of contribution per unit of limiting factor.

8.11   Example

Oddjobs Ltd manufactures special purpose gauges to customers' specifications. The highly skilled labour force is always working to full capacity and the budget for the next year shows:

	£	£
Sales		40,000
Direct materials	4,000	
Direct wages 3,200 hours @ £5	16,000	
Fixed overhead	10,000	
		30,000
Profit		10,000

An enquiry is received from XY Ltd for a gauge which would use £60 of direct materials and 40 labour hours.

(a)   What is the minimum price to quote to XY Ltd?

(b)   Would the minimum price be different if spare capacity were available but materials were subject to a quota of £4,000 per year?

8.12   Solution

(a)   The limiting factor is 3,200 labour hours and the budgeted contribution per hour is £20,000 ÷ 3,200 hours = £6.25 per hour. Minimum price is therefore:

	£
Materials	60
Wages 40 hours @ £5	200
	260
Add: Contribution 40 hours @ £6.25	250
Contract price	510

At the above price the contract will maintain the budgeted contribution (check by calculating the effect of devoting the whole 3,200 hours to XY Ltd.)

Note, however, that the budget probably represents a mixture of orders, some of which earn more than £6.25 per hour and some less. Acceptance of the XY order must displace other contracts, so the contribution rate of contracts displaced should be checked.

(b)   If the limiting factor is materials, budgeted contribution per £ of materials is £20,000 ÷ 4,000 = £5 per £1.

Minimum price is therefore:

	£
Materials/wages (as above)	260
Contribution £60 × 5	300
Contract price	560

Because materials are scarce, Oddjobs must aim to earn the maximum profit from its limited supply.

9   FURTHER PROCESSING DECISIONS

9.1   Introduction

In processing operations, particularly those involving more than one product, there is often a choice to be made between selling a product in an unfinished state (to another manufacturer) or to further process it into a finished product for sale to the consumer.

9.2   Relevant costs and revenues of further processing decisions

Relevant costs are those which are incurred as a consequence of the decision to further process the item.   Thus common costs incurred already, for example pre-separation costs, should always be ignored.

Relevant revenues are the extra revenues earned from selling the product in its further processed state instead of selling it in its semi-processed state.

9.3   Example

PST Ltd produces three products from a common process which costs £104,000 per month to operate.   Typical monthly outputs are:

Product	Output (litres)
P	10,000
S	5,000
T	8,000

Each of the products may be further processed.   Selling prices and further processing costs per litre are as follows:

	Product		
Cost/Revenues/litre	*P*	*S*	*T*
	£	£	£
Further processing	5.00	3.00	9.00
Selling price:			
Before further processing	11.00	14.00	13.00
After further processing	15.00	19.00	20.00

Advise PST Ltd whether it should further process any of its products.

9.4   Solution

The common cost is irrelevant, only the incremental costs and revenues should be considered:

	Product		
	P	*S*	*T*
	£	£	£
Selling price:			
Before further processing	11.00	14.00	13.00
After further processing	15.00	19.00	20.00
Incremental revenue	4.00	5.00	7.00
Further processing cost	(5.00)	(3.00)	(9.00)
Incremental contribution	(1.00)	2.00	(2.00)

The above table, based on values per litre, shows that the further processing of product S is the only further processing activity which leads to an increase in contribution.

Therefore, PST Ltd should further process product S, but should sell products P and T without further processing them.

9.5   Activity

Z Ltd operates a process which produces three products: X, Y, and Z. Each of these may be sold without further processing or refined and sold as higher quality products. The following costs/revenues have been determined:

		Product	
	X	*Y*	*Z*
Refining cost/litre (£)	3.00	2.50	3.50
Selling prices/litre (£):			
Refined	6.00	5.50	7.00
Unrefined	2.50	2.75	4.00

On the basis of the above, which products, if any, should Z Ltd refine?

9.6   Activity solution

		Product	
	X	*Y*	*Z*
	£	£	£
Incremental revenue/litre (£)	3.50	2.75	3.00
Incremental cost/litre (£)	(3.00)	(2.50)	(3.50)
	0.50	0.25	(0.50)

Products X and Y should be refined.

10   THE CHOICE BETWEEN INTERNAL SERVICE DEPARTMENTS AND EXTERNAL SERVICES

10.1   Introduction

Typically these decision choices are concerned with the administration function of a business, though it is possible to make these choices in other areas, for example in selling a choice may be made between using selling agents or company employees.

10.2   Relevant costs

The decision is very similar to that described earlier as make or buy, the difference being that it is likely that if internal service departments are to be used there will be a significant amount of fixed costs incurred whereas if external services are used the cost may be significantly variable.

10.3 . Example

KRS Ltd is considering whether to administer its own purchase ledger or to use an external accounting service. It has obtained the following cost estimates for each option:

Internal service department:

Purchase computer cost	£1,000
Purchase computer software	£600
Hardware/software maintenance	£750 per annum
Accounting stationery	£500 per annum
Part-time accounts clerk	£6,000 per annum

External services:

Processing of invoices/credit notes	£0.50 per document
Processing of cheque payments	£0.50 per cheque
Reconciling supplier accounts	£2.00 per supplier per month

KRS Ltd would have to assess the forecast volumes of transactions involved before making its decision.

10.4   Qualitative factors

Such decisions will also involve qualitative factors, such as:

- the reliability of supply;
- the quality of supply; and
- security of information.

11   CHAPTER SUMMARY

This chapter has considered a number of specific decision making situations, and illustrated which costs and revenues are relevant to their solution.

12   SELF TEST QUESTIONS

12.1   Distinguish between short and long term decision making. (1.2, 1.3)

12.2   List the qualitative factors in product line decisions. (2.2)

12.3   What is a limiting factor? (4.1)

12.4   What information is relevant in the decision to close down a segment of a business? (5.3)

13   EXAMINATION TYPE QUESTIONS

13.1   JEN Ltd

JEN Ltd manufactures three products, J, E and N, which undergo similar production processes and use similar materials and types of labour. The company's forecast profit statement for the forthcoming year, as submitted to the board, is as follows:

	Product J	*Product E*	*Product N*	*Total*
	£	£	£	£
Sales	1,344,000	840,000	680,000	2,864,000
Direct material	336,000	294,000	374,000	1,004,000
Direct labour	201,600	168,000	136,000	505,600
Variable overhead	268,800	168,000	204,000	640,800
	806,400	630,000	714,000	2,150,400
Contribution	537,600	210,000	(34,000)	713,600
Fixed overhead				113,600
Profit				600,000

At a board meeting, a decision was made to discontinue the production of Product N as demand was falling and there was no possibility of increasing the selling price. Prospects for the other two products, however, were bright and the company had, in the past, been unable to meet the demand. It was decided, therefore, that the labour force released should be used to increase production of Products J and E; 60% of the budgeted labour for Product N being transferred to J and the remainder to E. The increased production of J and E is not expected to change their cost/selling price relationships.

You are required to prepare the revised forecast profit statement and to comment briefly upon the effect of the Board's decision.

(20 marks)

13.2   Hard and soft

A company produces a hard grade and, by additional processing, a soft grade of its product.

A market research study for next year has indicated very good prospects not only for both the hard and soft grades but also for a light grade produced after still further processing.

The raw material is imported and there is a possibility that a quota system will be introduced allowing only a maximum of £300,000 pa of material to be imported.

The company's marketing policy has been to sell 60% of its capacity (or of its allocation of material if the quota is introduced) in the most profitable grade. It has been decided that this policy should continue if it is to produce three grades, but that only 15% of its capacity (or material allocation) should be sold in the least profitable grade.

The budgeted prime costs and selling prices per ton for each grade are as follows:

	Hard	*Soft*	*Light*
	£	£	£
Selling price	70	95	150
Direct material cost	15	20	25
Direct wages (@ £2.50 per hour)	15	25	45

For next year the company's annual production capacity is 225,000 direct labour hours and its fixed overhead is £500,000. Variable overhead is 20% of direct wages.

Fixed overhead is at present absorbed by a rate per ton produced.

You are required:

(a)   to state which of the three grades of product will be most profitable and which will be least profitable in the short term assuming that such volume as can be produced can be sold:

(i)   if the materials quota does not operate;
(ii)   if the materials quota does come into force.

(b)   if the materials quota does come into force, to calculate the budgeted profit for next year from the company's marketing policy if:

(i)   only light grade is produced;
(ii)   all three grades are produced in accordance with present policy.

14   ANSWERS TO EXAMINATION TYPE QUESTIONS

14.1   JEN Ltd

Note: a variable cost is a cost which changes in direct proportion with changes in the volume of production or sales. In this example we have to apply this definition in reverse ie, if we increase the direct labour cost (assumed to be variable) by a certain percentage, then the production volume will increase by the same percentage.

Revised profit statement

	Product J £	Product E £	Total £
Sales	1,888,000	1,112,000	3,000,000
Direct materials	472,000	389,200	861,200
Direct labour	283,200	222,400	505,600
Variable overhead	377,600	222,400	600,000
	1,132,800	834,000	1,966,800
Contribution	755,200	278,000	1,033,200
Fixed overhead			113,600
Profit			919,600

The following points are relevant to the Board's decision:

(a)   The change results in a substantial profit increase of £319,600;

(b)   It is necessary to consider whether there is sufficient additional demand for Products J and E to meet such large increases in volume;

(c)   If the products are at all complementary this may result in sales of Product J and E being adversely affected by not selling Product N;

(d)   Although the products use 'similar' labour it is necessary to confirm that the changes are acceptable to the employees and unions.

(e)   Also, is it reasonable to assume that the same level of efficiency will be maintained by the employees switching from Product N?

WORKINGS

	Product J £	Product E £
Additional direct labour		
£136,000 × 60%	81,600	
£136,000 × 40%		54,400
Existing direct labour	201,600	168,000
Percentage increase	$\dfrac{81,600}{210,600} \times 100$	$\dfrac{54,400}{168,000} \times 100$
	= 40.476%	= 32.381%

As direct labour is a variable cost and assuming the same level of efficiency the production and sales volume of Product J and Product E will increase by these respective percentages.

14.2   Hard and soft

(a)   In the short term, whatever decision the company makes regarding the mix of products to be produced and sold, the fixed overhead can be assumed to remain the same. It is necessary, therefore, to base the decision on the contribution earned by each product.

	Hard £ £	*Soft* £ £	*Light* £ £
Selling price	70	95	150
Direct material	15	20	25
Direct wages	15	25	45
Variable overhead	3	5	9
	33	50	79
Contribution	37	45	71
Hours per unit	6	10	18
Contribution per hour	£6.167	£4.500	£3.944
Contribution per £1 material	£2.467	£2.25	£2.84

(i)   If the materials quota does not operate, the company's production capacity is limited to 225,000 labour hours, in which case it must seek to obtain the greatest contribution for each labour hour. The hard grade gives the greatest contribution per hour and therefore this is the most profitable.

(ii)   If the materials quota comes into force, the company must obtain the maximum contribution from each £1 spent on material. The light grade gives the greatest contribution per £1 of material and this is therefore the most profitable.

Note: this applies only if the materials quota provides production which is within the production capacity of 900,000 hours. To test this:

$$\frac{£300,000}{£25} \times 18 = 216,000 \text{ hours}$$

As this is within the labour constraint, conclusion (ii) is correct.

(b)   (i)   *Light*

Material	£300,000
Budgeted units	12,000
Contribution per unit	£71

	£
Total contribution	852,000
Fixed overhead	500,000
Budgeted profit for year	352,000

(ii)

	Hard	*Soft*	*Light*	*Total* £
Material allocation	£75,000 (25%)	£45,000 (15%)	£180,000 (60%)	300,000
Budgeted units	5,000	2,250	7,200	
Contribution per unit	£37	£45	£71	
Total contribution	£185,000	£101,250	£511,200	797,450
Fixed overhead				500,000
Budgeted profit for year				297,450

16 DECISION MAKING - LINEAR PROGRAMMING

INTRODUCTION & LEARNING OBJECTIVES

Syllabus area 6b. Limiting factors, including problems requiring graphical linear programming solutions. (Ability required 2.)

November 1996 students

The syllabus requires you to tackle questions requiring graphical linear programming solutions. You must therefore study this chapter in full.

May 1997 students

The topic of linear programming is removed from the syllabus. You need only study sections 1 and 2 of this chapter, on scarce resources and single scarce resource problems. You need not study section 3 onwards, on linear programming.

Linear programming is an important technique that allows management to allocate resources effectively.

When you have studied this chapter you should be able to do the following:

- Identify scarce resources within a decision problem.
- Recognise when linear programming is required to solve the problem.
- Formulate a two-variable problem.
- Solve a two variable problem using graphical linear programming.

---

1 SCARCE RESOURCES

1.1 What is a scarce resource?

 Economics defines a scarce resource as a good or service which is in short supply. This definition is modified in the context of decision-making to a resource which is in short supply and which, because of this shortage, limits the ability of an organisation to provide greater numbers of products or service facilities.

1.2 Decision-making objectives

These are really organisational objectives which are many and varied; however, in order to evaluate a decision mathematically one single objective is assumed, that of profit maximisation.

Other factors may then be considered before a final decision is taken, but this is part of the management process after the profit maximising solution has been found.

2 SINGLE SCARCE RESOURCE PROBLEMS

2.1 Identifying the scarce resource

In any situation it can be argued that all of the resources required are scarce. What is important is to identify the key resource(s) which limit the ability of the organisation to produce an infinite quantity of goods or services.

2.2   Example

X Ltd makes a single product which requires £5 of materials and 2 hours labour. There are only 80 hours labour available each week and the maximum amount of material available each week is £500.

2.3   Solution

It can be said that the supply of both labour hours and materials are limited and that therefore they are both scarce resources. However, there is more to this problem than meets the eye. The maximum production within these constraints can be shown to be:

Materials:	£500/£5	=	100 units
Labour hours:	80 hours/2 hours	=	40 units

Thus the shortage of labour hours is the significant factor - the scarcity of the materials does not limit production.

In the context of the decision in this example the materials are not a scarce resource.

2.4   Multiple product situations

When more than one product or service is provided from the same pool of resources, profit is maximised by making the best use of the resources available.

2.5   Example

Z Ltd makes two products which both use the same type of materials and grades of labour, but in different quantities as shown by the table below:

	Product A	Product B
Labour hours/unit	3	4
Material/unit	£20	£15

During each week the maximum number of labour hours available is limited to 600; and the value of material available is limited to £6,000.

Each unit of product A made and sold earns Z Ltd £5 and product B earns £6 per unit. The demand for these products is unlimited.

Advise Z Ltd which product they should make.

2.6   Solution

Step 1   Determine the scarce resource.

Step 2   Calculate each product's benefit per unit of the scarce resource consumed by its manufacture.

Each resource restricts production as follows:

Labour hours	600/3	=	200 units of A; or
	600/4	=	150 units of B
Materials	£6,000/£20	=	300 units of A; or
	£6,000/£15	=	400 units of B

It can be seen that whichever product is chosen the production is limited by the shortage of labour hours, thus this is the limiting factor or scarce resource. (Again this is not an easy point to notice and the method used later will overcome the problem of identifying resources that are not limiting.)

Benefit per hour

Product A benefit per labour hour

$\quad\quad$ = £5/3 hours $\quad$ = £1.66 per hour

Product B benefit per labour hour

$\quad\quad$ = £6/4 hours $\quad$ = £1.50 per hour

Thus Z Ltd maximises its earnings by making and selling product A.

2.7 Conclusion

Where there is only one 'real' scarce resource the method above can be used to solve the problem, however where there are two or more resources in short supply which limit the organisation's activities, (for example if materials had been limited to £3,000 per week in the example above), then **linear programming** is required to find the solution.

2.8 Activity

A Ltd makes two products, X and Y. Both products use the same machine and the same raw material which are limited to 200 hours and £500 per week respectively. Individual product details are as follows:

	Product X	*Product Y*
Machine hours/unit	5	2.5
Materials/unit	£10	£5
Benefit/unit	£20	£15

Identify the limiting factor

2.9 Activity solution

Production is restricted as follows:

Machine hours	200/5	=	40 units of X; or
	200/2.5	=	80 units of Y
Materials	£500/£10	=	50 units of X; or
	£500/£5	=	100 units of Y

Therefore machine hours is the limiting factor since X's and Y's production are most severely limited by machine hours.

2.10 Activity

Using the data of the activity above recommend which product A Ltd should make and sell (assuming that demand is unlimited).

2.11 Activity solution

Benefit per machine hour:

Product X	£20/5 hours	=	£4/hour
Product Y	£15/2.5 hours	=	£6/hour

Product Y should be made.

MAY 1997 STUDENTS

You need not study this chapter further than this point

3   FORMULATION OF A LINEAR PROGRAMMING MODEL

3.1   Introduction

Linear programming is one of the most important post-war developments in **operations research**. It is in fact the most widely used of a group of mathematical programming techniques.

Linear programming can be thought of as a method of balancing many factors (eg, distance, time, production capacity) to obtain a predetermined objective (eg, minimum cost). Some of the factors are variable, while others are fixed.

In order to apply linear programming there must be, as its title suggests, a linear relationship between the factors. For example, the cost of shipping 5 extra units should be 5 times the cost of shipping one extra unit.

3.2   Field of application of linear programming

(a)   **Mixing problems**

A product is composed of several ingredients, and what is required is the least costly mix of the ingredients that will give a product of predetermined specification.

(b)   **Job assignment problems**

A number of jobs or products must be handled by various people and/or machines, and the least costly arrangement of assignments is required.

(c)   **Capacity allocation problems**

Limited capacity is allocated to products so as to yield maximum profits.

(d)   **Production scheduling**

An uneven sales demand is met by a production schedule over a period of time, with given penalties for storage, overtime, and short-time working.

(e)   **Transportation problems**

Various suppliers (or one company with several plants) throughout the country make the same products, which must be shipped to many outlets that are also widely distributed. This may involve different transportation costs and varying manufacturing costs. Linear programming can determine the best way to ship; it denotes which plant shall service any particular outlet. It can also evaluate whether it pays to open a new plant.

(f)   **Purchasing**

Multiple and complex bids can be evaluated, in order to ensure that the orders placed with suppliers comply with the lowest cost arrangement.

(g)   **Investment problems**

The results of alternative capital investments can be evaluated when finance is in short supply.

(h)   **Location problems**

Linear programming can help to select an optimum plant or warehouse location where a wide choice is possible.

3.3   Method of linear programming

Linear programming reduces the kind of problems outlined above to a series of linear expressions and then uses those expressions to discover the best solution to achieve a given objective. The student should appreciate that not all situations can be reduced to a linear form. Nevertheless, a surprising number of problems can be solved using this relatively straightforward technique.

3.4   Stages in linear programming – graphical method

> **Step 1**   Define the unknowns ie, the variables (that need to be determined).

> **Step 2**   Formulate the constraints ie, the limitations that must be placed on the variables.

> **Step 3**   Graph the constraints.

> **Step 4**   Define the objective function (that needs to be maximised or minimised).

> **Step 5**   Manipulate the objective function to find the optimal feasible solution.

We will now look at each of these steps in more detail by working through a comprehensive example

3.5   Step 1 - defining the unknowns

Hebrus Ltd manufactures summer-houses and garden sheds. Each product passes through a cutting process and an assembly process. One summer-house, which makes a contribution of £50, takes six hours cutting time and four hours assembly time; while one shed makes a contribution of £40, takes three hours cutting time and eight hours assembly time. There is a maximum of thirty-six cutting hours available each week and forty-eight assembly hours.

The variables that need to be determined in this example are the number of summer-houses and garden sheds to be produced each week.

Let x	=	number of summer-houses produced each week;
and y	=	number of garden sheds produced each week.

3.6   Further example

Alfred Ltd is preparing its plan for the coming month. It manufactures two products, the flaktrap and the saptrap. Details are as follows.

	Product		
	Flaktrap	*Saptrap*	*Price/wage rate*
Amount/unit:			
Selling price (£)	125	165	
Raw material (kg)	6	4	£5/kg
Labour hours:			
Skilled	10	10	£3/hour
Semi-skilled	5	25	£3/hour

The company's variable overhead rate is £1/labour hour (for both skilled and semi-skilled labour). The supply of skilled labour is limited to 2,000 hours/month and the supply of semi-skilled labour is limited to 2,500 hours/month. At the selling prices indicated, maximum demand for flaktraps is expected to be 150 units/month and the maximum demand for saptraps is expected to be 80 units/month. The directors of Alfred believe that demand for each product could be increased by advertising.

You are required to define the decision variables.

3.7   Example solution

The variables are:

(1)   The quantity of Flaktraps to produce per month.

(2)   The quantity of Saptraps to produce per month.

Let x   =   number of Flaktraps produced per month.
Let y   =   number of Saptraps produced per month.

3.8   Step 2 - define the constraints

As we saw earlier in the chapter most resources are limited to a certain degree which usually puts some limitation on what can be achieved. When formulating a linear programming problem those limitations are included as a set of conditions which any solution to the problem must satisfy and they are referred to as **constraints**.

The constraints (limitations) in our Hebrus example are the amounts of cutting and assembly time available.

If   1 summer-house requires 6 hours cutting time,
      x summer-houses require $6x$ hours cutting time.

If   1 shed requires 3 hours cutting time,
      y sheds require $3y$ hours cutting time.

Hence total cutting time required = 6x + 3y hours

Similarly, if 1 summer-house and 1 shed require 4 and 8 hours assembly time respectively, the total assembly time for x summer-houses and y sheds will be $4x + 8y$.

The conventional way of setting out the constraints is to place the units utilised on the left, and those available on the right; the inequality sign is the link.

Constraint		*Utilised*		*Available*
cutting time	(i)	6x + 3y	$\leq$	36
assembly time	(ii)	4x + 8y	$\leq$	48

In addition, two other logical constraints must be stated ie,

$$x \geq 0$$
$$y \geq 0$$

These simply state that negative amounts of garden sheds or summer-houses cannot be made.

3.9   Activity

Using the information in the previous example (Alfred Ltd), formulate the constraints.

3.10 Activity solution

Skilled labour	10x	+	10y	≤	2,000
Semi-skilled labour	5x	+	25y	≤	2,500
Flaktrap demand	x			≤	150
Saptrap demand			y	≤	80
Non-negative constraints {	x			≥	0
			y	≥	0

3.11 Step 3 - define the objective function

Definition The objective function is a quantified statement of what is trying to be achieved, for instance the minimisation of costs or maximisation of profit. The objective function is always expressed in terms of the unknown variables (defined in Step 1). In the Hebrus example, these are x and y. Hence, continuing this example:

The objective is to maximise contribution C, given by:

$$C = 50x + 40y$$

The company undoubtedly wishes to maximise profit, however, given the usual assumptions of linear programming (stated later), this is achieved by maximising contribution. Take care that the coefficients of x and y (ie, 50 and 40 respectively) represent the amount by which contribution (and hence profit) increases per unit of each item produced and sold.

3.12 Graphing a straight line

This section is for those students who have not done any basic mathematics for a while. This is a revision section on graphing a straight line, a technique which is required for evaluating linear programming problems.

Step 1 We must have a linear relationship between two measurements, in other words if we know the value for x we can work out the value for y.

Examples	y	=	3x + 1
	y	=	2x + 42 etc.

Note:

(1) To recognise a **linear** relationship the equation must have only 'x' not 'x' to the power of anything eg, x^2.

(2) A straight line has two characteristics.

(i) A slope or gradient - which measures the 'steepness' of the line.

(ii) A point at which it cuts the y axis - called the intercept.

y = slope × x + intercept

eg, y = 2x + 3

∴ the gradient is 2 and the point at which the line cuts the y axis is 3.

Step 2 To draw a straight line graph we only need to know two points which can then be joined.

Consider the following two equations.

(i) y = 2x + 3

(ii) y = 2x − 2

In order to draw the graphs of these equations it is necessary to decide on two values for x and then to calculate the corresponding values for y. Let us use x = 0 and 3. These calculations are best displayed in tabular form.

x		0	3
(1)	$y = 2x + 3$	3	9
(2)	$y = 2x - 2$	-2	4

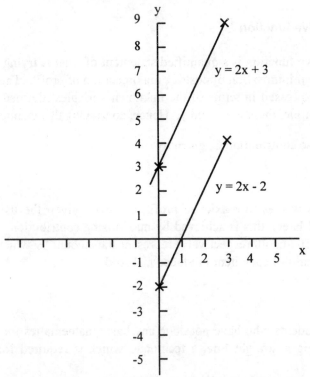

Note: the lines are parallel because the equations have the same gradient of 2.

3.13   Step 4 - graph the constraints

Having revised how to plot a straight line on a graph, we can now move on to graphing the constraints which are simply linear equations of the type we have just looked at.

In order to plot the constraints it is normally best to compute the intercepts of the equalities on the horizontal and vertical axes. Thus, x and y are each set equal to zero in turn and the value of y and x computed in these circumstances.

Returning to the Hebrus example.

For the equation $6x + 3y = 36$ - cutting time constraint

when x = 0, $y = \dfrac{36}{3} = 12$

when y = 0, $x = \dfrac{36}{6} = 6$

For the equation $4x + 8y = 48$ - assembly time constraint

when x = 0, $y = \dfrac{48}{8} = 6$

when y = 0, $x = \dfrac{48}{4} = 12$

The constraints can now be represented graphically:

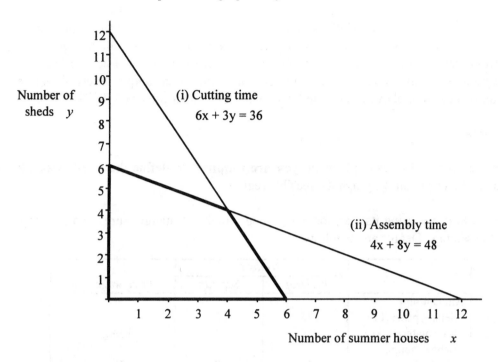

3.14   The feasible region

Having inserted the straight lines in the graph, we are then ready to work out what is called the **feasible region**.

If you recall each line inserted on the graph represents a constraint. In the Hebrus example, there can only be 36 hours of cutting time and no more and only 48 hours of assembly time and no more. Therefore the area on the graph **above** these lines is 'out of bounds' or more technically 'not feasible'. The area below these lines is therefore called the feasible region; it is possible for total cutting time and total assembly time to be any of these values up to and on the constraint line **but not above**.

Hence, the feasible region for Hebrus is as shown below.

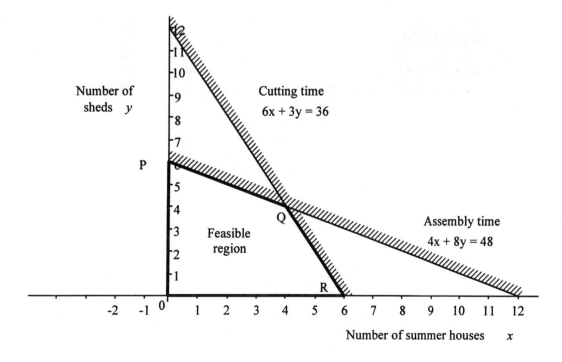

The area OPQR which is outlined in bold represents all feasible solutions ie, combinations of the two products which are achievable given the constraints. It is therefore called the **feasible region**.

To recognise that feasible solutions are, as in this case all **below** the constraint lines, it is normal practice to hatch **above** the line indicating that anything above is outside the feasible region. Some questions can be minimising problems eg, the objective function will be to minimise costs subject to minimum output levels. The constraints will be minimum output levels, therefore the feasible region will be on or above the line and will be hatched under the line.

3.15   Example

Using the Alfred Ltd example again **you are required** to define the constraints, plot them on a graph and indicate on the graph the feasible region.

Alfred Ltd is preparing its plan for the coming month. It manufactures two products, the flaktrap and the saptrap. Details are as follows.

	Product		Price/wage rate
	Flaktrap	Saptrap	
Amount/unit:			
Selling price (£)	125	165	
Raw material (kg)	6	4	£5/kg
Labour hours:			
Skilled	10	10	£3/hour
Semi-skilled	5	25	£3/hour

The company's variable overhead rate is £1/labour hour (for both skilled and semi-skilled labour). The supply of skilled labour is limited to 2,000 hours/month and the supply of semi-skilled labour is limited to 2,500 hours/month. At the selling prices indicated, maximum demand for flaktraps is expected to be 150 units/month and the maximum demand for saptraps is expected to be 80 units/month. The directors of Alfred believe that demand for each product could be increased by advertising.

3.16   Example solution

Let x be the number of flaktraps to be produced each month and y be the number of saptraps to be produced each month.

Skilled labour	:	$10x + 10y$	$\leq$	2,000
Semi-skilled labour	:	$5x + 25y$	$\leq$	2,500
Flaktrap demand	:	x	$\leq$	150
Saptrap demand	:	y	$\leq$	80
Non-negative constraints	:	x	$\geq$	0
	:	y	$\geq$	0

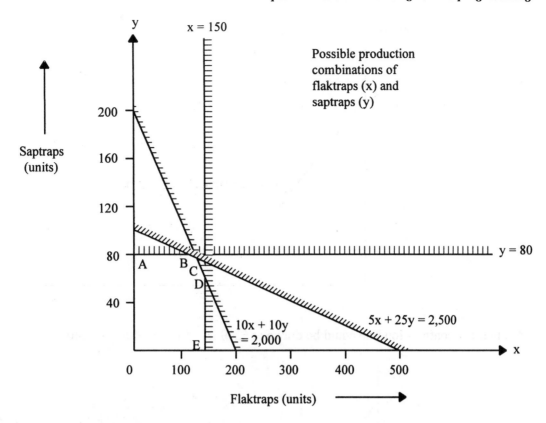

This give a feasibility region of OABCDE.

3.17   Step 5 - manipulate the objective function

Having found the feasible region the problem now is to find the optimal solution within this feasible region.

There are two approaches to this final stage:

(a)   by inspection it is clear that the maximum contribution will lie on one of the corners of the feasible region. In the Hebrus example the corners are P, Q, R (it could lie on the line PQ or the line QR) – the optimal solution can be reached simply by calculating the contributions at each; or

(b)   by drawing an **iso-contribution** line (an objective function for a particular value of C), which is a line where all points represent an equal contribution. This is the recommended approach, particularly for more complex problems.

Using the Hebrus example, consider a contribution of £200. This would give the contribution line $50x + 40y = 200$ and could be achieved by producing four summer-houses, or five sheds, or any combination on a straight line between the two.

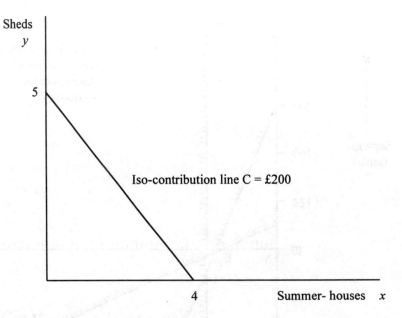

Another iso-contribution line could be drawn at £240 ie, $50x + 40y = 240$:

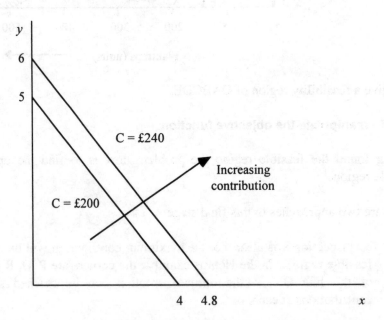

Clearly, iso-contribution lines move to and from the origin in parallel; the arrow indicates increasing contribution. The object is to get on the highest contribution line within (just touching) the binding constraints.

The point is found by drawing an example of an iso-contribution line on the diagram (any convenient value of C will do), and then placing a ruler against it. Then, by moving the ruler away from the origin (in the case of a maximisation problem) or towards the origin (in the case of a minimising problem) but keeping it parallel to the iso-contribution line, the last corner of the feasible solution space which is met represents the optimum solution.

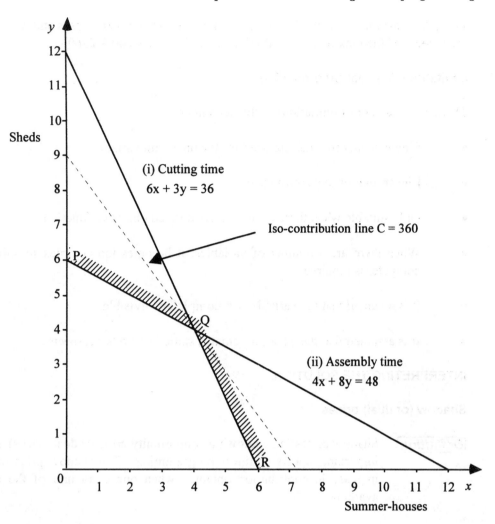

The highest available iso-contribution line occurs at $C = 360$, at point Q, where, reading from the graph, $x = 4$ and $y = 4$.

3.18   Evaluating the optimal solution using simultaneous equations

You may consider that the whole process would be easier by solving the constraints as sets of simultaneous equations and not bothering with a graph. This is possible and you may get the right answer, but such a technique should be used with caution and is not recommended until you have determined graphically which constraints are effective in determining the optimal solution. Furthermore if the question asks for a graphical solution, then a graph **must** be used.

The technique can however, be used as a check. For example using the Hebrus example the optimal solution can be checked by solving the two simultaneous equations for the two constraint boundaries.

Point Q is the intersection of the lines:

Constraint

$$6x + 3y \quad = \quad 36 \qquad \text{(i)}$$
$$4x + 8y \quad = \quad 48 \qquad \text{(ii)}$$

$3 \times \text{(ii)} - 2 \times \text{(i)}$ gives

$$18y \quad = \quad 72$$
$$y \quad = \quad 4$$

Substituting into (i)
$$x \quad = \quad 4$$

Thus, the maximum contribution is obtained when four summer-houses and four sheds per week are produced, and the maximum contribution is $4 \times £50 + 4 \times £40 = £360$.

3.19   Limitations to linear programming

There are a number of limitations to this technique.

- Single value estimates are used for the uncertain variables.

- Linear relationships must exist.

- Only suitable when there is one clearly defined objective function.

- When there are a number of variables, it becomes too complex to solve manually and a computer is required.

- It is assumed that the variables are completely divisible.

- It is assumed that the situation remains static in all other respects.

4   INTERPRETING THE SOLUTION

4.1   Shadow (or dual) prices

Definition   Shadow prices (also known as opportunity costs or dual prices) are one of the most important aspects of linear programming. The shadow price of a resource is the increase in contribution obtained when one extra unit of the constraint is made available.

4.2   Example

Refer back to the earlier example concerning Hebrus Ltd.

Suppose one extra hour was available for the cutting process each week.

By how much would contribution (and profit) be increased?

The extra hour would alter the constraints to:

Cutting   (i) $6x + 3y \le 37$; and

Assembly   (ii) $4x + 8y \le 48$;

To solve simultaneously multiply (ii) by 1.5.

(iii) $6x + 12y \le 72$

Solving as before:

Subtracting (i) from (iii) gives

$$9y = 35$$

and thus $y = 3\frac{8}{9}$

Inserting this value in (i) gives

$$6x + (3 \times 3\tfrac{8}{9}) \quad = \quad 37$$

$$6x + 11\tfrac{6}{9} \quad = \quad 37$$

$$6x \quad = \quad 25\tfrac{3}{9}$$

$$x \quad = \quad 4\tfrac{2}{9}$$

			£
C	=	$(£50 \times 4\tfrac{2}{9}) + (£40 \times 3\tfrac{8}{9})$ =	$366\tfrac{2}{3}$
Original contribution			360
Increase			$6\tfrac{2}{3}$

Thus, £6 $\tfrac{2}{3}$ is the shadow price of one hour in the cutting process.

Note: there is a great potential for rounding errors when finding dual prices. The problem has been avoided here by working in fractions. If decimals are used retain several decimal places.

Similarly the shadow price of assembly time may be found by keeping the cutting time constraint unchanged, but relaxing the assembly constraint by one unit so that it becomes:

Assembly $4x + 8y \leq 49$ (ii)

Whilst (i) remains as:

Cutting $6x + 3y \leq 36$ (i)

Solving as before:

$$3 \times (ii) - 2 \times (i) \quad \Rightarrow \quad 18y \quad = \quad 75$$

$$y \quad = \quad 4.16667 \qquad \text{(Keep this value in the memory of your calculator.)}$$

Substituting into (i) gives x = 3.91667

	£
Contribution C = (£50 × 3.91667) + (£40 × 4.16667) =	362.5
Original contribution =	360.0
Increase	2.5

Thus, the shadow price of assembly time = £2.5.

(Note: in view of these calculations it is important that no attempt is made to simplify the original constraints by cancelling, otherwise you will not be able to calculate correct values for the shadow prices.*)*

4.3 **Tabular approach**

An alternative method of arriving at the shadow price is to set out the two critical constraints (cutting and assembly) as a table:

	Column	(1)	(2)	
Cutting	Cu	$6x$ + $3y$ = 36		(i)
Assembly	As	$4x$ + $8y$ = 48		(ii)
	Contribution =	$50x$ +	$40y$	

The shadow prices are found by solving the **columns** (1) and (2), replacing x and y with the constraint symbols Cu and As.

	Column	*(1)*	*(2)*
replace x and y with Cu		6 Cu	3 Cu
replace x and y with As		4 As	8 As
Contribution		50	40

Turning these into equations:

$$6Cu + 4As = 50 \quad (1)$$
$$3Cu + 8As = 40 \quad (2)$$

Solve simultaneously

Multiply (1) by 2: $\quad\quad\quad\quad 12Cu + 8As = 100 \quad (3)$

Subtract (2) from (3):

$$9Cu = 60$$

$$Cu = \frac{60}{9} = £6\tfrac{2}{3} \text{ (the same solution as above for shadow price)}$$

Substituting in (2) gives: As = £2.5.

These shadow prices represent the amount of contribution forgone by **not** having one extra hour available in each department.

4.4 **Activity**

Using the following data, calculate the shadow prices of respectively one hour of machine time and one hour of finishing time.

(i) $\quad 20x + 25y \le 500 \quad$ (machining time)

(ii) $\quad 40x + 25y \le 800 \quad$ (finishing time)

$\quad\quad C = 80x + 75y \quad\quad$ (contribution)

Solution: x = 15, y = 8

Use the constraint alteration (incremental) method for machining time and the table method for finishing time.

4.5   Activity solution

Machining time - the constraints become:

(i) $20x + 25y \leq 501$

(ii) $40x + 25y \leq 800$

Subtracting (i) from (ii) gives

$20x = 299$

and thus x   =   14.95

Inserting into (i) gives

$(20 \times 14.95) + 25y = 501$

$25y = 202$

$y = 8.08$

Original contribution:

		£
$(15 \times £80) + (8 \times £75)$	=	1,800

Amended contribution

$(14.95 \times £80) + (8.08 \times £75)$	=	1,802

Increased contribution   2

The shadow price per machine hour is £2.

Finishing time:

Machining	M	$20x + 25y = 500$
Finishing	F	$40x + 25y = 800$
Contribution		$80x + 75y$

becomes:

(i) $20M + 40F = 80$

(ii) $25M + 25F = 75$

Multiply (i) by 1.25 gives

(iii) $25M + 50F = 100$

Subtracting (ii) from (iii) gives

$25F = 25$

$F = 1$

Thus the dual price of finishing time is £1.

4.6 Usefulness of shadow prices - conclusion

Shadow prices have the following relevance:

(a) The shadow price is the extra profit that may be earned by relaxing by one unit each of the constraints.

(b) It therefore represents the maximum **premium** which the firm should be willing to pay for one extra unit of each constraint.

(c) Since shadow prices indicate the effect of a one unit change in each of the constraints, they provide a measure of the sensitivity of the result (but see later).

The shadow price for any constraint which is not binding at the optimum solution is zero. In the above example suppose production of summer-houses and sheds was also limited by the amount of painting time available – each product took 4 hours to paint and only 40 hours a week were available.

Since the optimum plan involved production of 4 sheds and 4 summer-houses the painting time would only be 32 hours a week – consequently it would make no difference to the optimum solution if painting time availability either increased to 41 hours or decreased to 39. Under these circumstances the dual price of painting time is zero.

However, if the painting time was reduced to only 32 hours this too would become a binding constraint, and a reduction by one further hour, to 31 may affect the optimum solution. It should be noted that shadow prices are valid for only a small range of changes before, eventually, they become non-binding or make different resources critical. The shadow price of a non-binding resource is zero.

5 CHAPTER SUMMARY

This chapter has considered decision problems where activity is limited by the existence of one or more scarce resources.

The distinction between one or more scarce resource problems has been illustrated and solved, two variable problems have also been shown and solved using graphical linear programming techniques.

6 SELF TEST QUESTIONS

6.1 What is a scarce resource? (1.1)

6.2 What is linear programming? (3.1)

6.3 List some common applications of linear programming. (3.2)

6.4 What is the feasible region? (3.14)

6.5 What is an iso-contribution line? (3.17)

6.6 What are the limitations of linear programming? (3.19)

6.7 What is a shadow price? (4.1)

7   EXAMINATION TYPE QUESTION

7.1   Flintstones

The Flintstones are involved in the manufacture of two products, Chip and Dale. Due to an industrial dispute, which is expected to go on for some time, material B, which is required in the production of Dale, is expected to be limited to 300 units per week. Material A, required for both products, is freely available.

Flintstones are experiencing labour shortages and it is expected that only 800 hours of unskilled labour and 1,000 hours of skilled labour will be available in any week, in the short run.

Due to a transport problem, the Flintstones will be able to import only 400 Dinos into the country each week. This item is required in the manufacture of both Chip and Dale.

It is the company's policy to limit the production of Dale to not more than three times the production of Chip.

The following information is available:

	Chip £	*Dale* £
Material B (2 units for Dale only)	–	10
Material A	15	10
Labour – unskilled £3 per hour	12	15
– skilled £5 per hour	50	20
Dinos (£10 each)	20	20
Total cost	97	75
Selling price	127	100

Fixed costs each week amount to £3,000.

You are required to calculate the optimal plan for Flintstones together with the weekly profit which may be earned.

8   ANSWER TO EXAMINATION TYPE QUESTION

8.1   Flintstones

From the tabulated information given, per week:

No. of hours unskilled labour per Chip $= \dfrac{12}{3} =$ 4 hours

No. of hours unskilled labour per Dale $= \dfrac{15}{3} =$ 5 hours

No. of hours skilled labour per Chip $= \dfrac{50}{5} =$ 10 hours

No. of hours skilled labour per Dale $= \dfrac{20}{5} =$ 4 hours

No. of Dinos per Chip $= \dfrac{20}{10} =$ 2

No. of Dinos per Dale $= \dfrac{20}{10} =$ 2

Contribution per Chip $=$ £(127 – 97) $=$ £30

Contribution per Dale $=$ £(100 – 75) $=$ £25

As each Dale requires 2 units of B, and only 300 units of B are available, this limits the number of Dales to 150.

There is no constraint on the amount of material A.

Fixed costs will be the same, whatever mix of Chip and Dale is produced, hence they can be ignored for the purpose of obtaining the optimum product mix, but must be included in the calculation of profit.

Let C =   number of Chips produced per week.
Let D =   number of Dales produced per week.
Let Z =   total contributions per week.

The objective function then is to maximise contribution to fixed overheads ie,

Maximise: Z = $30C + 25D$

					Constraint Number	
Subject to:	$4C$	$+$	$5D$	$\leq$	800	(1)	Unskilled labour
	$10C$	$+$	$4D$	$\leq$	$1,000$	(2)	Skilled labour
	$2C$	$+$	$2D$	$\leq$	400	(3)	Dinos
			D	$\leq$	$3C$	(4)	Production policy
			$2D$	$\leq$	300	(5)	Material B
			C, D	$\geq$	0		

Note: that there is a constraint which appears confusing at first, that of company policy with regard to the production of Chips and Dales. However, it can be dealt with simply by taking the expression of the policy, as expressed in words, and turning it into symbols, thus:

The production of Dales is to be not more than (ie, less than or equal to) three times the production of Chips.

$$D \leq 3C$$

or $$-3C + D \leq 0$$

For graph see below. The feasibility region is CBAO (outlined in bold).

The solution is at the intersection of constraints (1) and (2), the two labour constraints. The solution can be found by solving (1) and (2) simultaneously.

$$4C + 5D = 800 \quad (1)$$
$$10C + 4D = 1,000 \quad (2)$$

$5 \times (2) - 4 \times (1)$ gives $34C = 1,800$

$$C = 52.94 \simeq 53$$

$$D = 117.65 \simeq 118$$

Contribution   = $30C + 25D$ = $£30 \times 53 + £25 \times 118$ = $\underline{£4,540}$

Thus, profit   = $£4,540 - £3,000$ = $\underline{£1,540}$ per week

Note: the non-integer solutions have been rounded up. Strictly speaking this puts the optimal solution outside the feasible region (52 and 117 might be more appropriate). The values of C and D have been rounded since, in any one week it is difficult to sell 117.65 Dales. However the Flintstones might consider making on average 117.65 Dales per week.

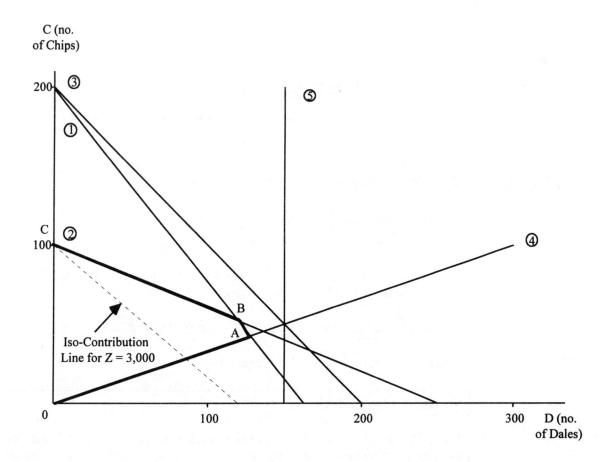

17 BUDGET PREPARATION

INTRODUCTION & LEARNING OBJECTIVES

Syllabus area 6c. The budget manual; preparation and monitoring procedures; reporting against actual financial data. (Ability required 3).

Preparation of functional budgets for operating and non-operating functions; cash budgets; the master budget. (Ability required 3).

Problems and techniques of forecasting. (Ability required 2).

Principal budget factors. (Ability required 3).

November 1996 students

The syllabus areas for budget preparation are as set out above, and include 'problems and techniques of forecasting'. This topic, in common with the others, must be studied in full.

May 1997 students

The syllabus item 'problems and techniques of forecasting' is deleted from the syllabus. You need not therefore study section 7 of this chapter.

This chapter is concerned with identifying an organisation's objectives, quantifying them and communicating them through plans for the future.

Such plans can be divided into long-term and short-term; short-term plans are often referred to as budgets.

When you have studied this chapter you should be able to do the following:

- List the objectives which an organisation may pursue and explain conflicts between them.
- Explain the purposes of planning.
- Explain the workings of the budgeting process.
- Prepare budgets based on given data.
- Explain the problems and techniques of forecasting.

1   WHY PLAN FOR THE FUTURE?

1.1   Introduction

Given the increasing complexity of business and the ever-changing environment faced by firms (social, economic, technological and political) it is doubtful whether any firm can survive by simply continuing to do what it has always done in the past. If the firm wishes to earn satisfactory levels of profit in the future, it must plan its course of action.

1.2   Corporate planning

[Definition]   Corporate planning is essentially a long run activity which seeks to determine the direction in which the firm should be moving in the future.

A frequently asked question in formulating the corporate plan is 'Where do we see ourselves in ten years time'. To answer this successfully the firm must consider:

(a)   what it wants to achieve (its objectives);
(b)   how it intends to get there (its strategy);
(c)   what resources will be required (its operating plans);
(d)   how well it is doing in comparison to the plan (control).

These areas are discussed below.

1.3   Objectives

[Definition]   Objectives are simply statements of what the firm wishes to achieve.

Traditionally it was assumed that all firms were only interested in the maximisation of profit (or the wealth of their shareholders). Nowadays it is recognised that for many firms profit is but one of the many objectives pursued. Examples include:

(a)   maximisation of sales (whilst earning a 'reasonable' level of profit);
(b)   growth (in sales, asset value, number of employees etc);
(c)   survival;
(d)   research and development leadership;
(e)   quality of service;
(f)   contented workforce;
(g)   respect for the environment;

Many of these non-profit goals can in fact be categorised as:

(a)   surrogates for profit (eg, quality of service);

(b)   necessary constraints on profit (eg, quality of service);

(c)   'sub-optimal' objectives that benefit individual parties in the firm rather than the firm as a whole (eg, managers might try to maximise sales as this would bring them greater personal rewards than maximising profit).

A variety of objectives can therefore be suggested for the firm and it is up to the individual company to make its own decisions. For corporate planning purposes it is essential that the objectives chosen are quantified and have a timescale attached to them. A statement such as maximise profits and increase sales would be of little use in corporate planning terms. The following would be far more helpful:

(a)   achieve a growth in EPS of 5% per annum over the coming ten year period;

(b)   obtain a turnover of £x million within six years;

(c)   launch at least two new products per year, etc.

Some objectives may be difficult to quantify (eg, contented workforce) but if no attempt is made there will be no yardstick against which to compare actual performance.

1.4   Strategy

Definition   Strategy is the overall approach that the company will adopt to meet its chosen objectives.

Strategy formulation usually involves:

(a)   an analysis of the environment in which the firm operates, a review of the strengths and weaknesses of the company and a consideration of the threats and opportunities facing it;

(b)   the results of the firm's existing operations are then projected forward and compared with stated objectives;

(c)   any differences between projected performance and objectives are defined as 'gaps'.

To bridge these gaps the firm will either change its objectives (because they are too optimistic) or attempt to change the firm's direction to improve performance. This change of direction is strategy formulation.

Formulation of strategy is largely a creative process, whereby the firm will consider the products it makes and the markets it serves. Policies are usually developed to represent the firm's strategy and cover basic areas such as:

(a)   product development policy (eg, new products, discontinuation of old products);

(b)   market development (continue in existing markets, develop new ones);

(c)   technology;

(d)   growth (ie, internally generated growth, or growth by acquisition).

These policies are sometimes known as 'missions'.

1.5   Operating plans

Definition   Strategic plans are essentially long term. Operating plans are the short-term tactics of the organisation.

A strategic plan might call for expansion in a particular market; whereas the operating plan will detail how the extra products are to be made and how much is to be spent on advertising. A military analogy is useful here - strategy is how to organise to win the war, operating plans (or tactics) are how to fight individual battles.

1.6   Control

Definition   It is not enough merely to make plans and implement them. Control is the comparison of the results of the plans and the stated objectives to assess the firm's performance, and the taking of action to remedy any differences in performance.

This is an essential activity as it highlights any weakness in the firm's corporate plan or its execution. Plans must be continually reviewed because as the environment changes so plans and objectives will need revision. Corporate planning is not a once-in-every-ten-years activity, but an on-going process which must react quickly to the changing circumstances of the firm.

1.7   Diagram of planning activities

The following diagram shows the relationships between planning and budgeting.

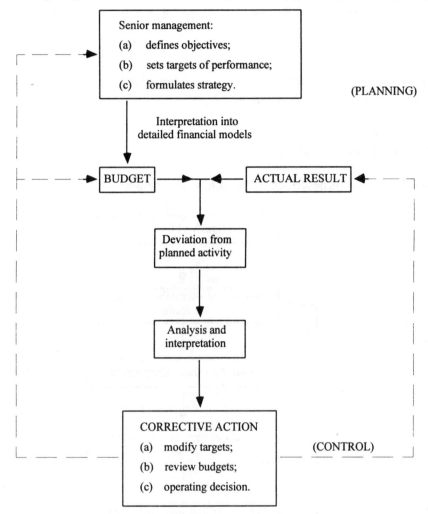

1.8   Importance of long-range planning for successful budgeting

No doubt some managers would argue that because long-range forecasting can never be completely accurate, it is pointless. However, a system of budgetary control introduced in isolation without any form of corporate or long-range planning is unlikely to yield its full potential benefit, and it is important to understand the reasons for this.

Firstly, a budget is not (or should not be) the same as a forecast. A forecast is a statement of what is expected to happen; a budget is a statement of what it is reasonable to believe can be made to happen. An organisation without a long-range plan probably starts with the sales forecast and perhaps tries to improve the expected results slightly by increasing the advertising budget. This modified sales forecast then becomes the budget on which the other budgets are based. However, this approach has several limitations, some of which are listed below:

(a)   In the absence of specified long-term objectives, there are no criteria against which to evaluate possible courses of action. Managers do not know what they should be trying to achieve.

(b)   Performance evaluation can only be on a superficial 'better/worse than last year' basis: no one has assessed the **potential** of the business.

(c)   Many decisions eg, capital expenditure decisions or the decision to introduce a new product, can only be taken on a long-term basis. Long-term forecasts may be inaccurate, but they are better than no forecast at all. A company with no long-range forecasting would be in dire straits when, sooner or later, sales of its existing products decline.

(d)   There is a limit to the influence a company can exert over events in the short term (eg, by increased advertising). If it wishes to improve its position markedly, it must think long term.

(e)   Eventually some factor other than sales may become the limiting factor eg, shortage of materials or labour. If the company has not anticipated the situation, it may simply have to live with the problem. With adequate long-range planning it might be able to avoid or overcome it.

1.9   Overview of the planning process

The overall planning process is described in the following diagram:

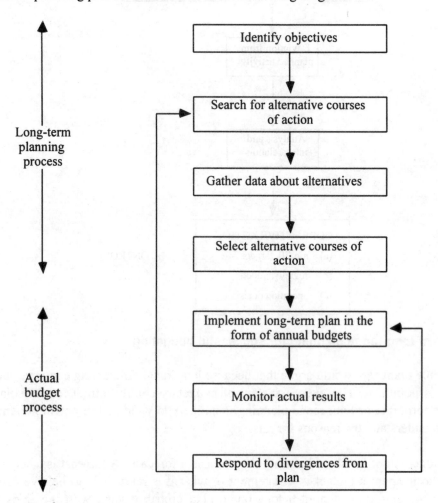

The seven stages are expanded below:

(a)   Identify objectives

This first stage requires the company to specify objectives towards which it is working. These objectives may be in terms of:

- economic targets;
- type of business;
- goods/services to be sold;

- markets to be served;
- market share;
- profit objectives; and
- required growth rates of sales, profits, assets.

(b) **Search for possible courses of action**

A series of specific strategies should be developed dealing particularly with:

- developing new markets for existing products;
- developing new products for existing markets; and
- developing new products for new markets.

(c) **Gathering data about alternatives and measuring pay-offs**

This is an information-gathering stage.

(d) **Select course of action**

Having made decisions, long-term plans based on those decisions are created.

(e) **Implementation of long-term plans**

This stage signals the move from long-term planning to annual budgeting. The budget provides the link between the strategic plans and their implementation in management decisions. The budget should be seen as an integral part of the long-term planning process.

(f) **Monitor actual outcomes**

This is the particular role of the cost accountant, keeping detailed financial and other records of actual performance compared with budget targets (variance accounting).

(g) **Respond to divergences from plan**

This is the control process in budgeting, responding to divergences from plan either through budget modifications or through identifying new courses of action.

1.10   What does management hope to get out of budgeting?

The principal advantages relate to:

(a)   planning and co-ordination;
(b)   authorising and delegating;
(c)   evaluating performance;
(d)   discerning trends;
(e)   communicating and motivating;
(f)   control.

1.11   Planning and co-ordination

Success in business is closely related to success in planning for the future. In this context the budget serves three functions:

(a)   It provides a formal planning framework that ensures planning does take place.

(b)   It co-ordinates the various separate aspects of the business by providing a master plan (the **master budget**) for the business as a whole (this is particularly important in a large organisation engaged in making several different products, where otherwise it is too easy for individual managers to concentrate on their own aspects of the business).

(c)   Though not all decisions can be anticipated, the budget provides a framework of reference within which later operating decisions can be taken.

1.12   Authorising and delegating

Adoption of a budget by management explicitly authorises the decisions made within it. This serves two functions:

(a)   the need continuously to ask for top management decisions is reduced;
(b)   the responsibility for carrying out the decisions is delegated to individual managers.

1.13   Evaluating performance

One of the functions of accounting information is that it provides a basis for the measurement of managerial performance. By setting targets for each manager to achieve, the budget provides a bench-mark, against which his actual performance can be assessed objectively.

Note, however, that before a budget can successfully be used for this purpose, it must be accepted as reasonable by the individual manager whose area of responsibility it covers and whose performance is to be evaluated.

1.14   Discerning trends

It is important that management should be made aware as soon as possible of any new trends, whether in relation to production or marketing. The budget, by providing specific expectations with which actual performance is continuously compared, supplies a mechanism for the early detection of any unexpected trend.

1.15   Communication and motivating

The application of budgeting within an organisation should lead to a good communications structure. Managers involved in the setting of budgets for their own responsibility need to have agreed strategies and policies communicated down to them. A good system of downwards communication should itself encourage good upwards and sideways communication in the organisation. Budgets that have been agreed by managers should provide some motivation towards their achievement.

Conclusion   When the goals have been set for the organisation, the management uses the budgetary system to control the running of the business to evaluate the extent to which those goals are achieved. By a continuous comparison of actual performance with planned results, deviations or variances are quickly identified and appropriate action initiated. This is a fundamental aspect of the whole process: if targets were set but little or no attempt were made to measure the extent to which they were achieved, then the advantages of budgeting would be severely curtailed.

There is, however, a danger in adhering to the budget too inflexibly. Circumstances may change, and the budget should change accordingly or the control system should identify separately the variances arising due to the changed conditions. Organisations operate within a dynamic environment, and the control systems need to be appropriately flexible.

2   REPORTING AGAINST ACTUAL FINANCIAL DATA

2.1   The concept of budgeting

> **Definition**   A budget is defined as a plan quantified in monetary terms, prepared and approved prior to a defined period of time, usually showing planned income to be generated and/or expenditure to be incurred during that period and the capital to be employed to attain a given objective.

Thus, budgeting may be regarded as **predictive accounting.**   A budget may stand on its own, but it is more useful if it is part of a control system. A control system is designed to control an operation so as to achieve desired objectives.

A simple closed control system is illustrated by an oven thermostat:

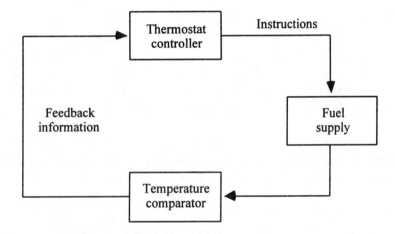

A budgetary control system is essentially similar:

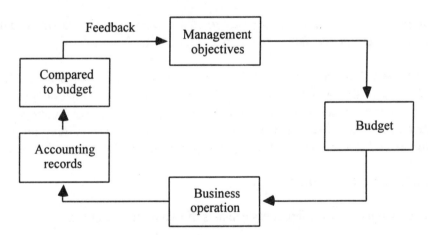

This is an oversimplified view, in that there are other factors and forecasts.

> **Definition**   A budgetary control system is defined as the establishment of budgets relating the responsibilities of executives to the requirements of a policy, and the continuous comparison of actual with budgeted results, either to secure by individual action the objective of that policy or to provide a basis for its revision.

The subject of budgetary control is vital to management accounting. The following sections provide an introduction.

2.2   The nature of budgets

In general, budgets are set for specific periods of time in the future, for example the budget for next year. Sometimes budgets are constructed for specific projects that are to be undertaken but again these can be analysed into the periods of time that the projects are expected to last. Thus, if a project is planned to last two years, the total budget for it can be split into that relating to the first year and that relating to the second year.

Budgets are plans expressed in financial and/or quantitative terms for either the whole of a business or for the various parts of a business for a specified period of time in the future. The budgets are prepared (**the planning activity**) within the framework of objectives (**targets or goals**) and policies that have been determined by senior management as part of its own planning activities.

2.3   Budget centres and budget periods

A **budget centre** is a clearly defined part of an organisation for the purposes of operating a budgetary control system. Each function within an organisation will be sub-divided into appropriate budget centres. In determining budget centres it is important to be able to define them in terms of management responsibility. The manager responsible for a budget centre (eg, the machining department within the production function) will be involved in the planning stage of setting the budget for his area of responsibility and he will be the recipient of control information in due course.

The **budget period** is the period of time for which a budget is prepared and over which the control aspect takes place. The length of such a period will depend on:

(a)   **The nature of the business** - in the ship-building or power supply industries budget periods of ten to twenty years may be appropriate; periods of less than one year may be appropriate for firms in the clothing and fashion industries.

(b)   **The part of the business being budgeted** - capital expenditure will usually be budgeted for longer periods ahead than the production output.

(c)   **The basis of control** - many businesses use a twelve month period as their basic budget period, but at the same time it is very common to find the annual budget broken down into quarterly or monthly sub-units. Such a breakdown is usually for control purposes because actual and budgeted results need to be monitored continuously. It is not practicable to wait until the end of a twelve month budget period before making control comparisons.

2.4   The budgetary control process

Essentially the budgetary control process consists of two distinct elements;

(a)   **Planning**

This involves the setting of the various budgets for the appropriate future period. Management at the various levels in an organisation should be involved in the budgetary planning stage for its own area of responsibility. In many medium and large businesses this activity can take a considerable amount of time. There is a need to co-ordinate the budgets of the various parts of a business to ensure that they are all complementary and in line with overall company objectives and policies.

(b)   **Control**

Once the budgets have been set and agreed for the future period under review, the formal control element of budgetary control is ready to start.

This control involves the comparison of the plan in the form of the budget with the actual results achieved for the appropriate period. Any significant divergences between the budgeted and the actual results should be reported to the appropriate management so that the necessary action can be taken.

2.5   Introduction of a budgetary control system

Before a budgetary control system can be introduced, it is essential that:

(a)   key executives are committed to the proposed system;

(b)   the long-term objectives of the organisation have been defined (as previously discussed);

(c)   there is an adequate foundation of data on which to base forecasts and costs;

(d)   an organisation chart should be drawn up, clearly defining areas of authority and responsibility. The organisation can then be logically divided into budget centres, such that each manager has a budget for, and is given control information about, the area which he can control. This is the essence of **responsibility accounting**.

(e)   a budget committee should be set up and a budget manual produced;

(f)   the limiting factor is identified (see below).

2.6   Stages in the budgetary process

These may be identified as follows:

(a)   **Communicating policy guidelines to preparers of budgets**

The long-term plan forms the framework within which the budget is prepared. It is therefore necessary to communicate the implications of that plan to the persons who actually prepare the budget.

(b)   **Determining the factor which restricts output**

Generally there will be one factor which restricts performance for a given period. Usually this will be sales, but it could be production capacity, or some special labour skills. This is the **principal budget factor.**

(c)   **Preparation of the sales budget**

On the assumption that sales is the principal budget factor, the next stage is to prepare the sales budget. This budget is very much dependent on forecast sales revenue. Various forecasting techniques may be used in this process eg, market research, sales personnel estimates, statistical forecasting, and so on.

(d)   **Initial preparation of budgets**

Ideally budgets should be prepared by managers responsible for achieving the targets contained therein - **participative budgeting.** The role of the finance specialists should be to assist in turning physical budget forecasts into financial budgets.

(e)   **Co-ordination and review of budgets**

At this stage the various budgets are integrated into the complete budget system. Any anomalies between the budgets must be resolved and the complete budget package subject to review. At this stage the budget profit and loss account and cash flow must be prepared to ensure that the package produces an acceptable result.

(f)   **Final acceptance of budgets**

All of the budgets are summarised into a master budget, which is presented to top management for final acceptance.

(g)   **Budget review**

The budget process involves regular comparison of budget with actual, and identifying causes for variances. This may involve modifying the budget as the period progresses - **planning changes**.

The mechanics of stages (e) and (f) are explained below; the detail of stage (g) dealt with later in the text.

2.7   Budget committee

A typical budget committee comprises the chief executive, the management accountant (acting as budget officer) and functional heads. The functions of the committee are to:

(a)   agree policy with regard to budgets;

(b)   co-ordinate budgets;

(c)   suggest amendments to budgets (eg, because there is inadequate profit);

(d)   approve budgets after amendment, as necessary;

(e)   examine comparisons of budgeted and actual results and recommend corrective action if this has not already been taken.

The budget officer is secretary to the committee and is responsible for seeing that the timetables are adhered to and for providing the necessary specialist assistance to the functional managers in drawing up their budgets and analysing results.

2.8   Budget manual

A budget manual is a document which sets out standing instructions governing the responsibilities of persons, and the procedures, forms and records relating to the preparation and use of budgets. It sets out the procedures to be observed in budgeting, the responsibilities of each person concerned, and the timetable to be observed.

2.9   Continuous v periodic budgeting

The effect of inflation on budgets can be very serious. In the past rapid inflation has led to widespread use of continuous rolling budgets. A budget is prepared for a year ahead (or whatever budget period has been chosen) and at the end of the first control period the budget for the remainder of the year is revised in the light of inflation to date or changed expectations concerning future inflation, in the light of which a budget is prepared for the first control period of the following year. This procedure is repeated after each control period, so that a budget for a year ahead is always available and budgets are as up-to-date as possible. This continual revision of budget figures leads to more up-to-date forecasts of future performance. Even though the days of hyper-inflation now seem to have gone, many firms still maintain a rolling budgeting system, regularly updating budgets for changes in the firm's circumstances.

While continuous budgets have a fixed planning horizon, periodic budgets have planning horizons which shorten as the period progresses. Periodic budgets are established for an accounting period, usually one year but can be as short as three months, and while the forecast for that year may change as the period progresses, the original periodic budget remains unchanged. This means that management will tend only to look to the end of the period for financial planning, while with continuous budgets they must always plan a full twelve months ahead. However, periodic budgets are used extensively in practice, mainly because they are less of an administrative burden. Continuous budgets may seem like a good idea, but periodic budgets are more practical.

2.10 Budget v actual compared

One of the purposes of preparing budgets is to provide feedback to managers concerning operational performance. This is achieved by comparing actual results against the budget as shown in the following example:

	Budget £	*Actual* £	*Difference* £
Sales	100,000	104,000	+4,000
Production costs	48,000	51,500	−3,500
Selling costs	13,500	14,000	−500
Administration costs	10,000	9,500	+500
PROFIT	28,500	29,000	+500

(*Note.* that the +/− in the difference column is stated by reference to the effect of that difference on profit.)

3 PREPARATION AND MONITORING PROCEDURES

3.1 How to budget - the seven steps

Preparation of the budget involves seven steps. These are illustrated diagrammatically below:

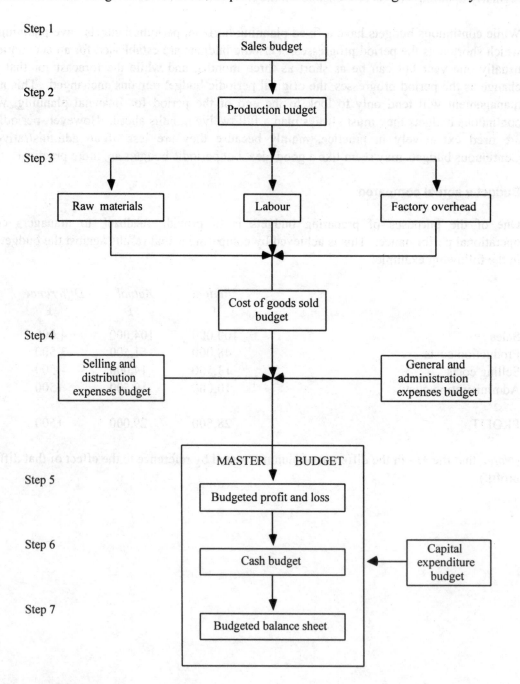

3.2 Principal budget factor

The sales budget is shown in the diagram because this is the pattern in most businesses, where it is the volume of the demand for the product which limits the scale of operation. It is possible, however, for there to be some other limiting factor eg, labour, material, cash or machinery. The limiting factor must be identified at the first stage of the budgeting process, since it will determine all the other budgets. In this context the limiting factor is referred to as the **principal budget factor.**

The determination and valuation of the principal budget factor is achieved using forecasting techniques. These are dealt with later in this chapter.

The budgeting process is, therefore, more fully described as follows:

(a)   Prepare:

- sales forecast;
- raw material availability forecast;
- cash availability forecast, etc.

(b)   Determine the principal budget factor.

(c)   Decide whether the limitations can be removed, and at what cost eg, by additional advertising expenditure, by intensive recruitment and training, etc. This is a matter for the budget committee.

(d)   Draw up budgets on the agreed basis.

4   PREPARATION OF THE BUDGETED PROFIT AND LOSS ACCOUNT

4.1   Illustration

The following data will be used to explain the technique of budget preparation

Hash Ltd makes two products - PS and TG. Sales for next year are budgeted at 5,000 units of PS and 1,000 units of TG. Planned selling prices are £65 and £100 respectively.

Hash Ltd has the following opening stock and required closing stock.

	PS units	TG units
Opening stock	100	50
Required closing stock	1,100	50

You are also given the following data about the materials required to produce PS and TG and the whittling and fettling processes involved in production.

	PS	TG
Finished products:		
Kg of raw material X, per unit of finished product	12	12
Kg of raw material Y, per unit of finished product	6	8
Direct labour hours per unit of finished product	8	12
Machine hours per unit - whittling	5	8
Machine hours per unit - fettling	3	4

	Raw material	
	X	Y
Direct materials:		
Desired closing stock in kg	6,000	1,000
Opening stock in kg	5,000	5,000

Standard rates and prices:

Direct labour	£2.20 per hour
Raw material X	£0.72 per kg
Raw material Y	£1.56 per kg

Production overheads:

Variable	£1.54 per labour hour
Fixed	£0.54 per labour hour
	£2.08 per labour hour

4.2   The sales budget

The sales budget represents the plan in terms of the quantity and value of sales, for sales management. In practice this is often the most difficult budget to calculate.

What is next year's sales budget?

The sales budget would be:

	Total	*PS*	*TG*
Sales units	6,000	5,000	1,000
Sales value	£425,000	£325,000	£100,000

In practice a business would market many more than two products. Moreover, the sales budget would probably be supported by subsidiary budgets to show analysis according to:

(a)   responsibility eg, Northern area, Western area, etc
(b)   type of customer eg, wholesale, retail, government, etc

4.3   The production budget

The production budget is usually expressed in quantity and represents the sales budget adjusted for opening/closing finished stocks and work in progress.

Production budget	*PS units*	*TG units*
Sales budget	5,000	1,000
Budgeted stock increase (1,100 – 100)/(50 – 50)	1,000	-
Production in units	6,000	1,000

The production budget needs to be translated into requirements for:

(a)   raw materials;
(b)   direct labour;
(c)   machine utilisation;
(d)   factory overheads;
(e)   closing stock levels.

4.4   The raw materials budget

(Remember that Hash Ltd is going to produce 6,000 units of PS and 1,000 units of TG.)

		X kg		*Y kg*
For production of PS	6,000 × 12 kg	72,000	6,000 × 6 kg	36,000
For production of TG	1,000 × 12 kg	12,000	1,000 × 8 kg	8,000
		84,000		44,000
Budgeted raw material stock increase/(decrease)	(6,000 – 5,000)	1,000	(1,000 – 5,000)	(4,000)
Raw materials required		85,000		40,000
		£		£
Budgeted value:				
X £0.72 per kg × 85,000		61,200		
Y £1.56 per kg × 40,000				62,400

4.5   The direct labour budget

		Hours		£
For PS	6,000 × 8 hrs	48,000		
For TG	1,000 × 12 hrs	12,000		
		60,000	@ £2.20	132,000

4.6   The machine utilisation budget

		whittling hours		fettling hours
For PS	6,000 × 5 hrs	30,000	6,000 × 3 hrs	18,000
For TG	1,000 × 8 hrs	8,000	1,000 × 4 hrs	4,000
		38,000		22,000
Total hours	=			60,000

4.7   Production overheads

		£
Variable costs	60,000 hours × £1.54	92,400
Fixed costs	60,000 hours × £0.54	32,400
		124,800

4.8   Opening and closing stocks

Remember that we are calculating the cost of sales. So far we have calculated the amounts of material, labour and overheads used in **production**. To arrive at the figures for cost of sales you have to remember that **production** is used not just for sales but also to increase/decrease stock levels - hence the need to adjust for the opening and closing stock position of both raw material and finished goods.

4.9   Closing stock of raw materials

		£
X	6,000 kg × £0.72	4,320
Y	1,000 kg × £1.56	1,560
		5,880

4.10   Closing stock of finished goods

		PS £		TG £
Standard cost of finished goods:				
Materials:				
X	12 kg × £0.72	8.64	12 kg × £0.72	8.64
Y	6 kg × £1.56	9.36	8 kg × £1.56	12.48
		18.00		21.12
Wages	8 hours × £2.20	17.60	12 hours × £2.20	26.40
Overhead	8 hours × £2.08	16.64	12 hours × £2.08	24.96
		52.24		72.48
Stock in units		1,100		50
Stock value		£57,464		£3,624

4.11   Activity

Calculate the values of the opening stocks of raw material and finished goods.

4.12   Activity solution

Raw material	X:	5,000 kg × £0.72	=	£3,600
Raw material	Y:	5,000 kg × £1.56	=	£7,800
Finished good	PS:	100 units × £52.24	=	£5,224
Finished good	TG:	50 units × £72.48	=	£3,624

4.13   Budgeted cost of sales

We can now bring all the above elements together.

	£	£
Opening stocks:		
Raw materials (3,600 + 7,800)	11,400	
Finished goods (5,224 + 3,624)	8,848	
		20,248
Raw materials (61,200 + 62,400)		123,600
Direct labour		132,000
Production overhead		124,800
		400,648
Less: Closing stocks:		
Raw materials	5,880	
Finished goods (57,464 + 3,624)	61,088	
		66,968
		333,680

4.14   Marketing and administration budget

Marketing and administration budgets will be a summary of the budget centres within those functions.

For the purposes of this example, the marketing/administration budget is assumed to be £45,000.

4.15   Budgeted profit and loss account

The budgeted profit and loss account is prepared by summarising the operating budgets.

Master budget - profit and loss account

	£	£
Sales		425,000
Cost of sales:		
Opening stocks	20,248	
Raw materials	123,600	
Direct labour	132,000	
Production overhead	124,800	
	400,648	
Closing stocks	66,968	
		333,680
Operating margin		91,320
Marketing/administration		45,000
Operating profit		46,320

Note: that the above budgets are presented to highlight planned requirements rather than for costing purposes. Most businesses will obviously be more complex than that illustrated and supporting analyses would be prepared as required eg,

> Production units by month or weeks
> Raw materials by supplier
> Direct labour by grade

4.16   Budgeted balance sheet

The total company plan will include a statement to show the financial situation at the end of the budget period. Subsidiary budgets will be prepared to analyse movements in fixed and working capital during the budget period based on the operating budgets and reflecting financial policy formulated by the budget committee.

4.17   Other budgets - capital expenditure

Obtaining finance for investment and selecting capital investment projects are aspects of long-term planning which are outside the syllabus. The capital expenditure included in the master budget will essentially be an extract from the long-term capital budget.

The cash required to finance the capital expenditure will be incorporated in the cash budget as illustrated later.

4.18   Other miscellaneous budgets

Depending on the requirements of management, additional budgets may be prepared for:

(a)   **Purchasing** - consolidates purchases of raw materials, supplies and services in raw materials/expense budgets, analysed to show when the goods are received (for control of supply) and also when they are paid for (for cash budget).

(b)   **Personnel (manpower)** - shows detailed requirements, month by month, for production and administration personnel.

(c)   **Stocks** - itemises quantity and value, month by month, of planned stock levels for raw materials, work in progress and finished goods.

(d)   **Debtors** - details time analysis of collections from sales suitably analysed by type of customer or type of product.

5   CASH BUDGETS

5.1   Objectives

(a)   Part of the budgeting process;

(b)   to anticipate cash shortages/surpluses and to provide information to assist management in short and medium-term cash planning and longer term financing for the organisation.

5.2   Method of preparation

(a)   Forecast sales;

(b)   forecast time-lag on converting debtors to cash, and hence forecast cash receipts from credit sales;

(c)   determine stock levels, and hence purchase requirements;

(d)   forecast time-lag on paying suppliers, and thus cash payments for purchases;

(e)   incorporate other cash payments and receipts, including such items as capital expenditure and tax payments;

(f)   collate all this cash flow information, so as to determine the net cash flows.

5.3   Layout

A tabular layout should be used, with:

(a)   columns for weeks, months or quarters (as appropriate);
(b)   rows for cash inflows and outflows.

5.4   Example

A wholesale company ends its financial year on 30 June. You have been requested, in early July 19X5, to assist in the preparation of a cash forecast. The following information is available regarding the company's operations:

(a)   Management believes that the 19X4/19X5 sales level and pattern are a reasonable estimate of 19X5/19X6 sales. Sales in 19X4/19X5 were as follows:

		£
19X4	July	360,000
	August	420,000
	September	600,000
	October	540,000
	November	480,000
	December	400,000
19X5	January	350,000
	February	550,000
	March	500,000
	April	400,000
	May	600,000
	June	800,000
	Total	6,000,000

(b)   The accounts receivable at 30 June 19X5 total £380,000. Sales collections are generally made as follows:

During month of sale	60%
In first subsequent month	30%
In second subsequent month	9%
Uncollectable	1%

(c)   The purchase cost of goods averages 60% of selling price. The cost of the stock on hand at 30 June 19X5 is £840,000, of which £30,000 is obsolete. Arrangements have been made to sell the obsolete stock in July at half the normal selling price on a cash on delivery basis. The company wishes to maintain the stock, as of the first of each month, at a level of three months' sales as determined by the sales forecast for the next three months. All purchases are paid for on the tenth of the following month. Accounts payable for purchases at 30 June 19X5 total £370,000.

(d)   Payments in respect of fixed and variable expenses are forecast for the first three months of 19X5/19X6 as follows:

	£
July	160,620
August	118,800
September	158,400

(e)   It is anticipated that cash dividends of £40,000 will be paid each half year, on the fifteenth day of September and March.

(f)   During the year unusual advertising costs will be incurred that will require cash payments of £10,000 in August and £15,000 in September. The advertising costs are in addition to the expenses in item (d) above.

(g)   Equipment replacements are made at a rate which requires a cash outlay of £3,000 per month. The equipment has an average estimated life of six years.

(h)   A £60,000 payment for corporation tax is to be made on 15 September 19X5.

(i)   At 30 June 19X5 the company had a bank loan with an unpaid balance of £280,000. The entire balance is due on 30 September 19X5, together with accumulated interest from 1 July 19X5 at the rate of 12% pa.

(j)   The cash balance at 30 June 19X5 is £100,000.

You are required to prepare a cash forecast statement, by months, for the first three months of the 19X5/19X6 financial year. The statement should show the amount of cash on hand (or deficiency of cash) at the end of each month. All computations and supporting schedules should be presented in clear and concise form.

5.5   Solution

The solution can be best approached as in the following paragraphs.

5.6   Activity

Work out the cash received from sales.

5.7   Activity solution

	Sales £	Cash received July £	August £	September £
May	600,000	54,000	-	-
June	800,000	240,000	72,000	-
July	360,000	216,000	108,000	32,400
August	420,000	-	252,000	126,000
September	600,000	-	-	360,000
		510,000	432,000	518,400

5.8   Obsolete stock

	£
Obsolete stock at cost	30,000
Normal sales price $\frac{100}{60} \times £30,000$	50,000
Realised ½ × £50,000	25,000

5.9   Payment to trade creditors

		£	£	£
(i)	10 July - Balance b/d			370,000
(ii)	10 August - sales in July		360,000	
	Cost of goods sold (60%)		216,000	
	Less: Opening stock	(840,000)		
	Less: Obsolete stock	30,000		
		(810,000)		
	Add: Closing stock 60%			
	(420,000 + 600,000 + 540,000)	936,000		
			126,000	
				342,000
(iii)	10 September - sales in August		420,000	
	Cost of goods sold (60%)		252,000	
	Less: Opening stock	(936,000)		
	Add: Closing stock 60%			
	(600,000 + 540,000			
	+ 480,000)	972,000		
			36,000	
				288,000

5.10   Cash budget

	July £	*August* £	*September* £
Receipts:			
Receipts from debtors	510,000	432,000	518,400
Obsolete stock	25,000	-	-
	535,000	432,000	518,400

	July £	*August* £	*September* £
Payments:			
Payments to creditors	370,000	342,000	288,000
Expenses	160,620	118,800	158,400
Dividends	-	-	40,000
Advertising	-	10,000	15,000
Capital expenditure	3,000	3,000	3,000
Corporation tax	-	-	60,000
Bank loan	-	-	288,400
	533,620	473,800	852,800
Net cash inflow/(outflow)	1,380	(41,800)	(334,400)
Balance	100,000	101,380	59,580
Balance/ (deficiency) at month end	101,380	59,580	(274,820)

5.11   Long-term cash budgeting

A short-term cash budget (say, for periods of up to one year) is prepared by first estimating sales and then considering the implications for cash if that level of sales is achieved. It is necessary to adopt a different method for the longer term, and the starting point can be the target figure of profit which the company has set itself as necessary for achievement of its long-term objectives. A suitable **pro forma** follows:

	£	£
Opening balance (from short-term forecast)		10,000
Add: Target profit	2,000	
Add back: Depreciation	500	
	———	2,500
		12,500
Less: Capital expenditure	1,000	
Tax payable	4,000	
Dividends payable	2,000	
	———	7,000
		5,500
± Changes in working capital		2,500
Closing balance		8,000

Plans should be laid to make good any shortfall of long-term funds by the issue of shares or by long-term borrowing. The function of the long-term budget is to give a general idea as to when such arrangements will be necessary to finance capital expenditure. The short-term budget, on the other hand, is primarily concerned with ensuring that sufficient cash is available for the day-to-day operations of the business. It is broken down into shorter periods than the long-term budget (generally monthly) and arrangements will be made to cover any short-term deficits by short-term borrowings.

6   COMPUTERISED CASH FLOW MODELS

6.1   Introduction

Computer models provide an easy way of monitoring cash flows. The most suitable format is that of various **spreadsheet** packages now available on most micros - Supercalc, Multiplan, Lotus 1-2-3, Jazz and Excel are among the better known.

The following simplified example is on Jazz, but similar results would be achieved with any of the above packages. In this example the cash flow data has been reduced to balance brought forward, receipts and payments:

	A	B	C	D	E
1		Jan	Feb	Mar	April
2					
3	Opening balance	1,000	1,100	1,000	550
4	Add: Receipts	700	800	500	850
5	Less: Payments	600	900	950	400
6					
7	Closing balance	1,100	1,000	550	1,000
8					

This table could equally well have been prepared manually, but in fact the columns containing balances consist of relationships, rather than numeric values:

	A	B	C	D	E
1		Jan	Feb	Mar	April
2					
3	Opening balance	1,000	=B7	=C7	=D7
4	Add: Receipts	700	800	500	850
5	Less: Payments	600	900	950	400
6					
7	Closing balance	=B3+B4–B5	=C3+C4–C5	=D3+D4–D5	=E3+E4–E5
8					

In order to understand the second table, it must be appreciated that the columns are labelled from left to right alphabetically, A, B, C, etc, and the rows numerically from the top down, 1, 2, 3, etc. Each cell is defined by the letter of the column and the number of the row, and calculations are by reference to cells rather than numbers.

Thus the opening balance for every month except January equals the previous month's closing balance. Similarly the closing balance is the Opening balance + Receipts – Payments.

The great advantage of this approach becomes apparent when applied to a large and complex flow projection:

(a)   this program can handle up to 8,192 rows and 234 columns, enough to accommodate a very complex model (though most micros would run out of memory if all the cells were used);

(b)   if any figure is amended, all the figures will be immediately recalculated;

(c)   the results can be printed out without going through an intermediate typing phase; and

(d)   most programs can also represent the results graphically eg, the above balances can be shown in a bar diagram:

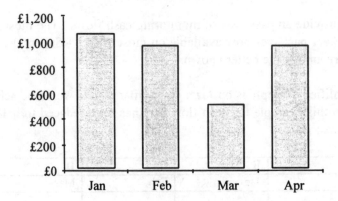

Closing cash balances

In total spreadsheet cash flow models represent a very powerful tool for use by the accountant.

6.2   Example of a cash budget

The following worksheet illustrates a screen showing part of a budgeting spreadsheet that has been set up for a cash budget.

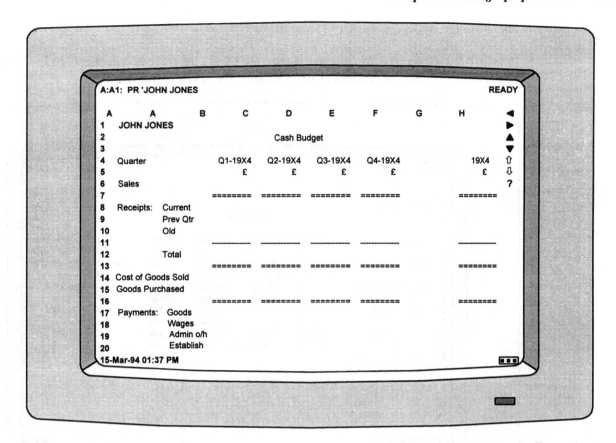

It is not the purpose of this examination or text to teach you how to use a spreadsheet. The following therefore simply attempts to give a good overview of how a spreadsheet can be used to produce part of a cash budget.

(a)   **Quarterly sales**

Sales are expected to be £60,000 in quarter 1, increasing in volume by 10% per quarter.

Thus insert £60,000 in C6. A formula can then be inserted into D6:

   +C6*1.1

This can be copied into E6 to G6 using:

   / C(opy) D6 ↵ E6..G6 ↵

The figures for quarters 2-4 should be:

   £66,000, £72,600, £79,860 (and £87,846 for the first quarter of 19X5 which will be needed to find purchases below. This 19X5 quarter is shown in column G.)

   Total sales revenue (@SUM(C6..F6)) is £278,460.

(b)   **Receipts**

50% of sales are expected to be received in the quarter that the sale is made, 40% is received one quarter later and 10% received two quarters later.)

The formulae: for cell F8 will be   F6*0.5

              for cell F9 will be   E6*0.4

              for cell F10 will be   D6*0.1

These can be copied into rows C, D and E.

In cells H8..H10 an @SUM function is required to add the total of columns C to F. In row 12 the three elements of receipts can be totalled. The result is shown below.

```
A:F10: U +D6/10                                                    READY

   A      A       B      C        D        E        F       G       H
 1  JOHN JONES
 2                                   Cash Budget
 3
 4  Quarter             Q1-19X4   Q2-19X4  Q3-19X4  Q4-19X4            19X4
 5                          £        £        £        £               £
 6  Sales               60,000   66,000   72,600   79,860   87,846  278,460
 7                     ======== ======== ======== ========         ========
 8  Receipts: Current   30,000   33,000   36,300   39,930          139,230
 9            Prev Qtr       0   24,000   26,400   29,040           79,440
10            Old            0        0    6,000    6,600           12,600
11                     -------- -------- -------- --------         --------
12            Total     30,000   57,000   68,700   75,570          231,270
13                     ======== ======== ======== ========         ========
14  Cost of Goods Sold
15  Goods Purchased
16                     ======== ======== ======== ========         ========
17  Payments: Goods
18            Wages
19            Admin o/h
20            Establish
15-Mar-94 01:47 PM
```

(c)   **Cost of sales and purchases**

The company will use a mark up on cost of 60%. 1½ months stock is to be held, therefore purchases in a quarter will correspond to 50% of the current quarter's cost of sales plus 50% of the next quarter's, the exception being quarter 1 of 19X4 when sufficient goods will be purchased to satisfy the next 4½ months.

The formula for cell C14 can be worked out by looking at the cost structure:

Cost of goods sold   +   profit   =   sales revenue

100   +   60   =   160

Cost of goods sold are $\frac{100}{160}$ times sales revenue.

The formula for cell C14 is:

+C6*100/160

When this is copied into rows D to G, the figures that appear are:

£37,500, £41,250, £45,375, £49,912.5 (and £54,903.75)

The cost of goods purchased shown in cell C15 must be:

+C14+D14/2

However in D15 (and copied into E and F) will be:

+D14/2 + E14/2

The totals can be shown in row H. The total of the Cost of Goods Sold is £174,037.50 (£278,460 × $\frac{100}{160}$) and of Goods Purchased £201,489.4.

(d) **Payments for goods**

Assume that 50% of purchases in each quarter are paid for in the quarter in which the purchases were made and 50% in the following quarter.

A similar approach can be adopted as for receipts by entering a formula in cell C17:

+C15/2 + B15/2

This can be copied into cells D17..F17 and the row summed to give the following worksheet.

```
A:H17: U @SUM(C17..F17)                                           READY

   A        A        B      C         D         E         F        G         H
1  JOHN JONES
2                                    Cash Budget
3
4  Quarter                        Q1-19X4   Q2-19X4   Q3-19X4   Q4-19X4            19X4
5                                    £         £         £         £                £
6  Sales                          60,000    66,000    72,600    79,860   87,846   278,460
7                                 ========  ========  ========  ========          ========
8  Receipts:  Current             30,000    33,000    36,300    39,930            139,230
9             Prev Qtr                 0    24,000    26,400    29,040             79,440
10            Old                      0         0     6,000     6,600             12,600
11                                --------  --------  --------  --------          --------
12            Total               30,000    57,000    68,700    75,570            231,270
13                                ========  ========  ========  ========          ========
14 Cost of Goods Sold             37,500    41,250    45,375   49,912.5  54,903.75 174,037.5
15 Goods Purchased                58,125   43,312.5  47,643.75 52,408.13          201,489.4
16                                ========  ========  ========  ========          ========
17 Payments:  Goods             29,062.5  50,718.75 45,478.13 50,025.94           175,285.3
18            Wages
19            Admin o/h
20            Establish

15-Mar-94 01:55 PM
```

7   PROBLEMS AND TECHNIQUES OF FORECASTING

November 1996 students

This topic is in the syllabus. You must study it.

May 1997 students

This topic is deleted from the syllabus. You need not study it.

Forecasting

Forecasting can be used to predict future data based on historical data. Although there are a number of techniques which can be used when forecasting, one should understand that the forecasts are just a prediction, and although they are expected to be a close approximation to the actual data, the forecast can never be 100% correct.

It is possible to produce sales forecasts and a forecast of costs by using a number of techniques, some of which are explained below.

Sales Forecasting

Market Research

Market Research is a study of consumer behaviour, it involves researching and surveying a number of people, businesses, areas etc, and collating this information to produce a forecast.

Time Series Models

A time series can be broken down into three major components. These being the trend, seasonal variation and the residual.

The trend and the seasonal variation are the 2 major parts of the series. The trend is calculated by using a technique of moving averages; this trend can then be extracted from the data, leaving the seasonal variation and the residual, both of which can be extracted in turn.

The trend shows the general direction of the data, where the seasonal variation shows how the data is affected over a 12 month period (ie, ice cream sales peak in the summer and drop heavily in the winter months).

Once this trend and seasonal variation have been established, this data can be used to forecast future sales.

Forecasting costs

Regression analysis allows us to establish a relationship between 2 variables and hence produce a regression line, which will in turn allow us to produce a forecast.

Eg, Total cost $Y = ax+b$

$$(Y) = a \times \text{units produced (x)} + b$$

If we had the regression line Total cost (£) = $2x + 8$

where x = no. of items produced.

If we wanted to calculate the expected total cost of producing 100 units.

Total cost	=	$2 \times 100 + 8$
	=	$200 + 8$
	=	£208

In conclusion then, forecasting can be used in relation to both sales and costs and hence to produce forecasted Profit & Loss a/c, cash flows etc.

8   A MORE COMPLEX BUDGETING EXAMPLE

8.1   Introduction

At this stage of your studies the examiner expects you to be able to prepare budgets from data using your knowledge of other areas of the cost accounting syllabus. The following example is taken from a past CIMA examination.

8.2   Example

The following data relate to Product Aye:

Budgeted data

	1 October to 31 December 19X5			1 January to 31 March 19X6		
Sales division	*1*	*2*	*3*	*1*	*2*	*3*
Sales of Aye (£)	54,000	342,000	228,000	60,000	360,000	240,000
Stocks of Aye:						
Opening units	90	320	260	100	350	250
Maximum units	150	500	350	150	500	350

Sales and production occur evenly each month during each budget quarter.

Debtors pay for sales in the month following that when sales occur.

Creditors are paid for materials in the second month following that when purchases occur.

On average, overhead incurred is paid for within the month following that in which incurred.

Wages are paid in the same month as earned.

Cash balance on 31 December 19X5, £(18,000).

Corporation tax of £50,000 is payable in January 19X6.

Special advertising compaign expenditure of £60,000 is due in March 19X6.

Standard cost data

Direct materials	DM1	10 kilos at £3 per kilo
	DM2	5 kilos at £2 per kilo
Direct wages	DW1	5 hours at £4 per hour
	DW2	2 hours at £5 per hour

Production overhead is absorbed as a labour hour rate, ie, £12 in respect of DW1 and £10 in respect of DW2.

Administration and selling overhead is recovered at 20% of production cost.

Profit is calculated at 10% of selling price.

Direct materials data

	Materials	
	DM1	*DM2*
Maximum consumption per week (kilos)	3,600	1,800
Minimum consumption per week (kilos)	2,400	1,200
Re-order quantity (kilos)	20,000	12,000
Stock at 30 September 19X5 (kilos)	24,500	13,650
Stock at 31 December 19X5 (kilos)	23,000	14,400
Lead time from suppliers (weeks):		
Maximum	6	5
Minimum	4	3

A major sales campaign is planned in the budget period beginning 1 April 19X6. In anticipation of an increase in sales, an advertising campaign will commence in the previous quarter. The production director has requested that stocks of raw materials be increased to maximum level by 1 April 19X6 and the sales director has requested that stocks of finished goods be increased to maximum level by 1 April 19X6.

You are required to prepare the following budgets for the three months ending 31 March 19X6:

(a)   production;

(10 marks)

(b)   purchases;

(10 marks)

(c)   production cost;

(15 marks)

(d)   cash (for each of the three months).

(5 marks)

8.3   Solution

This problem requires knowledge of standard cost cards and stock control systems as well as budgets.

(a)

$\boxed{\textbf{Step 1}}$ The question does not provide sales quantities or a selling price for Product Aye. Instead it gives sales values analysed by selling division. The divisional analysis is unnecessary to answer the question. The standard cost card must be prepared to determine the selling price, from this the sales quantity can be calculated.

Working: Calculation of standard cost and profit per unit

		£ per unit
Direct materials	DM1 (10 kgs × £3)	30
	DM2 (5 kgs × £2)	10
Direct wages	DW1 (5 hrs × £4)	20
	DW2 (2 hrs × £5)	10
Production overhead	DW1 - 5 hours × £12	60
	DW2 - 2 hours × £10	20
Total production cost		150
Administration and selling overhead - (20% of £150)		30
		180
Profit - 10% of selling price (therefore $^{10}/_{90}\%$ of cost of £180)		20
Selling price		200

Step 2   The sales quantity can now be determined and the production budget prepared.

Product Aye - Production budget for three months ending 31 March 19X6

		Units	*Units*
Sales units	- Division 1 (£60,000/£200)	300	
	- Division 2 (£360,000/£200)	1,800	
	- Division 3 (£240,000/£200)	1,200	
		——	
			3,300
Add required closing stock	- Division 1	150	
	- Division 2	500	
	- Division 3	350	
		——	
			1,000
			——
			4,300
Less opening stock	- Division 1	100	
	- Division 2	350	
	- Division 3	250	
		——	
			700
			——
Required production			3,600
			——

(b)

Step 3   In order to determine the raw material purchases it is necessary to calculate the required closing stock. This is to be at maximum and this has to be calculated using the stock control information given:

Maximum stock = reorder level + reorder quantity - (minimum usage × minimum lead time)

			DM1 *Kilos*	*DM2* *Kilos*
Reorder level =	Maximum × usage	Maximum lead time		
	DM1 = 3,600 × 6		21,600	
	DM2 = 1,800 × 5			9,000
Reorder quantity			20,000	12,000
			——	——
			41,600	21,000
Minimum usage × minimum lead time				
	DM1 = 2,400 × 4		9,600	
	DM2 = 1,200 × 3			3,600
			——	——
Maximum stocks			32,000	17,400
			——	——

Step 4   The direct material purchases budget can now be prepared:

Direct materials - purchases budget for the three months ending 31 March 19X6

	DM1 *Kilos*	*DM2* *Kilos*
Required closing stocks (maximum level)	32,000	17,400
Production requirements		
DM1 3,600 × 10kg	36,000	
DM2 3,600 × 5kg		18,000
	68,000	35,400
Less opening stock 31 December 19X5	23,000	14,400
Purchases	45,000	21,000
× standard price	£3	£2
	£135,000	£42,000

(c)

Step 5   The production cost budget can be prepared using the standard cost card details

Production cost budget for the three months ending 31 March 19X6

		£'000	£'000
Direct materials	- DM1 3,600 × £30	108	
	- DM2 3,600 × £10	36	
			144
Direct wages	- DW1 3,600 × £20	72	
	- DW2 3,600 × £10	36	
			108
Production overhead	- DW1 3,600 × £60	216	
	- DW2 3,600 × £20	72	
			288
Total production cost			540

(d)

Step 6   The material purchases for November and December must be calculated to determine the payments to be made to creditors. To do this the production budget for the quarter ended December must also be calculated:

Production for the three months ending 31 December 19X5:

	Aye *Units*
Closing stock	700
Sales for quarter (£54,000 + £342,000 + £228,000)/£200	3,120
	3,820
Less: Opening stock	670
Production units	3,150

Material purchases for the three months ending 31 December 19X5:

	DM1 *Kilos*	*DM2* *Kilos*
Closing stock	23,000	14,400
Used in production		
DM1 3,150 × 10 kilos	31,500	
DM2 3,150 × 5 kilos		15,750
	54,500	30,150
Less opening stock	24,500	13,650
Purchases	30,000	16,500
at standard price	£3	£2
	£90,000	£33,000
	£123,000	

Step 7   It is now assumed that:

- all overheads are cash items
- administration and selling overhead is incurred as it is recovered
- purchases of material occur evenly within each quarter

The cash budget can now be prepared:

Cash budget for the three months ending 31 March 19X6

	January *£'000*	*February* *£'000*	*March* *£'000*
Receipts from sales			
December sales	208		
Jan and Feb sales		220	220
	208	220	220
Payments			
Direct materials			
Nov and Dec purchases =			
$\dfrac{£123,000}{3}$	41	41	
Jan purchases =			
$\dfrac{£177,000}{3}$			59
Direct wages	36	36	36
Overhead			
December production	115.5		
Jan and Feb production		132	132
Corporation tax	50		
Advertising			60
	242.5	209	287
Net payment for month	(34.5)	11	(67)
Opening cash balance	(18)	(52.5)	(41.5)
Closing cash balance	(52.5)	(41.5)	(108.5)

9   CHAPTER SUMMARY

This chapter has considered the need for long term planning and conversion of these plans into short-term plans known as budgets.

The problems and techniques of forecasting have been introduced.

The techniques and organisation of budget preparation have been considered and finally the use of spreadsheets for budgeting have been introduced.

10   SELF TEST QUESTIONS

10.1   List five organisational objectives. (1.3)

10.2   What is the difference between a budget and a forecast? (1.8)

10.3   List the seven stages of the planning process. (1.9)

10.4   What are the advantages of budgeting? (1.10)

10.5   What is a budget? (2.1)

10.6   What is a budget centre? (2.5)

10.7   Why is it important to identify the principal budget factor? (3.2)

11   EXAMINATION TYPE QUESTIONS

11.1   Cash budget

From the following statements, prepare a month-by-month cash budget for the six months to 31 December.

(a)   **Revenue budget (ie, trading and profit and loss account)**

Six months to 31 December (all revenue/costs accrue evenly over the six months)

	£'000	£'000
Sales (cash received one month in arrear)		1,200
Cost of sales:		
Paid one month in arrear	900	
Paid in month of purchase	144	
Depreciation	72	
		1,116
Budgeted profit		84

(b)   **Capital budget**

	£'000	£'000
Payments for new plant:		
July	12	
August	25	
September	13	
November	50	
		100
Increase in stocks, payable August		20
		120
Receipts:		
New issue of share capital (October)		30

(c)   **Balance sheet**

		Actual 1 July
		£'000
Assets side:		
	Fixed assets	720
	Stocks	100
	Debtors	210
	Cash	40
		1,070
Liabilities side:		
	Capital and reserves	856
	Taxation (payable December)	30
	Creditors - trade	160
	Dividends (payable August)	24
		1,070

11.2   S Ltd

S Ltd manufactures three products - A, C and E - in two production departments - F and G - each of which employs two grades of labour. The cost accountant is preparing the annual budgets for Year 2 and he has asked you as his assistant to prepare, using the data given below:

(a)   the production budget in units for Products A, C and E;

(b)   the direct wages budget for Departments F and G with the labour costs of Products A, C and E and totals shown separately.

Data	Total	Product A	Product C	Product E
		£'000	£'000	£'000
Finished stocks:				
Budgeted stocks are:				
1 January, year 2		720	540	1,800
31 December, year 2		600	570	1,000
All stocks are valued at expected cost per unit		£24	£15	£20
Expected profit:				
Calculated as percentage of selling price		20%	25%	$16\frac{2}{3}$%
	£'000	£'000	£'000	£'000
Budgeted sales:				
South	6,600	1,200	1,800	3,600
Midlands	5,100	1,500	1,200	2,400
North	6,380	1,500	800	4,080
	18,080	4,200	3,800	10,080
Normal loss in production		10%	20%	5%

Expected labour times per
unit and expected rates

per hour	Rate £	Hours per unit	Hours per unit	Hours per unit
Department F:				
Grade 1	1.80	1.00	1.50	0.50
Grade 2	1.60	1.25	1.00	0.75
Department G:				
Grade 1	2.00	1.50	0.50	0.50
Grade 2	1.80	1.00	0.75	1.25

12   ANSWERS TO EXAMINATION TYPE QUESTIONS

12.1   Cash budget

	Jul £'000	Aug £'000	Sep £'000	Oct £'000	Nov £'000	Dec £'000	Total £'000
Receipts:							
Sales	210	200	200	200	200	200	1,210
New issue of share capital	-	-	-	30	-	-	30
Payments:							
Expenses and purchases	160	150	150	150	150	150	910
Expenses and purchases	24	24	24	24	24	24	144
Plant	12	25	13	-	50	-	100
Stock	-	20	-	-	-	-	20
Tax	-	-	-	-	-	30	30
Dividends	-	24	-	-	-	-	24
	196	243	187	174	224	204	1,228
Surplus/(deficiency)	14	(43)	13	56	(24)	(4)	12
Opening balance	40	54	11	24	80	56	52
Closing balance	54	11	24	80	56	52	64

12.2   S Ltd

(a)   **Production budget**

	Product A 000 units	Product C 000 units	Product E 000 units
Sales	140	190	420
Stock increase/(decrease)	(5)	2	(40)
Production required	135	192	380
Add: Excess to cover normal loss	15	48	20
Production budget	150	240	400

Notes:

(1)   Sales units $= \dfrac{\text{Budgeted sales value}}{\text{Expected selling price}}$

(2)   Expected selling price = Expected unit cost plus expected profit ie,

Product A	£24 × $\frac{100}{80}$	= £30
Product C	£15 × $\frac{100}{75}$	= £20
Product E	£20 × $\frac{100}{83\frac{1}{3}}$	= £24

(3)   Stock units = $\dfrac{\text{Budgeted stock values}}{\text{Expected unit costs}}$

(4)   Additional requirements to cover normal loss of production:

$$\text{Required production} \times \frac{\text{Loss percentage}}{\text{Normal production percentage}}$$

ie,			
	Product A	135 × $\frac{10}{90}$	= 15
	Product C	192 × $\frac{20}{80}$	= 48
	Product E	380 × $\frac{5}{95}$	= 20

(b)   **Direct wages budget**

	Product A 000 hours	£'000	Product C 000 hours	£'000	Product E 000 hours	£'000	Total £'000
Department F:							
Grade 1 (@ £1.80/hr)	150	270	360	648	200	360	1,278
Grade 2 (@ £1.60/hr)	187.5	180	240	384	300	480	1,044
		450		1,032		840	2,322
Department G:							
Grade 1 (@ £2.00/hr)	225	450	120	240	200	400	1,090
Grade 2 (@ £1.80/hr)	150	270	180	324	500	900	1,494
		720		564		1,300	2,584
Total budget		1,170		1,596		2,140	4,906

Note: hours budgeted represent production budget units at expected labour times.

18 BUDGETARY CONTROL

INTRODUCTION & LEARNING OBJECTIVES

Syllabus area 6c. Preparation and monitoring procedures; reporting against actual financial data. (Ability required 3).

Flexible budgets. (Ability required 3).

This chapter considers the use of budgets as part of an organisation's system of performance evaluation. It introduces the principles of comparing actual and target performance using variances and shows the importance of involving managers in the budgeting process.

When you have studied this chapter you should be able to do the following:

- Explain the principles of budgetary control.

- List and explain the criteria for budget reporting.

- Distinguish between fixed and flexible budgets.

- Explain the problems of budgeting and budgetary control in periods of rising prices.

---

1 BUDGETARY CONTROL

1.1 Systems theory

In order that control can be exercised, an understanding is required of the **system** over which or within which control is required. If the characteristics of a business system can be identified, a control process can be developed.

There are a number of ways in which systems can be classified. The most general sub-division is between:

(a)   closed systems; and
(b)   open systems.

> **Definition**   A **closed system** may be defined as one which does not take in anything from, or give out anything to, the environment.

The complete behaviour of the system takes place by interaction among the components of the system. It is completely self-contained and does not exchange material, information or energy with its environment. Conventional physics deals only with closed systems eg, the laws of thermo-dynamics are expressly stated to be applicable only to closed systems. Chemistry tells us about the reactions and chemical equilibriums established in a closed vessel into which certain reactants are brought together.

> **Definition**   An **open system** is open to the outside world: it takes in material, information or energy and can also give these out again.

In other words, open systems have **inputs** and **outputs.** All biological systems are open systems and they exist in a dynamic balance with their environment. Organisations are also examples of open systems and they too are able to adapt to changes in the environment in order to survive - only open systems have this quality.

As businesses are open systems, control must be capable of responding to changes in the environment as the system itself responds to changes. For example, an external influence on a business may be tighter safety standards required in a finished product by the European Community. Machine tolerances may thus become much finer. Quality control tests must therefore also become more precise.

1.2   Control systems

'A control system is a communications network that monitors activities within the organisation and provides the basis for corrective action in the future' (Drury). Control systems are best exemplified by simple mechanical control systems, such as the thermostat control over the temperature in a gas oven.

The essential features of a control system are: control (the automatic regulator), instructions, the process (burning gas) and feedback information (temperature). In a mechanical control system the process is essentially simple in that only one variable (temperature) is monitored, and only one process (burning of gas) is controlled.

The thermostat control, however, is essentially a closed system. It does not have many interfaces with the environment. A budgetary control system is much more complex in that there are many variables and a variety of processes. Also outcomes from specific actions cannot be known with certainty, and there are many factors outside the budget affecting outcomes. Nevertheless, it is possible to see certain similarities to the simple control system above.

It should be recognised that as business is an open system, the budgetary control system may need to be redesigned if the way the business operates changes.

A budgetary control system is widely regarded as the most important financial control system in an organisation. This section is primarily concerned with factors that affect the effectiveness of the budget as a control system.

1.3   Classification of controls

There is a widely accepted three-way classification of controls into **organisational, informal group** and **individual**. The table below compares these classes:

Type	Objectives	Performance criteria	Feedback	Incentives	
				Rewards or reinforcements	*Punishments or sanction*
Organisation	Profits, share of market: quality of service	Budgets, standard costs, past performance	Quantitative variances	Commendation, promotions, salary rises	Condemnation, dismissal, salary cuts
Informal group	Mutual commitment, group ideals	Group norms	Deviant behaviour	Peer approval, membership, leadership	Kidding, hostility, ostracism
Individual	Personal goals, aspirations	Expectations, interim targets	Reaching or missing targets	Self-satisfaction, elation	Disappointment self-hatred

Though the main concern in management accounting is with organisational controls, all three categories are relevant in the management process.

1.4   Concept of budgetary control

The budgetary control cycle can be illustrated as follows:

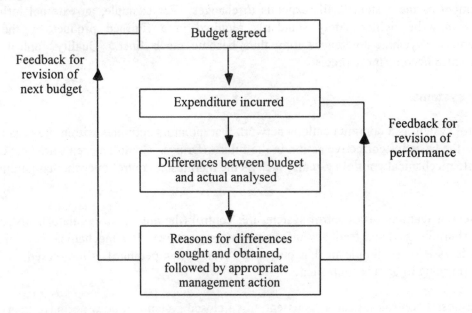

The various stages in the cycle will be discussed in turn.

1.5   Feedforward control

In order to have overall organisational control it is essential to have feedforward control as well as the feedback control that has been detailed in the previous sections of this lesson. Feedback control compares actual outputs with predetermined objectives, while in feedforward control predictions are made of what outputs are expected to be at some future time. In some ways all planning is a form of feedforward control. If the initial plans differ from what is desired at that time, control actions are implemented that will minimise these differences.

An important example of feedforward control is cash planning. This is especially important where an enterprise must work within predetermined overdraft limits. Failure to do so may result in the liquidation of the enterprise. Feedback control is not appropriate in these circumstances. The possibility of exceeding the overdraft limits must be appreciated in advance; it is of little use to know that the strict limits have been exceeded, which is how the information would be reported in a feedback control system. Stock control systems with minimum and maximum stores levels also require the use of feedforward control eg, system required to prevent 'stock-outs' of vital materials and components.

Feedforward controls give management warnings that they should not ignore.

1.6   Agreement of budget

The first stage is marked 'Budget agreed'. Budgets should not be imposed on those who have to work within them, but should be arrived at by a process of discussion between those who are to spend the money, their superiors and the finance department.

1.7   Analysis of variances

This is the stage marked 'Differences between budget and actual analysed'. This stage presents several problems: how often are the variances to be extracted (most businesses use monthly, weekly or even daily systems - a year is too long for control purposes) and how are they to be analysed? Variance analysis is described in detail later.

1.8   Use of variances

The aim of a budgetary control system is not to assign blame for past variances, which cannot be retrieved, but to use the knowledge gained from the explanation of those variances to:

(a)   take immediate action to improve current and future performance;
(b)   improve the plans for future periods.

The reporting of variances to appropriate managers within the organisation structure is a good example of the well-established concept of **management by exception.** This involves highlighting for the attention of management the deviations or exceptions from the plan, rather than inundating managers with a lot of information about actual results which are very much in line with the budgets. In this way the important items which require the attention of management are not camouflaged amongst the whole information package. This approach should reduce the delay and speed up the decision-making process.

1.9   Applicability of budgetary control

Budgetary control can be operated to a greater or lesser degree in most types of organisation. It may or may not be linked to a system of standard costing - a point that will be dealt with later. Budgeting is often discussed in the context of an industrial organisation where sales budgets usually dictate the levels of other budgets (the principal budget factor concept already discussed). However, non-trading organisations also operate budgetary control systems eg, local authorities budget their expenditure (and revenue) to fix the council tax and business premises rate in the pound of rateable value. It is then of great importance that expenditure levels are closely controlled, for it is difficult (and usually politically embarrassing) to attempt to impose supplementary charges at a later date in the same financial year. Budgetary control takes on a very important role in these circumstances.

1.10   Budget reporting

The feedback loop in the control system requires a formal reporting procedure. This link is vital in that the budget system may identify variances, and hence problems, but unless these are effectively communicated to management, that knowledge is ineffective. In the context of budget systems, feedback reports consist of comparisons of budget targets and actual financial achievements, with differences highlighted as variances.

General criteria may be laid down for such reports:

(a)   **Reports should be relevant to the information needs of their recipients.** This means that the report should contain all relevant information to the decisions to be made, and responsibilities exercised by the manager who receives the report. Generally, other information should be excluded although there is an argument for including background information on divisional/company performance.

(b)   **Reporting should be linked to responsibility.** This is discussed in more detail below.

(c)   **Reports should be timely.** One of the most frequent reporting problems is that reports are received after the decision for which they are required. In such cases managers must often rely on informal information sources outside the budget system. This may be less efficient, and also reduces the credibility of the budgetary control system in the eyes of that manager.

(d)   **Reports should be reliable.** The reports should be regarded as containing reliable information (though not necessarily exact to the penny). There may be a conflict between reliability and timeliness, and often as assessment must be made of what is an acceptable error rate and/or degree of approximation.

(e)   **Reports should be designed to communicate effectively.** Reports should be specifically designed to communicate effectively, often with managers who are not professional accountants. Reports should avoid jargon, be concise, but contain sufficient detail (often in supporting schedules). Maximum use should be made of graphical presentation.

(f)   **Reports should be cost-effective.** A report is only worthwhile if the benefits from its existence exceed the cost of producing it.

1.11   Control of non-manufacturing costs

Non-manufacturing costs present their own specific problems of budgetary control, in addition to those already discussed in the context of manufacturing costs. Such costs are unlikely to vary with the level of production activity, but they may represent a significant proportion of total costs. Therefore, specific budgetary control techniques must be developed to deal with such costs.

These costs would include research and development, administration and finance, marketing and distribution.

(a)   **Alternative activity measures**

Since the costs are not related to production activity, some alternative activity measure must be identified. Possible examples would be marketing costs per sales order and purchasing costs per delivery.

(b)   **Committed fixed costs**

Definition   These are fixed costs incurred for a series of accounting periods because of some past decision. An example would be lease costs as a result of entering into a lease agreement. Because of their implications for future accounting periods such costs must be considered in the same way as a capital expenditure proposal.

(c)   **Discretionary fixed costs**

Definition   These are costs which are fixed only in the sense that they are unaffected by the level of production; from a decisional point of view they are entirely within the discretion of management. Examples include advertising expenditure, research and development and training costs. In all of these cases there is no direct link between expenditure (input) and revenues (output).

This makes the task of defining an appropriate level of expenditure extremely difficult. Various approaches are possible, but they all have failings:

(i)   Past expenditure - but this may perpetuate past mistakes.
(ii)   Other similar companies - but they may have it wrong.
(iii) A percentage of sales - but the percentage selected must be arbitrary.

From the management control point of view, it is essential that such costs are controlled by fixed budgets that form ceilings on expenditure.

(d)   **Measuring effectiveness**

It follows from the above that controlling the effectiveness of non-manufacturing costs can be very difficult.   However, this is not to suggest that it is impossible, and the cost accountant should actively seek measures of effectiveness.   Examples would include percentage utilisation of training facilities/instructor's time, sales per marketing campaign, etc.

1.12   Control in non-profit organisations

The major problems of non-profit organisations are:

(a)   difficulty of quantifying objectives - eg, animal welfare may be a legitimate objective, but it is not easily amenable to quantification;

(b)   lack of outputs quantifiable in monetary terms - eg, if the output is improved health care in an Asian village, the gains may be real, but they are not monetary.

The largest examples of non-profit organisations are government bureaucracies, and effective budgetary control continues to create problems in these areas in spite of government's attempts to control expenditure.

1.13   Management audit

Management audits tend to have developed in the context of non-profit organisations, but can also be an effective management control in profit-orientated entities.   Their objective is to improve management performance by identifying waste and inefficiencies, and recommending corrective action.   In this sense management audits should be clearly distinguished from traditional financial audits.   A management audit would concentrate on the following specific aspects:

(a)   nature and functioning of the entity's managerial systems and procedures;
(b)   economy and efficiency with which entity's services are provided; and
(c)   the entity's effectiveness in achieving objectives.

Generally a management audit should consist of the following phases:

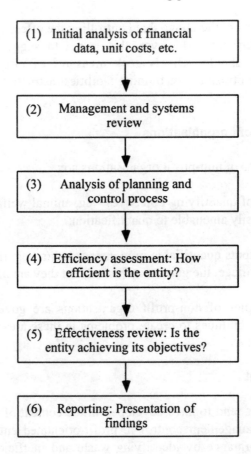

Management audits can be undertaken either by an internal team of specialists or by external consultants.

1.14   Responsibility accounting

Budgetary control and responsibility accounting are inseparable. It has already been stated that an organisation chart must be drawn up in order to implement a budgetary control system. It may even be necessary to revise the existing organisation structure before designing the system. The aim is to ensure that each manager has a well-defined area of responsibility and the authority to make decisions within that area, and that no parts of the organisation remain as 'grey' areas where it is uncertain who is responsible for them. This area of responsibility may be simply a **cost centre** or it may be a **profit centre** (implying that the manager has control over sales revenues as well as costs) or an **investment centre** (implying that the manager is empowered to take decisions about capital investment for his department). Once senior management have set up such a structure, with the degree of delegation implied, some form of responsibility accounting system is needed. Each centre will have its own budget, and the manager will receive control information relevant to that budget centre. Costs (and possibly revenue, assets and liabilities) must be traced to the person primarily responsible for taking the related decisions, and identified with the appropriate department.

Some accountants would go as far as to advocate charging ie, actually debiting, departments with costs that arise strictly as a result of decisions made by the management of those departments. For example, if the marketing department insists on a special rush order which necessitates overtime working in production departments, then the marketing department and not the production departments should be charged with the overtime premiums incurred. However, there are practical problems with such an approach:

(a)   The rush order itself might actually be produced during normal time because, from a production scheduling angle, it might be more convenient to do it then (eg, because it would not involve a clean-down of the machines as it was compatible with some other orders currently in production) - normal orders thereby actually being produced during the period of 'overtime'.

(b)   Re-charging costs to other departments can become a common occurrence because managers see it as a way of passing on not only the costs but also the associated responsibility eg, if the rush order is produced inefficiently in overtime, should the costs of the inefficiency also be charged to the marketing department?

(c)   Re-charging on a large scale can cause a lot of extra administration and explanation to the recipient department at the reporting stage.

It is worth concluding with the comment that all the managers do work for the same organisation and, if the costs are shunted around, there is a nil effect on the overall profit of the organisation (except to the extent of any extra costs incurred in operating such a recharging system).   Perhaps the effort expended on such a system could be more positively used to increase overall profit.

1.15   Controllable costs

Performance reports should concentrate only on **controllable costs.** Controllable costs are those costs controllable by a particular manager in a given time period.   Over a long enough time-span most costs are controllable by someone in the organisation eg, factory rental may be fixed for a number of years but there may eventually come an opportunity to move to other premises. Such a cost, therefore, is controllable in the long term by a manager fairly high in the organisation structure.   However, in the short term it is uncontrollable even by him, and certainly not by managers lower down in the organisation.

There is no clear-cut distinction between controllable and non-controllable costs for a given manager, who may in any case be exercising control jointly with another manager. The aim under a responsibility accounting system will be to assign and report on the cost to the person having **primary** responsibility. Most effective control is thereby achieved, since immediate action can be taken.

Some authorities would favour the alternative idea that reports should include all costs caused by a department, whether controllable or uncontrollable by the departmental manager. The idea here is that, even if he has no direct control, he might influence the manager who does have control. There is the danger of providing the manager with too much information and confusing him but, on the other hand, the uncontrollable element could be regarded as for 'information only', and in this way the manager obtains a fuller picture.

An illustration of the two different approaches is provided by raw materials. The production manager will have control over usage, but not over price, when buying is done by a separate department. For this reason the price and usage variances are separated and, under the first approach, the production manager would be told only about the usage variance, a separate report being made to the purchasing manager about the price variance. The alternative argument is that if the production manager is also told about the price variance, he may attempt to persuade the purchasing manager to try alternative sources of supply.

1.16   The problem of dual responsibility

A common problem is that the responsibility for a particular cost or item is shared between two (or more) managers. For example, the responsibility for payroll costs may be shared between the personnel and production departments; material costs between purchasing and production departments; and so on. The reporting system should be designed so that the responsibility for performance achievements (ie, better or worse than budget) is identified as that of a single manager.

The following guidelines may be applied:

(a)   If manager controls quantity **and** price - responsible for all expenditure variances.

(b)   If manager controls quantity but **not** price - only responsible for variances due to usage.

(c)   If manager controls price but **not** quantity - only responsible for variances due to input prices.

(d)   If manager controls **neither** quantity **nor** price - variances uncontrollable from the point of view of that manager.

1.17   Budgetary control and responsibility centres

The table below indicates how standard cost variances might be the responsibility of different responsibility centres:

Responsibility centre	A	B	C	D	E	F	G
1	x	x		x			
2		x			x	x	
3				x	x		x
4		x	x			x	

Thus, for all the products except A, C and G more than one centre is responsible for their production. Therefore, it is not possible for products B, D, E and F to make one centre exclusively responsible for variances in relation to that product. Instead the system must ensure that each centre is made responsible for the variances within its control.

1.18   Guidelines for reporting

There are several specific problems in relation to reporting which must be identified and dealt with:

(a)   **Levels of reporting**

The problem is how far down the management structure should responsibility centres be identified for reporting purposes? On the one hand, lower reporting levels encourage delegation and identify responsibility closer to the production process. On the other hand, more responsibility centres increase the number of reports and hence the cost of their production. One solution may be to combine small responsibility centres into groups (eg, departments) for reporting purposes.

(b)   **Frequency of reports and information to be reported**

The frequency of reports should be linked to the purposes for which they are required. This may well mean a variety of reports being produced to different time-scales for different purposes eg, some control information will be required weekly, or even daily. However, comprehensive budget reports are only likely to be required monthly.

The related problem is the content of such reports. It has been suggested that in computerised information systems the problem is often too much, rather than too little information. Generally, as reporting proceeds up the management pyramid, the breadth of the report should increase, and the detail should decrease. The following series of reports illustrate this principle:

	Budget		Variance	
	Current month	*Year to date*	*Current month*	*Year to date*

Managing director

Factory A
Factory B
Administration costs
Selling costs
Distribution costs
R&D costs

Production director Factory A

Machining department
Casting department
Assembly department
Inspection and quality control
Factory manager's office

Head of machining department

Direct materials
Direct labour
Indirect labour
Power
Maintenance
Other

The above layout should only be regarded as illustrative, but it does indicate how detail increases as span decreases.

2   FLEXIBLE BUDGETS

2.1   Introduction

Definition   A flexible budget is one which, by recognising the distinction between fixed and variable costs, is designed to change in response to changes in output.

The concept of responsibility accounting requires the use of flexible budgets for control purposes. Many of the costs under a manager's control are variable and will therefore change if the level of activity is different from that in the budget. It would be unreasonable to criticise a manager for incurring higher costs if these were a result of a higher than planned volume of activity. Conversely, if the level of activity is low, costs can be expected to fall and the original budget must be amended to reflect this.

A variance report based on a flexible budget therefore compares actual costs with the costs budgeted for the level of activity actually achieved. It does not explain any change in budgeted volume, which should be reported on separately.

2.2   Flexible budgeting

The key points to note are:

(a)   A fixed budget is set at the beginning of the period, based on estimated production. This is the original budget.

(b)   This is then **flexed** to correspond with the actual level of activity.

(c)   The result is compared with actual costs, and differences (variances) are reported to the managers responsible.

2.3   Example

Bug Ltd manufactures one uniform product only, and activity levels in the assembly department vary widely from month to month. The following statement shows the departmental overhead budget based on an average level of activity of 20,000 units production per four-week period and the actual results for four weeks in October.

	Budget average for four-week period £	Actual for 1 to 28 October £
Indirect labour - variable	20,000	19,540
Consumables - variable	800	1,000
Other variable overheads	4,200	3,660
Depreciation - fixed	10,000	10,000
Other fixed overheads	5,000	5,000
	40,000	39,200
Production (units)	20,000	17,600

You are required:

(a)   to prepare a columnar flexible four-week budget at 16,000, 20,000 and 24,000 unit levels of production;

(b)   to prepare two performance reports based on production of 17,600 units by the department in October, comparing actual with:

(i)   average four-week budget; and
(ii)   flexible four-week budget for 17,600 units of production;

(c)   to state which comparison ((b) (i) or (b) (ii)) would be the more helpful in assessing the foreman's effectiveness and why; and

(d)   to sketch a graph of how the flexible budget total behaves over the 16,000 to 24,000 unit range of production.

2.4   Solution

(a)

Production level	16,000 units	20,000 units	24,000 units
	£	£	£
Variable costs:			
Indirect labour	16,000	20,000	24,000
Consumables	640	800	960
Other overheads	3,360	4,200	5,040
	20,000	25,000	30,000
Fixed costs:			
Depreciation	10,000	10,000	10,000
Other overheads	5,000	5,000	5,000
	35,000	40,000	45,000

(b)   (i)

	Average four-week budget	Actual results	Variances fav./adv.)
	£	£	£
Indirect labour	20,000	19,540	460
Consumables	800	1,000	(200)
Other variable overheads	4,200	3,660	540
Depreciation	10,000	10,000	-
Other fixed overheads	5,000	5,000	-
	40,000	39,200	800

(ii)

	Flexed four-week budget	Actual results	Variances fav./(adv.)
Sales (units)	17,600	17,600	-
	£	£	£
Indirect labour	17,600	19,540	(1,940)
Consumables	704	1,000	(296)
Other variable overheads	3,696	3,660	36
Depreciation	10,000	10,000	-
Other fixed overheads	5,000	5,000	-
	37,000	39,200	(2,200)

(c)   The flexed budget provides more useful data for comparison because:

(i)   the fixed original budget makes no distinction between fixed and variable costs;

(ii)   hence no data is available concerning the appropriate level of costs at the actual production level;

(iii)   this would lead to the conclusion that the foreman had done well, when in fact costs had not fallen nearly as much as anticipated for the actual production;

(iv)   responsibility for the production shortfall is not known.

(d)   **Graph of costs in the production range 16,000 to 24,000 units**

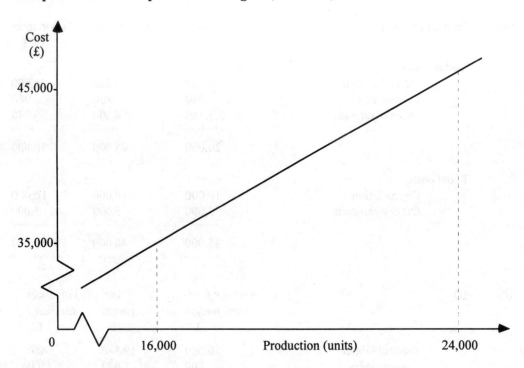

2.5   Flexible budgeting and management attitudes

The nature of cost behaviour patterns is not changed according to whether fixed or flexible budgets are used; what is changed is the way in which management view costs.

2.6   Example

The Alic Co Ltd has many small customers. Work measurement of the debtors' ledger shows that one clerk can handle 2,000 customer accounts. The company employs 30 clerks on the debtors' ledger at a salary of £3,600 each. The outlook for next year is of a decline in the number of customers from 59,900 to 56,300. However, management decides not to reduce the number of clerks.

Show the effect of this decision if debtors' ledger clerks' salaries are treated as:

(a)   variable expenses per customer per year;
(b)   fixed overhead.

2.7   Solution

		£
(a)	Allowed expense $56,300 \times \dfrac{£3,600}{2,000}$	101,340
	Actual expenditure $30 \times £3,600$	108,000
		6,660 A

		£
(b)	Allowed expense	108,000
	Actual expenditure	108,000
		Nil

Neither approach says whether the management decision was right. Approach (a), however, does give the cost of that decision.

Consequently the way costs are classified can influence the way management views costs, and ultimately the decisions that are made.

2.8   Activity

A company's production overhead budget is based on the principle that each unit of production incurs variable overhead cost of £5.40 and that each month fixed production overhead of £6,750 is incurred.

During June the budgeted output was 460 units and actual output was 455 units.

Calculate the allowed expense for June.

2.9   Activity solution

(455 units × £5.40) + £6,750 = £9,207

3   COPING WITH INFLATION

3.1   Inflation

Definition   Inflation may be defined alternatively as:

(a)   a general increase in prices; or
(b)   a fall in the value of money.

The effect is that money will buy less goods or, to put it another way, the same quantity of goods will cost more money.

3.2   Effect on budgets

In inflationary conditions budgeting is made more difficult because a prediction has to be made not only of future income and expenditure in real terms, but also an estimate of the level of inflation in order to arrive at a satisfactory value of the money which must be spent.

3.3   Example

LFC bought 500 tons of material for its production process last year at a cost of £2 per ton. It expects production levels to increase by 20% next year and inflation of 5% is expected to prevail. How much should LFC budget in respect of material?

Current situation	*Increase due to production*	*Budget in real terms*	*Inflation*	*Budget in money terms*
500 tons @ £2/ton = £1,000	20% × £1,000 = £200	£1,200	5% × £1,200 = £60	£1,260

Thus, if the price level remained constant LFC could expect to spend £1,200 on material. Because of inflation, however, an additional £60 must be budgeted, resulting in a total of £1,260.

3.4   Effect on control

Inflation will lead to changes in prices, as illustrated above. Because inflation is so difficult to predict, however, it is unlikely that estimates will in fact be met. Thus there is, almost inevitably, certain to be a price variance which is due to inflation - a situation outside the control of the company. It would be possible to isolate the effects of this inflation variance, but the cost of doing so may be prohibitive. Nevertheless, without such isolation the control function becomes much more difficult.

3.5   Effect on decisions

Decisions may become clouded in inflationary conditions for two reasons:

(a)   the problem of estimating: costs associated with different options may be wrongly adjusted for inflation;

(b)   different factors may have different rates of inflation associated with them.

For example, consider the following two options:

		Option (i) £	Option (ii) £
Costs:			
	Materials	8,000	3,500
	Labour	2,000	6,000
	Overheads	2,000	2,000
	Total	12,000	11,500

As option (ii) is cheaper, it would be selected.

Assume, however, that in the following year rates of inflation will be as follows:

	%
Material	Nil
Labour	25
Overheads	10

Forecasts for the next year would become:

	Option (i) £	Option (ii) £
Materials	8,000	3,500
Labour	2,500	7,500
Overheads	2,200	2,200
	12,700	13,200

Option (ii), as a result of the differing rates of inflation, is now the less attractive of the two options.

Other problem areas include:

(a)   Valuation of stock - inflation will erode the value of stock and a system such as FIFO will result in higher profit figures being recorded than may be applicable. Conversely, LIFO will result in an understatement of stock values.

(b)   Plant and machinery will be recorded at a value lower than their money value.

(c)   Prices will be difficult to set if a sufficient provision for inflation is to be allowed for.

4   CHAPTER SUMMARY

This chapter has introduced the principles of budgetary control using flexible budgets and variances.

5   SELF TEST QUESTIONS

5.1   What are the differences between a closed system and an open system? (1.1)

5.2   What is feedforward control? (1.5)

5.3   What is a variance? (1.7)

5.4   What is a committed fixed cost? (1.11)

5.5   What is a discretionary fixed cost? (1.11)

5.6   What is responsibility accounting? (1.14)

5.7   What are controllable costs? (1.15)

5.8   What is a flexible budget? (2.1)

5.9   What is inflation? (3.1)

6   EXAMINATION TYPE QUESTIONS

6.1   Principal budget factor

(a)   Define the term 'principal budget factor'. Say why the principal budget factor is important in the planning process.

(3 marks)

(b)   What are the differences between a fixed budget and a flexible budget? In what ways are fixed budgets and flexible budgets useful for planning and control?

(7 marks)

(c)   In its budgets for the period ahead, a company is considering two possible sales forecasts for its three products:

		Product A	Product B	Product C
(i)	Sales units	22,000	40,000	6,000
	Selling price per unit	£10.00	£6.00	£7.50
(ii)	Sales units	30,000	50,000	7,000
	Selling price per unit	£9.00	£5.70	£7.10

Variable costs per unit are expected to be the same at the different levels of possible sales. The variable costs per unit are as follows:

	Product A £	Product B £	Product C £
Direct materials	3.00	2.00	4.00
Direct labour	2.00	1.50	1.00
Variable overhead	1.00	0.50	0.50

Fixed overheads are expected to total £150,000. These are expected to be unaffected by the possible changes in activity which are being considered.

Due to recent high labour turnover and problems of recruitment, direct labour will be restricted to a maximum of £135,000 in the period. It can be assumed that all labour is of the same grade and is freely transferable between products. Other resources are expected to be generally available.

You are required to take each of the possible sales forecasts in turn.

(i)   Say what the principal budget factor is for each of the forecasts.

(ii)   For each forecast, calculate the sales budget that you would recommend to maximise profits.

(iii)   What profit would you expect from each sales budget?

In order to answer these questions you must assume that the three products must be sold either all at the higher prices or all at the lower prices.

(15 marks)

(Total: 25 marks)

6.2   C Ltd

(a)   Planning is expressed by the budgets which are prepared, but, prior to this, it is necessary to go through a forecasting exercise.

You are required to discuss briefly five problems which are likely to arise when forecasting for a business.

(10 marks)

(b)   C Ltd employs 300 people and has sales of £9 million. It has five producing departments, two service departments and manufactures one product.

No effective planning or financial control system has been established but after one of the directors had attended a CIMA course on 'Finance for Non-Financial Managers' he decided to introduce a budget system and performance reports related to responsibilities. Other directors and management had some reservations about the introduction of this system but they were persuaded to allow its introduction.

After the end of April, which was the first month of the current financial year, departmental performance reports were issued to all departmental supervisors. These took the form of that illustrated below for Production Department 'D' which was produced by the office manager - the senior person on the administrative staff. (A separate report was issued relating to direct material and direct labour.)

Monthly report: department 'D' - April 19X0

	Actual	Planning budget	Variance
Units produced	1,100	1,000	100
	£	£	£
Salaries and wages	10,000	10,500	500
Indirect labour	8,000	7,000	(1,000)*
Maintenance	3,500	2,750	(750)*
Overhead allocated	3,000	2,750	(250)*
Consumable stores	1,600	1,500	(100)*
Depreciation	2,500	2,500	0
Insurance	1,100	1,000	(100)*
Sundries	1,000	500	(500)*
	30,700	28,500	(2,200)

Note: considerable inefficiency; action should be taken to improve cost control in this department.

J, the supervisor for department D, was not pleased on receiving her report and declared she did not have time to bother with such paperwork and, in any case, the report was inaccurate and unfair. Her comment was typical of others who had received similar reports.

You are required:

(i)   to state what changes ought to be made to the report and why;

(10 marks)

(ii)   to assess the situation as it now stands in May and indicate what should be done in respect of the budget system and the departmental performance reports.

(5 marks)

(Total: 25 marks)
(CIMA May 1990)

7   ANSWERS TO EXAMINATION TYPE QUESTIONS

7.1   Principal budget factor

Notes:

(i)   Parts (a) and (b) are straightforward but remember part (b) is worth more than double the marks for part (a) and together they constitute 40% of the marks for the question. Make sure you **fully** answer the question.

(ii)   Part (c) is basically concerned with maximising profit within some limiting factor. However, it is not immediately apparent that one of the factors is sales demand. Also it is necessary to maximise contribution per £ spent on labour, not per labour hour as is usual in this type of question.

More a problem of interpretation, than of technical difficulty.

(a)   **Principal budget factor**

This is the constraint which limits the activity level of a business. The constraint is usually shortage-based eg, sales demand, skilled labour, raw materials, and it is essential to the planning process that the factor is identified at an early stage. Thus all the budgets produced must be in line with this constraint. For example there is little point in establishing a sales budget of 250,000 units when raw material shortages are limiting factory output to 200,000 units.

(b)   A **fixed budget** is one which is designed to remain unchanged irrespective of the volume of output or turnover attained. The fixed budget will be prepared for a single level of activity, usually that which is determined by the principal budget factor.

A **flexible budget** however is prepared for a range of activities and by recognising the difference in behaviour between fixed and variable costs in relation to fluctuations in output, turnover or other variable factors, is designed to change appropriately with such fluctuations.

A fixed budget is essentially a **planning** budget, setting the original targets towards which people should aim.   The flexible budget is more appropriate for **control** purposes. Variances produced using a budget which reflects the actual level of activity are more meaningful than those arising using a fixed budget.

(c)   *Note:*

From the data given in the question the only possible principal budget factors are either sales demand or labour.

£

(i)   Forecast (i): required labour -

			£
Product A,	22,000 × £2.00	=	44,000
Product B,	40,000 × £1.50	=	60,000
Product C,	6,000 × £1.00	=	6,000
			110,000

With a maximum of £135,000 available for labour, the constraint must be the sales demand.

£

Forecast (ii): required labour -

			£
Product A,	30,000 × £2.00	=	60,000
Product B,	50,000 × £1.50	=	75,000
Product C,	7,000 × £1.00	=	7,000
			142,000

There is insufficient labour to meet the demand and it is labour therefore which is the principal budget factor.

(ii) and (iii)   Forecast (i): set sales budget to meet sales demand

	22,000 units Product A £	40,000 units Product B £	6,000 units Product C £	Total £
Sales	220,000	240,000	45,000	
Variable cost	132,000	160,000	33,000	
Contribution	88,000	80,000	12,000	180,000
Fixed costs				150,000
Net profit				30,000

Forecast (ii): set sales budget to maximise the contribution per £1 of labour costs

	Product A £	*Product B* £	*Product C* £
Contribution per unit	3.00	1.70	1.60
Labour cost per unit	2.00	1.50	1.00
Contribution per £1 of labour	1.50	1.13	1.60
Ranking	(2)	(3)	(1)

	Product A	*Product B*	*Product C*
	30,000 units	45,333 units	7,000 units
Sales budget	£270,000	£258,398	£49,700
Use of labour	£60,000	£68,000 (Balance)	£7,000

Note:

£68,000 labour on product B enables $\left(\dfrac{£68,000}{£1.50}\right)$ = 45,333 units to be produced.

45,333 × £5.70 = Sales of £258,398.

Profit achieved from these sales would be:

	Product A £	*Product B* £	*Product C* £	*Total* £
Contribution	90,000	77,066	11,200	178,266
Fixed costs				150,000
Net profit				28,266

7.2 C Ltd

Note: all forecasting problems are linked to the fact that the future is uncertain. It therefore requires some hair splitting to come up with five separate forecasting problems but there is 18 minutes in which to do it!

(a) Forecasting is an attempt to predict what is likely to happen in the future. The future is by definition uncertain therefore most problems of forecasting are linked to that uncertainty:

Examples are (only five needed in exam)

(i) **New products**

There is no past experience so it is more difficult to predict the level of sales.

(ii) **New production methods**

Changes in the method of production can effect cost behaviour. Initial standard times may be difficult to establish and as workers become more familiar with procedures time taken is likely to decrease (the learning curve effect).

(iii) **Changes in structure of the business**

As a business expands into different products it may become more difficult to identify the costs of each product line.

(iv)   **The business environment**

It is very difficult to predict, for example, the level of interest rates, inflation rates, foreign exchange rates and the impact of these changes on the business; other one-off factors are even more difficult to take into account eg, outbreak of war.

(v)   **Competitors**

It may be difficult to predict competitor behaviour on such matters as pricing and new developments (and the impact of these developments on sales).

(vi)   **Research and development**

A particular problem arises if, for example, the business is involved with rapidly changing technology or developing drugs. This is particularly a problem if the product life cycle is short.

(vii)   **Customers**

Unpredictable changes in tastes may occur or if involved in food products, health scares may affect sales.

(b)   *Note:* this is very much a thinking question where the student has to apply knowledge of budgetary control and some common sense to identify the 'deliberate mistakes' made by the examiner.

(i)   The following changes ought to be made to the report:

(1)   The budgeted cost figures should be adjusted/flexed to allow for the effect of the 100 unit increase in the activity level on costs before variances are calculated. This will have the effect of increasing the budgeted variable costs to reflect the increase in the activity level. It would be easier for this purpose to separate costs into fixed and variable.

(2)   It would be helpful to provide a breakdown of the overhead allocated and sundries figures to obtain a clearer idea of which cost items have changed. It would also be useful to indicate where possible which costs are controllable by the cost centre manager.

(3)   There should be space on the report for the department supervisor to be able to explain why variances have occurred. It should not be assumed they are as a result of 'considerable inefficiency'. The current approach is rather insensitive to the feelings/opinions of the supervisor.

(4)   Budget and actual figures for the year to date would be useful.

(5)   It may be more relevant from the point of view of cost behaviour to measure the activity level for some of the costs in labour/machine hours.

(ii)   The budget system should be revised to take account of the above changes. In addition, action is necessary to improve the attitude of the supervisors to the system. They should have the purposes/benefits and mechanics of the system explained to them and senior management should also consider allowing supervisors the opportunity to participate in budget preparation to encourage better co-operation and motivation amongst the management team.

19 STANDARD COSTING

INTRODUCTION & LEARNING OBJECTIVES

Syllabus area 6d. Types of standard and sources of standard cost information. (Ability required 3.)

Evolution of standards; continuous improvement; keeping standards meaningful and relevant. (Ability required 3.)

This chapter considers the use of standard costing as an alternative to the use of budgets and budgetary control methods.

The concept of standard costs and the setting of standards is considered, and the difficulties of introducing standard costing into non-manufacturing and specific order environments are examined.

Finally the difficulties of ensuring that standards are meaningful and relevant is discussed.

When you have studied this chapter you should be able to do the following:

- Define standard costs.
- Explain the differences between different types of standard.
- Explain the relationship between standard costing and budgetary control.
- Recognise and explain the difficulties of using standard costing in non-manufacturing and specific order environments.
- Explain the importance and problems associated with ensuring that standards remain meaningful and relevant.

1 STANDARD COSTING

1.1 Introduction

Definition A method of cost accounting which incorporates standard costs and variances into the ledger accounts of the organisation.

1.2 Standard cost

Definition A standard cost is a standard expressed in money. It is built up from an assessment of the value of cost elements. Its main uses are providing bases for performance measurement, control by exception reporting, valuing stock and establishing prices.

1.3   Standard cost card

This shows the standard cost for a single unit of a product.

Standard cost card
Cost per unit of product X

			£
Raw materials:	5 kgs	P @ £2/kg	10.00
	3 kgs	Q @ £1.5/kg	4.50
Labour	4 hrs	grade A @ £4/hr	16.00
	1 hr	grade B @ £5.50/hr	5.50
			36.00

This standard cost is used as a basis of comparison with actual results.

1.4   The meaning of 'standard'

The term implies a fixed relationship which is assumed to hold good for the budget period or until it is deliberately revised. By the use of standards one measurement can be converted into another. When it is said that a journey of 90 miles from A to B takes three hours, a standard speed under prevailing traffic conditions of 30 miles per hour is assumed. It is thus possible to express distance in hours.

Therefore, if our standard speed of production is 50 items per hour, a transfer of 5,000 items into finished store may be said to represent 100 hours of work. Again, if the standard cost of raw materials is £2.50 per lb and the standard usage per item is 2 lb, the 5,000 items may be regarded either as representing 10,000 lb of raw material or as having a raw material content of £25,000.

A standard cost is calculated in relation to a prescribed set of working conditions ie, it reflects technical specifications and scientific measurement of the resources used to manufacture a product.

Standard costs represent target costs. As such they represent costs which are most likely to be useful for:

(a)   planning;
(b)   control;
(c)   motivation.

However carefully costs are predetermined (and one authority has referred to them as 'scientifically' predetermined costs), in the end they must be **somebody's** best estimate.

Nevertheless in one sense standard costs go beyond a best estimate: standard costs have been adopted as the firm's target - they become a statement of policy. For this reason it is necessary to think carefully about what sort of standards should be set.

1.5   The standard hour

Output is measured in terms of standard hours. A standard hour is a hypothetical unit which represents the amount of work which should be achieved in one hour at standard performance. Thus, if 50 articles are estimated to be made in a 'clock' hour, an output of 150 should take three 'clock' hours and would be valued at the standard cost of those three hours, irrespective of the actual time taken to manufacture them.

1.6   Activity

A factory in week 1 had an activity level of 120% with the following output:

	Units	Standard minutes each
Product F	5,100	6
Product C	2,520	10
Product A	3,150	12

The budgeted direct labour cost for budgeted output was £2,080.

You are required:

(a)   to calculate budgeted standard hours;
(b)   to calculate budgeted labour cost per standard hour.

1.7   Activity solution

(a)   Actual standard hours produced were:

Product F	$5,100 \times \dfrac{6}{60}$	=	510
Product C	$2,520 \times \dfrac{10}{60}$	=	420
Product A	$3,150 \times \dfrac{12}{60}$	=	630
			1,560

representing 120% of budgeted standard hours ie,

$$\text{Budgeted standard hours} = 1,560 \times \frac{100}{120} = 1,300$$

(b)   Budgeted labour cost per standard hour $= \dfrac{\text{Budgeted cost}}{\text{Budgeted standard hours}}$

$$= \frac{£2,080}{1,300}$$

$$= £1.60 \text{ per hour}$$

1.8   Activity

XYZ Ltd manufactures three different sized fridges. The expected (standard) number of labour hours per fridge is as follows:

Small	5 hours
Medium	7 hours
Large	10 hours

During February the following output was produced by working 130 hours more than the budgeted number of hours which was 470 hours:-

Small	28
Medium	32
Large	30

Calculate the number of standard hours produced during February.

1.9   Activity solution

$$(28 \times 5) + (32 \times 7) + (30 \times 10) = 664 \text{ standard hours}$$

1.10   Control ratios

These ratios may be used as a means of reporting performance without attributing monetary values to the differences between the actual and target results.

For these purposes the budget is assumed to represent available capacity and to be based on efficiency rated at 100%.

There are three ratios:-

(a)   volume;
(b)   capacity;
(c)   efficiency

1.11   Volume ratio

This compares the actual output (measured in standard hours) to the budget output (in standard hours) and expresses the ratio as a percentage.

Suppose the budget hours were 1,000 and the actual number of standard hours produced were 980. The ratio would be:-

$$\frac{\text{Standard hours produced}}{\text{Budget standard hours}} \times 100$$

$$= \frac{980}{1,000} \times 100 = 98\%$$

1.12   Capacity ratio

This measures the extent to which the budgeted capacity was actually used.

Suppose the actual hours worked in the above example were 950, the capacity ratio would be

$$\frac{\text{Standard worked}}{\text{Budget hours}} \times 100$$

$$= \frac{950}{1,000} \times 100 = 95\%$$

1.13   Efficiency (productivity) ratio

This measures the efficiency of the actual hours worked. Using the above data:

$$\frac{\text{Standard hours produced}}{\text{Actual hours worked}} \times 100$$

$$= \frac{980}{950} \times 100 = 103.16\%$$

1.14   Relationship between the ratios

The volume ratio is the overall effect of the capacity and efficiency ratios. This can be proven by multiplying the capacity and efficiency ratios to get the volume ratio:-

$$95\% \times 103.16\% = 98\%$$

1.15   Activity

Using the data from the previous activity calculate the three control ratios and prove that the volume ratio equals the capacity ratio multiplied by the efficiency ratio.

1.16   Activity solution

Volume ratio	141.28%
Capacity ratio	127.66%
Efficiency ratio	110.67%

Proof: $127.66\% \times 110.67\% = 141.28\%$

1.17   Setting standards

In general, a standard cost will be set for each product, comprising:

(a)   **Direct materials:** standard quantity (kgs, litres etc) × standard price per unit (kg, litre etc.)

(b)   **Direct wages:** standard labour hours × standard hourly rate.

(c)   **Variable overhead:** standard hours (labour or machine) × standard rate per hour.

(d)   **Fixed overhead:** budgeted overhead for the period ÷ budgeted standard hours (labour or machine) for the period.

2   TYPES OF STANDARDS

2.1   What sort of standards?

There is a whole range of bases upon which standards may be set within a standard costing system. The choice will be affected by the main purposes for which management see such a system operating. Five main alternative bases are possible:

(a)   basic standards;
(b)   ideal standards;
(c)   attainable standards;
(d)   historic standards;
(e)   loose standards.

2.2   Basic standards

[Definition]   'a standard established for use over a long period from which a current standard can be developed' CIMA, 1984.

Such standards do not change from year to year as a matter of course but they remain static and provide a base or yardstick against which to measure action (and expected) costs. The variances stemming from this system will reflect changes in price that have occurred since the base year as well as changes in efficiency over the same period. The price variance element may well dwarf any efficiency/usage variance.

Trends would be highlighted by a system incorporating basic standards, but for other management control purposes the information from the analysis between actual and standard would be limited. Most businesses operate in a dynamic world of continuously changing products and production methods. This would necessitate changes to standards and, therefore, to the base period.

Basic standards are not widely met in practice. However, as a means of monitoring any changes in efficiency/usage of standard costs, a reference to base year standards can be useful. This could be done as an 'off-line' annual comparison to see if the controllable elements of standards within an organisation are being tightened, slackened or remain unchanged.

2.3   Ideal standards

[Definition]   'Standards which can be attained under the most favourable conditions, with no allowance for normal losses, waste and machine downtime' CIMA, 1991.

These are standards set on the assumption of maximum efficiency. So, for example, no allowance for breakdowns, no wastage, working at full capacity would all be features of such ideal or theoretical standards. In other words, a perfect and ideal operating environment is assumed. Such standards would not be achieved and sustained for any significant period of time, if at all.

Large adverse variances are likely to be a feature of a standard costing system based on ideal standards. They would reflect a deviation not only from an expected level of activity and performance but also from the ideal.

An important feature of any control system is the impact that it has on managerial performance. Standard costing is only a means to an end in that variances and their analysis, as an example of management by exception, should lead management to appropriate action. A manager receiving a variance statement which is evolved from a system based on ideal standards would be unlikely to be motivated to improve performance and act in the best interests of the whole business. On the contrary, such a system might operate in the opposite manner and cause the manager to be demotivated.

If senior management want some measure of the extent to which the planned level of activity and efficiency falls below the ideal, then it might consider calculating this on a once-off annual basis as part of the analysis of the standards set for a given year prior to the start of that period. It is not recommended that such standards be built into the period-by-period detailed control system in an overall blanket way. However, for certain cost elements, the ideal or theoretical may correspond with the expected. This is more likely to occur with raw materials than with labour where, for example, standard costs may be based on the best theoretical mix of raw materials.

If standards are ideal then allowance would need to be made for the variances expected to arise in the budget period. The appropriate write-off of variances would need to be incorporated into the budgeted profit and loss account. This action is important in terms of all the master budgets, but perhaps particularly in respect of cash flow ones.

2.4   Attainable standards

 'A standard which can be attained if a standard unit of work is carried out efficiently, a machine properly operated or material properly used. Allowances are made for normal losses, waste and machine downtime' CIMA, 1991.

Such standards represent what should be achieved with a reasonable level of effort under normal efficient operating conditions. This does not mean that as such they are 'easy' standards. On the contrary, behavioural studies tend to suggest that they should include some element of 'target' in them. Managers at the operating levels in the organisation structure should be encouraged to set standards at the tightest level acceptable by themselves – in other words, at a degree of difficulty that they themselves see as acceptable.

In contrast with ideal standards, attainable standards do include allowances for such occurrences as the normal level of wastage, machine breakdowns and other non-productive time.

If there is any deviation between actual and standard, it is more likely to be such as to give marginally adverse variances rather than favourable. However, such variances are likely to be looked upon by the managers to whose area of responsibility they relate, as an appropriate measure of performance. Expected or currently attainable standards are those most commonly found in organisations operating standard costing systems because they can be seen to serve a range of advantages in terms of planning, control and motivation.

Variances from systems incorporating attainable standards are likely to be most relevant in terms of providing appropriate information to management.

2.5   Historic standards

A system of basing standards either on last period's actuals, or on the average of some previous periods, is not recommended generally. Over time, there could be just a tendency to relax standards in line with actual results rather than an encouragement to management to investigate why variances have arisen and to take the appropriate action. This presupposes adverse variances in the past and a lowering of standards in the future.

Past anomalies or inefficiencies tend to be built into future standards and treated as normal and any potential improvement in efficiency eg, due to technological change, may be overlooked. Inefficient use of resources would tend to go unnoticed.

The knowledge to management that this year's variances will be built automatically into next year's standards tend to undermine the importance of variance investigation and appropriate management action. In theory, as this year's standards would be based on actual results last year, the variances arising this year should be very small and insignificant. However, the effect of such a system may be to encourage a general lowering of standards over time and, therefore, a tendency towards small adverse variances.

2.6   Loose standards

There is some evidence that loosely set, easy-to-achieve standards could demotivate rather than motivate management. The element of target in standards, to an acceptable degree, is considered important.

Variances would always tend to be favourable in nature. In the long term, inefficiency would tend to be built into the standards as the norm. Loose standards are not recommended.

It is important that all managers are aware of the nature of the standards used as a base in any standard costing system so that the variances arising can be interpreted appropriately. Variances are not necessarily bad; this will depend upon the bases used to set the standards. It is suggested from the important motivational angle that standards based on expected operating conditions are used in a standard costing system ie, currently attainable standards.

2.7   Conclusions on standards

In the setting of standards, three aspects should be kept in mind:

(a)   their value for **control**;
(b)   their **motivational effect**; and
(c)   their usefulness for **planning** purposes

The five types of standard described above may be evaluated against these type of criteria:

Type of standard	Suitability for:		
	Control	Motivation	Planning
Basic	Unsuitable	Unsuitable	Unsuitable
Ideal	Unsuitable	May be suitable	Unsuitable
Attainable (note 1)	Very suitable	Less than optimal	Suitable
Historic	Unsuitable	Unsuitable	Unsuitable
Loose (note 2)	Unsuitable	Unsuitable	May be used

Notes:

(1)   It is assumed the attainable standards are set as defined by the CIMA, rather than somewhat above expectations, as would be preferred for motivational purposes;

(2)   It is assumed that loose standards are only slightly slacker than current standards.

From the above analysis it appears that no standard is optimal for all objectives, but attainable standards present the best compromise.

3   EVOLUTION OF STANDARDS

3.1   Continuous improvement

Organisations are continually seeking ways to improve efficiency, often by the installation of technologically superior equipment. When a standard costing system is in use the standard set is based upon the existing operating method.

If the method of operation changes the standard will be out of date and no longer relevant. A new standard is required which reflects the new method of working.

3.2   Keeping standards meaningful and relevant

An analysis of the causes of the variances between actual and standard performance may indicate the relevance of the standard to current operating conditions. In addition to the effects of method changes referred to earlier, significant price differences may affect the validity of the standard and affect its usefulness.

There is therefore an argument for revising the standard to reflect the present attainable conditions. However to do so presents difficulties:

(a)   the determination of the present attainable conditions as opposed to what is presently being attained; and

(b)   the implications for other parts of the planning process of frequent revisions to standard costs.

3.3   Performance evaluation

The purpose of standard costs as targets is to evaluate performance by making comparisons with actual results.

If the standard is no longer meaningful and relevant, then the results of comparing actual performance with those standards also has no meaning.

Variance reports which have been prepared following the comparison of actual results with existing standards may be used as the starting point in determining whether the present standards continue to be appropriate.

The reason or cause of the variance must be established and this may result in a recognition that the standard is no longer appropriate.

3.4   [Conclusion]   Standard costs need to be updated for changes in method as they occur, but changes in prices and similar factors are better highlighted through non-controllable variances if they occur during the planning period.

4   SOME ASPECTS OF IMPLEMENTATION AND OPERATION OF STANDARD COSTING

4.1   Standard costs and frequent price changes

Many organisations operating standard costing systems have set standards on an annual basis, the standards for next year are based on estimated average prices. In times of high inflation this approach can lead to large price variances in any particular control period, such variances tending to be favourable in the early part of the budget year and adverse in the later months. In many instances the changes in price levels will have been foreseen and incorporated into the overall standard set for the coming year, so the variances which arise (because the actuals are being compared with the average annual standard each period) may mask other variances which should be highlighted for the attention of management. An alternative approach to the problems associated with the annual standard in periods of high inflation is for the organisation to adopt **current standards**.

4.2   Current standard

[Definition]   A standard established for use over a short period of time, related to current conditions.

4.3   Establishment of current standards

Current standards should be set before the start of the budget year for each month or accounting period. This approach would allow a fully-phased annual budget to be evaluated. In practice the annual budget is often established first and subsequently phased into the individual budgets for each period by recognising the timing of price changes.

Some businesses have a few significant items of cost for which individual estimates are made for the timing and quantification of price level changes eg, organisations with a small number of raw materials which are subject to volatile market conditions. However, most organisations will try and predict accurately the timing and effect of pay increases to their own work force. With labour intensive types of operations this element of cost and the consequent labour cost variances are important and significant.

4.4   Applying control techniques to practical situations

It is impractical, if not impossible, to lay down a standard approach and/or common principles which can be universally applied to the problems of planning and control systems as each individual case is different.

4.5   Activity

Discuss the special problems which arise in establishing financial controls in a non-manufacturing (eg, a warehouse business or an advertising agency), as compared to a manufacturing business.

4.6   Activity solution

The special problems that arise in establishing financial controls in a non-manufacturing business stem from the fact that it is difficult to set standards which relate costs to activity in such businesses. In manufacturing industry a large part of the product cost is normally cost which can be allocated directly to the product. The product specification itself determines the quantities and costs of the material and operations to be incurred in manufacture, and therefore control of actual expenditure is facilitated. In non-manufacturing businesses, however, the bulk of costs are indirect and it is difficult to select a unit against which such costs can be measured.

In a warehousing business costs will tend to vary with sales activity but there will be a problem in selecting a unit to measure this activity. Weight and cubic capacity will be significant features, but shape and fragility, etc., may have a greater influence on handling costs. In an advertising agency salaries and accommodation are the major costs; these are difficult to measure in terms of activity.

It will be difficult, therefore, to establish for non-manufacturing businesses the standards and budgets which provide the basic financial controls in manufacturing industry. Managers in non-manufacturing businesses will have to rely on experience and personal judgement when authorising expenditure, so that control depends on the ability of the individual responsible for each cost centre and the relationship between that individual and top management.

Control of capital expenditure will present problems in non-manufacturing businesses, although the amount involved will be smaller than in manufacturing businesses. Problems arise in assessing the return on capital expenditure, as this is often of an intangible nature and difficult to measure. For example, an advertising agency cannot assess the monetary benefit to be derived from a scheme of office landscaping, and a warehouse cannot be specific as to the financial benefits occurring from the installation of an overhead crane.

Non-manufacturing businesses tend to suffer more from influences external to the firm than do manufacturing businesses, largely because the former are in service industries which are prone to disturbance or statutory control and/or whose services may be dispensed with in times of financial difficulty. Manufacturing tends to be carried on at a steady pace even though sales are seasonal and, thus, financial control of manufacturing businesses is insulated against external fluctuations, whilst activity in non-manufacturing businesses tends to be related far more closely to such fluctuations. It is difficult to budget accurately for external factors, so that financial control can be weakened by variances from plan which cannot be controlled by action within the company.

4.7   Relationship of standard costing to budgetary control

Historically, standard costing evolved as a parallel system to budgetary control, representing a different approach to the problem. Today, standard costing has become a subset of budgetary control, and is commonly used within an organisation as part of a budgetary control system.

Nevertheless, it is important to identify three factors that differentiate standard costing from other approaches to budgetary control:

(a)   Under standard costing, for costing purposes all stocks are valued at their standard costs.

(b)   Standard costs are incorporated in the ledger accounts; budgets are a memorandum record outside the ledger accounts.

(c)   Standard costs are set as unit costs; budgets tend to be set as total costs.

Thus although standard costing is a subset of budgeting, it has certain distinct features of its own.

5   CHAPTER SUMMARY

This chapter has explained how standard costing may be used to either supplement or replace a system of budgets and budgetary control.

The setting of different types of standard has been considered in terms of the uses of standard costs, and the difficulties of introducing standard costing into certain organisational environments examined.

Finally the evolution of standards was discussed.

6   SELF TEST QUESTIONS

6.1   What is standard costing? (1.1)

6.2   What is a standard cost? (1.2)

6.3   What is a standard hour? (1.5)

6.4   Identify the three control ratios (1.10)

6.5   What is the relationship between these control ratios? (1.14)

6.6   What is a basic standard? (2.2)

6.7   What is an ideal standard? (2.3)

6.8   What is an attainable standard? (2.4)

6.9   What is a historic standard? (2.5)

6.10   What is a loose standard? (2.6)

7   EXAMINATION TYPE QUESTIONS

7.1   Marketing cost budgets

(a)   Comment in detail on the factors you would observe and the steps you would take in constructing a marketing cost budget for a manufacturer of a widely distributed household durable product. Set out your points in brief numbered notes.

(b)   Arising from (a) above, what proposals can you make for setting standards to control such costs?

7.2   Specific order businesses

W Ltd is an engineering works wherein some of the departments manufacture standard products but most departments engage in one-off and small batch production. The financial director proposes to introduce budgetary control techniques into the business by gradual stages, starting with factory departmental performance and cost budgets. There are 60 budget centres in all in the factory, 35 of which are concerned with production. He is prepared to accept fixed budgets for departmental costs for a limited period, although he wants flexible budgeting to be introduced as quickly as possible.

Explain how you would develop a system of budgetary control for W Ltd, first using fixed budgets and then flexible budgets. How, in particular, would you tackle the problems of budgeting for the jobbing and small-batch production departments? On what bases do you see departmental budgets being flexed?

8   ANSWERS TO EXAMINATION TYPE QUESTIONS

8.1   Marketing cost budgets

(a)   As a preliminary to constructing a marketing cost budget, the following factors require consideration:

(i)   **Functional responsibilities**

The organisation structure should be analysed to define the activities embraced by the marketing function eg, packing costs may be considered part of the production budget or credit control part of the administration function.

(ii)   **Budget centres**

Budget centres should be developed to facilitate analysis of the budget in relation to executive responsibility. Sales executives may be responsible for particular areas or for specific types of customer, whereas managers within the distribution function are more likely to be allocated product responsibilities.

(iii)   **Integration with other budgets**

Distribution costs will largely be budgeted in relation to sales, but selling costs (apart from commission) will be budgeted in relation to planned sales effort. The two elements of the marketing budget, therefore, require different approaches.

(iv)   **External influences**

The budget will be affected by many factors outside the control of the executive responsible. These factors, such as economic conditions, corporate policy, statutory regulations, etc., should be analysed to assess their effect on the budget.

As indicated by (iii) above, separate selling and distribution budgets would be constructed as follows:

(i)   **Selling**

Assuming that sales responsibility is divided by geographical area, separate budgets would be prepared for each area, together with a budget to cover central sales administration. Within each area budget costs could be grouped between salesmen and establishment expenses, the former set in relation to planned effort and the latter representing fixed selling costs. If practical, the total advertising and promotion expense authorised would be allocated to represent area budgets. The separate budgets would be summarised for review and authorisation as the selling cost budget.

(ii)   **Distribution**

Budget centres would be set up for the activities within the distribution function. A substantial part of the costs would represent packing and transport, and a flexible budgeting approach could be used to control those costs, since a definite relationship exists between the level of costs and sales volume. Fixed administration costs could represent one budget centre controlled by the senior executive within the function.

(b)   Possible standards to control selling and distribution costs would include:

(i)   **Selling**

Apart from commission, which could be expressed as a standard percentage of sales value, selling costs would need to be measured against appropriate work units eg:

Cost item	*Unit*
Travel expenses	Mile or visit
Order processing	Order
Credit control	Account

Standards could be further analysed by area or class of trade for more effective control if the level of costs justified the work involved.

(ii)   **Distribution**

Similarly, standard costs per unit could be developed for different activities eg,

Activity	*Unit*	*Sub-analysis*
Warehousing	£100 factory cost	Product group
Packing	Order	Order size
Delivery	Ton-mile	Type of transport

Separate standards for the major cost items within each activity could be developed, if justifiable.

The above standards would be used for budget preparation and cost control/reduction.

8.2   Specific order businesses

The work of introducing budgetary control for the engineering factory is likely to be very extensive if the system is to operate successfully. For this reason a consultancy assignment is often required, since sufficient management time cannot usually be released to carry through successfully the implementation of such a system. The work can be broadly separated into three categories, viz. setting up the organisation to administer the budgetary control system, including the training of management and staff; preparing and introducing forms and records needed for the system; and carrying out the detailed analysis of records and preparing the required budgets.

(a)   **Setting up the organisation and preparation of forms**

    (i)   Budget centres are already in existence, but they should be formalised by organisation charts and responsibilities should be defined.

    (ii)   The information requirements of all levels of management should be determined.

    (iii)   Necessary changes and additions to accounting records should be made. In particular, coding and classification for the system should be identical to the coding to be used for historical recording, and the recording and reporting systems should be integrated.

    (iv)   Senior departmental heads should be appointed to a budget committee, the responsibilities and functions of which should be defined. The committee should be headed by the chief executive, and a representative of the accounting function should act in the secretarial and liaison position of budget officer.

    (v)   The budget timetable should be established, indicating when each subsidiary budget has to be prepared and approved, and when the master budget should be submitted to the board.

    (vi)   Formats for budget presentation and control reports should be designed.

    (vii)   All members of management and staff involved in the preparation and/or use of budgetary information should be trained, and their views incorporated in the design of the system.

    (viii)   Budget periods should be selected, long, medium and short term being integrated.

    (ix)   A budget manual should be prepared to formalise the system for future reference.

(b)   **Preparing the budgets**

    (i)   Past records should be examined, particularly the final accounts and sales records, to establish trends; and these should form the basis for discussion by the directors and budget committee of the forward plans of the company.

    (ii)   The principal budget factor should be established and the planned level of activity agreed. When flexible budgets are later introduced, the planned level of activity in any year will form the basis for budget flexing.

    (iii)   Prepare a sales budget based on current trends and plans, analysed by product.

    (iv)   Convert the sales budget into production budgets in total and in detail for parts and operations, taking into account existing and planned stock levels.

(v)   Identify spare capacity and limited capacity, and consult with the budget committee to determine courses of action.

(vi)   Prepare materials purchases budgets for direct and indirect materials, taking into account existing and planned raw materials stock levels.

(vii)   Prepare labour budgets and personnel budget.

(viii) Prepared budget centre overhead budgets and a general administrative overhead budget.

(ix)   Prepare capital expenditure and working capital budgets.

(x)   Prepare master budget to summarise detailed budgets.

(xi)   Check with budget committee and board of directors to discover if the completed budgets satisfy the original plans, and discuss in what ways the budgets need amendment.

(c)   **Flexible budgets**

The flexible budgets will take as a base the budgets at the planned level of activity, and these will be flexed to several alternative activity levels. In order to carry out this exercise, a detailed consideration of the performance of individual cost items at varying levels of activity will be needed. Variances, so far as these are measures of efficiency, should be calculated in relation to the flexed budgets. Total variances from the fixed or planned level budgets will also be useful to show the extent and cost of deviation from the plan.

(d)   **Jobbing and small batch production budgeting**

For this type of activity standards are often difficult to set for a large proportion of the work, though standards should be set wherever practicable. One-off jobs will involve some operations which are standard, though some operations will not be sufficiently typical to be regarded as standard. Assessment of the work content of one-off jobs, therefore, will be in the nature of estimating. In setting budgets, then, standards will be of relatively little help. The trend of orders and estimates of labour hour content will be most useful. Detailed consideration of the performance of individual costs will be needed, variable costs being related to labour hours where possible, and the activity levels for flexing will be based on estimated required man hours. Hourly overhead rates can be calculated, based on the fixed budget or expected level of activity as measured in estimated man hours.

20 VARIANCE ANALYSIS (1)

INTRODUCTION & LEARNING OBJECTIVES

Syllabus area 6d. Variance analysis covering material (price/usage), labour (rate/efficiency), variable overhead (expenditure/efficiency) variances.

This chapter is concerned with the comparison of actual and target performance using variance analysis.

1 VARIANCES

1.1 Introduction

Standard costing involves the setting of standard costs and the comparison of these with actual costs. This is, therefore, very similar to budgetary control, the difference being that in a standard costing system the variances are actually recorded in double entry ledger accounts.

Definition A variance is a difference between planned, budgeted, or standard cost and actual cost; and similarly for revenue.

Despite the use of the term 'standard costing', variances are also calculated in relation to sales, so that the differences between budgeted and actual profit can be completely analysed.

The diagram below summarises the major categories of cost variances:

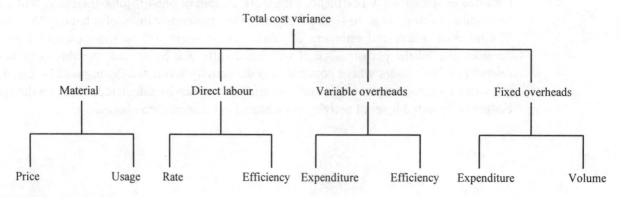

1.2 Variances in detail

(a) **Profit variances**

Definition the difference between budgeted profit and the actual profit.

This variance and its sub-divisions do not appear in a ledger account, as budgeted operating profit does not appear there.

The sub-divisions are:

- **Selling price variance** – the difference between the actual selling price per unit and the standard selling price per unit multiplied by the actual quantity sold.

- **Sales volume profit variance** – the difference between actual units sold and the budgeted quantity at the standard profit per unit.

(b)   Production cost variances

[Definition]   the difference between the standard cost of actual production volume, and the actual production cost incurred over the specified period.

This sub-divides as follows:

- **Direct materials price variance** – the difference between the standard price and the actual price for the actual quantity of material.

- **Direct materials usage variance** – the difference between the standard quantity specified for the actual production and the actual quantity used, at standard purchase prices.

- **Direct labour cost variance** – the difference between the standard direct labour cost and the actual direct labour cost incurred for the production achieved, which can be analysed into:

    - **Direct labour rate variance** – the difference between the standard and the actual direct labour rate per hour for the total hours worked; and

    - **Direct labour efficiency variance** – the difference between the standard hours for the actual production achieved and the hours actually worked valued at the standard hour rate.

- **Overhead total variance** – the difference between the standard overhead cost specified for the production achieved and the actual overhead cost incurred.

    Where overhead costs tend to vary with the amount of an input eg, actual labour hours, the overhead total variance may be subdivided into expenditure, efficiency and volume variances.

- **Variable production overheads**

    - **Variable production overhead expenditure variance** – the actual hours worked at standard overhead rate less the actual overhead expenditure. This is applicable when the production overhead rate varies with the hours worked.

    - **Variable production overhead efficiency variance** – the standard variable production overhead of the actual production less the actual hours worked at standard overhead rate. Again this is applicable when the production overhead rate varies with the hours worked.

- **Fixed production overheads**

    - **Fixed production overhead expenditure variance** – this is budgeted fixed production overhead less the actual fixed production overhead.

Fixed production overhead volume variance – this is the standard absorbed cost less the budgeted fixed production overhead.

1.3   The standard hour

Output may be measured in terms of standard hours. A standard hour is a hypothetical unit which represents the amount of work which should be performed in one hour at standard performance. Thus, if 50 articles are estimated to be made in a 'clock' hour, an output of 150 should take three 'clock' hours and would be valued at the standard cost of those three hours, irrespective of the actual time taken to manufacture them.

Output is usually expressed in standard hours rather than in units when more than one type of product is being made. It provides a more reasonable basis for apportioning fixed overheads (though, as already discussed, any such basis is bound to be arbitrary).

2   CALCULATION OF VARIANCES

2.1   Cost variances

Definition   A cost variance is a difference between planned, budgeted or standard cost and actual cost.

Cost variances occur when standard costs are compared to actual costs. There is one important feature of standard costing which must be remembered: standard costing carries out variance analysis using the normal, double entry ledger accounts. This is done by recording in the ledgers:

(a)   actual costs as inputs;
(b)   standard costs as outputs;
(c)   the difference as the variance.

2.2   Direct material cost variances

The purpose of calculating direct material cost variances is to quantify the effect on profit of actual direct material costs differing from standard direct material costs. This total effect is then analysed to quantify how much has been caused by a difference in the price paid for the material and how much by a difference in the quantity of material used.

2.3   Example

The following standard costs relate to a single unit of product X:

	£
Direct materials	10
Direct labour	8
Production overhead	5
	25

On the basis of the above standard costs if a unit of product X is sold for £30, the expected (or standard) profit would be £7 (£30 – £23).

However, if the **actual** direct material cost of making the unit of X were £12 then (assuming the other costs to be as per standard) the actual cost of product X would be:

	£
Direct materials	12
Direct labour	8
Production overhead	5
	25

Thus when the product is sold, the profit is only £5 (£30 – £25).

This reduction in profit is the effect of the difference between the actual and standard direct material cost of £2 (£12 – £10).

This simple example considered only one unit of product X, but it is the principle upon which variance calculations are made.

2.4   Direct material total cost variance

The purpose of this variance is to show the effect on profit for an accounting period of the actual direct material cost being different from the standard direct material cost.

2.5   Example

In July, 1,000 units of product X were manufactured, and sold for £30 each.

Using the data above,

(i)   the standard direct material cost of these 1,000 units of product X would be:

1,000 units × £10/unit = £10,000

(ii)   the actual direct material cost of these 1,000 units of product X would be:

1,000 units × £12/unit = £12,000

Assuming the other actual costs to be as expected in the standard, the actual profit and loss account would appear:

	£	£
Sales (1,000 × £30)		30,000
Direct materials (1,000 × £12)	12,000	
Direct labour (1,000 × £8)	8,000	
Production overhead (1,000 × £5)	5,000	
		25,000
Profit		5,000

The expected profit was £7 per unit (£30 – £23) so on sales of 1,000 units this would be:

1,000 units × £7/unit = £7,000.

Actual profit is £2,000 less than expected. Note that this is the same as the difference between the actual and standard direct material cost calculated earlier (£12,000 – £10,000).

This is known as the direct material total cost variance, and because it causes actual profits to be less than expected it is said to be an **adverse** variance.

Note that this total variance for the period can be shown to be equal to the difference of £2 per unit of X (calculated earlier) multiplied by 1,000 units.

2.6   Activity

The standard direct material cost of product A is £5. During August 600 units of product A were made, and the actual direct material cost was £3,200. Calculate the direct material total cost variance for the period.

2.7   Activity solution

		£
Standard direct material cost of 600 units:		
£5 × 600		3,000
Actual direct material cost		3,200
Direct material total cost variance - Adverse		200

2.8   Analysing the direct material total cost variance

When a standard material cost is determined for a unit of a product it is made up of two parts. These are estimates of:

(a)   the quantity of material to be used; and

(b)   the price to be paid per unit of material.

If we return to the earlier example concerning product X, the standard direct material cost per unit was stated to be £10. This was based on using 5 kg of a particular material to make each unit of product X and paying £2/kg for the material.

You should remember that the actual direct material cost incurred in making 1,000 units of product X was £12,000. The invoice for these costs shows:

4,800 kg @ £2.50/kg = £12,000.

It should be noted that this form of analysis corresponds to the two estimates which form the basis of the standard cost. It is this which allows the direct material total cost variance to be analysed.

2.9   Direct material price variance

The purpose of calculating this variance is to identify the extent to which profits will differ from those expected by reason of the actual price paid for direct materials being different from the standard price.

The standard price per kg of material was stated above to be £2/kg. This can be used to calculate the expected cost of the actual materials used to make 1,000 units of product X. On this basis the 4,800 kg of material should have cost:

4,800 kg × £2/kg = £9,600.

The actual cost of these materials was £12,000 which is £2,400 (£12,000 − £9,600) more than expected. Since the actual price was greater than expected this will cause the profit to be lower than expected. This variance, known as the direct material price variance, is adverse.

2.11   Activity solution

		£
Standard cost of 2,300 litres:		
2,300 litres × £1.30/litre		2,990
Actual cost of 2,300 litres		3,128
Direct material price variance - Adverse		138

2.12   Direct material usage variance

The purpose of this variance is to quantify the effect on profit of using a different quantity of raw material from that expected for the actual production achieved.

Returning to our example concerning product X, it was stated that each unit of product X had a standard direct material usage of 5 kgs. This can be used to calculate the amount of direct material (in kgs) which should be used for the actual production achieved.

1,000 units of X @ 5 kgs of direct material each = 5,000 kgs.

You should remember that the analysis of the actual cost showed that 4,800 kgs of direct material were actually used.

Thus a saving of 200 kgs (5,000 – 4,800) was achieved.

This saving of materials must be valued to show the effect on profit. If the original standard direct material cost were revised to reflect this saving of material it would become:

4.8 kgs (4,800/1,000) @ £2/kg = £9.60.

This is £0.40 per unit of product X less than the original standard and profit would therefore increase by this amount for every unit of product X produced. This has a total value of

1,000 units × £0.40 = £400.

We achieve the same result by multiplying the saving in quantity by the standard price:

200 kgs × £2/kg = £400.

In this case profits will be higher than expected because less material was used than expected in the standard. Therefore the variance is said to be favourable.

2.14   Activity solution

Standard usage of 500 units of K:	
500 × 0.4 tonnes	200 tonnes
Actual usage	223 tonnes
Excess usage	23 tonnes

Valued at standard price of £30/tonne:

Direct material usage variance is:

23 tonnes × £30/tonne = £690 Adverse

2.15   Raw material stocks

The earlier example has assumed that the quantity of materials purchased equalled the quantity of materials used by production. Whilst this is possible it is not always certain to occur. Where this does not occur profit will be affected by the change in the level of stock. The extent to which this affects the calculation of direct material variances depends on the methods chosen to value stock. Stocks may be valued either using:

(a)   the standard price for the material; or
(b)   the actual price (as applies from using FIFO, LIFO, etc).

2.16   Stocks valued at standard price

This is the most common method when using a standard costing system because it eliminates the need to record value based movements of stock on stores ledger cards (since all movements, both receipts and issues, will be valued at the standard price).

The effect of this valuation method is that price variances are calculated based on the quantity purchased rather than the quantity of materials used. This is illustrated by the following example.

2.17   Example

Product P requires 4 kg of material Z per unit. The standard price of material Z is £8/kg. During September 16,000 kgs of Z were bought for £134,400. There was no opening stock of material Z but at the end of September 1,400 kgs of Z remained in stock. Stocks of Z are valued at standard prices.

The price variance is based on the quantity purchased (ie, 16,000 kgs). The standard cost of these materials can be calculated:

	£
16,000 kgs × £8/kg	128,000
Actual cost of 16,000 kgs	134,400
Direct material price variance - Adverse	6,400

2.18   Stock account

Continuing the above example the issues of material Z of 14,600 kgs (16,000 − 1,400) would be valued at the standard price of £8/kg.

The value of the issues debited to work in progress would thus be:

14,600 kgs × £8/kg = £116,800.

The stock account would appear thus:

Raw material Z

	£		£
Creditor	134,400	Work in progress	116,800
		Price variance	6,400
		Bal c/d	11,200
	134,400		134,400

Note that the balance c/d comprises the closing stock of 1,400 kgs valued at the standard price of £8/kg.

1,400 kgs × £8/kg = £11,200.

The entry representing the price variance is shown as a credit in the raw material account because it is an adverse variance. The corresponding entry is made to a price variance account, the balance of which is transferred to profit and loss at the end of the year: The price variance account is as follows:

Raw material price variance

	£		£
Raw material Z	6,400		

2.19   Stocks valued at actual price

If this stock valuation method is used it means that any price variance is recognised not at the time of purchase but at the time of issue.

When using this method issues are made from stock at actual prices (using, FIFO, LIFO, etc) with the consequence that detailed stores ledger cards must be kept. The price variance is calculated based upon the quantity used.

2.20   Example

Using the data concerning material Z above, calculations of the value of issues and closing stock can be made as follows:

$$\text{Actual cost 1 kg} = \frac{£134,400}{16,000} \quad = \quad £8.40$$

$$\begin{aligned} \text{Value of issues (at actual cost)} \quad &= \quad 14,600 \text{ kgs} \times £8.40 \\ &= \quad £122,640 \end{aligned}$$

$$\begin{aligned} \text{Closing stock value (at actual cost)} \quad &= \quad 1,400 \text{ kgs} \times £8.40 \\ &= \quad £11,760. \end{aligned}$$

The direct material price variance based on the issues quantity can be calculated:

	£
Standard cost of 14,600 kgs:	
14,600 kgs × £8/kg	116,800
Actual cost of 14,600 kgs (above)	122,640
Direct material price variance - Adverse	5,840

2.21 Stock account

If stock is valued using actual prices, the stock account will be as follows:

Raw material Z

	£		£
Creditor	134,400	Work in progress	122,640
		Balance c/d	11,760
	134,400		134,400

Note that the closing balance comprises:

	£
1,400 kgs × standard price of £8/kg	11,200
Adverse price variance not yet recognised:	
1,400 kgs × (£8.40 – £8.00)	560
	11,760

The price variance is shown in the work in progress account with the corresponding entry as before:

Work in progress

	£		£
Raw material Z	122,640	Direct material price variance	5,840

2.22 Direct labour cost variances

The purpose of calculating direct labour cost variances is to quantify the effect on profit of actual direct labour costs differing from standard direct labour costs.

This total effect is then analysed to quantify how much has been caused by a difference in the wage rate paid to employees and how much by a difference in the number of hours.

2.23 Example

The following standard costs relate to a single unit of product Q:

	£
Direct materials	8
Direct labour	12
Production overhead	6
	26

On the basis of these standard costs if a unit of product Q is sold for £35, the expected (or standard) profit would be £9 (35 – £26).

However, if the actual direct labour cost of making the unit of Q were £10, then (assuming the other costs to be as per standard) the actual cost of product Q would be:

	£
Direct materials	8
Direct labour	10
Production overhead	6
	24

Thus when the product is sold the profit is £11 (£35 – £24).

This increase in profit is the effect of the difference between the actual and standard direct labour cost of £2 (£12 – £10).

This simple example considered only one unit of product Q, but it is the principle upon which variance calculations are made.

2.24   Direct labour total cost variance

The purpose of this variance is to show the effect on profit for an accounting period of the actual direct labour cost being different from the standard direct labour cost.

2.25   Example

In August, 800 units of product Q were manufactured, and sold for £35 each.

Using the data above,

(i)   the standard direct labour cost of these 800 units of product Q would be:

800 units × £12/unit = £9,600

(ii)   the actual direct labour cost of these 800 units of product Q would be:

800 units × £10/unit = £8,000.

Assuming the other actual costs to be as expected in the standard, the actual profit and loss account would appear:

	£	£
Sales (800 × £35)		28,000
Direct materials (800 × £8)	6,400	
Direct labour (800 × £10)	8,000	
Production overhead (800 × £6)	4,800	
		19,200
Profit		8,800

The expected profit was £9 per unit (£35 – £26) so on sales of 800 units this would be:

800 units × £9/unit = £7,200.

Actual profit is £1,600 more than expected. Note that this is the same as the difference between the actual and standard direct labour cost calculated earlier (£9,600 – £8,000).

This is known as the direct labour total cost variance, and because it causes actual profits to be more than expected it is said to be a favourable variance.

Note that this total variance for the period can be shown to be equal to the difference of £2 per unit of Q (calculated earlier) multiplied by 800 units.

2.26   Activity

The standard direct labour cost of product H is £7. During January 450 units of product H were made, and the actual direct labour cost was £3,450. Calculate the direct labour total cost variance of the period.

2.27   Activity solution

	£
Standard direct labour cost of 450 units:	
£7 × 450	3,150
Actual direct labour cost	3,450
Direct labour total cost variance - Adverse	300

2.28   Analysing the direct labour total cost variance

When a standard labour cost is determined for a unit of a product it is made up of two parts. These are estimates of:

(a)   the number of hours required per unit; and

(b)   the hourly wage rate.

If we return to the example concerning product Q, the standard direct labour cost per unit was stated to be £12. This was based on 4 direct labour hours being required per unit of Q and paying a wage rate of £3/hour.

You should remember that the actual direct labour cost incurred in making 800 units of product Q was £8,000. An analysis of the payroll records shows:

2,000 hours @ £4/hour = £8,000.

It should be noted that this corresponds to the two estimates which form the basis of the standard cost. It is this which allows the direct labour total cost variance to be analysed.

2.29   Direct labour rate variance

The purpose of calculating this variance is to identify the extent to which profits will differ from those expected by reason of the actual wage rate per hour being different from the standard.

The standard wage rate per hour was stated to be £3. This can be used to calculate the expected cost of the actual hours taken to make 800 units of product Q. On this basis the 2,000 hours should have cost:

2,000 hours × £3/hour = £6,000.

The actual labour cost was £8,000 which is £2,000 (£8,000 – £6,000) more than expected.

Since the actual rate was greater than expected, this will cause the profit to be lower than expected. This variance, known as the direct labour rate variance, is adverse.

2.30   Direct labour efficiency variance

The purpose of this variance is to quantify the effect on profit of using a different number of hours than expected for the actual production achieved.

Continuing with our example concerning product Q, it was stated that each unit of product Q would require 4 direct labour hours. This can be used to calculate the number of direct labour hours which should be required for the actual production achieved.

> 800 units of Q × 4 direct labour hours each = 3,200 direct labour hours

You should remember that the analysis of the actual cost showed that 2,000 hours were used.

Thus a saving of 1,200 direct labour hours (3,200 – 2,000) was achieved.

This saving of labour hours must be valued to show the effect on profit. We do this by multiplying the difference in hours by the standard hourly rate:

> 1,200 direct labour hours × £3/hr = £3,600.

In this case profit will be higher than expected because fewer hours were used. Therefore the variance is favourable.

2.31   Activity

The following data relates to product C

Actual production of C (units)	700
Standard wage rate/hour	£4.00
Standard time allowance per unit of C (hours)	1.50
Actual hours worked	1,000
Actual wage cost	£4,200

Calculate the direct labour rate and efficiency variances from the above data.

2.32   Activity solution

	£
Expected cost of actual hours worked:	
1,000 hours × £4/hr	4,000
Actual wage cost	4,200
Direct labour rate variance - Adverse	200
Expected hours for actual production:	
700 units × 1.50 hours/unit	1,050
Actual hours	1,000
A saving (in hours) of	50

These are valued at the standard wage rate/hour.

Direct labour efficiency variance is:

> 50 hours × £4/hour = £200 Favourable.

3   VARIABLE OVERHEAD VARIANCES

3.1   Introduction

These variances are very similar to those for material and labour because, like these direct costs, the variable overhead cost also changes when activity changes.

The most common examination question assumes that variable overhead costs vary with labour hours worked. This results in the calculation of two variable overhead variances which are illustrated by the following example.

3.2   Example

K Limited has a budgeted variable overhead cost for August of £84,000. Budgeted production is 20,000 units of its finished product and direct labour hours are expected to be 40,000 hours.

During August the actual production was 20,500 units. Actual hours worked were 41,600 hours and the variable overhead cost incurred amounted to £86,700.

3.3   Variable overhead total variance

In order to calculate the total variance it is necessary to calculate the standard variable overhead cost for the actual production achieved.

The budgeted variable overhead cost per hour is calculated by:

$$\frac{\text{Budgeted cost}}{\text{Budgeted hours}} = \frac{£84,000}{40,000} = £2.10 \text{ per hour}$$

Actual production was 20,500 units which is the equivalent of 41,000 standard hours. (According to the budget each unit should require 2 hours ie, 40,000 hours/20,000 units.)

	£
The standard cost of 41,000 hours at £2.10 per hour is	86,100
Actual cost	86,700
Variance	600 (A)

The variance is adverse because the actual cost exceeded the standard cost and therefore profits would be lower than expected.

3.4   Variable overhead expenditure variance

This variance measures the effect on profit of the actual variable overhead cost per hour differing from the standard hourly cost.

The actual hours worked were 41,600.

	£
If these had cost £2.10/hour as expected the cost would have been	87,360
This is the standard cost of actual hours.	
The actual cost was	86,700
Variance	660 (F)

This results in a favourable expenditure variance of £660.

3.5   Variable overhead efficiency variance

This variance measures the effect on profit of the actual hours worked differing from the standard hours produced.

Standard hours produced	41,000
Actual hours worked	41,600
Difference	600

This difference in hours is valued at the standard variable overhead cost/hour:

$600 \times £2.10 = £1,260$ (A).

The variance is adverse because actual hours exceeded standard hours.

3.6   Proof of total variance

Note that the sum of these sub-variances, representing expenditure and efficiency equals the total variance:

£660 (F) + £1,260 (A) = £600 (A).

3.7   When variable overhead cost varies with volume

If variable overhead cost changes not as a result of a change in direct labour hours, but as a result of a change in production volume it is not possible to calculate the sub-variances illustrated above.

Instead only the total variance can be calculated using the standard variable overhead cost/unit:

$$\frac{\text{Budgeted cost}}{\text{Budgeted units}} = \frac{£84,000}{20,000} = £4.20 \text{ per unit}$$

	£
Standard cost of actual production 20,500 units × £4.20/unit	86,100
Actual cost	86,700
Total variance (as before)	600 (A)

4   SELF TEST QUESTION

4.1   What is a variance? (1.1)

21 VARIANCE ANALYSIS (2)

INTRODUCTION & LEARNING OBJECTIVES

Syllabus area 6d. Variance analysis covering fixed overhead (expenditure/volume) and sales (price/volume) variances. (Ability required 3).

Standard cost book-keeping. (Ability required 3).

The causes and reporting of variances are considered followed by an explanation of the techniques used to identify which variances should be investigated.

Finally standard costing and budgetary control are compared.

When you have studied this chapter you should be able to do the following:

- Reconcile budget profit with actual profit using variances.

- Explain the importance of establishing the cause(s) of a variance.

- Comment on the internal and external reporting implications of using standard costing.

---

1 FIXED OVERHEAD VARIANCES

1.1 Introduction

These variances show the effect on profit of differences between actual and expected fixed overhead costs. By definition these costs do not change when there is a change in the level of activity, consequently many of the variances are calculated based upon budgets; however, the effect on profit depends upon whether a marginal or absorption costing system is being used. In the variance calculations which follow firstly an absorption costing system is assumed. These are then compared with the variances which would arise if a marginal costing system were used.

1.2 Marginal v absorption costing - a reminder

The difference between these costing methods lies in their treatment of fixed production overheads. Whereas absorption costing relates such costs to cost units using absorption rates, marginal costing treats the cost as a period cost and writes it off to profit and loss as it is incurred.

1.3 Fixed overhead total variance

Assuming an absorption costing system, this is the effect on profit of there being a difference between the actual cost incurred and the amount absorbed by the use of the absorption rate based on budgeted costs and activity. This is illustrated by the following example.

1.4   Example

Q Limited has completed its budget for October, the following data have been extracted:

Budgeted fixed overhead cost	£100,000
Budgeted production	20,000 units
Budgeted machine hours	25,000

A machine hour absorption rate is used.

The actual fixed overhead cost incurred was £98,500. Actual production was 20,300 units using 25,700 machine hours.

1.5   Solution

The absorption rate per machine hour (based upon the budget) is given by:

$$\frac{\text{Budgeted fixed overhead cost}}{\text{Budgeted machine hours}}$$

$$= \frac{£100,000}{25,000} = £4 \text{ per machine hour}$$

This would be used to determine the fixed overhead cost absorbed (ie, attributed to the actual production achieved).

In a standard costing system the actual production achieved is measured in standard hours, in this case standard machine hours.

According to the budget 20,000 units should require 25,000 machine hours, this is the equivalent of 1.25 machine hours per unit (25,000/20,000).

Thus the actual production of 20,300 units is equivalent to

$20,300 \times 1.25 = 25,375$ standard machine hours.

The amount absorbed is therefore:

25,375 standard machine hours × £4/machine hour

$= £101,500$

This is the standard cost of the actual production (using absorption costing). It is compared with the actual cost to find the total variance:

	£
Standard cost	101,500
Actual cost	98,500
Variance	3,000 (F)

Since the actual cost is less than the standard cost it is a favourable variance.

1.6   Over/under absorptions and the total variance

The comparison of actual fixed overhead cost incurred and the amount of fixed overhead cost absorbed is not new, it was used in your earlier studies to determine the extent of any under/over absorption. Often this is done using a fixed production overhead control account which is shown below based upon the above figures:

Fixed production overhead control a/c

	£		£
Creditors	98,500	Work in progress	101,500
P & L (over absorption)	3,000		
	101,500		101,500

You should note that the over absorption is equal to the total variance.

1.7   Activity

TP has the following data concerning its fixed production overheads:

Budget cost	£44,000
Budget production	8,000 units
Budget labour hours	16,000
Actual cost	£47,500
Actual production	8,450 units
Actual labour hours	16,600

Calculate the fixed overhead total variance assuming an absorption system based upon labour hours.

1.8   Activity solution

$$\text{Absorption rate} = \frac{\text{Budgeted cost}}{\text{Budgeted hours}} = \frac{£44,000}{16,000} = £2.75$$

Actual output in standard hours $= 8,450 \times \dfrac{16,000}{8,000} =$	16,900
Amount absorbed $= 16,900 \times £2.75 =$	£46,475
Actual cost $=$	£47,500
Variance	1,025 (A)

1.9   Analysing the total variance

In the same way that any over/under absorption can be analysed into the causes known as expenditure and volume, the same analysis can be made of the total variance. The same terminology is used, and the method of calculation is the same as you learnt earlier in this text. The example we used earlier (reproduced below) will be used to show this.

1.10   Example

Q Limited has completed its budget for October, the following data have been extracted:

Budgeted fixed overhead cost	£100,000
Budgeted production	20,000 units
Budgeted machine hours	25,000

A machine hour absorption rate is used.

The actual fixed overhead cost incurred was £98,500. Actual production was 20,300 units using 25,700 machine hours.

1.11   Fixed overhead expenditure variance

This variance shows the effect on profit of the actual fixed overhead expenditure differing from the budgeted value:

	£
Budgeted expenditure	100,000
Actual expenditure	98,500
Variance	1,500 (F)

The variance is favourable because the actual expenditure is less than that budgeted.

1.12   Fixed overhead volume variance

This variance measures the difference between the amount actually absorbed based upon actual production (in standard hours) compared to the amount expected to be absorbed based upon budgeted production (in standard hours).

Budgeted production (standard machine hours)	25,000
Actual production (standard machine hours)	25,375
Difference	375

This difference of 375 standard machine hours is valued at the absorption rate of £4/hr:

375 hours × £4/hr = £1,500 (F).

This variance is favourable because the actual output exceeded the expected output. Since the cost is fixed, the actual cost/unit is lowered by making greater production and profits will therefore increase.

1.13   The total variance and the sub-variances

Note that the sum of the fixed overhead expenditure and volume variances equals the fixed overhead total variance:

£1,500 (F) + £1,500 (F) = £3,000 (F).

1.14   Activity

Analyse the total variance you calculated in the previous activity into the fixed overhead expenditure and volume variances. (The data is reproduced below for convenience.)

TP has the following data concerning its fixed production overheads:

Budget cost	£44,000
Budget production	8,000 units
Budget labour hours	16,000
Actual cost	£47,500
Actual production	8,450 units
Actual labour hours	16,600

1.15   Activity solution

Fixed overhead expenditure variance:

		£
Budget cost		44,000
Actual cost		47,500
		3,500 (A)

Fixed overhead volume variance:

Budget production (labour hours)	16,000
Actual production (standard hours)	16,900
	900

900 hours × £2.75 = £2,475 (F)

Proof of total:

£3,500 (A) + £2,475 (F) = £1,025 (A)

1.16   Fixed overhead variances and marginal costing

As was stated earlier, marginal costing does not relate fixed production overhead costs to cost units. The amount shown in the profit and loss account is the cost incurred. Since the cost is a fixed cost it is not expected to change when activity changes thus the expected cost of any level of production is always the budgeted cost.

The purpose of variance analysis is to calculate the effect on profit of actual performance differing from that expected, consequently, under marginal costing this will be the difference between the actual and budgeted expenditure.

Thus under marginal costing the total fixed production overhead variance will always equal the fixed production overhead expenditure variance which is calculated in the same way as for absorption costing systems (above).

2   NON-PRODUCTION OVERHEADS

2.1   Introduction

Since the purpose of variance analysis is to show the effect on profit of actual results differing from those expected, it is also necessary to compare the costs of non-production overheads such as selling, marketing and administration.

2.2   Non-production overhead variances

These costs are not related to the cost unit (even in an absorption costing system) so the calculation of variances for these items is exactly the same as that for fixed production overheads in a marginal costing system.

In other words the only variance is expenditure which is simply the difference between actual and budgeted expenditure. It is usual for separate variances to be calculated for each function (ie, selling, marketing, administration).

3   SALES VARIANCES

3.1   Introduction

The purpose of calculating sales variances is to show their effect when a comparison is made between budget and actual profit. There are two causes of sales variances, a difference in the selling price and a difference in the sales volume.

3.2   Sales price variance

This variance shows the effect on profit of selling at a different price from that expected. The following example is used to illustrate its calculation.

3.3   Example

TZ has the following data regarding its sales for March:

Budgeted sales	1,000 units
Budgeted selling price	£10/unit
Standard variable cost	£6/unit
Budgeted fixed cost	£2/unit*

* based upon annual fixed costs and activity levels

Actual sales	940 units
Actual selling price	£10.50/unit

If the actual sales volume had been sold at the budgeted selling price the sales revenue would have been

940 units × £10 =	£9,400

But actual sales revenue was

940 units × £10.50 =	£9,870
Variance	470 (F)

The variance is favourable because the higher actual selling price causes an increase in revenue and a consequent increase in profit.

3.4   Sales volume variance

The purpose of this variance is to calculate the effect on profit of the actual sales volume being difference from that budgeted. The effect on profit will differ depending upon whether a marginal or absorption costing system is being used.

Under absorption costing all production costs are attributed to the cost unit, and the fixed production overhead volume variance accounts for the effects of actual volumes differing from those expected. Whereas under marginal costing contribution is emphasised (ie, the difference between the selling price and the variable cost).

This affects the calculation of the sales volume variance, under absorption costing any difference in units is valued at the standard profit per unit, whereas under marginal costing such a difference in units is valued at the standard contribution per unit.

In neither case is the standard selling price used. This is because when volumes change so do production costs and the purpose of calculating the variance is to find the effect on profit.

3.5   Sales volume variance - absorption costing

Using the data from the example above:

Budgeted sales	1,000 units
Actual sales	940 units
Difference	60 units

These 60 units are valued at the standard profit of £2/unit (£10-£6-£2)

60 units × £2 = £120 (A).

The variance is adverse because actual sales volume was less than expected.

3.6   Sales volume variance - marginal costing

The difference of 60 units (as above) is valued at the standard contribution of £4/unit (£10-£6):

60 units × £4 = £240 (A).

3.7   Reconciling the sales volume variances under absorption and marginal costing

Using the above example:

Variance under	- absorption costing	£120 (A)
	- marginal costing	£240 (A)

There is a difference between these variances of £120 (A).

Earlier in this chapter we learnt how to calculate fixed overhead variances. These too were affected by the choice of costing method. Absorption costing required the calculation of both an expenditure and a volume variance, whereas marginal costing only required an expenditure variance.

Continuing with the data from the above example there is a volume difference of 60 units. The fixed cost is absorbed at a rate equivalent to £2/unit.

Thus the fixed production overhead volume variance would be

60 units × £2/unit = £120 (A)

The variance would be adverse because actual volume was less than expected and, since the cost is fixed this would increase the cost per unit and so decrease profit.

Thus when reconciling the profits, the absorption and marginal systems would show:

	Absorption	*Marginal*
Variances:		
Sales volume	£120 (A)	£240 (A)
Fixed production overhead volume	£120 (A)	Not applicable
	£240 (A)	£240 (A)

All other cost variances and the sales price variance would be identical under both systems.

The reconciliation of profits is covered in more depth later in this chapter.

3.8   Activity

Budgeted sales	500 units
Actual sales	480 units
Budgeted selling price	£100
Actual selling price	£110
Standard variable cost	£50/unit
Budgeted fixed cost	£15/unit

Calculate:

(i)   the selling price variance;
(ii)   the sales volume variance assuming an absorption costing system;
(iii)   the sales volume variance assuming a marginal costing system.

3.9   Activity solution

(i)   480 units × (£110 – £100) = £4,800 (F)
(ii)   20 units × (£100 – 50 – 15) = £700 (A)
(iii)   20 units × (£100 – 50) = £1,000 (A)

4   RECONCILIATION OF BUDGET AND ACTUAL PROFITS

4.1   Introduction

The purpose of calculating variances is to identify the different effects of each item of cost/income on profit compared to the expected profit. These variances are summarised in a reconciliation statement.

4.2   The reconciliation statement

The example which follows shows how such a statement reconciles the budget and actual profit of a period, based on absorption costing.

The statement commences with the budgeted profit which is based upon budgeted cost and activity levels.

This is then adjusted by the sales volume variance to reflect any difference in actual and budgeted activity. The result, which is referred to as the 'Standard profit on actual sales' represents the profit which would be achieved if:

(i)   the selling price was as budgeted; and
(ii)   all variable costs were as per the standard unit cost; and
(iii)   all fixed costs were as budgeted.

The selling price and cost variances are then included under the headings of adverse and favourable as appropriate. The total of these should reconcile the actual profit to the standard profit on actual sales.

4.3   Example

The following example illustrates the variances defined above.

Chapel Ltd manufactures a chemical protective called Rustnot. The following standard costs apply for the production of 100 cylinders:

		£
Materials	500 kgs @ 80p per kg	400
Labour	20 hours @ £1.50 per hour	30
Fixed overheads	20 hours @ £1.00 per hour	20
		450

The monthly production/sales budget is 10,000 cylinders. Selling price = £6 per cylinder.

For the month of November the following production and sales information is available:

Produced/sold	10,600 cylinders
Sales value	£63,000
Material purchased and used 53,200 kgs	£42,500
Labour 2,040 hours	£3,100
Fixed overheads	£2,200

You are required to prepare an operating statement for November detailing all the variances.

4.4   Solution

	£
Budgeted profit (10,000 cylinders) (W(a))	15,000
Add: Sales volume variance (W(f))	900
Standard profit on actual sales (10,600 cylinders) (W(c))	15,900

Less: Variances (W(f) – (i)):	*Adv.*	*Fav.*	
	£	£	
Sales price (f)	600		
Material price (g)		60	
Wages rate (h)	40		
Fixed overhead expenditure (i)	200		
Material usage (g)	160		
Labour efficiency (h)		120	
Fixed overhead volume (i)		120	
	1,000	300	
			700
Actual profit (W(b))			15,200

WORKINGS

		£	£
(a)	**Budgeted profit**		
	10,000 cylinders @ £1.50		15,000
(b)	**Actual profit**		
	Sales		63,000
	Less: Materials	42,500	
	Labour	3,100	
	Fixed overheads	2,200	
			47,800
			15,200

(c)   **Actual units/standard profit**

Sales value 10,600 × £6	63,600
Less: Standard cost of sales 10,600 × £4.50	47,700
	15,900

(d)   **Standard hours**

10,600 cylinders × 0.2 hours = 2,120 hours

(e)   **Budgeted hours**

10,000 × 0.2 = 2,000 hours

Variances

(f)   **Sales**

The budgeted selling price is £6 per cylinder. Actual sales were 10,600 cylinders for £63,000. If the actual cylinders sold had been sold at the budgeted selling price of £6 then sales would have been

10,600 × £6 = £63,600.

Thus the difference in selling price resulted in a lower sales value by £600. This is an adverse selling price variance.

The budgeted volume was 10,000 cylinders costing £4.50 each. At the budgeted selling price of £6 each this is a budgeted profit of £1.50 per cylinder.

Actual sales volume was 10,600 cylinders, 600 more than budget. These extra 600 cylinders will increase profit by

600 × £1.50 = £900.

This is a favourable sales volume variance.

(g)   **Raw materials**

The standard price of the raw material is £0.80 per kg. If the actual quantity of 53,200 kg had been bought at the standard price this would have been

53,200 kg × £0.80/kg = £42,560.

The actual cost was £42,500. This is a saving caused by price, it is a favourable price variance of £60.

Each 100 cylinders should use 500 kgs of material. Therefore the 10,600 cylinders produced should use

10,600 × 500 kg/100 = 53,000 kgs

The actual usage was 53,200 kgs. These additional 200 kgs of material have a value (using standard prices) of

200 kgs × £0.80 = £160.

This is an adverse material usage variance.

(h)   **Labour**

The standard labour rate is £1.50 per hour. The actual labour hours was 2,040 hours, so if they had been paid at the standard rate per hour, the wage cost would have been

$$2,040 \times £1.50 = £3,060.$$

The actual wage cost was £3,100. This extra £40 is the adverse wage rate variance.

Each 100 cylinders should take 20 hours to produce. The actual production was 10,600 cylinders so these should have taken

$$10,600 \times 20/100 = 2,120 \text{ hours}$$

Actual hours were 2,040 hours, a saving of 80 hours. These hours (valued at the standard rate) are worth

$$80 \times £1.50 = £120.$$

This is a favourable labour efficiency.

(i)   **Fixed overheads**

The standard fixed overhead cost is £20 per 100 cylinders. Monthly production is budgeted at 10,000 cylinders. Therefore the budgeted fixed overhead cost is

$$10,000 \times £20/100 = £2,000.$$

The actual cost was £2,200. The extra cost of £200 is an adverse fixed overhead expenditure variance.

But the actual production was 10,600 cylinders, 600 more than budgeted. This extra volume of 600 units (valued at the standard absorption rate of £20/100 units) is

$$600 \times £20/100 = £120$$

This is a favourable fixed overhead volume variance.

4.5   Marginal costing reconciliation

The above presentation was based on absorption costing; on a marginal costing basis it would appear as:

	Adv £	Fav £	£
Budgeted profit			15,000
Add: Sales volume variance (j)			1,020
Standard contribution on actual sales (Wj)			16,020
Less: Variances (W(f)-(i)):			
Sales price (f)	600		
Material price (g)		60	
Wages rate (h)	40		
Fixed overhead expenditure (i)	200		
Material usage (g)	160		
Labour efficiency (h)		120	
	1,000	180	
			820
Actual profit (W(b))			15,200

WORKING

(a) to (i) are as in the previous example.

(j) $600 \times$ contribution of £1.70 each = £1,020 (F)

Contribution/unit = $£6 - \left(\dfrac{£400 + £30}{100} \right)$ =   £1.70/unit

5   CAUSES OF VARIANCES

5.1   Introduction

The calculation of variances is only the first stage. Management wants information to plan and control operations. It is not sufficient to know that a variance has arisen: we must try to establish why. The figures themselves do not provide the answers, but they point to some of the questions that should be asked.

5.2   Possible causes

Possible causes of the individual variances are now discussed. In addition to the causes suggested, any of the variances could be due to poor initial standard-setting.

(a)   **Material price variance**

This could be due to:
- different source of supply;
- unexpected general price increase;
- alteration in quantity discounts;
- substitution of a different grade of material;
- standard set at mid-year price so one would expect a favourable price variance in the early months and an adverse variance in the later months of the year.

(b)   **Material usage variance**

This could be due to:
- higher/lower incidence of scrap;
- alteration to product design;
- substitution of a different grade of material.

(c)   **Wages rate variance**

Possible causes:
- unexpected national wage award;
- overtime/bonus payments different from plan;
- substitution of a different grade of labour.

(d)   **Labour efficiency variance**

Possible causes:
- improvement in methods or working conditions;
- variations in unavoidable idle time;
- introduction of incentive scheme;
- substitution of a different grade of labour.

(e)   **Variable overhead variance**

Possible causes:

- unexpected price changes for overhead items;
- labour efficiency variances, (see above).

(f)   **Fixed overhead expenditure variance**

Possible causes:

- changes in prices relating to fixed overhead items eg, rent increase;

- seasonal effects eg, heat/light in winter. (This arises where the annual budget is divided into four equal quarters of thirteen equal four-weekly periods without allowances for seasonal factors. Over a whole year the seasonal effects would cancel out.)

(g)   **Fixed overhead volume**

Possible causes:

- change in production volume due to change in demand or alterations to stockholding policy;

- changes in productivity of labour or machinery;

- production lost through strikes, etc.

(h)   **Operating profit variance due to selling prices**

Possible causes:

- unplanned price increase;
- unplanned price reduction eg, to try and attract additional business.

(i)   **Operating profit variance due to sales volume**

This is obviously caused by a change in sales volume, which may be due to:

- unexpected fall in demand due to recession;
- additional demand attracted by reduced prices;
- failure to satisfy demand due to production difficulties.

5.3   Interdependence of variances

The cause of a particular variance may affect another variance in a corresponding or opposite way.

(a)   If supplies of a specified material are not available, this may lead to a favourable price variance (cheaper material used), an adverse usage variance (cheaper material caused more wastage), an adverse fixed overhead volume variance (production delayed while material was unavailable) and an adverse sales volume variance (unable to meet demand due to production difficulties).

(b)   A new improved machine becomes available which causes an adverse fixed overhead expenditure variance (because this machine is more expensive and depreciation is higher) offset by favourable wages efficiency and fixed overhead volume variances (higher productivity).

(c)   Workers trying to improve productivity (favourable labour efficiency variance) might become careless and waste more material (adverse material usage variance).

6 STANDARD COSTING AND INTERNAL REPORTING

6.1 Reporting back to managers

The control information reported back to managers at regular intervals is an important aspect of standard costing. This is the stage where managers are made aware of the effect of any deviations between the actual results and the pre-determined standards. Normally, variances should not come as a surprise to a manager as they only represent the monetary quantification of the effect on profits of any deviations that have occurred. A conscientious manager would have a number of his own sub-systems monitoring what is happening within his area of responsibility day-by-day or even hour-by-hour. These controls would normally be in terms of physical units (kg used, wasted; hours, etc.). The manager would have to make decisions on matters arising, all the time.

In reporting variances, the concept of responsibility accounting would normally be followed so a variance report to an individual manager should only include figures relating to his own area of responsibility ie, within his area of control. If more figures are given, then they are usually reported in the form of 'for information only' as a help to a manager in seeing the total picture or context in which his figures arise.

Variance reporting associated with a standard costing system complies with the principle of **management by exception**. Variances represent deviations (or exceptions) between actuals and standards. By drawing the attention of management to the variances, the management accountant is concentrating on what is not going according to plan (standard) and highlighting the fact rather than producing masses of information about what is in line with what was expected. It is the former that is more likely to require management action than the latter.

The reporting frequency must be related to the particular needs of management. Monthly, weekly, daily or any other time period for variance reporting may be appropriate.

The amount of detail included in reports will vary according to the needs of management. As a guide, they should be in sufficient detail to motivate the individual manager to take the most appropriate action in all the circumstances. If a report lacks the required amount of detail, then an individual manager should request this from the management accountant.

6.2 Example of a report

Machining department
Performance report for week ended 7 July 19X4

	Actual £	Standard £	Variance £	Comments
Controllable costs:				
Direct labour time	220	175	45 A	Idle time due to machine failure
Raw materials usage	120	110	10 A	No explanation
Repairs	50	20	30 A	Machine failure
Power consumption	40	50	10 F	Idle time due to machine failure
	430	355	75 A	

6.3 Periodic reporting to top management

(a) Top management is likely to be concerned only with significant variances. A form of exception reporting can be used, only specifying significant variances (the question of what is significant is considered later).

(b)   It is not enough merely to report variances without some attempt to investigate their causes.

6.4   Example

X Ltd – Profit and loss account for November 19X4

		Ref. to notes	£	£
	Budgeted profit			17,500
	Loss of profit due to:			
(1)	Failure to achieve budgeted volume		2,100	
(2)	Wage rate variance		450	
(3)	Raw materials price variance		800	
	Sundry adverse variances not reported individually		700	
				4,050
				13,450
	Improved profit due to:			
(4)	Sales price increase		1,500	
(5)	Favourable labour efficiency variance		400	
	Sundry favourable variances not reported individually		300	
				2,200
	Actual profit for period			15,650

Comments on variances

(1)   Primarily due to credit restrictions imposed during October. See marketing department report dated 21 October 19X4.

(2)   Negotiated national pay increase.

(3)   Failure to anticipate effects of inflation when setting standards.

(4)   Agreed price increase due to higher raw material cost.

(5)   Badly set standard under review.

Note: the above comments are indications of the type of points that might be raised. In a real situation these would be enlarged and might well include recommendations for action.

7   STANDARD COSTING AND EXTERNAL REPORTING

7.1   Use of standard costs in ledger accounts

It was noted earlier that a special feature of standard costing was the use of standard figures in the ledger accounts. This procedure has the result that stocks and work in progress are generally carried at standard cost (depending on the treatment of material price variances discussed earlier). This poses two questions:

(a)   Are standard costs a proper basis for valuing stocks for external reporting?

(b)   If not, is their use in the ledgers still justified?

7.2   Example

The entries which would appear in the following ledger accounts of Chapel Ltd (from the example earlier in this chapter) show how standard cost book-keeping applies in an integrated accounting system:

Raw material control a/c

	£		£
Creditors	42,500	Work-in-progress	42,560
Raw material price variance	60		
	42,560		42,560

Work-in-progress control a/c

	£		£
Raw material control	42,560	Raw material usage variance	160
Wages control	3,100	Wage rate variance	40
Labour efficiency variance	120	Finished goods/Cost of sales	47,700
Production overhead control	2,120		
	47,900		47,900

Production overhead control a/c

	£		£
Creditor	2,200	Expenditure variance	200
Fixed overhead volume		Work-in-progress	2,120
variance	120		
	2,320		2,320

Profit & Loss

	£		£
Cost of sales	47,700	Sales	63,000
Material usage variance	160	Material price variance	60
Wage rate variance	40	Labour efficiency variance	120
Overhead expenditure variance	200	Fixed overhead volume variance	120
Net profit	15,200		
	63,300		63,300

7.3   Advantages of using standard costs in ledgers

There are three major advantages:

(a)   Bookkeeping is made simpler – the problems of similar stock items having different values is avoided.

(b)   Variances are automatically segregated without further work and without the possibility of discrepancies between financial and cost statements.

(c)   Experience shows that managers take variances more seriously if they are included in the financial accounts.

7.4   Importance of the types of standard used

Amongst the types of standard, **high but attainable** is the most generally useful (see below). From the point of view of stock valuation, the **attainable** suggests acceptability. However, the term 'high but attainable' obviously allows a degree of variation between the tight and loose standards. From a valuation point of view loose standards are preferable in that they represent the most realistic estimates. On the other hand, from a control point of view, tight standards, making only the minimum allowance for inefficiency, may be desirable.

7.5   Variances and stock valuations

Consider again the implications of raw materials price variance on raw materials stock value when the variance is calculated at purchase.

(a)   Adverse variance – standard cost lower than actual. Raw materials stocks carried at below actual cost, and difference written off as price variance in reporting period.

(b)   Favourable variance – standard cost higher than actual. Raw materials carried at above actual cost, and difference taken as a credit in current reporting period.

Similar analysis could be applied to all variances (remembering that work in progress and finished goods valuations must include conversion cost): adverse variances indicate conservative valuations, favourable variances inflated valuations.

Since one of the fundamental accounting concepts specified in SSAP 2 is prudence, the usual treatment is to make no adjustments for adverse variances, but to write back favourable variances so as to reduce stock values.

Conclusion   It is common, and generally accepted, to use standard costs for stock valuation (see, for example, paras 11 & 12 SSAP 9). This is based on the view that all methods of inventory valuation are to some extent arbitrary and, provided standard costs are realistic, they represent a reasonable valuation basis. The key word, however, is **realistic**: the test lies in the variances that arise. The usual approach to variances has been indicated above. However, any large variances suggest inadequacies in the standards as a basis for valuation and will require further investigation.

8   RELATIONSHIP BETWEEN STANDARD COSTING AND BUDGETARY CONTROL

8.1   Comparison

Historically, budgeting and standard costing developed as distinct techniques, though both were concerned with the same problems of financial control. Today, standard costing is normally thought of as a specific technique within the overall concept of budgetary control; often both standard costing and budgeting are used, as appropriate, for different types of cost within one entity.

Nevertheless, standard costing retains three distinct features which do not apply to other budget techniques:

(a)   Under standard costing, **all stocks are valued at standard**. This applies to raw materials, WIP, and finished goods, and is essential to the concept of standard costing. This is because at each stage variances are identified and segregated as they arise.

(b)   The **variance analysis is carried out within the ledger accounting system**. This is in contrast to other forms of budgeting, where only actual data is recorded in the accounts, and variance analysis is carried out in separate memorandum records. However, the significance of this distinction is likely to diminish as accounting data is increasingly regarded as data base within a computer system, from which various reports are extracted.

(c)   Standard costs are **planned unit costs**. Budgets normally start as total costs estimates, though they may work down to unit costs.

These differences justify regarding standard costing as a distinct technique, though within the overall budget system.

8.2   Circumstances under which each technique may be applied

The circumstances under which each of the techniques may be used are, in general terms, as below:

(a)   **Standard costing**

This may be most effectively utilised where output or production is routine and regular and can, therefore, be easily and accurately measured. The principal advantage of standard costing is to enable a detailed comparison of individual inputs of materials, labour and other production costs to be made with the standard inputs which should be used for a given level of output. A superior variance analysis is, therefore, possible.

(b)   **Budgetary control**

This can be used for all activities within an organisation where costs and revenues can be predicted and actual results compared. Budgetary control is, therefore, of use in the control of overhead costs and service department costs, and also perhaps in the control of sales activity. The technique is broader in its application than standard costing, and budgets may be considered to be a more basic control tool generally.

The use of flexible budgets is suitable for cost centres where output or volume of activity has an effect on costs and in this situation there is a closer correlation with standard costing, although a broader measure of the level of output or activity will be used.

9   SPREADSHEETS AND VARIANCE ANALYSIS

We studied earlier how spreadsheets may be used to prepare budgets. By keying actual results into the spreadsheet we can automatically calculate variances using formulae and even produce a written report. The report could include tables of figures and graphs which may be imported from the spreadsheet.

One of the fundamental principles of calculating variances based on budgets is that the original budget must be flexed to the actual level of activity. To do this costs must be identified as either fixed or variable, with only the variable costs being flexed. The flexed costs may then be compared with the actual costs and the variance calculated. The spreadsheet layout below shows how this may be done:

	A	B	C	D	E
1		Budget	Flexed budget	Actual	Variance
2	Activity level	☐	+D2	☐	
3					
4	Variable costs	☐	(C2/B2)*B4	☐	+C4–D4
5	Fixed costs	☐	+B5	☐	+C5–D5
6	Total costs	+B4+B5	+C4+C5	+D4+D5	+C6–D6

☐ denotes keyed data that is keyed into the spreadsheet.

The budget values would either be keyed in or imported from the budget preparation spreadsheet. In reality costs would be identified in more detail than shown by separating materials, labour and so on. However the principle is that fixed and variable costs must be separated. When the actual data is known, this is keyed in and the formulae then flex the original budget and calculate the variances.

The above example uses marginal costing principles and only calculates total cost variances. By including other data (eg, units of material, labour hours) as well as the costs, sub-variances may be calculated.

If variances are to be based on standard costs, then column B could be used for standard costs per unit, column C would then multiply the standard costs per unit by the actual activity before calculating the variances as before.

10   CHAPTER SUMMARY

This chapter has explained how variances are calculated under both absorption and marginal costing systems, and their recording in ledgers has been illustrated.

The causes of variances have then been considered and the importance of including the causes as part of the reporting process discussed.

11   SELF TEST QUESTIONS

11.1   What is the difference between standard absorption costing and standard marginal costing? (1.16)

11.2   What is 'management by exception?' (6.1)

11.3   What are the implications of variances on stock valuations and SSAP 9? (7.5)

12   EXAMINATION TYPE QUESTIONS

12.1   Department 7

Shown below is the previous month's overhead expenditure and activity, both budget and actual, for department 7 in a manufacturing company:

	Month's budget	Month's actual
Activity:		
Standard hours	8,000	8,400
	£	£
Fixed overheads:		
Salaries	6,750	6,400
Maintenance	3,250	3,315
Variable overheads:		
Power	17,600	20,140
Consumable materials	6,000	5,960
Indirect labour	4,400	4,480
Total overheads	38,000	40,295

The budgeted overheads shown above are based upon the anticipated activity of 8,000 standard hours and it should be assumed that the department's budgeted overhead expenditure and activity occur evenly throughout the year. Variable overheads vary with standard hours produced.

You are required:

(a)   to calculate the following variances incurred by the department during the previous month:

  (i)   Fixed overhead volume variance;
  (ii)   Fixed overhead expenditure variance; and
  (iii)   Variable overhead expenditure variance.

  (9 marks)

(b)   to draft a suitable operating statement which will assist management in controlling the department's overheads.

  (9 marks)

(c)   to explain carefully why the difference between budgeted and actual activity will cause a change in the anticipated profit by the amount of the volume variance calculated in (a) above.

  (4 marks)

  (Total: 22 marks)

12.2   Gunge

The standard cost per gallon of Gunge, the only product manufactured by Chemit plc, is shown below:

	£
Direct material (4kg @ £3/kg)	12
Direct labour (5 hours @ £4/hour)	20
Variable overhead	5
Fixed overhead	15
Standard cost per gallon	52

The standard selling price of Gunge is £60/gallon and the budgeted quantity to be produced and sold in each period is 10,000 gallons. It may be assumed that variable overheads vary directly with the number of gallons produced.

The actual results achieved during period 4 were:

	£	£
Sales (9,500 gallons)		588,500
Cost of sales:		
Direct material (37,000 kg)	120,000	
Direct labour (49,000 hours)	200,000	
Variable overhead	47,000	
Fixed overhead	145,000	
		512,000
Profit		76,500

There were no stocks of work-in-progress or finished goods at the beginning or end of the period.

You are required:

(a) to calculate the relevant manufacturing cost variances for period 4; and

(14 marks)

(b) to calculate the appropriate sales variances for period 4, showing the effect on budgeted profit of actual sales being different from those specified, and prepare a statement reconciling the budgeted and the actual profit for the period.

(8 marks)

(Total: 22 marks)

13 ANSWERS TO EXAMINATION TYPE QUESTIONS

13.1 Department 7

(a) **Calculation of variance**

(F = Favourable; A = Adverse)

Fixed overhead volume variance

	Budget		Actual	Variance
	8,000	-	8,400	$= 400 \text{ hours} \times \dfrac{6,750 + 3,250}{8,000}$

$$= 400 \times 1.25 = £500 \text{ (F)}$$

Fixed overhead expenditure variance

Flexed budget	Actual	Variance
6,750	6,400	
3,250	3,315	
10,000	9,715	£285 (F)

Variable overhead expenditure variance

Flexed budget	Actual	Variance
17,600	20,140	
6,000	5,960	
4,400	4,480	
$28,000 \times \dfrac{8,400}{8,000} = 29,400$	30,580	£1,180 (A)

(b)   **Operating statement for control of department overheads**

	Flexed budget	Actual	Variance
Fixed overhead:			
Salaries	6,750	6,400	350 (F)
Maintenance	3,250	3,315	65 (A)
Total	10,000	9,715	285 (F)
Variable overhead:			
Power	$17,600 \times \dfrac{8,400}{8,000} = 18,480$	20,140	1,660 (A)
Consumable materials	$6,000 \times \dfrac{8,400}{8,000} = 6,300$	5,960	340 (F)
Indirect labour	$4,400 \times \dfrac{8,400}{8,000} = 4,620$	4,480	140 (F)
Total	29,400	30,580	1,180 (A)
Overall total	39,400	40,295	895 (A)

Strictly an 'operating statement' should include information relating to sales and to prime costs but information was not provided by the examiner.

A further point is that in practice variances would normally be stated for the previous month and for the budget period to date.

(c)   In this case the business uses a standard absorption costing system which involves absorbing fixed as well as variable overhead to production and therefore stock is valued inclusive of fixed production overhead.

As fixed overheads are, by definition, unaffected by changes in volume of output, an over-recovery will arise where volume increases above budget - called here a fixed overhead volume variance.

The way in which profit is affected depends on the relationship between production and sales. Firstly, if production increases but sales volume remains in line with budget, there will be an increase in the amount of fixed overhead included in stock equal to the amount of the fixed overhead volume variance. Hence profit would be higher by that amount.

Secondly, if sales and production increase by the same amount, then the overall effect of the increase will be an increase in contribution amounting to the increase in sales volume multiplied by the contribution per unit. In an absorption costing system this contribution is shown as two separate items ie,

(1)   sales volume variance valued at the standard profit per unit; and
(2)   fixed overhead volume variance valued at the standard fixed overhead per unit.

Hence in this second situation where sales volume increases, profit increases by more than the amount of the fixed overhead volume variance.

Note: if sales and production change by differing amounts, then a combination of the two effects will influence profits eg,

	Budget units	Actual units
Sales	100	150
Production	100	160

Here the sales volume variance would be 50 units @ the standard profit per unit, whereas the fixed overhead volume variance would be 60 units @ the standard absorption rate. This would comprise 50 units relating to the sales volume increase and 10 units relating to the stock increase.

13.2   Gunge

(a)   Direct material

	£	
Actual quantity at actual price	120,000	Price variance £9,000 A
Actual quantity at standard price 37,000 kg @ £3/kg	111,000	
Standard quantity at standard price (9,500 × 4) @ £3/kg	114,000	Usage variance £3,000 F

Direct labour

	£	
Actual hours at actual rate	200,000	Rate variance £4,000 A
Actual hours at standard rate 49,000 hours @ £4/hour	196,000	
Standard hours at standard rate (9,500 × 5) @ £4/hour	190,000	Efficiency variance £6,000 A

Variable overhead

	£	
Actual cost	47,000	Expenditure variance £500 F
Standard cost: 9,500 galls. @ £5/gall.	47,500	

Fixed overhead

	£	
Actual cost	145,000	Expenditure variance £5,000 F
Budgeted cost: 10,000 galls. @ £15/gall.	150,000	
Standard cost (overhead absorbed) 9,500 galls. @ £15/gall.	142,500	Volume variance £7,500 A

(b)   **Sales margin variance**

	£	
Actual quantity at actual price	588,500	⎞
Actual quantity at standard price		⎬ Price variance
9,500 galls. @ £60/gall.	570,000	⎠ £18,500 F
Actual quantity at standard margin	76,000	
9,500 galls. @ £(60 − 52)		⎞ Volume variance
Budgeted quantity at standard margin		⎬ £4,000 A
10,000 galls. @ £8/gall.	80,000	⎠

Profit reconciliation statement
Period 4

	£	£
Budgeted profit		80,000
Sales margin volume variance		4,000 A
Standard profit on actual volume sold		76,000
Sales margin price variance		18,500 F
Cost variances: Materials	6,000 A	
Labour	10,000 A	
Variable overhead	500 F	
Fixed overhead	2,500 A	
		18,000 A
Actual profit		76,500

| CIMA AT FOULKS LYNCH | HOTLINES
Telephone: 0181 844 0667
Fax: 0181 831 9991 | AT FOULKS LYNCH LTD
Number 4, The Griffin Centre
Staines Road, Feltham
Middlesex TW14 0HS |

Intended Examination Date: November 96 ☐ May 97 ☐	Textbooks	Exam Kits	Lynchpins	Distance Learning (Includes all materials)
Stage One				
1 Financial Accounting Fundamentals	£17 ☐	£8 ☐	£4 ☐	£85 ☐
2 Cost Accounting & Quantitative Methods	£17 ☐	£8 ☐	£4 ☐	£85 ☐
3 Economic Environment	£17 ☐	£8 ☐	£4 ☐	£85 ☐
4 Business Environment & Info Technology	£17 ☐	£8 ☐	£4 ☐	£85 ☐
Stage Two				
5 Financial Accounting	£17 ☐	£8 ☐	£4 ☐	£85 ☐
6 Operational Cost Accounting	£17 ☐	£8 ☐	£4 ☐	£85 ☐
7 Management Science Applications	£17 ☐	£8 ☐	£4 ☐	£85 ☐
8 Business & Company Law	£17 ☐	£8 ☐	£4 ☐	£85 ☐
Stage Three				
9 Financial Reporting	£18 ☐	£9 ☐	£4 ☐	£85 ☐
10 Management Accounting Applications	£18 ☐	£9 ☐	£4 ☐	£85 ☐
11 Organisational Management & Development	£18 ☐	£9 ☐	£4 ☐	£85 ☐
12 Business Taxation (Finance Act 1996)	£18 ☐	£9 ☐	£4 ☐	£85 ☐
Stage Four				
13 Strategic Financial Management	£18 ☐	£9 ☐	£4 ☐	£85 ☐
14 Strategic Mgt Accountancy & Marketing	£18 ☐	£9 ☐	£4 ☐	£85 ☐
15 Information Management	£18 ☐	£9 ☐	£4 ☐	£85 ☐
16 Management Accounting Control Systems	£18 ☐	£9 ☐	£4 ☐	£85 ☐

TOTAL	Sub Total £			
	Postage £			
	Total £			

POSTAGE	UK Mainland	£2.00/book	£1.00/book	£1.00/book	£5.00/pack
	NI, ROI & Europe	£5.00/book	£3.00/book	£3.00/book	£15.00/pack
	Rest of World Standard Service	£10.00/book	£8.00/book	£8.00/book	£25.00/pack
COURIER	China & Asia	£20.00/book	£18.00/book	£12.00/book	£44.00/pack
	West Indies & Africa	£23.00/book	£20.00/book	£14.00/book	£47.00/pack
	Far East & Middle East	£17.00/book	£16.00/book	£11.00/book	£34.00/pack
SINGLE ITEM POSTAGE		For orders of 1 item only, add £2.50 (UK & Europe) or £10.00 (Rest of World)			

DELIVERY DETAILS

Student's name (print)

Delivery address

Postcode

Country   Tel (Home)

Tel (Day)   Fax

Note: All delivery times subject to stock availability.
Signature required on receipt.
Allow: 5 working days - work address (UK mainland)
10 working days - home address (UK mainland)
6 weeks for Overseas Standard Service

DECLARATION

I agree to pay as indicated on this form and understand that AT Foulks Lynch Ltd Terms and Conditions apply (available on request). I understand that AT Foulks Lynch Ltd are not liable for non-delivery if the Rest of World Standard Air Service is used.

Signature   Date

PAYMENT OPTIONS

1. I enclose Cheque/PO/Bankers Draft for £_____

Please make cheques payable to AT Foulks Lynch Ltd.

2. Charge Access/Visa Account Number

Expiry Date | | | |

Signature   Date

3. Please invoice employer. Minimum order of £150.
30 days credit. I agree to pay fees of £_____

Name (print)

Position

Signature

Company Name

Invoice Address

Post Code   Country

Telephone   Fax

All details correct at time of printing.   *Source: CMTXJ6*